TWENTY YEARS AFTER COMMUNISM

Twenty Years After Communism

THE POLITICS OF MEMORY AND COMMEMORATION

Edited by Michael Bernhard and Jan Kubik

OXFORD
UNIVERSITY PRESS

OXFORD

UNIVERSITY PRESS

Oxford University Press is a department of the University of Oxford.
It furthers the University's objective of excellence in research, scholarship,
and education by publishing worldwide.

Oxford   New York
Auckland   Cape Town   Dar es Salaam   Hong Kong   Karachi
Kuala Lumpur   Madrid   Melbourne   Mexico City   Nairobi
New Delhi   Shanghai   Taipei   Toronto

With offices in
Argentina   Austria   Brazil   Chile   Czech Republic   France   Greece
Guatemala   Hungary   Italy   Japan   Poland   Portugal   Singapore
South Korea   Switzerland   Thailand   Turkey   Ukraine   Vietnam

Published in the United States of America by
Oxford University Press
198 Madison Avenue, New York, NY 10016

Library of Congress Cataloging-in-Publication Data
Twenty years after communism : the politics of memory and commemoration / edited by
Michael Bernhard and Jan Kubik.
pages cm
Includes bibliographical references and index.
ISBN 978-0-19-937513-4 (hardcover)—ISBN 978-0-19-937514-1 (paperback)   1. Collective
memory—Political aspects—Europe, Eastern—Case studies.   2. Memorialization—Political aspects—Europe,
Eastern—Case studies.   3. Post-communism—Europe, Eastern—Case studies.   4. Europe, Eastern—Politics
and government—1989—Case studies.   I. Bernhard, Michael H.   II. Kubik, Jan, 1953–
DJK51.T89 2014
943.0009'049—dc23
2013049616

9 8 7 6 5 4 3 2 1
Printed in the United States of America
on acid-free paper

Memory Shapes Nations

What is a Nation? It is collective memory, which in one way or another extends to all of us, via school, but also through a variety of common traditions—monuments, songs, anthems, music, and literature. All of this makes us a single nation. Thanks to everything that is memory we live as a distinct whole.

That is the reason why ideological conflicts often play out through the manipulation of memory. Each nation, every European nation, has in its history rather inglorious pages. We try to minimalize these events somehow, even forget about them, by various acts of manipulation.

—Leszek Kołakowski (2008). Translation by Michael Bernhard and Jan Kubik

Contents

List of Figures and Tables

Figures

Tables

List of Pictures

Acknowledgments

THANKS ARE DUE to the University of Florida Foundation for providing the bulk of the funding for this project through its support of the Miriam and Raymond Ehrlich Chair. Additional support was provided by the Center for European Studies and the Department of Political Science at the University of Florida. Personal thanks are due to the respective heads of the Department of Political Science and Center for European Studies at the time of the Conference, Michael Martinez and Amie Kreppel, as well to Dean Paul D'Anieri of the College of Liberal Arts and Sciences. Three graduate assistants at the University of Florida, Dong-Joon Jung, Tristan Vellinga, and Keith Weghorst, as well as Debbie Wallen, the former department administrator, worked hard to make sure that the logistical side of the project went smoothly and we thank them for their contribution in making it a success.

Several present or former faculty members at UF—Dietmar Schirmer, Bryon Moraski, Katrina Schwartz, Petia Kostadinova, and Amie Kreppel—provided useful comments and suggestions on the chapters. Additionally, Stephen Hanson provided challenging feedback on our conclusions at the Conference of European Studies meetings in Boston in March 2012 and Giovanni Capoccia shared with us his critical thoughts on the theoretical framework early in the process. In Warsaw, Barbara Szacka listened to two presentations, at the beginning and at the end of the project, and was always a source of precise criticism and matchless encouragement. Kazimierz Wójcicki helped to sharpen several issues in a splendid conversation.

Eviatar Zerubavel read the theory chapter and conclusions with a sharp critical eye and offered stimulating comments, as did several other members of the 2012-14 faculty seminar on "Contested Memories and the Politics of Change" at the Allen and Joan Bildner Center for the Study of Jewish Life at Rutgers. Joanna Kurczewska invited Kubik to present our work to her seminar at the Polish Academy of Sciences, which turned out to be a perfect testing ground for many ideas. Her sharp remarks and warm support are much appreciated. At the International Interdisciplinary Conference "Still Postsocialism? Cultural Memory and Social Transformations," held at Kazan Federal University, Russia, we received many excellent comments and want to thank in particular Alexander Etkind, Chris Hann, Caroline Humphrey, Marina Mogilner, Ilya Gerasimov, and Yaroslav Hrytsak. Barbara Törnquist-Plewa and her crew at Lund University, Sweden, offered many incisive comments and a lot of support, particularly during a wonderful conference "Beyond Transition? New Directions in Eastern and Central European Studies." At Rutgers, several of Kubik's colleagues at the Comparative Politics Seminar, most memorably Robert Kaufman, Mona Krook, and Paul Poast, welcomed the work with a perfect mix of critical attention and encouragement.

With certain trepidation, as we do not want to omit any of the many friends and colleagues who offered criticism and support, we want to thank Amy Linch, Grzegorz Ekiert, Carsten Schneider, Andrij Portnov, Diana Mincyte, Florian Bieber, Valerie Bunce, Chip Gagnon, Nermina Mujagic, Asim Mujkic, Tanja Petrovic, Jelena Subotic, Veljko Vujacic, Tim Haughton, Branislav Kovalčík, Sune Bechmann Pedersen, Holly Raynard, and Ingrid Kleespies, Darina Malová, Christine Cannata, Zora Bútorová (and her colleagues at the Institute for Public Affairs), and Claudiu Tufis, all of whom gave us critical readings of individual chapters. Finally, thanks are due to Krzysztof Jasiewicz for organizing a roundtable on the twentieth anniversary of the Polish Roundtable at the Association for Slavic, East European, and Eurasian Studies meeting in 2009, at which we first discussed these issues, and for his comments on the Polish chapter.

About the Contributors

LAURA ARDAVA is a doctoral candidate in the Department of Communication Studies at the University of Latvia. She also works as a Researcher at Institute for Advanced Social and Political Research (ASPRI), University of Latvia. In her thesis she examines the meaning of the Latvian Third Awakening period (1988–1991) on national identity and how it has been formed and maintained by various commemorative rituals and media events in the past twenty years. Her work is supported by the European Social Fund. Her main research interests lie in the areas of media events, media rituals, commemoration, social memory, and national identity.

DAVID ART is an Associate Professor of Political Science at Tufts University. He is the author of *The Politics of the Nazi Past in Germany and Austria* (Cambridge University Press, 2006) and of *Inside the Radical Right: The Development of Anti-Immigrant Parties in Western Europe* (Cambridge University Press, 2011). Art is co-convener of the European Consortium for Political Research's Standing Group on Extremism and Democracy. His articles have been published in such journals as *Comparative Politics, German Politics and Society, Party Politics,* and *West European Politics*, and his research has been supported by the German Academic Exchange Service (DAAD), the Center for European Studies at Harvard University, and the Max Weber Program at the European University Institute. His research interests include the origins and consequences of political extremism, the production and influence of historical memory, and the development of authoritarian regimes.

MICHAEL BERNHARD is Ehrlich Professor of Political Science at the University of Florida. He is the author of *Institutions and the Fate of Democracy: Germany and Poland in the Twentieth Century* (University of Pittsburgh Press, 2005) and *The Origins of Democratization in Poland: Workers, Intellectuals, and Oppositional Politics, 1976–1980* (Columbia University Press, 1993). His work has appeared in *The Journal of Conflict Resolution, World Politics,*

Comparative Politics, Perspectives on Politics, Angelaki, Conflict Management and Peace Science, International Studies Quarterly, Theory and Society, Comparative Political Studies, The Journal of Politics, Journal of European Area Studies, East European Politics and Societies, Communist and Post-Communist Studies, Political Science Quarterly, Studies in Comparative International Development, Foreign Affairs, and *Krytyka.* His research interests include the role of civil society in democratization, institutional choice in new democracies, the political economy of democratic survival, and the legacy of extreme forms of dictatorship.

KEVIN DEEGAN-KRAUSE is Associate Professor of Political Science at Wayne State University, with a Ph.D. in Government from the University of Notre Dame (2000). His publications include *Elected Affinities: Democracy and Party Competition in Slovakia and the Czech Republic* (Stanford University Press, 2006), *The Structure of Political Competition in Western Europe,* (co-edited with Zsolt Enyedi, in *West European Politics* and Routledge, 2010), and *The Handbook of Political Change in Eastern Europe* (co-edited with Sten Berglund, Joakim Ekman and Terje Knutsen, Ashgate, 2013), "New Dimensions of Political Cleavage" in the *Oxford Handbook of Political Science* and articles in *Party Politics, The Journal of Democracy, East European Politics and Societies, Communist and Post-Communist Studies, Nations and Nationalism,* and chapters in many edited volumes. He is co-editor of the *European Journal of Political Research Political Data Yearbook* and its new online database, http://www.politicaldatayearbook.com. His primary research concerns party transformation and political divides.

DAINA S. EGLITIS is Associate Professor of Sociology and International Affairs at the George Washington University in Washington, D.C. She is the author of *Imagining the Nation: History, Modernity, and Revolution in Latvia* (Pennsylvania State University Press, 2002). Her articles on issues of post-communism, including poverty, social stratification, family change, electoral politics, and gender, have appeared in *Cultural Sociology, Acta Sociologica, Nationalities Papers, Slavic Review, East European Politics and Societies,* and the *Journal of Baltic Studies.* She has been a Fulbright Scholar (2007–2008) and Fulbright Senior Specialist (2003) in Latvia and an International Scholar with the Open Society Institute's Higher Education Support Program in Armenia (2011–2013). Professor Eglitis's current research projects focus on gender and collective memory.

VENELIN I. GANEV obtained his Ph.D. in Political Science from the University of Chicago in 2000 and is now an Associate Professor at Miami University of Ohio and a Faculty Associate of the Havighurst Center for Russian and Post-Soviet Studies. His publications have appeared in *East European Constitutional Review, American Journal of Comparative Law, Journal of Democracy, East European Politics and Societies, Communist and Postcommunist Studies, Slavic Review, Comparative Studies in Society and History,* and *Europe-Asia Studies.* He has also contributed chapters to several volumes that explore various aspects of institution-building in contemporary Europe. His is the author of *Preying on the State: The Transformation of Postcommunist Bulgaria* (Cornell University Press, 2007).

AIDA A. HOZIĆ is an Associate Professor of Political Science at the University of Florida. She is the author of *Hollyworld: Space, Power and Fantasy in the American Economy* (Cornell University Press, 2001). Her current work focuses on the relationship between states and their crimes in the former Yugoslavia.

JAN KUBIK is Chairman and Professor of Political Science, Rutgers, the State University of New Jersey, and serves also as a Recurring Visiting Professor of Sociology, Centre for Social

Studies, Polish Academy of Sciences, Warsaw. He received his B.A. and M.A. from the Jagiellonian University in Krakow, Poland, and his Ph.D. (with distinction) from Columbia University. In 2006–2007 he served as the Distinguished Fulbright Chair in East European Studies, Warsaw University. He is the author of many book chapters and articles published in major journals, mostly in English and Polish, as well as two award-winning books: *The Power of Symbols against the Symbols of Power: The Rise of Solidarity and the Fall of State Socialism in Poland* (Pennsylvania State University Press, 1994) and (with Grzegorz Ekiert) *Rebellious Civil Society: Popular Protest and Democratic Consolidation in Poland, 1989–1993* (University of Michigan Press, 1999). He has recently co-authored (with Myron Aronoff) *Anthropology and Political Science: A Convergent Approach* (Berghahn Books, 2013) and co-edited (with Amy Linch) *Postcommunism from Within: Social Justice, Mobilization, and Hegemony* (SSRC/NYU Press, 2013).

CAROL SKALNIK LEFF is Associate Professor of Political Science at the University of Illinois, Urbana-Champaign. Her research focus is comparative communist and post-communist politics in East Central Europe, especially the Czech Republic and Slovakia. She is the author of two books: *The Czech and Slovak Republics: Nation vs. State* and *National Conflict in Czechoslovakia: The Making and Remaking of a State, 1918–1987*. She also has published articles on regime change, post-communist state dissolution, transnational influences on regime change, and ethnic politics. Her current research is on elite transformation in post-communist Eastern Europe.

CONOR O'DWYER is Associate Professor of Political Science at the University of Florida. His first book examined the relationship between party-building and state-building in new democracies, looking specifically at the relationship between party competition and patronage politics in post-communist Eastern Europe: *Runaway State-Building: Patronage Politics and Democratic Development* (Johns Hopkins University Press, 2006). His current research explores how the expansion of the European Union affects the terrain of domestic politics in the post-communist member-states. This research focuses in particular on the development of gay rights movements in the region. He has been an Academy Scholar at the Weatherhead Center for International Affairs at Harvard University (2003–2004 and 2006–2007) and has published in *World Politics, Studies in Comparative International Development, East European Politics and Societies, East European Politics, Comparative European Politics,* and *the Journal of European Integration.*

GRIGORE POP-ELECHES is Associate Professor of Politics and International Affairs at Princeton University. His main research interests lie at the intersection between political economy and comparative political behavior, with a particular interest in Eastern Europe and Latin America. He has worked on the politics of IMF programs in Eastern Europe and Latin America, the rise of unorthodox parties in Eastern Europe, and the role of historical legacies in post-communist regime change. His first book, *From Economic Crisis to Reform: IMF Programs in Latin America and Eastern Europe,* was published by Princeton University Press in February 2009. His work has also appeared in a variety of academic journals, including *The Journal of Politics, World Politics, Comparative Political Studies, Comparative Politics, International Studies Quarterly, Journal of Democracy, Studies in Comparative International Development,* and *East European Politics and Societies.*

ANNA SELENY is Professor of the Practice at the Fletcher School of Law and Diplomacy, Tufts University; she also taught at Princeton University from 1993 to 2002. Her research in comparative politics and political economy has mostly focused on Eastern European and other post-socialist states. She is the author of *The Political Economy of State-Society Relations in Hungary and Poland: From Communism to the European Union* (Cambridge University Press, 2006) and articles in *Perspectives on Politics, World Politics, Comparative Politics, Journal of Democracy, International Studies Quarterly,* and *Law and Politics,* among others, as well as several book chapters. She spent a year at the Institute for Advanced Studies in Princeton, and has received awards and fellowships from the German Marshall Foundation, Fulbright-Hayes, the MacArthur Foundation, and the American Council of Learned Societies, among others. Seleny received her Ph.D. from MIT and her M.A. from Johns Hopkins/SAIS. Other professional experience includes international banking, international development work in Central Asia and Latin America, and experience in both nonprofit and government agencies.

OXANA SHEVEL is an Associate Professor of Political Science at Tufts University and an associate at the Davis Center for Russian and Eurasian Studies at Harvard and at the Harvard Ukrainian Research Institute. She is also a member of the Program on New Approaches to Research and Security in Eurasia (PONARS Eurasia) scholarly network, and a member of the EUDO Citizenship expert group as a country expert on Ukraine. Her research focuses on issues of nation- and state-building, the politics of citizenship and migration, memory politics, and the influence of international institutions on democratization in post-communist Europe. She is the author of *Migration, Refugee Policy, and State Building in Postcommunist Europe* (Cambridge University Press, 2011), in which she examines how the politics of national identity and strategies of the UNHCR shape refugee admission policies in the post-communist region. She is currently working on a comparative study of the sources of citizenship policies in fifteen former Soviet republics. Her research has appeared in *Comparative Politics, East European Politics and Societies, Europe-Asia Studies, Slavic Review, Political Science Quarterly, Post-Soviet Affairs, Nationality Papers,* and in edited volumes. She holds a Ph.D. in Government from Harvard University, and an M.Phil. in International Relations from the University of Cambridge in England.

SHARON L. WOLCHIK is a Professor of Political Science and International Affairs at the George Washington University. She has served as director of the Russian and East European Studies Program and the Masters in International Policy and Practice Program at the Elliott School of International Affairs and is a member of the Institute for European, Russian, and Eurasian Studies. She has served on the board of the American Association for Slavic Studies and as the chair of the Board of the National Council for Eurasian and East European Research. She is the author of *Czechoslovakia in Transition: Politics, Societies, and Economics* (Leicester University Press, 1992), the co-author of *Defeating Authoritarian Leaders in Postcommunist Countries* (Cambridge University Press, 2011) , and is co-editor of *Domestic and Foreign Policies in Eastern Europe in the 1980s* (St. Martin's Press,1983); *Women, State, and Party in Eastern Europe* (Duke University Press, 1985); *Women in Power in Post-Communist Parliaments* (Indiana University Press 2009); *The Social Legacies of Communism* (Cambridge University Press, 1994); and *Central and East European Politics: From Communism to Democracy* (Rowman and Littlefield, 2007, 2010). She has also authored articles in the *Slavic Review, Comparative Political Studies, World Politics, Journal of Democracy, Studies in Comparative Communism, the Journal of Communist and Post-Communist Studies,* and *East European Politics and Societies.*

TWENTY YEARS AFTER COMMUNISM

Introduction

Michael Bernhard and Jan Kubik

THIS PROJECT GREW out of discussions of the twentieth anniversary of the 1989 Roundtable Accord in Poland. The commemorations of that event, generally understood as a momentous historical turning point in the history of the world, were highly contested events. Their significance was the subject of radically different interpretations and a focal point of many political struggles. The irony of this was that Polish politics was entering into a phase in which the post-communist Left had collapsed and the political scene was dominated by two post-Solidarity parties, the Civic Platform (PO) and the Law and Justice Party (PiS). The memory of the Solidarity breakthrough at the Roundtable deeply divided the two parties, and this split carried over into the commemoration of the regime-shattering June 1989 elections.

The year 1989 was a turning point in history. The way in which such moments are remembered is central to the understanding of politics in their aftermath. To the Western liberal mind it was an *annus mirabilis,* a moment in which human freedom triumphed. But the anniversaries that were celebrated across the former Soviet Bloc in the last quarter of 2009 revealed a different and often conflicted view of the events of 1989. Whereas in many Western countries the fall of the Berlin Wall on November 9, 1989, was cause for positive recollection twenty years later, there seemed to be less enthusiasm in the countries that experienced the original events. We decided that the ways in which 1989 was commemorated twenty years hence was worth studying as an important moment that would yield new insights into both the "politics of memory" and post-communist politics in general. We also decided that it would be worthwhile to include in our deliberations some subset of the successor states to the Soviet Union, whose separation anniversary would come in 2011.[1]

The criterion we used in deciding which post-Soviet cases to cover was the existence of minimal level of democracy. We did so because we felt that the nature of memory politics would differ across democratic and authoritarian regimes, based on the autonomy of actors and the level of control over freedom of expression. We thus chose to include the Baltic States and Ukraine. While many have argued that the trajectory of Ukraine is no longer democratic as the country careens toward a new competitive authoritarian regime under Yanukovych, we believe that it is sufficiently competitive to provide us with a boundary case for our analysis.

We thought about adding Russia, but the degree of Putin's control over the media and his increasingly restrictive policy toward autonomous actors in civil society (Levitsky and Way 2010; Fish 2005; Robertson 2011) made the use of a framework for memory politics that was designed for democratic polities not applicable for an increasingly consolidated authoritarian regime. There was no official commemoration of the events of August 1991, and neither Prime Minister Putin nor President Medvedev made public statements.[2] The opposition did hold a small rally in Moscow in August 2011. On the twentieth anniversary of the breakup of the USSR in December 2011 there were no major public commemorations, even though there were extensive demonstrations to protest the non-competitiveness of the elections held that month. These were the largest popular protests since August 1991. While many commentators noted that these protests and the popular resistance to the hard-line coup of August 1991 shared a similar spirit, they were not commemoratory in nature (Volkov 2012).

This volume is about the explosion of the politics of memory triggered by the twentieth anniversary of the fall of state socialism in Eastern Europe. In the neighboring disciplines, especially history and sociology, there has been a long tradition of investigating the sources and implications of memory for society (Assmann 1995; Halbwachs 1950; Hobsbawm and Ranger, eds. 1983; Müller 2002; Nora 1989; Olick 1999; Olick, Vinitzky-Seroussi, and Levy, eds. 2011; Zerubavel 1996). Within political science the study of memory has not been totally neglected, but the existing works focus predominantly on questions of historical and transitional justice and tend to have more of a normative focus (Popovski and Serrano, eds. 2012; Aguilar and Humlebaek 2002; Appel 2005; De Brito, Enriquez, and Aguilar, eds. 2001; Nalepa 2010; Norval 1999; Shevel 2011; Brendese 2013).

Mainstream comparative politics has been slower to explore the role of memory in political competition among actors. We seek to move its consideration to the mainstream of studies on post-communist politics. The project is founded on a few simple premises. First, people always strive to come to terms with the past of their communities in order to generate a sense of order in their personal and collective lives. Second, new leaders often find it advantageous to call for the punishment of the political and coercive authorities of fallen regimes. Whether and how they do so depends heavily on their interpretation and assessment of the collective past. Third, remembering the past, particularly collectively, is always a political process; thus the politics of memory and commemoration needs to be studied as an integral part of the establishment of new collective identities and new principles of political legitimacy.

In post-communist Eastern Europe, the way people remember state socialism is closely intertwined with the manner in which they envision historical justice. For many people the assessment of the fallen system—something that is neither uniform in or across countries—is a prerequisite for fashioning standards of justice necessary for governing in a new system, particularly when it is a democracy. While there exist a number of studies on historical justice, there is no study that offers a theoretically informed and rigorously comparative analysis of the politics of memory in the post-communist states. This volume fills the gap.

We recognize that there are many layers of public memory, as different institutions and various groups in the society remember the old system and the regime transformation differently. But we focus in this study only on the way the old system and its demise are commemorated in public ceremonies designed by major political actors, such as governments and political parties. After offering detailed descriptions and analyses of the commemorations in seventeen countries, we explain the variance among them by examining several factors, including the types of political actors involved in the politics of memory, constellations of political forces at the moment of commemoration, and the cultural traditions of a given country that influence the way in which official collective memory is constructed. It is important to emphasize that we are not interested in judging the events of 1989/1991, but to better understand the events as milestones in the histories of the respective societies, as well as the role that their recollection plays in politics today.

Comparative politics has much to contribute to the study of the politics of memory. First, it treats the study of memory not just as a normative dilemma, but also as an empirical and analytical issue. The shift to an empirical research strategy allows us to foreground how the understanding of the past shapes the pursuit and exercise of power. And among the tools that comparative politics has at its disposal, actor-centered models that look at the self-interest of politicians as the motivating force for the generation of political regimes are a proven form of investigation (O'Donnell and Schmitter 1986; Przeworski 1991). An actor-centered approach is ideally suited for both our theoretical framework and case studies.

In political science there has been sprinkling of outstanding single-country monographs (Art 2006; Nalepa 2010), some well-placed articles (Cruz 2000; Bielasiak

2010; Capoccia 2010), and useful chapter contributions (Lebow, Kansteiner, and Fogu 2006). Clearly this is an emergent area of research that is just beginning to establish itself.

What this volume provides is a novel theoretical framework for understanding the importance of memory for politics on a general level, as well as a series of case studies that address the aftermath of one of the most important historical events of the late twentieth century, the end of European communist systems. Following this introduction, we present the original theoretical framework that provides guidance for the study of the politics of memory across the cases covered in the book. There are two conceptual components to this framework. First, we propose the idea of *mnemonic actors*. They are political forces that are interested in a specific interpretation of the past. They often treat history instrumentally in order to construct a vision of the past that they assume will generate the most effective legitimation for their efforts to gain and hold power. To generate a typology of mnemonic actors we use Lasswell's definition of politics, "*who* gets *what, when*, and *how*" (and add "*why*" to his list) and apply it to the question of how political forces use the interpretation of the past. We identify and characterize four different kinds of actors: mnemonic warriors, mnemonic pluralists, mnemonic abnegators, and mnemonic prospectives.

Second, we develop the idea of *mnemonic regime*, the dominant pattern of memory politics that exists in a given society at a given moment in reference to a specific highly consequential past event or process. Memory regimes constitute the building blocks of the official field of (collective or historical) memory. The type of memory regime is dictated by the characteristics of the actors prevailing in the field of memory politics and the salience of the specific past event whose commemoration they are attempting to use to their advantage at that specific juncture. We identify three different types of memory regimes: fractured, pillarized, and unified. We specify the mix of actors that generate each type and outline the main features of memory politics under each regime.

The third and final component of our framework is a theory of the emergence of specific mnemonic regime types. After a careful analysis of our cases, we determined that the dependent variable of this study should be *the political form of the memory regime*, which is defined as a configuration of strategic choices and has three values: (1) a fractured regime when at least one actor is a warrior, (2) a pillarized regime when there is no warrior in the mix and at least one actor is a pluralist, and (3) a unified regime when no actor is a warrior or a pluralist (that is, all are abnegators). There are three groups of independent variables that we study: (1) the range of structural constrains the actors face in the post-1989/1991 political environments, for example related to the type of regime transformation typical for a given country; (2) several cultural constraints related to the "past" of a specific actor or the existence and salience of specific cleavages in a given country (for example, ethnic); and (3) a set of cultural (as distinct from strategic-political) choices that actors can make, such as the choice of post-communist political identity or the choice to engage in mnemonic contests revolving around other past events (in our terminology, the decision is to engage or not engage in mnemonic layering).

The bulk of the volume is devoted to testing the empirical utility of our framework. However, in both the introduction and the conclusion we explore the ramifications of memory politics for new democracies such as those in Eastern Europe. We find that fractured memory regimes contribute to political polarization and thus can, but do not necessarily, have a negative impact on the quality of democracy and its consolidation. While deciding how to study the commemorative events twenty years later, we chose to do an in-depth investigation of each case. We recruited a team of researchers, all of whom were exceptionally knowledgeable about the history of the individual countries and who could conduct original research in the required languages.[3]

To ensure that the team did not work at cross-purposes, we provided each author with a first draft of the theoretical framework and a model case study (Poland) before they began their work. They were asked not only to consider using our theoretical framework to inform their case studies but also to provide feedback on the limitations of our theorizing. We thus asked each author to execute a theoretically informed case study (Lijphart 1971; Gerring 2004), that is, a study that applies a theoretical framework to a specific case to make sense of it.

As a result, the case chapters are organized in a similar fashion to facilitate comparison. Each chapter begins with a short synopsis of the event(s) in 1989 or 1991 that was the subject of commemoration, followed by a discussion of the commemoration twenty years later, and an analysis of the politics of the commemoration. Our intent in using similar narrative and analytical structures is to focus on the same causal factors, as suggested by George and Bennett (2005) in their discussion of structured-focused comparison. This both facilitates the use of the case material in the qualitative comparative analysis (QCA) that we employ in the concluding chapter and makes the chapters more accessible to readers. Our intention here was to produce a multi-authored work that is analytically coherent and to facilitate inter-case comparison, allowing for well-supported conclusions.

The volume that follows reflects this structure. It begins with the theoretical framework developed for the purposes of interpreting the individual cases and facilitating cross-case comparisons to produce a set of generalizations. It then presents the individual case analyses and concludes with a chapter that uses them in a rigorous QCA that allows us to develop systematic conclusions about the politics of memory, both in the post-communist context and more generally.

NOTES

1. We included all the countries of "Cold War" Eastern Europe except Albania. We also included Germany due to the centrality of the events that took place at the Berlin Wall and their role in the unification of the German Democratic Republic and the Federal Republic of Germany.

2. Putin stated in 2005 that the collapse of the USSR was "the greatest geopolitical catastrophe of the [20th] century (Kuchins 2005).

3. In order to facilitate a focused and consistent book, rather than a collection of uncoordinated chapters, each with its own individualized analytical framework, we organized a small conference/workshop. The conference was held at the University of Florida in February 2011. All participants in the conference read each other's papers in advance and provided feedback. We also held an extended discussion on the utility of the theoretical framework. The results of this discussion were incorporated into a subsequent version that was distributed early in the revision process.

1 A Theory of the Politics of Memory
Jan Kubik and Michael Bernhard

POLITICS OF MEMORY has become a fashionable and important object of scholarly investigations in the last thirty or so years,[1] particularly in history, sociology, and cultural studies, but also in journalism.[2] Political scientists have come to this topic a bit later, but by now a number of important works have been published.[3] There is also no paucity of fresh theorizing on the sociological mechanisms of collective remembrance (Olick 1999; Olick and Robbins 1998; Assmann 1995; Zerubavel 2003a, 2003b) that goes well beyond the classical formulations of Maurice Halbwachs (1950, 1952), the undisputed father of the field. Following Nora, the sociology of memory may be construed as an attempt to come to terms with the need to study situations when there is "a will to remember.... Without this intention to remember, *lieux de mémoire* would be indistinguishable from *lieux d'histoire*" (1989, 19). Thus, sociology studies *the social mechanisms involved in the emergence and organization of this intention to remember*. Political science has a different, narrower task; it needs to focus on *strategies that political actors employ to make others remember in certain, specific ways and the effects of such mnemonic manipulations*. Scholars who work on the politics of memory offer many fragmentary theoretical insights, gripping examples, fascinating descriptions, and often brilliant interpretations, but politics of memory as a separate field of inquiry seems to be weaker on two counts: the lack of systematic theory and the paucity of systematic comparative studies. Our project is designed to contribute to these two areas, as we offer a systematization of several theoretical motifs and a rigorous comparative study of seventeen cases coming from the post-communist world.

Students of the politics of memory train their attention on several objects of study. Nets-Zehngut identifies five types of collective memory in the literature: popular, official, autobiographical, historical, and cultural (2012, 254–255). In this study we are mostly interested in official memory (propagated by the state but also by political parties and other actors in the public space), and cultural memory ("defined by Assmann as the way the society views its past via newspaper articles, memorials, monuments, films, and buildings" [2012, 255]). To this list we add commemorations that definitely belong to cultural memory and that sometimes are "official," when organized by the state or important political actors (for example, political parties), and sometimes are not.

We propose a theoretical framework to investigate the politics of memory, a central albeit understudied aspect of post-communist politics. The impetus to address more systematically the importance of this phenomenon came with the observation that commemoration of the breakthrough of 1989 on its twenty-year anniversary was an intensely politicized event. In contrast to the celebratory nature of the commemoration in the West, in several post-communist states the commemorations of 1989 and 1991 were not occasions for national celebration but for political recrimination.

The central concepts of our investigations are *memory regime* and *mnemonic actor.* Soon we will define both concepts and develop a set of types as basic tools for our analysis. But before we go into detail on our analytic framework, a few caveats are in order. A radical regime change, such as that experienced in Eastern Europe in 1989, is not only about the reconfiguration of economic interests, redistribution of political power, and reordering of social relations. It is also about the *reformulation of collective identities* and the *introduction or reinvigoration of the principles of legitimizing power.*[4] These two tasks cannot be realized without a re-examination of the group's past—their historical memory.[5] The creation of historical memory is rarely a simple attempt to formulate a "truthful" reconstruction of the past; it is usually about creating a specific vision of it for instrumental reasons. In other words, the purposive use of selective remembering and forgetting shapes a group's historical memory (Yerushalmi 1982; Olick and Robbins 1998). A number of observers have noted that the writing of history is entwined with power (Müller 2002), and that in the age of mass politics many states have sponsored the formation and propagation of useful traditions (Starr 1991).[6] Historical memory and the practice of history as a discipline are distinct, though the work of historians can be and is often deployed in the construction of historical memory, seen as the central component of "national tradition," whose "essence" various cultural entrepreneurs often try to capture and emulate in "elemental narratives" (Wóycicki 2009). The purpose of such tradition formation was to justify rule in an age when legitimacy was subject to new challenges due to the incorporation of larger populations into the polity. Elemental narratives became new "civic religions" closely associated with the legitimation of power. Since then, the manipulation of public memory has been a part of the legitimation strategy of all mass-incorporating regimes (Hobsbawm and Ranger 1983, Gellner 1983, Mosse 1975).

We proceed from an "instrumentalist," actor-centered view of the development of historical memory. Actor-centered approaches have been used effectively in understanding other problems in the study of democratization in political science (O'Donnell and Schmitter 1986; Przeworski 1991; Linz and Stepan 1996).[7] However, we are also aware that the manipulation of history is subject to constraints of historically developed, socially transmitted, and culturally framed credibility (Olick and Robbins 1998, 128–130; Müller 2002; Kubik 1994). Mnemonic actors often try to treat history instrumentally, as they tend to construct a vision of the past that they assume will generate the most effective legitimation for their efforts to gain or hold power. But they are not totally free in their construction of "history," if they want to remain credible for their target audience(s). Each audience (public) cultivates a certain vision of the past that it considers valid.[8] In short, there are limits of malleability in the presentation of the cultural/historical material that are imposed by the visions of history that resonate in the discursive field of the target group. The line between credible and incredible visions of the past is not easy to specify, and it shifts; once it is crossed, however, the entrepreneur's claim to legitimacy in a given context fails or is weakened. On the other hand, proposing a vision of history, however instrumental such activity can be, contributes to the solidification of a body of interpretations that this version represents.

The "history" that constitutes a powerful constraint on the interpretive/representational strategies of the mnemonic actors must be conceptualized, however, not as an inertial "weight of the past" or an (immutable) "tradition," but rather as a set of discourses about the past, produced by a multitude of actors and accepted in a given group (public) as valid ("natural," "obvious," "convincing," "authentic," "reasonable," etc.). Examples of key mnemonic entrepreneurs and actors include parents, teachers, professional historians, artists (poets, novelists, visual artists), journalists, intellectuals, politicians, priests, and so on. "History," in other words, is always made in the present by various actors who may and often do present its various versions.

In short, the moderate instrumentalist approach holds that while change in historical memory can be a product of the work of historians, the uncovering of new artifacts, or developing new lines of historical argument, it is also subject to manipulation on the basis of the self-interest of those in power and those contesting power (for instance, see Lowenthal 1986). Academic and more popular genres of "history" are often deployed as elements in the struggle between political actors who seek to cultivate and disseminate views of the past conducive to the attainment of their political ends (Art 2006; Maier 1988; Lebow et al. 2006; Lasansky 2004; Hobsbawm and Ranger 1983).

For political scientists interested in the politics of memory, historical memory is conveniently approached as a product of power struggles between advocates of instrumental persistence and instrumental change in the public presentation of the past. However, thinking of this as a two-sided struggle can lead to oversimplification. There can be, of course, more than two contending parties, and any one may prefer a combination of status quo and non–status quo positions. Moreover, some mechanisms of social memory formation may not be politicized.[9] We proceed from the assumption that the commemoration of regime-forming events is fertile ground for "memory entrepreneurs." Investigation of the changing contours of historical memory as the product of political struggle is one area where political scientists may have a comparative advantage over historians, sociologists, and philosophers.

We set out to investigate the political mechanisms implicated in the formation, transmission, and reception of collective memory, particularly via public commemorative ceremonies, but we try not to lose sight of social and cultural mechanisms. We are operating at the "social" level of analysis but reject the notion that there is any sort of collective consciousness (or subconscious) that is an attribute of a group.[10] Individuals alone are the carriers of historical memory, but shared historical beliefs are the products of complex social, cultural, and political mechanisms (Brubaker et al. 2006). It is important to note, though, that individual memory is composed of both personal memory and individual historical memory. The former refers to recollections of one's personal life, and the latter is the representation of the collective past that the individual holds.[11] Individual historical memory is closely related to a vision of the collective past of any group with which a person identifies and holds to be true.

It is important to remember that the main object of our study is the official memory regime (defined below) composed of the "constructed" recollections of 1989 or 1991 from the perspective of twenty years later. We choose to focus on this moment in time because for the societies that experienced 1989/1991 as a critical event, the twentieth anniversary was an occasion to evaluate the consequences of the change of system. The changing representations of 1989/1991 produced in earlier periods of the twenty years of post-communism are not the principal object of study, but nevertheless are consequential in terms of influencing the understanding of 1989/1991 in 2009/2011 and thus are also investigated.

Now to our model: as we noted earlier, we expand on the notion of what the installation of a new political regime entails by adding to the mix the idea of memory regimes and the memory field. To flesh out this idea we proceed in four steps. First, we develop a typology of what we call *mnemonic actors*. Second, we introduce a typology of memory regimes and present their characteristics in some detail. Third, we propose factors that influence the formation of mnemonic actors and mnemonic regimes (with special attention to the factors most relevant to outcomes in post-communist countries). Fourth, we sketch a set of observations on the impact that various memory regimes may have on the quality of democracy.

Typology of Mnemonic Actors

There are two variables of central interest in this project: the types of mnemonic actors and the type of memory regime that emerges as a result of their interaction (dominated either by coexistence or conflict). We suggest that there are four ideal-types of such actors (individuals, parties, organizations, etc.): mnemonic warriors, mnemonic pluralists, mnemonic abnegators, and mnemonic prospectives. In the next section we will talk about how the mix of actors determines the nature of the mnemonic regime. Of these four, prospectives are rare in the region. Such a perspective is typical of a revolutionary Left that is scarce and/or of little political consequence in the post-communist cases that we investigate in this volume, at least at the moment. Contemporary neo-communist successor parties are not prospective in orientation but tend to be nostalgic defenders of an idealized past and the loss of the security it provided.

Each political entrepreneur chooses a particular strategy or—to use different wording—engages in specific practices. When actors consider a particular political stance or orientation, they consider its impact on their political fortunes. But how does an actor choose to take up a position as a warrior, a pluralist or an abnegator on a specific issue? Broadly speaking, there are two types of strategies (or practices) to consider: positional (political) and cultural (semiotic). For example, when an actor considers its choice, it takes into account how that might affect support from society at large and what sort of response it might provoke from other actors. Will a specific (mnemonic) action enhance political support from the electorate and/or change the range of political alliances with and between other actors? Actors need to make two important calculations in such choices. One—positional—is based strictly on the grounds of the (political) cost/benefit analysis (e.g., "Do I improve my electoral chances by inviting 'them' to form a coalition?"). The second consideration—semiotic—is about the cultural consequences of such a decision (e.g., "What kinds of meanings can be attached to my decision of forming this coalition?"). In this second calculation, a set of possible interpretations of one's actions is considered. The most successful politicians calculate political efficacy and cultural significance simultaneously. And sometimes they deliberately engage in specific cultural manipulation to increase political efficacy. This is precisely why the field of mnemonic politics is so fascinating: it is here that political success depends heavily on skillful interweaving of "realpolitik" maneuvers (often behind the scenes) with an effective formulation and communication of cultural interpretations, including public presentation of mnemonic positions. Effective positions are those that are consonant with the cultural terrain of target groups, those that resonate with their images of the past.

Gaining control of institutions in the post-transition period is often an effective strategy of shaping the political culture (including the mnemonic field) that emerges following communism. While institutions cannot fully control people's minds (to which the Eastern European experience with communism is perhaps the best evidence), the ability and will (thus strategizing) to remake things like school curricula and the media environment, including the distribution of state assets such as newspapers and television and radio outlets, are nonetheless consequential for post-transition mnemonic regimes. There are numerous examples of post-communist political actors spending considerable resources on gaining control of the media to promote specific visions of history (Törnquist-Plewa and Stala 2011) or creating national institutions (various institutes of national remembrance or museums of oppression) whose goal is orchestrated propagation of a specific vision of the nation's past (Mink and Neumayer 2013; Stan 2013; Nalepa 2010).

From the point of view of our analysis, the most important decision concerns the choice of mnemonic stance or strategy (on a given issue). We cannot, of course, know all the factors that influence a given political actor, but we theorize that in general there are three sets of factors that influence actors' decisions when it comes to the choice of their mnemonic strategy: (1) cultural constraints imposed by the meanings, values, and identities "enshrined" in the discourses (narratives, culture) actors know and consider using[12]; (2) cultural choices that actors make within these constraints (for example, assumption of specific political-cultural identities or use of specific ideological themes); and (3) structural-institutional constraints of the political field in which they act. We discuss these factors in detail below.

To analyze the characteristics of the each type of mnemonic actors, we utilize Harold Lasswell's definition of politics: "*who* gets *what, when*, and *how.*" We add "*why*" to his list of questions to also consider the dominant mode of justification of the other decisions. Such justifications are the essence of legitimacy. In our analysis of politically relevant discourses, we are guided by this set of Lasswellian questions. In particular, we observe how each question is answered *within* the discourses about the past proposed by each ideal type of political actor.

Let us begin with mnemonic warriors. To answer the question "who" is to capture the idea of how such actors construe themselves as protagonists in a discourse that they construct about the past and how they are expected to relate to other types of actors who are assumed to populate the field of memory politics. Mnemonic warriors tend to draw a sharp line between themselves (the proprietors of the "true" vision of the past) and other actors who cultivate "wrong" or "false" versions of history. They usually believe that the historical truth is attainable and that once it is attained it needs to become the foundation of social and political life. So, for them the contest in the field of memory politics is between "us"—the guardians of the truth—and "them"—the obfuscators, perpetuators of "falsehoods," or the opportunists who do not know or care about the "proper" shape of collective memory. The content of collective memory appears to warriors as largely non-negotiable; the only problem is how to make others accept their "true" vision of the past.

Mnemonic warriors tend to espouse a single, unidirectional, mythologized vision of time. In this conception, the meaning of events is often determined by their relation to some "paradise lost" or—negatively—an "aberrant past." Additionally, in such mythical constructions of time the distinction between the past, present, and future is sometimes collapsed. The present is construed as permeated by the "spirit" of the past, and if this spirit is defective, the foundations of the polity are corrupted. Another argument often deployed by mnemonic warriors is that the problems of the present (and the future) cannot be effectively addressed unless the whole polity is set on the proper foundation, constructed according to the "true" vision of history. The alternative visions of the past—by definition "distorted"—need to be delegitimized or destroyed. The proponents of such visions need to repent or leave public life. As the holders of the truth, mnemonic warriors tend to be, therefore, proselytizers.

By contrast, mnemonic pluralists accept that, in addition to "us" and our vision of history, there are "them" with their own visions of the past. Most important, the pluralists believe that the others *are entitled* to their own visions. If they disagree with those visions, they are ready to engage in a dialogue whose principal aim is the orderly pursuit of "the truth," discovery of the areas of overlap among the competing visions, and articulation of common *mnemonic fundamentals* that allow discussion among competing versions. The pluralists are comfortable with the possibility of multiple notions of time; for example, there may be a time within which one strives for expiation, but there is also a time within which one designs and implements "pragmatic" policy measures. A serious concern for the pluralists is how to construct a field of memory politics that accommodates competing visions and provides a platform for a dialogue among them. The type of mnemonic field they privilege can be called *pillarized*. In a pillarized memory regime, competing visions of the past "peacefully coexist." Mnemonic actors either accept this state of affairs or engage in a dialogue whose goal is a compromise in the form of a mnemonic reconciliation.

Mnemonic abnegators avoid memory politics. They are either uninterested or see no advantage in engaging in them. This may happen for two, distinct, reasons. In the first situation, the country has (or abnegators assume that it has) one strongly unified and broadly shared vision of the past. Consequently, the questions of collective memory are taken off the political agenda as not much can be gained from costly efforts to create and propagate an alternative vision of the past. Of course, such a mnemonic equilibrium holds until some political entrepreneur finds an effective discursive strategy to champion a hitherto marginalized, counter-hegemonic vision that challenges the premises of the dominant view of the past. The second situation occurs when a political actor chooses to stay away from the field of memory politics (or a specific memory regime), regardless of what other actors do. Mnemonic abnegators tend to be uninterested in thinking in terms of mythical time, treat the past as a reservoir of useful tests of practical solutions, focus on the present, and strive to avoid participating in cultural (including mnemonic) wars. A politics of convenient or purposive forgetting—chosen, for example, by actors who directly or indirectly (via their political precursors) may be held responsible for the past social traumas—may also underlay a stance of abnegation.

Prospectives believe that they have solved the riddle of history and thus have the key to a better future. They assume that, on the basis of the correct understanding of what is wrong with both past and present, people led by them can transcend the woes of the world by building a desirable post-historical end-state. When out of power they are implacable enemies of the detested status quo, and when in power, they maintain that the political system over which they preside is the best, if not the only, road to this transhistorical end. This is a teleological vision of human development. Once in power, prospectives truck no opposition, but try to mobilize the entire population in the "struggle" to achieve their desired end state. In political contest and in establishing their rule, prospectives' strategy is aggressive, very much like that of the warriors. But their actions are justified not by anchoring them in the past, but by prospects of a "better" future. If they invoke the past, it is either to emphasize historical wrongs whose putative logic underpins their utopian vision of the future or to celebrate historical resistance to those wrongs. Table 1.1 summarizes our typology of mnemonic actors.

Typology of Memory Regimes

The concept of "memory regime" in this study refers to a set of cultural and institutional practices that are designed to publicly commemorate and/or remember a single event, a relatively clearly delineated and interrelated set of events, or

TABLE I.I

	Types of Mnemonic Actors and Their Dominant Strategies			
	Mnemonic warriors	Mnemonic pluralists	Mnemonic abnegators	Mnemonic prospectives
Who are the participants in memory politics	Us versus them.	Us and them.	Those who dwell on the past, not us.	Expansive and exhaustive us.
What is the predominant vision of collective memory?	Memory is non-negotiable, as there is only one "true" vision of the past.	Negotiation on memory issues but within an agreement on the fundamentals of mnemonic politics.	Low salience of memory issues for politics.	The riddle of history has been solved; both the past and the future are known.
When are the events to be remembered happening?	**In a single mythical past** (wrongs of the past are part of the tissue of present politics).	(Probably) in **multiple pasts**. Different interpretations of the past exist.	**Never** mind when, it is not important. There is no time like the present.	**In the future.** Teleological orientation. There is an inevitable or desirable and attainable end state.
How is the mnemonic contest to be carried out? What are the culturally prescribed strategies of action?	Defeat, deny power to, delegitimize alternative visions of the past. Do not negotiate, avoid compromise.	Practice respect, toleration for alternative views of the past on the basis of a common understanding of the fundamentals. Be ready to negotiate or disagree.	Avoid mnemonic contests. They are a waste of time.	Focus political energy on building a "brighter" future and challenge competing visions of the past in the name of the correct, revolutionary interpretation.
Why is it worthwhile or not worthwhile to engage in mnemonic struggle?	**Fundamentalism:** our "true" vision of the past legitimizes our claim to power.	**Pluralism:** there are several visions of the past that are acceptable. Our claim to power rests on our effort to institutionalize a frame for their coexistence.	**Pragmatism:** propagating a predominant vision of the past is not seen as worthwhile in comparison to responding to present-day problems.	**Utopianism:** An idealized future is attainable but requires action in the present.

a distinguishable past process. We are particularly interested in *official memory regimes*, that is, memory regimes whose formulation and propagation involve the intensive participation of state institutions and/or political society (the authorities and major political actors such as parties, who are organized to hold and contest state power).[13] While our observations in the book are focused on a specific set of commemorations, not all memory regimes are generated by anniversaries. Memory regimes can be created through conflicts generated in other spheres of the polity or society.[14] The whole set of official regimes existing in a given country in a given period can be called the *official field of (collective or historical) memory.*

Memory regimes belong to more mutable components of culture, including political culture, especially in relatively new political regimes.[15] There are several reasons for fluidity of memory regimes. First, the entry and exit of actors can change the constellation of power in any memory regime. This can be a product of the realignment of the political field or generational change. Second, the salience of memory issues can change over time. This can be the product of things as routine as the passage of time and the occurrence of anniversaries (the tyranny of the mnemonic calendar), as well as exogenous shocks. Shocks could include traumatic events, the realignment of foreign policy, or revelations from professional historical debates.[16] Third, actors dissatisfied with the existing state of collective memory pertaining to a specific issue may develop and deploy new interpretations of the past in an attempt to produce results more politically beneficial for them. In doing so, they usually provoke a mnemonic conflict and force other actors to (re)define their positions. This, in turn, leads to the reconfiguration of the existing memory regime or the emergence of a new one, and as a consequence causes a shift in the memory field. Fourth, salience may vary depending on which political actor or coalition of actors is holding power at a given moment. For instance, incumbents who pursue agendas addressing past injustices will make memory issues instantly salient and the challengers will have to develop their own mnemonic positions. Other incumbents will be more or less vulnerable on memory issues and this will affect the behavior of challengers, who—most likely— will develop and publicly present visions of the past that are politically damaging to the power holders. Finally, memory of a specific issue (or event) as an aspect of the political agenda may recede into the background and lose salience when other issues become pressing. Examples include war or economic crises. As a result of such fluctuations, it is essential not to think of the field of collective memory as set in stone, but to begin analysis by considering its state at a given moment in time.

To recap, when we talk about the memory regime, we focus on (1) an organized way of remembering a specific issue, event, or process (2) at a given moment or period. When a government and/or the major political parties are involved in this process the memory regime becomes "official." An ensemble of memory regimes, understood as the organized way of remembering *all salient issues* in a given country in a given period, can be conveniently referred to as "the field of memory" or "mnemonic field."[17] Given different actor positions on different issues and the varying degree of salience of different issues over time, the analysis of such a field is best conducted inductively, one memory regime at a time, before assessing the state of the memory field as a whole.

The position that an actor takes in a given memory regime and in the mnemonic field depends to large degree on his or her calculation of the political benefits resulting from raising a specific "memory issue," given this issue's saliency at a given point. In short, the positions that actors take on such issues (within a specific memory regime) are dependent on their assessment of what position is most politically advantageous. When a particular issue is salient, an actor may find it advantageous to take a warrior position on it. However, on other issues at other times, the same actor may find it advantageous to take a pluralist stand or to disengage from the politics of memory altogether. This means that in politics, actor orientations (including the position on the past) are to a large degree context-dependent strategic choices. This does not seem to hold for a subset of extreme warriors who are reflexively dogmatic.

Memory regimes that emerge when a mnemonic warrior enters a debate on a particular issue are called *fractured*.[18] To be more precise, if we observe that among the component discourses of the mnemonic regime there is at least one that is construed with an *intention* of drawing a sharp line between its authors, the guardians of the "true" version of the past, and "them"—the prevaricators or opportunists who do not know or care about the "proper" shape of collective memory—we call the author(s) of such discourses "mnemonic warriors" and the resulting mnemonic regime *fractured*.

By contrast, a memory regime without warriors is either *pillarized* or *unified*. The specific type depends on the balance between abnegators and/or pluralists. In a pillarized regime there will be differences between actors over their interpretations of the past, but toleration of differences of opinion or indifference over memory issues will prevent the partisan politicization of such interpretations. Such regimes permit an easier coexistence of differences, despite disagreements over the past. Pillarized memory regimes are populated by a mixture of pluralists and abnegators.

Finally, memory regimes that are predicated on agreement over the interpretation of the past and thus are largely free of mnemonic conflicts are called *unified*. In such situations, all actors are de facto abnegators. Unified memory regimes may follow one of two distinct logics. It is possible that there would be a high degree of consensus about the past and for that reason memory issues are simply not salient.[19] A second logic of universal abnegation can emerge because of the potential danger of politicizing the past. There may be a kind of self-enforcing equilibrium, in which all actors see the costs of politicizing the past as prohibitive given high risks and low payoffs.[20] It is important to remember that such decisions are issue specific. That is, an actor may decide not to participate in the politicization of a specific past issue or event but may engage in the politicization of another.

Actors belonging to all four types usually populate the field of democratic memory politics, but warriors have the advantage in setting the tone of mnemonic contests since they confront not only other warriors, but also pluralists, abnegators, and prospectives.[21] We expect the dynamics of mnemonic contests in non-democratic regimes to be different from those in democratic polities. In this volume we have chosen to concentrate on cases that are largely democratic. The only chapter in which authoritarianism emerges as a potential concern is Shevel's account of Ukraine (Chapter 7), which many observers see as having a trajectory toward competitive authoritarianism.

In democratic polities, mnemonic contests are difficult to settle and often produce unintended consequences, sometimes harmful even for their instigators. Consider, for example, a situation in which pluralists attempt to create a pillarized mnemonic regime and are thwarted by "fundamentalist" mnemonic warriors seeking to establish a hegemonic memory regime. Pursuing hegemonic goals in a democratic polity, in which there is neither consensus nor apathy about the past, will inevitably lead to the formation of the fractured memory field. Or one can analyze the following hypothetical scenario: if, say, three mnemonic pluralists and one mnemonic warrior populate the field of memory politics, initially the memory regime is fractured, but its ultimate tenor over time will depend on the relative power of each type of actor. Regardless of the content of the competing visions of the past, if the pluralists are strong, they may marginalize the warriors by blocking the salience of questions of historical memory, effectively turning them into abnegators for whom engaging on that issue is disadvantageous. However, if the warrior is able to ignite a memory conflict, that particular memory regime will remain fractured.

We next set out to identify and analyze specific factors that we hypothesize may affect the emergence of mnemonic actors and regimes. In the next section we present a general threefold typology of such factors and discuss examples of each from post-communist context.

Factors Influencing the Choices of Mnemonic Actors and the Emergence of Mnemonic Regimes

Olick and Robbins do not treat "collective memory as a thing" and thus counsel us to study "distinct sets of mnemonic practices in various social sites" (1998, 112). We are particularly interested in specific sets of such practices that we refer to as mnemonic regimes (defined earlier). Furthermore, we posit that mnemonic practices are usefully analyzed as composed of two components: *semiotic practices* (Wedeen 2002) involved in the formulation of the content of collective memory and accompanying *institutional practices* needed to organize and propagate a specific vision of the past. On the one hand, both semiotic and institutional practices are mutable as frequent foci of interpretive and political contests. But they are also subject to constraints posited by the larger cultural field in which memory politics take place; they are constricted by broader cultural-political processes, often of long duration and considerable inertia.

Nets-Zehngut's conceptualization is similar. In his analysis of mnemonic politics, he identifies two broad sets of factors: *cultural* and *instrumental-political*. As he argues: "Collective memory is powerfully influenced by the present via two main paths: first, culturally, through the inevitable impact of the culture on the way people view the past. Second, instrumentally, through the conscious deliberate manipulation of the past for the interests of the present. This latter path, also referred to as creating a 'useable past,' influences the collective memory through activities of various institutions" (2011, 326).[22] We share Nets-Zehngut's distinction between cultural and institutional factors, but mindful of the literature on the dual nature of practices (whose essence is a precarious balance between structural and strategic dimensions), we propose a more elaborate analytical scheme. Political actors engaging in mnemonic politics have strategic *choices* and face (historical) *constraints* in two dimensions: *cultural* and *structural/institutional*.

The dependent variable of this study is *the political form of the official memory regime* (in short: memory regime), a configuration of strategic choices or, as we call them, positional orientations. Earlier we decided that three such orientations are relevant for post-communist memory politics: warrior, pluralist, and abnegator. Memory regime has three values: (1) a fractured regime when at least one actor is a warrior, (2) a pillarized regime when there is no warrior in the mix and at least one actor is a pluralist, and (3) a unified regime when no actor is a warrior or a pluralist (that is, all are abnegators).[23] Our independent variables are a range of structural and cultural constraints as well as the range of cultural (as distinct from positional) choices that actors face. We discuss them in some detail in the following sections. Figure 1.1 depicts our argument in graphic form.[24]

Structural Constraints

Mnemonic actors face many constraints beyond their control. Such constraints are either structural (including institutional) or cultural. In this section we consider

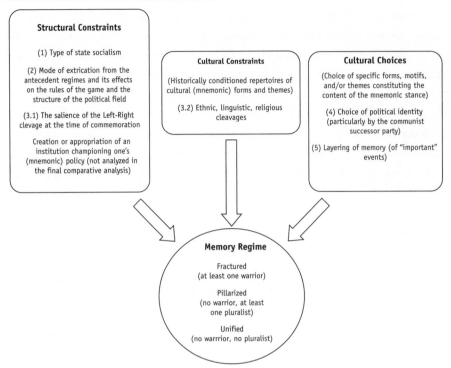

FIGURE I.I Factors Influencing Choice of Actor's Strategy and Type of Mnemonic Regime

the former. Generally speaking, a party's relative power compared to other actors in the system is a powerful factor influencing this party's ability to engage effectively in memory politics. More specifically, in a new democracy a party's relative power at the moment of power transfer has a medium- to long-term effect on its political chances—also in the mnemonic field—during the consolidation period. These are *structural* (non-cultural) constraints; they restrict actors' ability to maneuver, regardless of the interpretive frame they or others impose on such constraints.

The formation of mnemonic politics in post-communist regimes is influenced by several unique *structural (institutional) constraints* of this sort. First, we consider the type of state socialism. In the expert literature on post-communism there is a consensus that there was no single state socialism but rather state socialisms. There is no agreement, however, how to identify, name, and classify the various types. We decided to sidestep these discussions and focus only on a very simple, yet almost unanimously accepted generalization that there were two main types of state socialist regimes: *liberalized* and *hard-line*.[25] Liberalized regimes (reformist) were sufficiently "relaxed" to allow a modicum of political competition (if only within the Communist Party), tended to be more active in the area of economic reform, and relaxed somewhat their monopoly on information as well as social and political organization. Countries with such reformist histories are more likely to produce post-breakthrough political actors who have greater experience in political competition and symbolic manipulation. Such actors will tend to be more effective players of the game of mnemonic politics than those who come to the game *de novo*. The distinction between reformist and hard-line communist systems has important ramifications for the nature of the extrication from communism. The former were much more likely to negotiate with their opponents, whereas the latter were more resistant to change, and this difference has powerful repercussions for the games of memory politics after the breakthrough.

Given this, we also analyze the mode of extrication from the old regime. The actual sequence of events in that process and those leading up to it should have important ramifications for the type and intensity of mnemonic politics and the nature of a memory regime that emerges.[26] Thus we investigate how the mode of extrication, whether that is a *rupture* with the ancient regime, or a *reform*, or some variant that falls between the two, contributes to the establishment and subsequent evolution of the memory regime.[27] For example, it seems that the more violent the break with the past, the easier it is to break decisively with the legitimating historical myths of the previous regime and propose new variants of collective memory. In negotiated extrication, based on compromise that preserves a role for former regime incumbents in politics, those actors who negotiated with incumbents (challengers-negotiators) are vulnerable to political attacks by memory warriors who abstained from negotiating (former oppositional recalcitrants) and often challenge the legitimacy of negotiation and a new political order based on it.

Negotiated ends to dictatorship may also include institutional guarantees for the former incumbents as a way to get them to agree to share or leave power (Przeworski 1991). The struggle to remove such guarantees in the subsequent period is often intense and may become the central axis of political conflict (Bernhard 2005, 195–198). Not only do such guarantees have an effect on who holds power in the early stages of a democratization process; they often become the basis of claims that negotiating partners in compromise were colluding in a division of power and assets.

Thus the strength of the actors at the point of extrication is an important consideration. Whether representatives of the old regime, the opposition, or a coalition of forces from both sides control the government, the media, and school curricula determines the tenor of the initial, trend-setting discussions to make sense of the past and to determine its significance for the present. Quite often, especially when they are out of power, former anti-communist oppositions will have an interest in depicting the communist past (particularly during important commemorations) in negative terms, whereas the regime incumbents or their successors will generally have an interest in minimizing the negative recollection of their time in power under the old regime. Severe critical judgments about a political actor's past can function as a rationale for excluding them from the new political system.

The strength of actors at particular points in time can determine who gains control of such institutions as schools, newspapers, and television and radio outlets. The disposition of such institutional and cultural assets following regime change creates both opportunities and constraints for political actors.[28]

Finally, the ideological balance of political forces at the time of commemoration in 2009 or 2011 seem to pose an important structural constraint on how actors engage in commemoration. In particular, the existence of a salient and strong Left-Right political cleavage seems to feed into a propensity to engage in mnemonic warfare. The persistence of this cleavage is often the product of the reaction to extensive "capitalist" reforms of the economic system, related to the differential impact of the reforms on various sectors of society (the winners and losers of reform), and the fate of the successor parties. If this cleavage is strongly salient at the time of commemoration, it often plays into the vision of the past of important political actors.[29]

Cultural Constraints

In a given country, the set of historical-cultural factors that define actors' understanding of the world and constrain their strategic choices is best conceptualized as a *historically formed repertoire of cultural (mnemonic) forms and themes*. There is no "national character" or "collective consciousness" somehow encoded in the population's genes or mysteriously handed over from one generation to another. There exist, however, several official systems of social communication and education that deliberately manufacture and disseminate sets of "official" narratives about the national past[30] and equally powerful sets of "unofficial" narratives generated and reproduced within personal networks, which may be at odds or only partially congruent with official narratives. Each country's official and popular memories are composed from myriads of such narratives, transmitted in many different media, from school textbooks, films, theater performances, musical compositions (consider the significance of national operas in the nineteenth century), and monuments, to—particularly importantly for this project—public ceremonies that are designed to commemorate "important" past events.

Let's examine briefly several examples. The culture of a group is usefully construed as a set of common "points of concern" (Laitin 1988) rather than a set of shared values. One does not need to believe in the immaculate conception of the Virgin Mary to be a Pole; but one must know who she is and have at least rudimentary knowledge of some narratives about her (for example, as the "Mother of the Nation") to be recognized by others as a "legitimate" member of the nation. Otherwise, one's claim to "Polishness" is open to challenge.

Mnemonic (or—more broadly—political) entrepreneurs are free to construct their narratives out of the available "national" repertoire but are limited in their choices by its boundaries. If they choose elements outside this repertoire, they appear to be alien and not credible to their potential constituents. A Hungarian politician who decides to play the game of mnemonic politics may choose not to feature 1956 in his or her rhetoric, but cannot afford to show a lack of knowledge of what that year means in the Hungarian culture and would be ill-advised to ignore or ridicule its significance.

It would be odd for a Czech politician to couch a political statement in a heroic-romantic and religiously suffused idiom, whereas such a strategy makes perfect sense in the Polish context. Czech culture has over the years acquired a down-to-earth, pragmatic tenor with a lot of room for self-distance and even self-mockery. In Poland, such a cultural code is "admissible" mostly in narrow circles of intellectuals and artists, while the dominant tenor of Polish political culture is different: dramatic, "romantic" grand gestures, often infused with religious (Catholic) imagery, are quite routine and would not strike most Poles as out of place. But there exists also another set of tropes—positivistic—emphasizing pragmatic, "organic" work and taking care of national problems through sustained systematic effort whose goal is the "improvement" of the material condition of the nation. A mnemonic entrepreneur has here a clear choice: romanticism (of grand gestures) or positivism (of "organic" work), but the choice must be within the boundaries of the "proper" repertoire. Choosing outside this repertoire would make the actors claim to "Polishness" unconvincing to many "insiders."[31]

Consider the complexities of using the term "socialist" in the post-Soviet world. An actor self-defined as, say, "socialist" or "social-democrat" can try to ignore the existing set of discourses on socialism in a given country, but other actors can always define him or her using these discourses, thus turning them into cultural (including mnemonic) weapons. The origins, features, and consequences of "socialism," particularly of "really existing socialism," are defined and debated in these discourses that—when taken together—constitute a context that a political entrepreneur in a democracy cannot control; it is a *historical-cultural* constraint that influences how a given actor is portrayed by others in mnemonic battles.

Generally speaking, a political actor's genealogy poses constraints on the cultural strategy that he or she assumes, particularly in the short to medium term. And in new democracies an identity stemming back to the old power structure is a powerful constraint. Authoritarian incumbents have a difficult time recasting themselves as defenders of human rights, and communist successor parties are hard pressed to justify themselves as libertarian defenders of private property. In the post-communist context, communist successor parties and politicians face a different set of issues when it comes to self-definition and credible self-presentation than descendants of the anti-communist opposition or new actors.

Each political actor entering the field of mnemonic (or—more broadly—cultural) politics is constrained by the existing cultural repertoire, whose formation and propagation are outside of this actor's full control. Radical breaks with existing repertoires of earlier interpretations of the past are risky. The attempt to deploy a completely novel interpretation of the past that does not resonate with any of the elements of the established national historical repertoire as a strategic gambit in mnemonic contestation has a high probability of failure. While the payoff of a successful move of this sort may be high, an actor attempting it will face problems in gaining traction with the population and is likely to end up on the margins of the country's cultural field.

The case studies collected in this volume and our comparative analysis show that while most cultural constraints discussed thus far influence the *content* of mnemonic contests and play a role in determining whether a given actor is considered as a legitimate mnemonic actor, only one of them—cultural cleavage (ethnic, linguistic, or religious)—seems to have a powerful role in generating the patterns we discovered in our analysis of the *political-institutional form* of mnemonic regimes (fractured, pillarized, unified). This form is determined by specific combinations of values of the variables listed in Figure 1.1.

After preliminary analysis of our cases, we chose to focus on one particular historical-cultural constraint: the salience and strength of the religious, ethnic, or linguistic cleavages. In a number of the cases in the volume, tensions generated across such cleavages are central to mnemonic politics. The way in which different ethnic and religious groups have fared since the fall of communism will strongly affect the way in which that past is remembered. This is particularly acute in those countries for whom the fall of communism led to the attainment of independence, such as the former Yugoslavia and the Baltic states. Here the reordering of societies into the titular nationality and ethnic, linguistic, and/or religious minorities is an important cleavage, which, if politicized, has an important impact on memory politics.

Cultural Strategies

A selection of institutional (political) strategy (warrior, pluralist, abnegator or prospective) is independent of the choice of cultural strategy, that is, the choice of specific themes from the available set of narratives about the past that constitutes a "nation's heritage" and the cultural (also aesthetic) form of their presentation. As we argued earlier, the rejection of the national character concept is not tantamount to negating the existence of a relatively stable, accumulated over time, repertoire of themes and forms that comprise a semiotic (cultural) field that members of a given group (for example, a nation) are socialized to recognize as "theirs." While the repertoire of available forms and themes imposes a constraint on the actor, there are choices *within* it, and they have major political consequences. They determine to a large degree an actor's credibility, reputation, and legitimacy. For example, if narratives of victimhood are salient in a "national culture" and are central (*elemental*) to the "national story," an actor who wants to be "taken seriously" is ill advised to ignore their existence. But there is a choice. A mnemonic entrepreneur can contribute to increasing the centrality or marginality of such narratives, a decision driven either by strategic calculations or principled commitment to a version of the nation's history. Either way, the decision has political consequences and cultural repercussions for all actors involved in the public life of a given group (nation).

Take, for example, the identity of the actor who is in control of the government at the time of the twentieth anniversary. The content of that identity can affect whether the anniversary is celebrated and, if so, how it is celebrated and what interpretation is put on past events. The government's choice in turn will have a very important impact on how other actors participate in or respond to the commemoration and the picture of the past it presents.

Mnemonic entrepreneurs are also free to choose a form of emplotment for their narrative, though here also they want to stay within the boundaries of the historically sanctioned national repertoire of "traditional" forms in order to be politically effective. One possible analytical tool that can be employed in the analysis of mnemonic rhetoric is the typology of narrative styles proposed by Hayden White (1978). He distinguished between four modes of emplotment: romance, comedy, tragedy, and satire. While he argues that these modes correspond, however loosely, to distinct ideologies, we did not detect such an automatic correspondence between modes and ideological position in our cases. That, however, does not render such distinctions any less potentially useful from a descriptive or a theoretical viewpoint. Anthropologist F. G. Bailey offers an alternative typology of forms. He distinguished between logical reasoning, deliberative rhetoric, and hortatory rhetoric (Bailey 1981, summary in Aronoff and Kubik 2013, 75–76). While the first type is most common in scholarly debates, the second seems to correspond closely to the style favored by mnemonic pluralists. Hortatory rhetoric is expected to be a weapon of choice for mnemonic warriors.[32]

Arguably the single most important (and interesting) political issue in the study of post-communism, including mnemonic politics, is the strategic decision on new political identity made by the successor of the former ruling party.[33]

Ex-communist successor parties or politicians are constrained by their communist past (discussed earlier), but in addition to this constraint they are also free in their choice of new political identities. Ex-communists in the region followed one of three different political strategies to remain politically relevant in the period following transition. Those who rejected reform of the system can be thought of as *neo-communists* (initially the Communist Party of Bohemia and Moravia, the Communist Party of the Ukraine). Others took the route of pursuing intraparty reform in the quest to relegitimize their participation in the political system as *social democrats* (MSzP in Hungary, SdRP in Poland, Democratic Labor Party of Lithuania).

Finally, there is a third group that can most succinctly be described as "parties of power." Their functionaries, almost all of them ex-communists, are able to convert their positions of power in the party-state into positions of influence in the post-communist economy and politics. Some of them try to cast themselves as *nationalists* in articulating their claims on power (PDS in Romania, BSP in Bulgaria, Kuchma in Ukraine); others continue to rule without commitment to any particular ideology other than the pursuit of power itself (the fluctuating formations around Yeltsin and Putin in Russia, Lukashenko in Belarus, Kravchuk and Yanukovych in Ukraine). These could be described as "statist" in orientation. In general, ex-communists transform themselves into social democrats or neo-communists when they lose power during transitions. When they manage to keep their power, they re-legitimize themselves through adopting a statist position, often cloaked in a nationalist ideology.

The nature of the main successor party and its relationship to power can affect the basic dynamic of the contest to establish post-transitional memory regimes. Statist parties of power have tended to hold on to and not relinquish their power. Most of them try to invoke a logic of *raison d'état* that stresses unity over divisive recollections. They try to promote memory regimes that downplay repressive and ideological aspects of the pre-breakthrough polities and play up the accomplishments of the communist state. Such efforts are abetted by the degree to which such regimes are authoritarian. Ultimately, if and when the dominant party of power becomes vulnerable, it inevitably faces challenges concerning its role in the past and its selective reading of history.

Parties of power that rely on nationalist discourses attempt to legitimize their claims to rule by selectively embracing elements of the communist past that enhanced national prowess and prestige.[34] They may embrace the modernizing impact of communist rule, survival of the nation, and experience in governing. At the same time, they selectively castigate elements of the past such as inept policy performance, limitations on national sovereignty, and corrupt political behavior by the elites they have replaced. Often in such narratives, the blame for past wrongs and failures will be laid at the feet of the last leader of the old regime.

Generally speaking, parties of power provide convenient cover for what Ganev (2007) has called political capitalism. Former state assets are often converted into private property that in turn is used in patrimonial networks that support the party in power. Parties that emerged from anti-communist opposition often view such practices as the corrupt attainment of material advantage. We expect polities in which the main successor party is a party of power to provide its opposition with opportunities to effectively make use of a warrior strategy. Groups in opposition to successor parties of power will be able to derive political advantage by recollecting/ uncovering past wrongs and linking this specific mnemonic strategy to questioning whether the distribution of property and the benefits of the market following communism are just.

Social-democratic successor parties will seek to break with their communist past by adopting the democratic and reformist socialist model of the mass-based parties of the Center Left in Western Europe. At times their discourse about the past may be ambivalent and vague because of the difficulties of distancing themselves completely from their own communist "pre-history." But, by and large, these parties will want to abandon their pasts, often strongly criticizing communist rule and arguing that from transition onward their true democratic and reformist character has emerged. They often claim that this true nature was impossible to express when national sovereignty was constrained by the power politics of the Soviet Bloc. Often such parties will take a defensive pluralist stand about the past to fend off attacks that impugn their own reconstruction of the past. To the extent that they are able to control the struggle over memory, they favor a pillarized regime that treats the different interpretations of the past as mutually acceptable or at least tolerated representations of the nation's past.[35]

Opposition parties may be able to exploit the pasts of social democratic successor parties from the position of memory warriors, accusing them of preserving at least some privileges of the old system in a new guise, and leveling claims of injustice. Such groups may also reject the pillarization of memory and advocate an ideology of "no real change" or "hijacked revolution" that also can be used against other non-communist politicians who were partners in compromise with the former communists. Such rhetorical attacks, when they gain traction, lead to a fractured memory regime.

Finally, neo-communist successor parties have no choice but celebrate at least some aspects of the defunct system while often trying to blame past problems and failures on the previous leadership of the party. Other parties usually treat them as pariahs, and as long as they do not capture a sufficiently large share of seats in the parliament they do not have much of an effect on memory politics. Such parties will tend to try to capitalize on nostalgia for the communist past among "losers" of the transition, and play up political and economic difficulties of the pre-communist past. Here pointing out underdevelopment, gross inequality, and a history of pre-communist dictatorship works to their advantage.

Neo-communists tend to adopt a pluralist stance as they seek toleration of their more positive vision of the communist past. As they gain strength, they have the tendency to polarize other actors. Ideologically proximate parties may be tempted to enter into alliance with them, and this provokes even stronger reactions from anti-communist parties. Should neo-communist parties come close to power, either through electoral victory or through coalition with other parties, the memory regime will tend to fracture as non-successor parties will try to portray the successor parties' visions of the past and their return to power as beyond the bounds of what is acceptable.

Another important cultural choice revolves around the degree to which remembrance of a particular historical event is compartmentalized and stands alone or is influenced by commemoration of other events or issues. A phenomenon that attracted our attention early on during this study was the combining or mixing of a commemoration of one event with the cultivation of memories of another event or events; in our terminology, it is a strategy of linking different memory regimes. We call this strategy *layering*. For example, in Hungary many celebrations are layered with the memory of 1956. Or in Germany the anniversary of the fall of the Berlin Wall in 1989 came on the same day as the declaration of the Weimar Republic in 1918, the Beer Hall Putsch in 1923, and Kristallnacht in 1936. In the former Yugoslavia we observe layering with respect to the traumatic events of World War II and the Yugoslav Revolution, or the Yugoslav Wars of the 1990s and the genocidal acts committed in both. In the Baltic states, commemorations of the Baltic Way of 1989 were layered with memorialization of the Molotov-Ribbentrop Pact that led to the loss of independence in 1940. Layering can either weaken or strengthen the social, cultural, and political impact of a given commemoration (or another form of mnemonic practice).[36] And in some cases it can negate the impact of anniversaries and minimize their commemoration altogether.

Implications of Different Memory Regimes for the Quality of Democracy

Fractured, pillarized, and unified memory regimes have different ramifications for the quality of democracy. Unified memory regimes are most likely to exist in democracies in the long term only on the basis of a broad cultural consensus that is nonetheless hard to achieve and once attained very prone to breakdowns. Under such conditions, issues of public memory become depoliticized until a political and/ or mnemonic actor sees an advantage in challenging the mnemonic consensus. In the short term, unified memory regimes are likely to emerge only under specific sets of conditions in which actors face strong inhibitions about raising issues of the recent past. If actors see no political advantage in political competition from politicizing memory issues, then a universal stance of abnegation is possible.

Our expectation for post-communist democracies is that memory regimes will fluctuate between pillarized and unified on the one hand, and fractured on the other. There will be periods when competing political forces will be able to bracket questions about the past and the main axes of political struggle will be articulated across other issues. However, there will also be many periods when different interpretations of the past will become highly salient for their own sake or will be intertwined with other issues (e.g. transitional justice, economic performance, corruption, social issues, etc.). We expect new democracies to have turbulent mnemonic politics as they come to terms with pasts that are often difficult, and to experience periodic fracturing of the memory field fairly often.

What are the potential implications of the periodic fracturing of memory? First, the differences between pillarized/unified and fractured memory regimes (and fields) will have implications for the stability of both the *national discursive field* and the *polity's institutional framework*. Battles over the past will be directly related to the contests over which actors are legitimate and thus who has the right to frame institutions. To the extent that any party is deemed "illegitimate" by one side, any institutional compromise that is seen as protecting the interests of that party will be subject to sharp questioning and the possibility of revision.

Second, we believe that the differences between pillarized/unified and fractured memory regimes/fields will have implications for the *stability of the party system*. There are three reasons for this. To begin, when electoral campaigns are waged in terms that question the legitimacy of opponents, successful attacks may seriously and negatively impact the entire party system (Wasilewski 2010). Because of the high-stakes nature of political conflict under such conditions, mnemonic warfare produces higher volatility in the party system and contributes to the enfeeblement or even the extinction of some parties. Such campaigns may well cripple or destroy opponents, perhaps even driving them out of the political field. Finally, political conflicts that are waged in terms of painting the opponent as the "enemy," rather than a "competitor," are dangerous for the attacker as well. By defining the stakes of the political contest as dire, failure by the party making the attack makes it seem incompetent in the face of danger, and may lead to a weakening of its support.

Third, we believe that a fractured memory regime complicates issues of *governability*. The existence of a highly politicized mnemonic cleavage along with a more "normal" Left-Right ideological cleavage has two effects. First, when a memory field is composed of a large number of fractured—as opposed to a pillarized or unified—memory regimes,[37] questions potentially articulated in terms of different interpretations of the past become non-negotiable and tend to generate politics defined as a contest of maximalist demands. Such a pattern of demands contributes to centrifugal pressures in the whole political system. Second, differences on questions of memory may divide potential partners in adjacent issue spaces, complicating the process of coalition formation for governments or exacerbating the fragility of existing coalitions. Thus we expect fractured memory regimes and fields to be associated with more polarized, as opposed to moderate, forms of party pluralism (Sartori 1976; Capoccia 2007; Wasilewski 2010).

Fourth, more fractured memory regimes/fields should produce more *contentious civil societies*. Non-negotiable issues should generate greater consternation about unaddressed or unsuccessfully resolved disputes. As the stakes of the battle over interest articulation and satisfaction go up, more intense and even violent forms of collective action (riots, destruction of property) should become more common. We should also see greater instances of direct physical conflict between contending forces in the public space.

Fifth, the existence of fractured memory regimes/fields contributes to lowering the levels of *interpersonal trust* (Rothstein 2000). Mutually irreconcilable interpretations of the past stigmatize different parts of the body politic as holding illegitimate views or as not having legitimate claims to fully participate in politics. Thus, contending political forces that cultivate irreconcilable visions of the past trust each other less. This, in turn, contributes to the underdevelopment of both cultural and social capital, shown to be often beneficial for economic growth (Sen 2004; Woolcock 1998; Woolcock and Narayan 2000; Petro 2001, 2004).

What to Expect in the Chapters That Follow

In this volume we are studying the commemorations of 1989/1991 in 2009/2011 as key components of the "1989/1991 memory regimes" in several post-communist countries. What we want to explain is the variance in the nature of these mnemonic regimes (fractured, unified, pillarized). We asked the authors of country case studies to utilize our analytical frame, paying close attention to the nature of the mnemonic actors (warriors, abnegators, and pluralists) engaged in the politics of the twentieth anniversary commemorations, the political pedigree and stances characteristic of such actors, and the substance of their discourses about the past. We also asked them to explain why particular actors took the stances that they did.

After the presentation of the country casework that utilizes our analytical framework, we return to our attempt to explain the patterns of memory politics revealed by close examination of the twentieth anniversary commemorations. After a careful examination of case studies, we concluded that in our final comparative analysis we need to include the following set of explanatory variables: (1) the type of state socialism that existed in a given country, (2) the mode of extrication from state socialism, (3) the nature of the cleavage structure at the time of commemoration (Left-Right; ethnic, religious, linguistic; both, or neither), (4) the nature of the communist successor party, and (5) the existence of memory layering during commemoration and its nature. While the authors of case study chapters often consider a broader range of explanatory variables, in the concluding chapter we systematically compare only these factors and offer several generalizations, which we obtained by using qualitative comparative analysis (QCA) belonging to a group of methods and techniques sometimes referred to as configurational comparative methods (CCM) (Rihoux and Ragin 2009, xix).

NOTES

1. Nora writes: "The explosion of memory was worldwide. For multiple reasons and in various forms, it touched all areas of civilization and every country. It occurred a little earlier in France than in other countries... [as around 1975 this country was pushed-JK and MB] from a historical awareness of itself into an awareness of memory" (2001, x).

2. See, for example: Nora 1989; Lebow, Kansteiner, and Fogu, eds. 2006; Maier 1988; Pakier and Starth, eds. 2010; Olick, Vinitzky-Seroussi, and Levy, eds. 2011. See also Żakowski 2002 for a serious journalistic study augmented by several interviews with major thinkers working on collective memory.

3. See Wilde 1999; Cruz 2000; Davis 2005; Art 2006; Petro 2001, 2004; Rossi 2009; Nalepa 2010; Shevel 2011; Stan 2013; Mink and Neumayer 2013.

4. As Cruz argues: "we cannot grasp the nature and dynamics of political identity—and collective identity more broadly—unless we understand the rhetorical frames that emerge as dominant at critical junctures in the history of a group or a nation" (2000, 276). See also Assmann 1995; Gillis 1994; Davis 2005; and Gawin 2010 on legitimacy and memory.

5. Matsuda summarizes Renan's famous musings on the formation of the nation. He reminds us, *inter alia*, that for Renan "the memory of a 'collective' was the memory of the forging of that collective..." (1996, 206).

6. By the writing of history we mean the production of representations of the past in a variety of mediums. Such production is not limited to the actual writing of historical narratives, but also includes fiction, art, and mass media.

7. Nalepa (2010) has been an important voice in advocating a more instrumental approach to the study of transitional justice. Such an instrumentalist approach is practiced not only by political scientists. Nancy Wood, a media scholar, develops an analytical framework in which

she treats collective memory as "essentially *performative*—i.e. as only coming to existence at a given time and place through specific kinds of memorial activity." She further observes: "If particular representations of the past have permeated the public domain, it is because they embody an intentionality—social, political, institutional and so on—that promotes and authorizes their entry" (1999, 2). See also Yael Zerubavel (1995, 3–12); such an approach also informs the work of historian James Mark (2011).

8. Such visions evolve and sometimes even get radically modified in a complex process involving a play of mutual adjustment between what the mnemonic entrepreneur proposes and what a given audience is prepared to accept.

9. See Olick and Robbins (1998, 128–130) for an excellent discussion of these issues from multiple perspectives.

10. Kansteiner (2002) provides a thorough discussion of the difference between psychological and social mechanisms of memory. See, in particular pages 185–190.

11. Assmann's distinction (1995) between "communicative memory" and "cultural memory" is relevant here.

12. Collective memory understood as a "frame" "symbolically structures the political claim-making which is always both strategic and constitutive of politics" (Müller 2002, 26).

13. See Linz and Stepan (1996) and Ekiert (1996) for a fuller discussion of political society as a constituent component of the polity.

14. For instance, the current "culture of contrition" in Germany concerning the Holocaust was stimulated by a public debate that began as an exchange between prominent intellectuals. See Maier 1988; Art 2006. Similarly, the Polish memory regime of World War II was transformed by the debate over the Jedwabne massacre provoked by the publication of a book on the subject by Jan Gross (2001). Also see Polonsky and Michlic (2004).

15. Cultural change can certainly be accelerated through traumatic events such as revolution or war, but lasting change is usually measured in terms of generations rather than years (Verba 1965). See also Swidler (1986) on cultural change in unsettled periods.

16. An example of a traumatic event that transformed the politics of memory would include the crash of the airplane carrying Polish president Kaczyński and many high-ranking Polish functionaries to a Katyń commemoration on April 10, 2010. The impact was to further politicize "the Katyń case" and increase the degree of national trauma associated with the original event. A foreign policy realignment example would include the creation of the European Union and how the French and Germans now view their antithetic past. Examples of spillover effects from historical debates include the *Historikerstreit* in Germany, or the Jedwabne controversy in Poland, discussed in the note above.

17. Some memory regimes constituting a mnemonic field are official—when the authorities and/or major political actors are central in their construction—and some are not.

18. The relationship between the entrance of a warrior and the nature of the resulting mnemonic regime can be determined in two ways: either by definition or via an empirical study. We can decide that the field of memory politics populated by at least one mnemonic warrior will be called *fractured*. In contrast, we can pursue an empirical strategy, which requires that we look for an empirical relationship between the presence of a warrior and the type of regime (defined by different criteria). Such empirical study is based on the hypothesis that any mix of at least one politically relevant memory warrior with other warriors, pluralists, or abnegators will dramatically increase the probability of emergence of intense mnemonic struggles and thus a fractured/

contentious memory regime (which must be defined independently of the mix of actors). We adopt the definitional strategy.

19. Such unity could also emerge through hegemony, but we believe that mnemonic hegemony is not compatible with democracy. The dynamics of mnemonic contests in non-democratic regimes is different than in democratic polities and requires separate treatment.

20. This seems to be the situation in Spain where major political actors negotiated a Pact on Forgetting, which according to Encarnación (2014) promoted the post-1975 consolidation of democracy. The Pact, which was in place until 2007, prevented the politicization of potentially divisive memories of the Civil War and Francoist repression.

21. It strikes us that in contexts different from the post-communist cases considered here, prospectives could also function as warriors of a different sort, and would have the same fracturing effect on memory regimes. Given the paucity of prospectives in our set of cases, we are unable to substantiate this empirically.

22. Yael Zerubavel writes: "Collective memory continuously negotiates between available historical records and current social and political agendas" (1995, 5).

23. The logic here is simple. If in the mix of actors there is one pluralist (by definition accepting the mnemonic decisions of others) and the rest are abnegators, the resulting mnemonic regime is pillarized.

24. The figure is not exhaustive—for the sake of clarity of presentation, only a few illustrative factors, especially those central to a consideration of the commemoration of the fall of communism, are listed here.

25. There are three factors that contribute to the generation of liberalized regimes: (1) the presence of strong dissident movements with cross-class alliances, (2) a somewhat liberalized official political culture (selectively accepting the discourse on civil rights), and (3) less oppressive communist rule (including relative openness to the West).

26. We avoid use of the term "transition to democracy" here because there is variation in regime type across the sample of countries we study in the volume. All of the cases are competitive polities. Along with several long-established democracies, there are some that have fluctuated between democracy and competitive authoritarianism (Romania, Slovakia, Ukraine, Serbia, Croatia).

27. The literature on the relationship between the type of extrication and the transitory justice regime is extensive (Huntington 1991; Kraus 1995; Moran 1994; Nedelsky 2004; Stan and Nedelsky 2012; Stan 2013). We want to contribute to a related yet understudied field: the relationship between the type of extrication and the type of mnemonic regime.

28. It has to be acknowledged that skillful actors pursue control of such assets as part of their strategy as mnemonic actors. Both pluralists and warriors might well seek control of the process of coming to terms with crimes and injustices of the old regime and the institutions that oversee this process. Skillful tactics of this sort may make one's mnemonic strategy more effective, or may blunt the strategy of opponents.

29. Since the salience and importance of the Left-Right cleavage varied considerably over the first twenty years of post-communist transformations and we believe that it is reasonable to think of them as having a short-term impact. We focus on them at the time of twentieth anniversary commemorations in 2009/2011.

30. See, for example, Rusu (2011) and Dutceac Segesten (2011) on the evolution of Romanian history textbooks both before and after 1989.

31. This is not to say that such repertoires are fixed or unchanging in the long run. They may evolve over time, or new ones may emerge in periods of rapid or disjunctive cultural change.

32. Rather than focus on the type of rhetoric in this study, we choose to analyze the strategically chosen forms and particular content of mnemonic pronouncements and performances. Our goal is to see how these choices are related to what we call positional strategic choices of actors.

33. Given the strong similarities between the political systems and to a much more limited extent the political cultures of European communist regimes, we believe that they will share some problems as new post-communist memory regimes emerge.

34. State socialist regimes often invoked nationalistic/patriotic motifs in their attempts to legitimize their power, though with varying degrees of success. See Verdery (1991) on Romania, Ramet (1992) on Yugoslavia, or Kubik on Poland (1994) as well as on Poland and Russia (2003).

35. The preamble of the Polish Constitution is an excellent example of such a pillarized formulation. It was written when the post-communists, the SdRP, controlled the parliament. However, it was subject to contestation by anti-communist political forces and the Catholic Church. After a protracted deliberation, the following compromise formulation found its way into the final document: "Having regard for the existence and future of our Homeland, which recovered, in 1989, the possibility of a sovereign and democratic determination of its fate, we, the Polish Nation—all citizens of the Republic, both those who believe in God as the source of truth, justice, good and beauty, as well as those not sharing such faith but respecting those universal values as arising from other sources, equal in rights and obligations towards the common good—Poland..." For details on the struggle, see Bernhard 2005, 206.

36. The phenomenon of memory layering can be also studied as a constraint (for example, a layered tradition), not as a strategy. We have chosen to emphasize the strategic dimension of layering since we are focusing on what actors are doing during a specific event (commemorations of the fall of state socialism).

37. Memory fields are fractured (unified, pillarized) when most of the component regimes are fractured (unified, pillarized) or when a predominant cleavage in the polity is wholly or in part based on a fractured (unified, pillarized) memory regime.

1 Fractured Memory Regimes

2 Revolutionary Road

1956 AND THE FRACTURING OF HUNGARIAN HISTORICAL MEMORY

Anna Seleny

Introduction

Annus mirabilis, some called it—the year of miracles—when the previously unimaginable came to seem inexorable. In 1989, Hungarians and the citizens of other Eastern European countries assembled en masse in streets and squares, and independent political parties across the ideological spectrum emerged from a nascent civil society. As in Poland in 1989, opposition parties and the government negotiated the delicate transition to democracy. The Hungarian Third Republic was born on October 23, 1989. A Center-Right coalition won the country's first free elections since 1947, and the former Communist Party, in coalition with a liberal party of anti-communist dissidents, began its new role as the minority party in parliament.

Even before the elections, there had been other notable events during 1989. In the spring, the Hungarian government began dismantling parts of the barbed wire on its western border, followed in June 1989 by a meeting of the Hungarian and Austrian foreign ministers at the border, where they symbolically cut a section of the wire separating their countries. Encouraged by press photos of the event, thousands of East German vacationers converged on Hungary in hopes of crossing through Austria to West Germany. In August 1989, at a celebration that opposition groups had planned at the border, hundreds of East German tourists crossed through a simple wooden gate into Austria, testing Gorbachev's reassurances that he would not use Soviet troops to intervene in the domestic affairs of other socialist countries. In September, Hungary opened the border for good, and tens of thousands of East Germans traveled to West Germany via Austria. A little over a year later, on the eve of German unification, Helmut Kohl declared: "that was when the first stone was knocked out of the Wall" (1990, 264).

Twenty years later, in the summer of 2009, near the town where the East Germans crossed the border, Hungarians celebrated at a multi-day festival and again received accolades from the assembled international dignitaries for their country's role in bringing down the wall. That autumn, the nation formally commemorated but hardly celebrated its transition to democracy on October 23, 1989. The choice of this date for the birthday of the Hungarian Third Republic anchored it to another much darker one: the anniversary of the beginning of the 1956 revolution.

The political and cultural construction of Hungarian collective memory returns time and again to the 1956 uprising against Soviet occupation and its violent suppression by the Red Army. Not even the epochal events of 1989 or their commemoration in 2009 escaped its shadow. This chapter argues that political entrepreneurs transformed the uprising of 1956, a pivotal historical moment of national unity, into a source of extreme political polarization that fractured Hungarians' understanding of the 1989 transition, rendered a unified commemoration in 2009 virtually impossible, and ultimately weakened Hungarian democracy. These developments are especially puzzling since Hungary was long regarded as one of the most successful examples of stable democratic consolidation in the post-communist world.

How was this possible? Part of the answer points to the instrumental side of the politics of memory, and part points to the challenges that mnemonic actors face when dealing with a long-suppressed past and its ambiguous legacies. In 1989, new mnemonic warriors and belated pluralists alike seized the democratic transition as a strategic opportunity to define and instrumentalize 1956 and its aftermath. Neither group succeeded at the time. Rather, the contestation of 1956 became the polity's central point of reference—an unresolved struggle whose imagery and passions continued to prove indispensable to key political actors as they set out to decode and expose motivations, assign merit and blame, and articulate collective visions of the future. Mnemonic abnegators and pluralists—party reformers and liberal opposition groups alike—framed Hungary's consensus-based transition to democracy as an "us *and* them" process. Nevertheless, by the twentieth anniversary of the transition, mnemonic warriors would dominate a profoundly fractured memory regime. Political entrepreneurs on the Right and extreme Right cast Hungarian politics as a return to a revolutionary road punctuated by "us *versus* them" struggles that would ultimately vindicate the 1956 revolution. Key to the Right's framing of these battles was the theme of a revolution twice betrayed: first by the communists and their Soviet overlords, and then decades later by a "pseudo-transition" that failed to sweep away the socialists and provide the moral clarity that they perceived to be the driving force of 1956.

And yet the sense of a nation united in opposition masks the political complexities of a revolution fought by a large, unruly, and ideologically diverse group. The uprising of 1956 began as a movement to reform socialism, and quickly evolved into something larger. The diversity and the ambiguities of the revolution partly explain why all major political actors since the 1989 transition sought to stake their rightful claim as the true heirs of 1956. Such a claim, however, could be certified only by definitively establishing the meaning of the revolution itself. For the mnemonic warriors, the task was clear: to craft a credible and exclusive narrative of irreconcilable antagonism along the communist/anti-communist divide. The pluralists needed to stake their claim as well, or be left out of the game. Their task was more complicated, however, since pluralist narratives tend to be more nuanced and thus are vulnerable to the logic of simplification inherent in the warriors' alternative.

The enduring power of 1956 also derives from the decades-long suppression of its memory, and from the profound ambiguities—the blurring of identities, interests, and ideology—that resulted from the post-1956 coerced bargain between state and society. For more than forty years, the Hungarian Socialist Workers' Party (MSzMP) enforced an official story that depicted the uprising as a counterrevolution orchestrated through foreign subversion. Most Hungarians came to accept a relatively peaceful *modus vivendi* with the party-state: an acceptably high standard of living, increasing economic and cultural freedom, more opportunity to travel, and a marginal expansion of political freedom in exchange for respect for the political order.

The trauma of 1956 thus became central to the nation's "public forgetting" (Livitz 2006–2007). This forced compromise—an implicit "pact" between state and society—left most Hungarians in a morally equivocal relationship with the regime, but it produced many positive outcomes. From the 1960s on, the pact allowed reform-minded Communists to work with a range of societal groups to create a degree of flexibility and prosperity unknown elsewhere in the Soviet bloc. Unlike its counterparts in other countries of the region, by the late 1980s the Hungarian Socialist Worker's Party had already scrapped most restrictions on the private sector and had established the comprehensive legal foundations for a modern capitalist economy. The compromise produced meaningful legal-institutional changes and even political pluralism within the confines of the one-party state. By 1988, in fact, there was no single Communist Party, except in name. The remaining hard-liners—old mnemonic warriors from the 1950s—had settled into an opportunistic stance, willing to distort the past to their advantage but no longer willing to wage overt battles on the field of orthodoxy. Reformers, for their part, had become the dominant force within the party, but they preferred to avoid memory politics on pragmatic grounds.

By the late 1980s, however, some of these mnemonic abnegators emerged as pluralists, and during the transition they revised the official history of 1956 in an attempt to draw on the revolution's legitimating power. An emergent opposition party, the Alliance of Young Democrats (Fidesz, later Fidesz/Hungarian Civic Union), sought instead to highlight rifts obscured by the compromise, invoking 1956 to sharpen political identities and ideological divisions. Fidesz would eventually seek to construct its own revolution out of two key events: the riots and demonstrations of 2006—the first of their kind the country had seen since 1956—and its own decisive electoral victory in 2010. As we will see, for Fidesz—and for the extremist party Jobbik (Movement for a Better Hungary)—2006 represented a signal moment in the struggle for ideological-moral clarity that would ultimately accomplish what neither 1956 nor 1989 could: to vanquish the socialists and their legacy.

This chapter, then, weaves this dual narrative of 1956 and 1989 into the analysis of the twentieth anniversary of the latter. The first section looks back at the main events of the transition from Communism in 1988–1989, and shows the ways in which political actors sought to harness the legacy of the 1956 revolution to their purposes. The second section examines the salient themes in the 2009 twentieth anniversary commemorations, and shows that even after twenty years, the commemoration of 1989 remained entwined with—even overpowered by—1956. The third section identifies sources of Hungarians' conflicting understandings of their history, and highlights some of the events that have produced a profoundly fractured memory regime. The chapter concludes with an analysis of how these differing interpretations came alive in the growing polarization of contemporary party politics and a rising tide of right-wing, ethno-nationalist, and extremist forces.

The Transition: 1988–1989

The year 1988 saw more mass demonstrations than any year since 1956. The first of these harkened back to yet another revolutionary landmark in the nation's past. On March 15, 1988, the one hundred fortieth anniversary of the 1848 uprising against Austria, tens of thousands marched in unauthorized demonstrations and rallies in Budapest. This civic mobilization strengthened the legitimacy of opposition groups' demands for reform, and persuaded the party to begin negotiations with opposition groups. A week later, the Opposition Roundtable—a group representing the most important opposition parties, proto-parties, and civil society organizations—was founded. This was followed by other mass demonstrations against external targets and seemingly non-political causes: protesting the Ceaușescu government's attempt at ethnic cleansing of the Hungarian minority in Transylvania, and marching for environmental protection and in opposition to the long-planned Hungarian-Czechoslovak dam and power station at Nagymaros-Gabčikovo.

Against this backdrop of civic mobilization, in January 1989, the parliament laid the legal foundations for a multiparty system and legislated the right of assembly and religion, as well as the right to strike. By May, MSzMP reformers had forced the aged János Kádár to resign from the post of general secretary of the party's central committee, which he had occupied since 1956. Replacing Kádár would prove decisive in opening space to reclaim key historical memories, including his responsibility for the murder of the former prime minister Imre Nagy and other leaders of the revolution in 1958. By the spring of 1988, friends and supporters of Nagy had established the Committee for Historical Justice, and on the thirtieth anniversary of his murder held a small commemoration at the unmarked grave in the Kerepesi cemetery where he was buried.

The Trilateral Opposition Roundtable

The Hungarian transition, as Csaba Békés points out, was unique in the sense that the opposition and the MSzMP shared a key objective: the elimination of the Brezhnev Doctrine. The party's eye was on the forthcoming elections. Polls showed that the MSzMP could win between 36 and 40 percent of the votes, which in turn meant that the party might realistically hope to rely not on Soviet support but on electoral legitimacy (Békés 2002, 244). This coincidence of interests partly accounts, in the words of Miklós Haraszti, for the "handshake transition" itself, and for the overarching spirit of compromise that characterized the Opposition Roundtable Talks (Haraszti 2011, 7).

But party reformers' decision to change the long-standing official narrative about 1956 also facilitated compromise. According to the revised version, 1956 was in fact not a "counterrevolution" but a "popular uprising" aimed at a "debasing" system of "oligarchic rule." The changes amounted to an important admission of the revolution's legitimacy (Ash 1990, 42) and opened the way for the previously unthinkable: the exhumation and reburial of the remains of Nagy and the other leaders of the revolution. This meant revisiting the most sensitive aspect of the trauma of 1956 and reopening the wound inflicted on Hungary's national identity. The overthrow and murder of Imre Nagy, after all, bound together powerful themes in which the nation and the man became as one—an autonomous spirit crushed by a foreign power, a Hungarian betrayed by brethren, a martyred hero confined to oblivion.

Indeed, the MSzMP leadership was keenly aware of Nagy's symbolic power. The party's move in 1989 from mnemonic abnegation to recognition was a calculated risk that reformers took in hopes of gaining popular support. Their hopes were not realized. For if 1956 was not to be condemned as a counterrevolution that undermined Hungarian socialism and universal communist ideals, then what was the justification for the execution of Nagy and other revolutionaries? The shift did, however, have a major impact on the 1989 transition, since the reinterpreting of 1956 and the rehabilitation of its heroes helped smooth the way for the Roundtable Talks.

The Roundtable, intended to create a united front among the diverse opposition groups as they negotiated with the MSzMP, ended in a historic agreement signed on September 18, 1989, and produced six draft laws, including laws mandating free elections to be held in March 1990, a full review and revision of the Constitution, and the establishment of a Constitutional Court.

The talks proceeded in a charged political context. Gorbachev's more relaxed stance toward Eastern Europe, the Polish Roundtable Talks, the earlier reforms undertaken by the MSzMP itself, and an emergent civil society all helped to create an environment in which possibilities previously unimaginable now loomed large on the public stage. And among those possibilities, none stoked passions or offered as much opportunity for political entrepreneurs as the reburial of Nagy, which took place three days after the start of the Roundtable Talks, and further emboldened the opposition in their negotiations. Indeed, the reburial not only symbolically created a historical context for ongoing political discourse, but afterward, any unreconstructed Communists remaining in the MSzMP were in effect admitting that they or their predecessors had acted as "unjust executioners in the popular uprising, the leaders of which they were forced to honor at the reburial" (Livitz 2006–2007).

The Reburial

On June 16, some 300,000 people attended the funeral ceremony for Nagy and five of his closest associates. A number of foreign dignitaries and MSzMP officials honored the martyrs, while millions watched the event live on television. Hungarian flags with hammer and sickle torn out of the center—the symbol of the 1956 revolution—hung from colonnades, and ceremonial fires burned next to the six coffins (the sixth for the "unknown insurgent"). The emotion of the moment can hardly be overstated: Imre Mécs, who in 1956 narrowly escaped execution by the Communists, believed that the reburial brought the nation together in the same way that the revolution itself had 33 years earlier.

Opposition speakers seized the opportunity to demand national sovereignty and democracy, and drew on the revolutions of 1848 and 1956 to frame their vision of the nation's political future. Mécs, who was to become a leader of the Free Democrats, asked mourners to commit to the words of Sándor Petőfi, the 1848 revolutionary: "no more shall we be slaves!" and to promise Imre Nagy, as if he were the nation's patron saint, to vindicate "the achievements of the Revolution" (Ash 1990, 51; Rév 1995, 31).

Fidesz's Viktor Orbán used 1956 to paint reform communists and hard-liners as equally deserving of deep suspicion. In a speech that energized the somber crowd and presaged themes to which he would repeatedly return over the next two decades, the emerging mnemonic warrior attacked the MSzMP for "suppressing our revolution," and for burdening the nation with a "bankrupt state.":

> We cannot understand that those who were eager to slander the Revolution and its prime minister have suddenly changed into great supporters of Imre Nagy. Nor can we understand that the party leaders, who made us study from books, which falsified the Revolution, now rush to touch the coffins, as if they were charms of good luck. (Benziger, 9–10)

Orbán's speech, and the repeated applause from the crowd, intensified the aura of isolation surrounding the reform communists, who had been late in their efforts to "repossess" Nagy's symbol. Now, ironically, they found themselves identified with the old hard-liners.

Hungarian intellectuals, as well as domestic and foreign scholars, understandably tend to emphasize the pivotal role of the Opposition Roundtable in the establishment of Hungary's post-Communist democracy (Bozóki 2002). After all, these talks framed—and in large measure forced—the MSzMP's peaceful exit from power, and led to direct elections. But it is noteworthy that even during the talks, the opposition used 1956 and the figure of Nagy to stake out an unequivocal position. During the talks' Plenary Session, three days before the reburial, on June 13, 1989, Imre Kónya of the Hungarian Democratic Forum (MDF) and the opposition's main spokesman, connected the upcoming ceremony to the body politic: "Burying the martyrs of the Revolution and commencing these talks can mark the beginning of national reconciliation. Real reconciliation, however, can only be achieved by burying the existing dictatorial power system" (Benziger, 10).

Despite a newly expanded opportunity structure, key political actors continued to place 1956 at the very center of the democratic transition. Two other moments stand out. The first came when the president of the new democracy, Mátyás Szűrös, symbolically retraced Nagy's fateful steps. On October 23, 1989—the thirty-third anniversary of the beginning of the anti-Soviet revolution—Szűrös stood on the same balcony of the parliament building from which Nagy had made his historic address to the nation in 1956. To cheering crowds in the square below, Szűrös proclaimed the Hungarian Republic an independent, democratic state. More significant still, he invoked the revolution to legitimate the new rules of the game. "The new constitution," he intoned, was "motivated by the lessons of the historic uprising and national independence movement of 1956" (Ash 1993, 59).

The second moment came in 1990 when the first post-communist democratic parliament drafted as its first bill a declaration of 1956 as a "War of Independence," signaling the government's determination to block further historical reinterpretations by the socialists. The mistrust was not hard to understand. For in its death throes, as late as September 1989 and months after the reburial, hard-liners in the MSzMP had tried to discredit Nagy.[1] These men, to be sure, would soon fade into irrelevance, yet the mnemonic landscape was not without contradictions. On July 6, less than a month after the reburial of the men he betrayed, János Kádár died, not in obscurity or disgrace, but mourned by thousands of ordinary citizens who attended the state funeral. Many wept openly. Despite the dramatic rehabilitation of the 1956 martyred heroes, Kádár's legacy was not banished from memory. And indeed. in the elections of 1994, the new democratic socialist party was elected in a landslide, and was re-elected twice, in 2002 and 2006.

Celebrating and Contesting 1989: The Commemorations of 2009

Parliament, June 27, 2009

If Hungarians could agree on anything in 2009, it was that the country had torn the first hole in the Iron Curtain between Western and Eastern Europe. It is unsurprising, then, that the most enthusiastic twentieth anniversary commemorations were those focused on the spring and summer of 1989, when the government's decisions set in motion events that ended with the dismantling of the Berlin Wall.

It began with the socialist government's decision to dismantle the alarm system and take down the barbed wire on the border with Austria in May and June 1989. Thus, in June 2009, hundreds of guests gathered in the upper chamber of the country's gothic parliament on the Danube embankment to celebrate the twentieth anniversary of what President László Sólyom called the day the "partitioning of Europe came to an end." The presidents of Germany, Austria, Switzerland, Finland, and Slovenia, along with high-ranking officials like the president of the Polish Sejm and the speaker of the British House of Lords, representatives of more than twenty other countries and of the European Council, attended the special commemorative session of parliament, and later a gala at the Hungarian State Opera House. There was the obligatory military parade and the parade of flags from the countries whose representatives were present. The national anthem was played, followed by the anthem of the European Union, Beethoven's *Ode to Joy*.

Hungarians and their guests were commemorating without ambivalence or qualms a ceremony that in 1989 had been planned as a modest public relations event, and whose geopolitical ramifications had been unforeseen. On June 27 the Hungarian foreign minister Gyúla Horn and his Austrian counterpart Alois Mock cut a small section of barbed wire on the border. But when the photos of the ceremony were published in newspapers around the world, tens of thousands of East Germans, many of whom had for years vacationed at Hungary's Lake Balaton or in other Eastern European countries, sought temporary refuge in Hungary, Poland, or Czechoslovakia in hopes of traveling to West Germany. By summer's end, thousands of East German "tourists" were living in tents outside the West German Embassy and elsewhere in Budapest, and in towns nearer the border. This was the precursor to the so-called Pan European Picnic.

The Pan European Picnic

The city of Sopron, on the border between Hungary and Austria, celebrated the twentieth anniversary of the Pan-European picnic held on August 18–19, 1989, when Hungary's border with Austria was briefly opened, and hundreds of East Germans crossed freely to the west for the first time since the Berlin Wall was constructed in 1961. An elaborate two-day official ceremony was held to mark the occasion in 2009 at Sopronpuszta, a field outside Sopron. Prime Minister Gordon Bajnai and visiting German chancellor Angela Merkel, among others, made commemorative speeches, and President Sólyom unveiled a white marble monument called "Breakthrough" in memory of those who had risked their lives to cross the Iron Curtain. The dignitaries also met with a number of the East Germans who had crossed the border in 1989, and mounted numerous photo exhibits at an anniversary conference, which included speakers like the patrons of the Pan-European picnic Otto Hapsburg and Imre Pozsgay, as well as former East German prime minister Lothar de Maizière.

Twenty years prior, when the Wall still stood, the Hungarian border patrol had simply stepped aside and made no attempt to stop hundreds of mostly young East Germans participating in the Pan-European Picnic when they attempted to cross the border into Austria. The Picnic had been organized by members of the anti-communist opposition parties, with the support of Otto von Hapsburg, president of the Pan-European Union, and his daughter Walburga. Minister of State Imre Pozsgay also threw his support behind the plan, which was intended to promote friendship between East and West. The Austrians and Hungarians had decided to demonstrate this friendship by opening a short stretch of the common border at Sopronpuszta for three hours one afternoon, and to allow small groups from both sides of the border to conduct "an ordinary exchange of greetings between local populations" (Kiscsatári 2009, 13).

It was no accident, however, that hundreds of East Germans had arrived at the picnic hoping to walk across the border into Austria. Word had spread that during the previous spring, Hungary had signed the 1951 UN Convention on Refugees because of the increasing number of refugees arriving from Transylvania. Prime Minister Németh recalled in 2009 that he decided that Hungary should sign the convention so as not to be forced to turn them back, since it provided that no one seeking asylum could be sent back to his country of origin against his will (UNHCR 2012, 3).

Thus, after Austria and Hungary began dismantling the border defenses in late June 1989, the number of East Germans flowing into Hungary continued to grow. Invoking the 1969 extradition agreement between the German Democratic Republic (GDR) and Hungary, the East German authorities demanded the extradition of the "tourists" who wanted to leave the GDR. But public opinion in Hungary was in sympathy with the refugees, and the Hungarian leadership flatly refused Honecker's demands.

Németh's plan had been to permit a small number of East Germans to cross the border at the picnic, and he let it be known that "if on 19 August they 'just happened' to be staying in the area around Sopron, they were free to leave unimpeded." "...[M]aps, flyers and press releases" invited Hungarians and Austrians to the picnic. Less officially, East German tourists were also invited (Kiscsatári 2009, 13). Thousands of people came, and the fields around Sopron turned into the "largest garden party in the world" (László Nagy, organizer, quoted in Kiscsatári 2009). As the news of the Picnic spread, the number of East Germans coming to Hungary and refusing to go home grew almost overnight by several thousand. On August 25, Németh and Horn secretly flew to Bonn to meet Chancellor Kohl and Foreign Minister Genscher at Gymnich Castle. Németh told his hosts that he would open the borders "unless some external force prevents us" (Balogh 2009b).

The key point here is that the role of Hungary's last socialist government in the opening of the border before the democratic transition—and Németh's determination in particular—was well-known among the political elite; the facts were not in dispute. And yet already at the tenth anniversary of the occasion in 1999, for instance, when Fidesz was in power for the first time, the government drew a veil of silence over that part of history. In a telling move, Fidesz invited West German chancellor Helmut Kohl and his foreign minister, Hans Dietrich Genscher, but asked them not to give speeches; which may be why neither attended. Fidesz also asked the socialist Németh and his former foreign minister Gyúla Horn not to speak.

As political entrepreneurs, Fidesz's leaders showed a consistent appreciation for the symbolic capital that is often at stake in momentous public occasions. In 1989, Fidesz had demanded a place among the speakers at Nagy's reburial. Ten years later, however, its political leadership denied a voice to key protagonists in the opening of the border. Twenty years later, even at one of the few truly festive commemorative events in 2009, the Europa Concert in Sopron, József Szájer, leader of the Fidesz parliamentary faction, denied the socialist reformers any credit for the instrumental role they had played in the border opening in 1989. It was the people, according to Szájer, who had made possible a united community of Hungarians, Austrians, and Germans. In Szájer's view, the socialists had done little more than fight freedom and oppose the founding of Fidesz. These enemies of freedom, Szájer asserted, were still in political life. They were even among the celebrants. Hungarians' dreams of freedom had yet to be fulfilled, Szájer concluded, and he envisioned a struggle ahead (Szájer 2009).

With each passing year, Fidesz only hardened its exclusionary line, and rebuffed the socialists and liberals in their public calls for a more inclusive approach to the political and cultural construction of memory. Perhaps the clearest articulation of that approach remains Prime Minister Gordon Bajnai's speech at the Opera House in June 2009. As Eva S. Balogh recounts, on that occasion, Bajnai depicted the regime change of 1989 not as the product of a clash between two irreconcilable forces but as "the common cause" of the Németh government and the participants in the Roundtable discussions. Bajnai took care to mention the most important actors in the drama, including Orbán. More broadly still, Bajnai advocated a vision of politics as a constructive enterprise. "The most successful periods in Hungarian history," he said, "occurred when there was cooperation and compromise between the government and the opposition" (Balogh 2009b). His appeal fell on deaf ears.

By then, the country was deeply polarized, partly as a result of its fall from grace. For approximately fifteen years after 1989, Hungary had exemplified the successful transition to democracy and market. It enjoyed political stability and had made significant economic progress. By 2006, however, what many experts already knew was becoming clear to the public: Hungary's public finances were in shambles.

The country's financial woes, though an important factor, could not by themselves account for the polarizing dynamic that ensued in 2006. Events of that year tapped a deeper source. On September 17, 2006, via a leaked tape of a closed-door meeting of the MSzP's caucus that May, Hungarians heard Prime Minister Ferenc Gyurcsány admit that he and his ex-communist Hungarian Socialist Party (MSzP) had lied about the state of the country's finances. Though rich in electoral capital, the socialist leader knew that the party could not hide the worsening fiscal imbalance for much longer. In a darkly memorable phrase, Gyurcsány alluded to a famous

October 31, 1956, radio broadcast during which the announcer had admitted that "[w]e lied in the morning, we lied in the evening, and we lied the whole day on all the wavelengths" under the communists, and promised never to do so again. Many Hungarians found the premier's phrasing unforgivably cynical, since unlike the radio broadcasters in 1956, neither Gyurcsány nor his party had been forced to lie.

Only a few sentences of the rather lengthy "lies speech," as it became widely known, were released the day after, but the reaction was immediate. Budapest saw real riots for the first time since 1956, including arson attacks near the parliament at the national public television building on Freedom Square. The police faced angry mobs for hours and, in their efforts to contain them, became violent. Approximately two hundred people were injured. For weeks afterward, skinheads and extreme right-wing groups demonstrated in front of the parliament, threatening death by hanging to "Jewish traitors" and spitting on socialist and liberal parliamentarians coming in and out of the building (Marsovszky 2011, 1–2).

After extensive public debate about whether these protests constituted free speech, Kossuth Square was cleared just in time to celebrate the fiftieth anniversary of the 1956 revolution. On October 23, 2006, most of the commemorations reflected the solemnity and seriousness of the occasion, but it was not a unified event. Fidesz's Orbán gave a separate speech to supporters at a crowded intersection in Budapest. By the evening and in the following days, Budapest was again rocked by thousands of protesters, some of whom threw Molotov cocktails and set parked cars on fire. Police erected barricades and resorted to tear gas, rubber bullets, and water cannons, injuring hundreds and reawakening distressing memories of police actions against peaceful demonstrations in the years prior to 1989.

Not all the protests were violent, but at least initially, the crowds were large and dramatic. The demonstrators' target was a government that had lied to them. But other factors were in play as well. The prime minister's use of 1956 language proved catalytic because its historical resonance combined in explosive ways with the Socialist Party's hybrid political identity. On the one hand, the party's Center-Left, social democratic credentials were solid, and had helped them win re-election. On the other hand, the party was also heir to all the complex legacies of its predecessor, the Communist MSzMP. Fidesz and Jobbik repeatedly drew parallels between the 2006 deception and 1956—a comparison that resonated with some of the protesters.

On the night of September 18, for instance, protesters attacked the Soviet Memorial honoring Hungary's liberation at the end of World War II. Singing the Hungarian national anthem, the protesters removed the Soviet insignia from the memorial and threw it into the Danube. A video that emerged online offers a glimpse into the perpetrators' understanding of the attack's symbolic connection to 1956.

The soundtrack features 'the Marseillaise'…'freedom fighters' are at work here.…[The choreographed attack] imitate[s] well-known photos from the Revolution of 1956, [when] the Soviet memorial was also attacked. These old photos are also edited into the video. In both 1956 and 2006, the Soviet coat of arms was similarly pried away with iron rods. [The] iconographic parallels [are clear] (Marsovszky 2011, 2).

For other Hungarians, however, the association evoked the fascists of the Arrow Cross Party, who executed thousands of Jews on the riverfront and threw their bodies into the Danube. At the very least, it was not hard to see the re-emergence of the anti-Semitism common to Eastern European countries, which equates Bolsheviks with Jews. By symbolic extension, then, their ideological heirs, the socialists, were being tossed into the river.

The political rhetoric of the right-wing parties, and especially of Jobbik, which had turned acrimonious well before 2006, had by then become vicious, and was clearly intended to dehumanize the governing socialists. Demonstrators in 2006 repeatedly chanted "Gyurcsány: cockroach!" while print media and online outlets of radical right-wing parties began displaying graphics that portrayed left-wing liberal politicians as worms. By the time the 2010 elections rolled around, police had to protect a campaigning Gábor Demszky, the liberal mayor of Budapest, from verbal anti-Semitic abuse and harassment by Jobbik supporters and passersby (Marsovszky 2011, 2–3, 11).

The year 2006, then, marked a new radical phase in the deterioration of political discourse and mnemonic fragmentation. Demonstrations—some violent—took place every October 23 thereafter. Gyurcsány survived politically, largely because it is very difficult to unseat a prime minister in Hungary, since only a constructive vote of no-confidence is possible. But the sense of "moral crisis," to borrow President Sólyom's term, only deepened.

Jobbik and Fidesz both continued to play on the desire of a significant segment of the population for national pride and ethnic unity, and both used the 1956 revolution in their quest for the ideological-moral clarity missing from the prolonged transition to democracy and market. The 1956 revolution remained *the* historical touchstone for both, and Fidesz's Orbán had often used it successfully to mobilize support for what he called his "revolution of the voting booths" (Haraszti 2011, 9). Already in 2005, for instance, he felt confident enough to claim that he and his supporters were sufficiently strong to mob the government, and that he could already "smell the gunpowder in the air" (Orbán 2005). Even against this backdrop, Hungarians were able to commemorate the Pan-European Picnic without overt discord. The commemoration of October 23—the date of both the beginning of the 1956 revolution and the Hungarian Third Republic and democracy in 1989—was another matter.

October 23, 2009: A Dual Anniversary

President László Sólyom, Prime Minister Gordon Bajnai, and other politicians from the governing Socialist Party, as well as foreign dignitaries, attended the commemorative services at the Parliament and laid wreaths on Nagy's memorial. But the public was sparsely represented; at Parliament's Kossuth Square and later that day at the 1956-ers Square, the mood was somber (Picture 2.1).

That afternoon, not far away at Deák Square, riot police stood by as some 5,000 people assembled in the square and on the streets opening from it. They were there to hear the leaders of Jobbik and invited representatives from the other European Far-Right parties, such as the French National Front and the British National Party.[2]

The event, forward-looking in ambition, drew its energy from the past. Specifically, Jobbik's speakers were there to claim that the past disqualified the socialists from Hungarian politics. Party leader Gábor Vona, who was introduced as the future prime minister, told the assembled thousands that Jobbik would soon be the "strongest party in Hungary." Then Vona roused his audience by spilling vitriol on Tibor Draskovics, the Minister of Justice and Law Enforcement in the socialist government at the time. Draskovics's offense had been to warn Jobbik not to allow the Hungarian Guard—right-wing vigilantes—to appear at the twentieth anniversary

PICTURE 2.1 A guard of honor plays the trumpet during a commemoration of the twentieth anniversary of the reburial of the 1956 revolution's Prime Minister Imre Nagy beside his statue in Budapest, Hungary, June 16, 2009.

Source: AP Photo/Bela Szandelszky.

commemorations. Outraged, Vona, who also was head of the Guard, demanded rhetorically: "How does this man dare to instruct *our kind*, and the Guardists, about democracy? [He's from] that bunch who 50 years ago and [then again in 2006] shot at us in the crowd. [That bunch] who in 1956 left in exile and came back with Soviet tanks!" [*sic*]

For Vona, 1956 became the line that separated those who belonged in public life and those who did not: "So the question is not what the Guardists are doing at a celebration of 1956, since that is clear: *they belong there.* The question is what the hell are *you* doing, *Draskovics*, at a remembrance of 1956?" As the crowd cheered wildly, he continued: "in a normal country, it's not the Guardists they would ban....In a country with any self-respect...everyone [w]ould spit on [the Draskovics types].[3]

After the cheers subsided, Vona went on to predict that in the parliamentary elections Jobbik would "sweep away the socialists" much like it "had swept the SzDSz (Free Democrats) off the face of the Hungarian political palette." And then "what will they do in parliament," he demanded, "when they have to face [not just two] but dozens of us; when finally they are forced to face the truth; when Hungarians finally make it into their own parliament; when someone finally forces them to face the anger of the Hungarians and someone reads them the verdict of the Hungarian people?" (Vona 2009).

That night, at the Parliament, Jobbik held another well-attended rally. The lead speaker at this event was lawyer and European Parliament member Krisztina Morvai. The broad thematic frame of her speech was one of power abuse by the socialists and victimization of Jobbik. In a sullen tone, she explained that she wished she could offer an uplifting speech on the anniversary of October 23rd, but that it was impossible, because a number of their compatriots, including György Budaházy, sat in jail. As the crowd erupted in a chant of "Budaházy," she reminded them that on the fiftieth anniversary of the 1956 revolution in 2006, the socialist government "beat and arrested innocent, peaceful demonstrators." She requested the help of those assembled in finding information about what she knew to be the "shameful way those innocents had been hauled off," so that she could further press their case in Hungary and at the European Parliament. And finally, as if still living in pre-1989 Hungary, she recounted a phone conversation with Budaházy from jail, in which she told him that she was well aware that "the comrades are listening," but added defiantly that she "*wanted* them to hear."

The struggle between communists and anti-communists, for Morvai, was not over. The socialists, she warned, were trying to drive a wedge between Jobbik and the "silent majority" by frightening people with talk of "vandals," "extremists," and "terrorists." But Morvai reassured the crowd. "The future," she said, "belongs to the likes of us" (Morvai 2009).[4]

Neither Vona nor Morvai mentioned 1989, except occasionally to refer sarcastically to "the so-called transition," or the "so-called regime change," and virtually nothing was said about Hungary's achievements in the twenty years prior. Fidesz, for its part, opted to distance itself from Prime Minister Gordon Bajnai's socialist-backed caretaker government, which it deemed illegitimate; and held its own commemorative event—10 kilometers away. The symbolism was not lost on observers: Fidesz's ceremony took place in Nagytétény, as far removed as possible from the socialists without going outside the greater Budapest area.

Fidesz's event, moreover, focused not on 1989 but on 1956 and its relevance for the upcoming 2010 elections. Like Vona at the Jobbik gathering, Orbán was introduced to the audience as the future prime minister of Hungary. And like Vona, Orbán moved deliberately in his effort to connect with 1956. Orbán's connecting thread was the "sobriety" of the Hungarian national character: "The true voice of Hungary is not extremism, not dictatorship, not money, not the voice of hate, but that of well meaning and acting Hungarian people." Significantly, however, he did not target Jobbik's extremism, but, as in so many of Orbán's speeches and articles over the years, the "dictatorship" of the governing socialists. In Orbán's characterization of the Hungarian political field, the socialists represented the very opposite of the "sober" 1956 revolutionaries. The latter, Orbán claimed, had chosen to build rather than destroy, while the former, the extremist socialist government, opted for destruction, "break[ing] everything in sight into smithereens" (Balogh 2009c).

From there, Orbán went on to project an image of the future in which the socialists would suffer the fate of past offenders. Here the [Stalinist] Rákosi regime served as exemplar of socialist oppression and destructiveness. That regime not only had "lost touch with the people", but violated their "wishes and interests." It was in the face of such injustice, Orbán suggested, that the 1956 revolutionaries had emerged to bring about the regime's "collapse." The analogy became clear. The governing socialists, who Orbán said did not listen to the people and were concerned only with the "dictates of money," would fail in the upcoming 2010 elections. They had not learned from the mistakes of the pre-1956 communists. Now they were doomed to relive their fate at the hands of the new revolutionaries: Fidesz and "the new united Hungary would sweep them away" (Balogh 2009c).

For Orbán, as for the leaders of Jobbik, the socialists deserved no legitimate place in Hungary's political future. Even after their electoral loss, Orbán warned, the socialists could still be a threat, because they would have "the temerity" to seek an electoral comeback." Such comebacks, of course, are part and parcel of democratic competition. But democracy was not the point of the speech. Like Vona of Jobbik, Orbán hardly mentioned the democratic transition of 1989, or the beginning of Hungary's Third Republic (Balogh 2009c).

If any group actually focused on 1989, it was Hungarian intellectuals and scholars. In an effort to promote dispassionate public discussion of the transition, its long-term consequences, and lessons learned, the country's preeminent academic institutions and several foundations held conferences and initiated projects. There were also television and radio retrospectives on 1989. The Open Society Foundation initiated the "Was there a 1989?" project at the Open Society Archive (Rainer 2009, 17), while the Central European University held its "Annus Mirabilis: Commemorating the 20th Anniversary of the Transitions in Central and Eastern Europe."

But for intellectuals, too, 1956 remained a compelling memory and an inescapable referent. The 1956 Institute in Budapest, for instance, seized the opportunity to educate citizens about the revolution and modern Hungarian history through its oral history project, multimedia exhibits, and publications. And the Hungarian Academy of Sciences held a commemorative conference on the day before the twentieth anniversary of Nagy's reburial. Participants included Péter Kende, the well-known Paris-based historian, János Rainer, head of the 1956 Institute, the filmmaker Ferenc Kósa, as well as Nagy's niece, Katalin Jánosi. The tenor of the conference was sober, not unlike that of the socialist government's official commemorations. Jánosi, for instance, noted with regret that in the twenty years that had passed since the reburial, two generations of Hungarian youth had grown up knowing little of the 1956 revolution, or of Nagy. For this reason, she said, the Imre Nagy Foundation published a volume on the twentieth anniversary documenting the events leading up to June 16th, the exhumation of the revolutionary martyrs' remains, and the historic reburial itself (Tasi 2009b).

At the same conference, the historian Péter Kende posed the question of whether Hungarian society had made good use of the opportunity that the transition presented, and whether or not it had come closer to achieving freedom. Several speakers noted that June 16th commemorated not only the revolutionary heroes, but also the death of the old regime and its symbolic burial. But Kósa, the filmmaker, responded in the negative to Kende's query. Contemporary politics, he said, had betrayed the revolution's legacy. How could it not? Nagy himself, Kósa added, was too left-wing for the Right and too nationalist for the Left (Tasi 2009a),

Analysis: The Past Within the Past

Remembering the country's part in bringing down the Wall was the only relatively uncomplicated aspect of the 2009 commemoration of 1989, though discordant notes were heard even on that occasion. The ceremonies, as we have seen, took place in the context of a society that had become increasingly polarized as mnemonic politics reached a fever pitch in 2006. Commemoration of the 1989 transition to democracy was relegated to the background at best, and was denigrated at worst. Especially after 2006, it became increasingly commonplace to hear the opposition refer sarcastically to "the so-called transition" or the "so-called regime change." It also became less clear whether Fidesz and Jobbik were in tacit alliance, or whether Orbán truly believed that he would be able to control Jobbik once in power. It was Jobbik's leaders, to be sure, who repeatedly referred to the socialists as "degenerate," "moral corpses," and "weeds to be eradicated," and who spoke openly of the selling of Hungary by "red capitalists" while portraying the European Union as an "imperial" power. But Fidesz's leadership was only slightly less extreme in attitude and rhetoric, often making its views known indirectly through partisan newspapers like *Magyar Nemzet*, which in September 2008 had published an article entitled "The Architects of Imperium Europae. Blood-ritual Murder Against the Nation-State: The Attempt to Realize a Super-Government in Brussels" (Marsovszky 2011, 6).

The socialists were increasingly on the defensive, which explains in part the tenor of the commemorations of the democratic transition on October 23, 2009. Listen, for instance, to President Sólyom's lament at the 2009 commemorations of the Pan-European Picnic on the Austrian border—by all accounts a cheerful occasion, and highly festive compared to the October ceremony.

> Ever since the change in regime, we have had to fight for the past. Who does the past belong to? Who made the regime change? What is the relationship between the new democratic system and the Kádár regime? How often have I had to stand up and point out that there is no continuity between the two! How often have I had to argue that there was only one 1956! This memorial sculpture also proclaims that it was the people of our country who played the decisive role in the regime change. The roundtable was not merely the negotiations of politicians, and what was accomplished was not some sort of reform communist program. (Sólyom 2009)

He was clearly addressing the prevailing political narrative of the opposition parties Fidesz and the Christian Democrats (KDNP), as well as Jobbik and its growing group of supporters. Momentum, however, was now on the side of the mnemonic warriors. This was partly due to citizens' assessment of their post-communist fortunes, which had turned increasingly negative.

But momentum also favored the mnemonic warriors because the more that political elites across the spectrum rendered 1956 the polity's dominant mnemonic referent, the more polarized politics became. Whereas the reform socialists and the liberals saw the legacy of the 1956 Revolution as an injunction to build a nation of us *and* them—the people, reform-minded socialists, and other political parties coexisting in the context of a competitive democracy—the ethno-nationalist Right saw it as us (exclusively) *versus* them. On the Left, Prime Minister Gordon Bajnai, for instance, speaking at a conference in Parliament on the democratic changes, openly recognized that 1989—whose seeds, as he put it, had been planted by the revolution of 1956—had ushered in decades of mixed results, combining progress and disappointment. The promise of 1956, in fact, remained unfulfilled. But for Bajnai, this was the responsibility of all the post-1989 governments, and not just of any one particular party. In contrast, in the April 2010 elections, a victorious Fidesz and its leader Victor Orbán arrived to "clean up" the remnants of the communist past which, they averred, had been very much in evidence during the socialists' eight years of rule (2002-2010). Indeed, they claimed that the socialists represented a continuation of the old regime: now privatizing instead of nationalizing, to be sure, but benefiting just as before from their proximity to external networks of power—now international banks and multinational corporations instead of the Soviet Union.

In this context, it became increasingly common to hear references to the EU as the new "colonizer." Perhaps it was not so surprising that many who had high expectations of achieving a Western European standard of living in relatively short order were disappointed. And after the financial crisis of 2008, some of the very trends that had raised Hungarians' standard of living now left the middle class endangered— saddled, for instance, with mortgages denominated in Swiss francs or other foreign currencies.[5] As the Hungarian sociologist László Lengyel put it, "Brussels and Berlin have no answers to their cries for help. It's no longer the losers who are rioting—it's the people who until now have been winners. They are now the ones looking for scapegoats." While Euro-skepticism is certainly not unique to Hungary, it has been sharpened there by what Lengyel called the "third wave" of nationalism (2009). And as we have seen, Fidesz and Jobbik cast the socialists not only as the scapegoat for Hungarians' economic disappointments, but for their fears that Hungarian culture and the nation itself were being eclipsed by the EU in particular and globalization in general.

Having created a clear villain, Fidesz won a landslide in the parliamentary elections of 2010; indeed, with 52.7 percent of the votes, Fidesz and its junior coalition partner, the Christian Democratic Party (KDNP), won 68.8 percent of the seats, which translated into a two-thirds majority in parliament. Thus, Orbán declared, he had a "historic mandate" for a complete overhaul of the corrupt Hungarian political and economic system: the "true revolution" had finally arrived. This theme remained dominant. In September 2011, Tibor Navracsics, the deputy prime minister and Fidesz party leader, made this argument explicitly in a presentation that he delivered to a group of American academics and students in Budapest. "*This* is the true beginning of democracy," he proclaimed (Navracsics 2011).

Fidesz had become the quintessential mnemonic warrior on two key counts. As in their separate commemoration of the twentieth anniversary of 1989, party leaders drew a severe and irrevocable line between themselves—the owners of the "true" vision of the past—and the socialist purveyors of a false history. Second, they sought to make of their vision the polity's "proper foundation." Thus Fidesz took upon itself the historic responsibility of leading the country to a *genuine* break with the past, a stance it has since used, along with its supermajority, to justify many radical changes and a great deal of extraordinary rhetoric and behavior. Orbán had made it plain prior to the elections of April 2010 that in order for Fidesz to achieve its aims and set the Hungarian polity on the right path, the party would need to be in power for at least fifteen to twenty years. It was, after all, Fidesz's historic responsibility to keep the "obfuscators, perpetrators of 'falsehoods' ... [those] who do not care about the proper shape of memory" out of government.[6] Once in power, the government proceeded at lightning speed to make major institutional changes that increased the likelihood of precisely such an outcome.

While Hungary's new media law became widely known after the furor it caused in the European Union, it is but one aspect of Fidesz's radical "reforms" of Hungary's democratic institutions, which include fundamental constitutional and other sweeping legal-institutional changes.[7] Many political analysts in Hungary and abroad worried that these changes might be irreversible. The economist János Kornai, who until 2009 had served as a non-partisan adviser to every government since 1990 and is not known for alarmist statements, wrote that Fidesz had achieved "a level of centralization...comparable only to the propaganda machine of communist dictatorships." A mere eight months after Fidesz took power, Kornai declared in the pages of one of the country's major newspapers that Hungary was no longer a democracy: it was now, he plainly stated, an autocracy.[8]

Fidesz's radical changes continued apace after its ascent to power, including a new electoral law that, once enacted, would make it extremely difficult to mount a successful political challenge to the government. The socialists, for their part, grew increasingly and perhaps irreparably divided, and the former small liberal party that had governed in coalition with the socialists until 2008, the Free Democrats (SzDSz), was essentially defunct. The mnemonic warriors had won the political battle; now they were well positioned to win the war.

Conclusion

Political actors everywhere operate in a "field of imaginable possibilities" (Cruz 2005, 25). In 1989, as their country made the transition to democracy, Hungarians across the political spectrum summoned the power of public discourse and collective symbols to reclaim and instrumentalize the forbidden memory of 1956. In that expansive moment, the unimaginable became the dominant reality. By the end of the transition, the revolution of 1956, once relegated to enforced oblivion, had become the central mnemonic referent of the new democracy. In the coming decades, political actors would repeatedly struggle to appropriate the meaning of the revolution and its legacy and, just as important, to define themselves and others accordingly. The fractured memory regime that emerged pitted two visions of the past and of government against one another: the mnemonic warriors' dichotomy between existential antagonists versus the pluralists' understanding of the democratic transition and its aftermath as inclusive processes—that is to say, politics as the realm of us *and* them.

That Hungarians became increasingly aligned for the first time since 1956 along the communist/anti-communist divide is a measure of the mnemonic warriors' success. The upshot was a deeply polarized political and civil society that grew only more so between 2006 and 2009. It would be easy to attribute this trend to economic stress, but political polarization began well ahead of Hungary's economic crisis, and was in significant measure the result of mnemonic warriors' strategic choices.

A unified celebration of the democratic transition's twentieth anniversary was hardly possible. If anything, the twenty years that followed 1989 tell a cautionary tale of the dangers of a fractured memory regime. By 2009, mnemonic warriors had gained ground in Hungarian politics, and in parliamentary elections the following year, emerged dominant to successfully promote a zero-sum political discourse and implement radical institutional change. With an absolute majority in parliament, Fidesz proceeded rapidly to alter and dilute the democratic game until it teetered dangerously on the verge of authoritarianism. The consensus politics of the transition and the early post-communist governments might in any case have proved unsuited to the stresses of unfettered political and economic competition. But this tradition had older and deeper roots in Hungarian politics, prevailing for much of the last two decades prior to transition. Many factors weakened it, just as incompetence and corruption on both sides of the political spectrum weakened the economy and the public's trust in democracy. But until Fidesz began dismantling them, the country's democratic institutions were strong.[9] Nor did the tradition of consensus building die a natural death. Its extinction required sustained effort by dedicated mnemonic warriors who managed to recast the socialists' remarkable record of successful post-transition economic reform as collusion with rapacious international financiers, and their democratic credentials as cover for nefarious plans to compromise the country's sovereignty. None of this could have been accomplished—Fidesz could not have won the war—without first winning the battle to define and shape the legacy of the revolution of 1956 as an existential political encounter.

And if the revolution is being threatened, then winner-take-all tactics are justified. Fidesz has used democratic institutions to badly weaken—some say destroy—Hungarian democracy, in order to save the "nation." Liberal analysts of Hungarian politics often make reference to the 1930s in Hungary or to Weimar Germany. Many have compared Orbán's Hungary to Putin's Russia.[10] There is truth in each of these analogies. But like most historical metaphors and comparisons, they are imperfect, and we can only hope that Marx will be proven correct at least in his well-known aphorism that history repeats itself, the first time as tragedy, the second time as farce.

NOTES

1. They had requested a file on his activities from the head of the Soviet KGB (Gorbachev apparently received it from KGB chief Kryuchkov on June 16, 1989—the very day of Nagy's funeral.) Party Secretary Károly Grósz accused Nagy of "having been personally responsible for the imprisonment and eventual execution of dozens of innocent Communists." The evidence was equivocal; see Rév (1995, 15–16). Whatever the facts, for most Hungarians, Nagy remained a potent symbol of Hungarian national sovereignty and resistance to foreign domination—and heir to the legacy of 1848.

2. Some view Jobbik as the successor to the Arrow Cross Party, in power for a few months near the end of World War II. Jobbik's paramilitary guard, its attacks on the Roma, and its rhetoric contribute to this perception. On the anniversary of 1956 in 2008, for instance, Gábor Vona said: "I send the message to [TV2 and RTL Klub] that they should be afraid of the day when Jobbik can decide their fate because we have already made our decision.... We will close TV2 and RTL Klub. But because we are very, very angry that will not be all. We will show their owners and editors where the exit is from this country and we will raze their headquarters to the ground...Once history sweeps away this liberal rubble our time will come. And then Hungary to the last ounce of soil, to the last drop of water, to the last man will be ours" (Balogh 2009b).

3. This was partially unintelligible from the video (Vona 2009).

4. At the time, Jobbik held three of Hungary's 22 seats in the European Parliament. After campaigning on an xenophobic, anti-Roma, anti-EU platform, Jobbik in fact did very well in the April 2010 elections, winning 47 of 386 seats in Hungary's unicameral parliament. In comparison, the Socialists won 59 seats and Fidesz 262, more than the 258 needed for a two-thirds majority.

5. When the Hungarian forint was devalued, many could no longer make their payments.

6. See Jan Kubik and Michael Bernhard, "A Theory of the Politics of Memory," Chapter 1 of this volume.

7. Kornai wrote: "The head of the media authority can issue decrees, and...apply financial penalties. They...control not only the state-owned, but also privately owned media, not only television and radio, but also the printed press, internet portals and blogs. The [media authority] exclusively made up of Fidesz delegates regulates the distribution of technical television and radio frequencies, [and] their rejection of an application equals...[a] death sentence..." (Kornai 2010).

8. "...The parliament has turned into a voting machine producing laws...[at] incredible speed. The president of Hungary is an obedient party devotee. The key office of the Chief Prosecutor is filled by a supporter of the ruling party...The powers of the Constitutional Court...were brutally restricted...When daring to criticize the government plans, the independent Fiscal Council

was dissolved. [A] faithful member of the ruling political group was appointed head of the State Audit office…" (Kornai 2010).

9. In a recent article, Eva Balogh asked "Were the socialist-liberal governments between 2002 and 2010 that bad? No, they were not. Expectations of the population were too great and pressure from Orbán in opposition was merciless and vicious. In his relentless attacks on the government Orbán was expressing his fundamental political philosophy. When April H. Foley, the U.S. Ambassador to Hungary between 2006 and 2009, called his attention to the fact that in a democracy the opposition is supposed to work out compromises with the government parties, Orbán's answer was that it may be so in the West but not in Hungary where there is only one political goal: to win elections. According to Orbán, not only does Fidesz need to be in power for several decades, but 'dual power,' meaning a political system in which the opposition has a significant role to play, leads only to superfluous bickering which impedes effective governing" (Balogh 2011).

10. Miklós Haraszti and Gábor Halmai both compared Orbán's power with Putin's, the former noting that the Hungarian leader did "what Putin always has dreamed about but actually never managed"; see Scheppele (2012b) at 1:30:19.

3 Roundtable Discord

THE CONTESTED LEGACY OF 1989 IN POLAND

Michael Bernhard and Jan Kubik

Introduction

Poland's exit from communist rule in 1989 was the first in the region. Earlier, after the suppression of Solidarity in 1981, Polish politics settled into uncomfortable stagnation. The party-state regime under General Wojciech Jaruzelski was incapable of normalizing the country, having to contend with a diminished but unbowed underground Solidarity and a sluggish economy. Faced with growing strike activity in 1987 and 1988, the regime entered into negotiation with the Solidarity leadership, in the hope of enlisting its support for further liberalization and reform.

Formal negotiations that ran from early February to early April 1989 yielded a Roundtable Agreement, which opened the way for Poland's exit from communist rule. Whereas the Solidarity leadership had initially hoped to secure the union's relegalization, the two sides eventually agreed to hold semi-competitive elections that were meant to compel Solidarity to share power while keeping control in the hands of the party-state. However, the elections turned into a referendum on the party-state, and their result was a lopsided Solidarity victory in that part of the election that was truly contested. Solidarity won all the seats it was allowed to contest in the Sejm and 99 out of the 100 seats in a newly created Senate. When the United Peasant Party and the Democratic Party, satellite parties that had been subordinated to the ruling Polish United Workers' Party (PZPR) since the 1940s, defected from the regime it could not form a government. A deal was soon struck in which communists gave their consent to a Solidarity-led government in return for Solidarity's support for Jaruzelski's assumption of the newly created office of president.

The protracted and complex nature of power transfer in Poland meant that there was more than one milestone event in 1989. Thus both the signing of the Roundtable Agreement in April and the elections of June 1989 were commemorated in 2009. And both events provoked controversies and were contested by various political forces, albeit in different ways. The celebration of the twentieth anniversary of the Roundtable Agreement produced a fractured memory regime with many actors taking different positions. The celebration of the elections was also fractured and contentious but produced a bipolar configuration, with political actors falling into two distinct camps.

The remainder of this chapter has two parts. First, we discuss how the events of 1989 were commemorated in 2009. Then we analyze the politics of commemoration in Poland, highlighting the fractured nature of collective memory about the foundation of Polish democracy and what it has meant for contemporary politics. We first turn to the Roundtable commemoration.

February 2009: Roundtable Discord

Almost from its inception, the Roundtable Agreement has been a highly contested and polarizing issue in Polish historical memory. In February 2009 two separate and very different commemorative conferences were held to mark the twentieth anniversary of the opening of the negotiations. We identified *five and one-half* different interpretations of what happened.

The Ex-communists: Partners in the Roundtable as the "Path to Europe"

The larger of the two commemorative conferences, "Dialogue, Compromise, Agreement" (*Dialog-Kompromis-Porozumienie*), took place on February 5, 2009, in the Hall of Columns at the Sejm. Many of the major participants from both sides of the Roundtable Negotiations took part or attended as observers. It was sponsored by the Center for Political Analyses, a left of center think tank whose board was drawn heavily from important figures of the Democratic Left Alliance (SLD). The Center was headed by Janusz Reykowski, the main party negotiator at the political reform working group during the talks (Centrum Politycznych Analiz 2010a, 2010c).

The daylong conference included opening remarks from both the speaker of the Sejm, Bronisław Komorowski, and his deputy Jerzy Szmajdziński and five separate hour-long discussions. Given its location and the participation of the leadership of the Sejm and several representatives of the party caucuses, it had a quasi-official nature, despite being organized by a partisan think tank. The party-state side of the negotiations was represented by Aleksander Kwaśniewski, Stanisław Ciosek, Janusz Reykowski, and Jerzy Wiatr. The Solidarity side was also represented by the prominent 1989 negotiators: Tadeusz Mazowiecki, Adam Michnik, Władysław Frasyniuk, Andrzej Stelmachowski, and Zbigniew Bujak. A number of historians, political scientists, and former activists provided commentary on the presentations by the participants (Centrum Politycznych Analiz 2010b).

A minute of silence was held in memory of two famous Solidarity negotiators who had died since the tenth anniversary—Jacek Kuroń and Bronisław Geremek (Gazeta Wyborcza 2009m). The tone of this commemoration was celebratory. Many of the participants had played major roles in Polish politics in the early years after 1989, though in later years they had become politically inactive. Thus much of what was said at this event was reputational, rather than directly political, except for a handful of participants who were active in the since defunct Left and Democrats (LiD) coalition.

The most positive assessments were made by those who were associated with the PZPR side of the negotiations, many of whom went on to political careers with the post-communist Democratic Left Alliance (SLD). Former President Aleksander Kwaśniewski painted the Roundtable in glowing terms, drawing a direct path from the negotiations to democracy, national sovereignty, the market economy, and membership in both the European Union and the North Atlantic Treaty Organization (Gazeta Wyborcza 2009g). Kwaśniewski glanced over the fact that the Roundtable included non-democratic guarantees for the PZPR and that only the cataclysmic defeat suffered in the June elections had made rapid democratization possible. Major communist defeat was remolded into a national victory twenty years later. In a radio interview around the time of the commemoration, he described the Roundtable as a two-sided meeting of patriots, in which it was clear from the beginning that the authorities were going to "limit their power" (Gazeta Wyborcza 2009f).

The idea that both sides of the Roundtable were equal partners committed to democratic reform was also reiterated during the commemoration at the Sejm. Stanisław Ciosek, a former PZPR Politburo member, co-organizer of the Roundtable Talks, and later a close advisor to President Kwaśniewski, followed a similar line. He talked about how neither side had been capable of resolving the political impasse on its own. He gushed that the "Roundtable brought together the entire flower of the Polish intelligentsia in order seek a way out of oppression for Poland" (Okrągły

stół zebrał cały kwiat polskiej inteligencji, by wspólnie szukać wyjścia Polski z opresji)
(Wprost 2009b). Here we have the essence of the ex-communist retrospective view
of the Roundtable—two former enemies came together, became earnest if reluctant
allies, and saved Poland.

In their recollection of the Roundtable Talks, the former PZPR participants often
justified their actions by wrapping them in the approval of their former antagonists—the United States and the Catholic Church. At the Sejm commemoration,
Ciosek noted: "In the change of system the Church played a fundamental and vital
role" (*W przemianach ustrojowych Kosciół odegrał fundamentalną i zasadniczą rolę*)
(Wprost 2009b). Longin Pastusiak, a communist-era expert on the United States
and a former marshal of the Senate, noted the approving cables that US ambassador Richard Davies wrote home about the Roundtable: "Poland surprised the entire
world by that, and corrected the view of Poles as impulsive and romantics. It turned
out that Poles managed to acknowledge the economic facts, and showed that understanding and mutual toleration is not foreign to them" (Wprost 2009b).[1] Wojciech
Jaruzelski's retrospective justification for his decision to stand for the presidency,
delivered in a television interview around the time of the commemoration, also fits
with this pattern. He laid the responsibility at the feet of George Bush: "I had a long
[telephone] conversation with him, in which he convinced me that I needed to be a
candidate for president" (Gazeta Wyborcza 2009d).

In this presentation of the Roundtable Agreement as the foundational event
of Polish democracy, the prominent ex-communists fail to mention that the final
agreement included strong non-democratic guarantees for the regime. This presentation is meant to defend the contemporary Polish Left from uncomfortable
reminders that its founders were reluctant democrats who negotiated on the basis
of their self-interest, rather than a commitment to democracy. By treating the unintended unraveling of the agreement as an effect of deliberate design, it constituted
an attempt to establish democratic credentials for the ex-communist Left and prop
up its legitimacy. Very few in the former PZPR camp were prepared to admit that
the Roundtable Agreement was an imperfect start to a conflictual democratization
process. Jerzy Wiatr came close in his statement that the regime was not aiming to
hand over power, but to share it (Olczyk and Wiatr 2009).

The Mazowiecki Camp: "The Philosophy of the Roundtable" as a Foundation for Reconciliation

At the Sejm commemoration, a second major interpretation of the Roundtable was
posed by the Solidarity participants in the negotiations. Like the PZPR negotiators, this group held a strongly positive view of the Roundtable Agreement. It was

composed of leaders and activists who had supported the Mazowiecki government during the "War at the Top" (*Wojna na górze*). The split between the prime minister's supporters and Wałęsa's broke out over the latter's attempts to force the resignation of then-President Jaruzelski, and after its success, the presidential campaign to succeed him in 1990. The tensions between the two groups, characterized as the reformist and revolutionary factions by Ekiert and Kubik (1999, 164–166), represented a fundamental difference over whether to continue to be true to the terms of the Roundtable Agreement or to push more rapidly for the economic reforms and the isolation of the ex-communists in the political life of the country. The latter position has been described in Polish as the "acceleration" (*przyspieszenie*) of change. The reformist group around Mazowiecki that lost the political battle to Wałęsa and the revolutionaries is now less active in politics, but is still a strong presence in the public sphere. The group's position at the twentieth anniversary commemoration was succinctly summarized in the "philosophy of the Roundtable" (*filozofia okrągłego stołu*) (Gazeta Wyborcza 2009a).

The essence of this philosophy is a spirit of compromise, pragmatism, remaining true to one's word, and forgiveness for the wrongs of the past. And indeed, much of this rhetoric is geared at justifying the stances taken by the reformist group from 1989 to the period when the post-communist Left returned to power in 1993. During this period they proposed drawing a "thick line" (*gruba kreska*), broadly interpreted as an attempt to separate the communist past from the present, and argued to honor the letter of Solidarity's agreement with the party-state, including Jaruzelski's assumption of the presidency.

The philosophy of compromise was defended by former Prime Minister Mazowiecki at the commemoration: "The rational and moral perspectives demanded the drawing of a thick line" (Stróżyk 2009a). The reformists have argued that their caution was rational, given their position as the first non-communist government in the former Soviet Bloc and their uncertainty over the potential Soviet responses (Gazeta Wyborcza 20090: 94; Merkel 1999). And they claimed that it was both principled in that they attempted to live up to the promises they made at the Roundtable, and moral in its intent to create a new national community based on reconciliation rather than retribution.

The commemoration included several gestures of reconciliation, including one that involved Adam Michnik, the long-time editor of the national daily *Gazeta Wyborcza*, and General Czesław Kiszczak, Minister of Internal Affairs during Martial Law, whom Michnik famously skewered in one of his most visceral *Letters from Prison* (1985). At the commemoration, Michnik praised Kiszczak as committed to compromise and lamented the approbrium to which he is still subjected (Gazeta Wyborcza 2009a).

An even broader notion of reconciliation was proposed by Władysław Frasyniuk, whose Democratic Party had entered into a now-defunct electoral alliance with the parties of the Left (LiD) in 2007. He, too, praised the PZPR leadership around Jaruzelski for making the Roundtable possible and reminded the audience how the alternatives (presumably hard-liners) within the party would not have taken these steps or risks. He also acknowledged that both sides had support within society and that each side's perspective had some value. In talking about his hometown, the former Solidarity leader stated: "In Wrocław there is a large traffic circle named after Ronald Reagan and a small street named after Kuroń, but the scale of this should be reversed. We should erect monuments to Wałesa and Jaruzelski" (Stróżyk 2009a). And he added: "today, the participants in the roundtable should stop explaining themselves, and accept that nobody of a sound mind should criticize the Roundtable" (Wprost 2009b). And it is to that criticism that we next turn.

PiS: The Roundtable as a Corrupt Bargain

President Kaczyński organized his own event to mark the twenty years since the opening of the Roundtable negotiations. It was entitled "1989—The Origins of Freedom" and took place on February 6, 2009, at the Presidential Palace in Warsaw. Billed as a "debate of historians," it was the more contentious and critical of the two events. Participants did include a large number of historians,[2] but also several prominent figures in the president's party, Law and Justice (PiS), including the president himself, the highly controversial Antoni Macierewicz, and Wojciech Roszkowski, a historian and PiS deputy to the European Parliament.

In convening his own commemoration, the president created a public platform for espousing a largely negative view of the Roundtable. This framing is often explicitly linked to the idea that the democratization process in Poland has been flawed and thus requires correction by those clever enough to see through the corrupt nature of the Roundtable. Such rhetoric was often heard in the PiS campaign for parliament and Lech Kaczyński's presidential campaign. Both campaigns effectively played on popular dissatisfaction with the level of corruption during the previous SLD government. The strategy was to link together the embourgeoisement of former communists with the growing dissatisfaction with their corrupt practices. The highly publicized Rywin Affair was used to argue that the PiS's competitors from within Solidarity were complicit in SLD's corruption (notably Adam Michnik, who was exonerated in this case). Given President Kaczyński's role at the Roundtable, he by and large distanced himself from such arguments, but used some of their elements to attack his political opponents (more on his personal stance later).

A more measured negative assessment was articulated by Wojciech Roszkowski, who painted the Roundtable as an agreement between elites that denied voice to the people.[3] He argued that real democratization did not ensue until the elections of June of 1989, when the voice of the people finally was unconstrained. Andrzej Grajewski also argued that popular preferences were usurped because the Solidarity side did not represent the union's opinions, but only those of Lech Wałęsa and his advisors (Office of the President 2009, 40). Roszkowski did not completely disregard the significance of the Roundtable, conceding that it was a compromise based on the conditions at that time. He emphasized, however, that the conditions that gave rise to it changed quickly with events in the former Soviet Bloc and the USSR itself, therefore opening room for reconsideration of the terms of the Roundtable Agreement. This represents a critique of the Mazowiecki government group and its willingness to live up to the agreement, particularly after "one side of the Roundtable Agreement ceased to exist" (Office of the President 2009, 12–13; Gazeta Wyborcza 2009l; Rzeczpospolita 2009a).

Whereas Roszkowski's argument that the elections of 1989 drove the democratization process beyond the confines posed by the Roundtable Agreement is, from a historian's perspective, quite reasonable, Macierewicz's presentation raised many doubts. Macierewicz, who has a long oppositional pedigree, was a founding member of KOR and one of the leaders of its conservative faction. He was also a Solidarity advisor in 1980–1981 and has held a number of important positions in post-communist Poland, including Interior Minister in the government of Jan Olszewski, whose short duration was in no small part a product of Macierewicz's provocative style. He has been associated with half a dozen different conservative or right-wing parties since 1989.

His interpretation of the Roundtable was classic Macierewicz. He has a proclivity to unveil supposedly unknown evidence at critical moments, which unsurprisingly, if true, would cast his opponents in the worst possible light. Macierewicz went as far as to call the Roundtable a "national betrayal" (*zdrada narodu*). He argued that the only group to benefit from the Roundtable was that part of the opposition elite that managed to become part of the new power elite after 1989. Here, of course, he is not only attacking his old KOR comrades who constituted the intellectual elite of the reform wing of Solidarity, but also the centrist ruling party, Civic Platform (PO). Macierewicz claimed to have seen secret coded messages between the Polish ambassador in Moscow and the Ministry of Internal Affairs, which showed that the whole Roundtable process was overseen by Moscow (Gazeta Wyborcza 2009k; Rzeczpospolita 2009a; Office of the President 2009, 15).

The long hand of Moscow surfaced also in the comments of Andrzej Nowak, a conservative historian, who pointed to a letter supposedly sent by Bronisław

Geremek to Mikhail Gorbachev in 1988. The document, clearly not a letter but a six-point memorandum, only one of which addresses Soviet-Polish relations, is written in French and is addressed to George Soros. The level of evidence substantiating a claim of some sort of cooperation, let alone even indirect contact between the highest levels of the Soviet leadership and Solidarity, is speculative at best.[4] Nowak himself qualified the addressee in his discussion of the "letter" twice, describing Gorbachev as the "most likely" candidate (Office of the President 2009, 18).[5]

Macierewicz's sentiments, while a minority position, do have some resonance on the Right. One particularly alienated long-time oppositionist, former Solidarity leader Andrzej Gwiazda, also made public statements in which he roundly condemned the Roundtable as an attempt to deny voice to the people to the political and financial benefit of its participants (Stróżyk 2009b). Politicians on the Far Right have little chance of winning an outright majority in the Polish political system, but can benefit if such allegations discredit the center and sow polarization of the political system. Polarization strengthens the Far Right, but what was the motivation of Lech Kaczyński in sponsoring this? The Kaczyńskis were the first politicians to effectively court and use extreme parties (both the League of Polish Families and Self-Defense) as part of a ruling coalition. It remains unclear whether this strategy of using the extreme Right to weaken the Center was anything more than a short-term gambit that could pay off under circumstances other than the crisis of corruption in which the left of center SLD crippled itself.

Presidents Wałęsa and Kaczyński: The Moral Ambiguity of the Roundtable

A fourth set of actors presented the legacy of the Roundtable in decidedly mixed terms or as a necessary, but troubling, compromise. They included many of the politicians from the revolutionary wing of Solidarity who sided with Lech Wałęsa during the War at the Top, including some, like Lech Kaczyński, who participated in the Roundtable Talks. Given their participation, a total condemnation of the Roundtable would have not been credible and even might have worked to undermine their own position. At the same time, the success of the ex-communist political camp, both in politics and the economy, troubled these politicians and thus they felt obligated to criticize the substance of Poland's democratization process. Such a position allowed them to attack their competitors from the reformist wing of Solidarity for enabling and benefiting from the embourgeoisement of the nomenklatura and the incomplete nature of the political revolution. This was presented as a product of the leniency associated with the "thick-line" strategy of the Mazowiecki government.

While Lech Wałęsa had grown increasingly marginal to political outcomes in Poland, he projected himself conspicuously into the Roundtable anniversary by refusing to participate in either of the two commemorations. Instead, he delivered a speech in Konin. The man whom Poles most strongly associated with the memory of the Roundtable refused to commemorate it officially and distanced himself from it in his public pronouncements.

The speech was classic Wałęsa—a charismatic orator saying seemingly contradictory things in his very colorful way. He began by noting that he had wanted to settle accounts with communism during his presidency but had lacked the means. Then he warned that politicians should not participate in settling accounts, but should leave that to state prosecutors. Finally, he observed that with time it might be possible to talk positively about generals Jaruzelski and Kiszczak but that it was still too early (Gazeta Wyborcza 20090; Rzecpospolita 2009a).

Wałęsa then turned to the official commemorations: "I don't take part in academic events, because of the distaste I feel. Having a moral hangover, I do not want to take part in them. I have avoided them, I avoid them, and I will avoid them." In Konin, he described everyone who took part in the Roundtable as heroes, but at the same time said that the process was not fair, because the participants had tried to deceive each other. Wałęsa talked about his own pangs of conscience for breaking the agreement. He mentioned the shortening of Jaruzelski's term of office in this regard (Gazeta Wyborcza 2009p; Polska Agencja Prasowa 2009). He then added, "I signed it with one hand, and with the other thought to choke myself" (Stróżyk 2009a).

Wałęsa's position on the Roundtable had no direct political significance. His stance was mostly reputational. It was Wałęsa who broke decisively with the Roundtable Agreement, despite being one of its framers. By doing so, he moved Poland more quickly and decisively into an era of full-fledged democracy. Yet, at the same time, as the first president in the democratic era that he inaugurated, he was hardly a political success. He was ineffective in translating his preferences into policy once the SLD and its allies assumed control of the government after the elections of 1993.

The idea that the Roundtable was a historic and strategic success, albeit achieved at the cost of ethical "impurity" that had to be subsequently erased, justifies Wałęsa's declaration of the War at the Top, pushing Jaruzelski out of power, and convoking fully competitive elections for the presidency and the National Assembly. At the same time, it provides a justification for his failure. While he was able to overcome some of the legacies of the Roundtable, his failures in office can be explained in terms of the business that it left unfinished.

Sitting president Lech Kaczyński publicly articulated a mixed assessment of the Roundtable as well. The ambiguity and hybridity of this position is why we refer to five and *one-half* different positions on the Roundtable. Despite his going on record as having a mixed view, on some occasions he pronounced negative assessments. One such occasion was the commemoration that he organized. In a powerfully symbolic act, on the anniversary of the Roundtable, the president signed legislation stripping pension rights from former agents of the communist-era secret police and members of the Military Council for National Salvation (WRON), the body that Jaruzelski convened to implement Martial Law in 1981 (Stróżyk 2009b).

Yet publicly the president usually took care to strike a balanced personal position on the Roundtable, noting both its negatives and positives. He characterized it as a move forward toward the recovery of Polish sovereignty, but an incomplete one, and while describing the negotiations as a "conversation with the usurper" (*rozmowy z uzurpatorem*), he also saw them as necessary and "tactical" (Gazeta Wyborcza 2009k; Rzeczpospolita 2009a).

In his public remarks he noted that there were two retrospective assessments of the talks and that the difference in interpretation revolves around two very similar Polish words, *umowa* (agreement) and *zmowa* (collusion). He noted that one side presents the Roundtable Agreement as the rebirth of the "republic" (*rzeczpospolita*),[6] whereas the other criticizes it as a "social collusion of elites" (*społeczna zmowa elit*) that inhibited democratization. Kaczyński disagreed with the second view, but also maintained that the Roundtable reflected a particular set of political circumstances. And while disavowing collusion, he decried the fraternization that occurred between the two sides (Gazeta Wyborca 2009k; Rzeczpospolita 2009a). More generally, mentioning both sides served his purposes; the positive spin meant that his role in the Roundtable did not discredit him, whereas the negative assessment supported his contention that the process of transformation in Poland needed renewed impetus.

Kaczyński elaborated on the theories he was supposedly disavowing by mentioning an interpretation that the Solidarity side protected the PZPR and gave it economic privileges. Again, he reiterated that as a participant in the Roundtable talks he did not believe this, rejecting the idea that the Roundtable was a betrayal and refuting rumors that the Solidarity elite was given assurances of power in return for promises made to the communists with regard to property (Gazeta Wyborcza 2009i, 2009k; Rzeczpospolita 2009a; Office of the President 2009, 4). Yet at the same time, in an essay published in the daily *Rzeczpospolita*, Kaczyński made the accusation that "[a] part of the nomenklatura was striving to exchange its political privileges for economic ones" (Kaczyński 2009). In this he seems to be close to the public pronouncements of the sociologist Jadwiga Staniszkis, who argued: "on the one hand, the [Roundtable] agreement brought about democracy. On the other, it brought about the nomenklatura buyout that allowed this group to assume the most important positions in the economy" (Stróżyk 2009a).

Finally, the president, along with several others at the presidential commemoration, propounded a theory of a lost opportunity in the aftermath of the election of June 1989. They argued that the collapse of the system and the PZPR presented an opening to accelerate the pace of change (Office of the President 2009, 5). Of course, Wałęsa's War at the Top and his assumption of the presidency in 1990—in which the Kaczyński brothers and their party at that time, the Center Alliance (Porozumienie Centrum), were central actors—were supposed to be precisely about acceleration. This line of reasoning is implicitly critical of Wałęsa for not accelerating the pace of change enough during his presidency, thus necessitating radical action to overcome the Roundtable's effects (Office of the President 2009, 13).

The president's mixed assessment is summed up succinctly in the following statement: "One can and needs to criticize (the Roundtable), but as a stage in the struggle it was necessary" (Władyka 2009). For the Kaczyński brothers, this stance justified their support of Wałęsa in the War at the Top. In their assessment of the split in Solidarity, Lech Kaczyński contrasted his own more confrontational positions on breaking the terms of the Roundtable to those of Wałęsa's other advisors, who ultimately supported Mazowiecki. With regard to the breakthrough elections of June 1989, he maintained that he favored a more confrontational and plebiscitary approach to the elections than either Geremek or Michnik, whose positions he stigmatized as favoring "kontraktowe" (pacted) elections (Kaczyński 2009).

Tusk and the Government: Silence Is Golden

After the demise of the political parties that emerged from the reformist wing of Solidarity and the Mazowiecki campaign—the Democratic Union (UD) and the Union of Freedom (UW)—the current governing party, the Civic Platform (PO), has taken up the mantle of pragmatic reformism. Interestingly, they were nearly absent from the public commemorations of the Roundtable in 2009. While they obviously consented to the celebration of the Roundtable at the Sejm, and Speaker Komorowski did make welcoming remarks on that occasion, their major politicians stayed out of the controversy. In fact, one comes away with the impression that the major leaders of PO avoided commenting at all.[7]

In his remarks, Prime Minister Donald Tusk avoided engaging in the debate and instead tried to stay above the controversy. His speech was prefaced by the reminder that "the government did not budget gigantic sums of money for the organization of anniversary celebrations" in the midst of an economic crisis. He also emphasized that it was important to remind Europe about Poland's role in the fall of communism. His position was that it was better to highlight the twentieth anniversary of the June elections of 1989 (Stróżyk 2009b).

The interesting question here is why PO remained unengaged in this debate. Our belief is that PO saw only disadvantages in engaging in the rhetorical battles couched in terms of old divides. Defending the Roundtable would allow PiS to charge that PO was collaborating with the ex-communists and was thus complicit in their corruption. So, PO saw no advantage in the mud-slinging that mnemonic warfare offered. Rather, its politicians seemed to have assumed that their party's advantage was best served by playing the role of *mnemonic abnegators*, staying above the fray for the most part and looking like they were trying to avoid engagement in the divisive politics of memory. As a party that tries to bill itself above all as competent, uncontroversial, and moderate, staying out of fights about the past served it well. However, during the second round of commemoration of the events of 1989, the anniversary of the June elections, it changed in orientation to that of a mnemonic pluralist and continued to frustrate the warrior stance of PiS, albeit through a new strategy.

The Commemoration of the June Elections

The elections of June 1989 are generally seen by historians as a massive victory for Solidarity and a disaster for the PZPR.[8] Yet, the seemingly uncontroversial, historical victory became a hotly contested object of mnemonic politics. In 2009, it pitted President Lech Kaczyński against the government led by Donald Tusk, though on an ideological level it could also be conceptualized as a struggle between partisans of the Third and Fourth Polish Republics.

The distinction between the Third and Fourth Republics is an ideological formulation used by the Polish Right. The first two republics were the original Polish-Lithuanian Commonwealth, partitioned in late eighteenth century, and the interwar republic that was partitioned in 1939. "The Third Republic" commonly denotes the democratic republic created after the collapse of the communist Polish People's Republic in 1989. For sections of the Polish Right, the Third Republic was flawed from the outset because of its origins in the corrupt compromise between the PZPR and the reform faction in Solidarity. Partisans of a "Fourth Republic" speak of the necessity of a new set of radical measures to purge Poland of the remnants of the rotten deal struck at the Roundtable.[9]

This ideological divide grew out of the earlier division in Solidarity between the supporters of Mazowiecki and Wałęsa. The coalition of forces calling for an acceleration of change, arrayed around Wałęsa, fell apart during Jan Olszewski's six-month tenure as prime minister in 1991–1992. When his Interior Minister, Antoni Macierewicz, threatened to expose many important public figures, including President Wałęsa, as former collaborators of the communist-era secret police, the government was quickly terminated by a vote of no-confidence. This incident led to a split between Wałęsa and his more radical supporters, including the Kaczyński brothers. Since then, much ink has been spilled trying to substantiate Macierewicz's claims regarding Wałęsa (Cenckiewicz and Gontarczyk 2008; Zyzak 2009).

Those who broke with Wałęsa after the collapse of the Olszewski government continue to play public roles as partisans of the Fourth Republic. In their worldview, all other political forces in Poland, including their former Solidarity allies, are enemies who have resisted the "acceleration" of change necessary to create a true democracy in Poland. For them, only two governments have been truly reformist— the Olszewski government and that of Jarosław Kaczyński (2006–2007), which was replaced by the present government of Donald Tusk, who is the first post-1989 prime minister to win two elections in a row. The disputes over the twentieth anniversary of the June 1989 elections were arrayed along these lines. The side behind President Kaczyński and PiS was more confrontational in their tactics, and bereft of significant political allies. Prime Minister Tusk was classically mnemonic pluralist, conciliatory and inclusive in his approach. He also enjoyed the support of a more expansive range of political parties and figures.

Within the theoretical framework of this book, we argue that the memory regime moved from *fractured and multipolar* to *fractured and bipolar*. The symbolic conflict between the adherents of the two dominant visions of the origins of the post-communist Poland was fought out during the celebrations commemorating the June 4 elections. We identified five major events in the latter round of celebrations. The commemoratory exhibit and film screening at the Sejm in Warsaw was a spectacularly contested event. Two events, the celebration at the Gdańsk Shipyard and the protest march in Katowice, were strongly associated with the Kaczyński forces, whereas the celebratory Mass at the cathedral in Kraków and the celebration at Symphony Hall in Gdańsk were associated with Prime Minister Tusk and his political camp. These celebrations were more expansive in nature and included a broad spectrum of contemporary politicians and a diverse array of historical figures, both Polish and foreign.

Warsaw: The Polish Road to Independence, June 3, 2009

The first event commemorating the 1989 elections was held at the Sejm on June 3. It was the ceremonial opening of an exhibition and film entitled *The Polish Road to Independence, 1980–9*. It was meant to be a highly inclusive and celebratory event, but a strong element of partisanship raised its head at this event. Both President Kaczyński and Prime Minister Tusk attended the opening of the exhibition, but they did not take part in a celebratory joint session of the Sejm and Senate. When asked by journalists why he was leaving and not attending the parliamentary session, Kaczyński replied that he had other plans, and would be in Gdańsk on the fourth. When pressed by journalists about what they should tell the members of parliament, the president replied, "It is hard for me to say. Disputes in politics are a normal thing. On the other hand, the means by which it is carried out, for example by Representative Palikot or Marshal Niesiołowski, crosses the boundaries of what is acceptable in a democracy" (Gazeta Wyborcza 2009n, 2009q).[10]

The parliamentary session was attended by past presidents Lech Wałęsa and Aleksander Kwaśniewski, as well as former Prime Minister Mazowiecki. Also attending was Hans-Gert Poettering, the president of the European Parliament, as well as the representatives of twenty-four European national parliaments. It also included several important Eastern European oppositional and independence figures, including Vytautus Landsbergis from Lithuania, Russian dissident Sergei Kovalev, Ján Čarnogurský of Slovakia, and Arnold Vaatz of the former German Democratic Republic (GDR). The event celebrated Poland's pioneering role in the ending of communism and the dismantling of divisions in Europe. This event strongly linked Poland and Europe, a theme that was featured in the opening address given by the marshal of the Sejm, Bronisław Komorowski, as well as in speeches by both Wałęsa and Mazowiecki. An important element of this commemoration was participation by a well-known actress, author, and public figure, Joanna Szczepkowska.[11] Twenty years earlier, she uttered words to the effect that the elections of June 1989 "finished off communism in Poland" live on Polish television. She reflected on that moment and what it meant for the next two decades (Gazeta Wyborcza 2009n, 2009q).

Gdańsk I: Kaczyński

In Gdańsk on June 4, President Kaczyński attended a ceremony at the Headquarters of Solidarity, where he awarded medals to forty trade union activists for their contributions to the democratic transformation of Poland. While the ceremony highlighted the contributions of Solidarity to democracy in Poland, elements of political contestation crept in. The president stated, "It is sad, that in this hall, of all the highest office holders of the Republic only I am present. Truly, irrespective of our differences, I would like this to be otherwise." One of the trade unionists receiving the award, Jan Hałas, the leader of the strike at the Gdańsk Port in 1980 and a deputy chairman of Solidarity in the 1990s, refused to accept the decoration from the president. He was strongly against the organization of separate commemorations, did not think that this was what he had fought for, and was fed up (*Wprost* 2009a; Katka et al. 2009; Gazeta Wyborcza 2009c).

Following the ceremony, the President attended an outdoor Mass celebrated by the primate of Poland, Cardinal Józef Glemp, at the Monument to the Fallen

Shipyard Workers in Solidarity Square. The event, attended by about three thousand people, was dominated by members of Solidarity and PiS, including a large number of PiS politicians, led by party chairman Jarosław Kaczyński. Whereas PiS leaders were met with applause, activists and politicians from other parties who arrived at the scene were greeted with whistles and hoots.

Also present were Archbishop Sławoj Leszek Głódz, the metropolitan of Gdańsk; Janusz Śniadek, the leader of the trade union; Waldemar Pawlak, the deputy prime minister and leader of the Polish Peasant Party; Jan Kozłowski, the provincial marshall (PO); and Paweł Adamowicz, the mayor of Gdańsk (PO). When Archbishop Głódz greeted several of these public speakers, the crowd responded again with whistles. Members of the crowd also unfurled a banner mixing Polish with German that was hostile to the mayor, "Herr Adam Owitz z Gdańska Raus" (Mr. Adam-Owitz get out of Gdańsk). These actions troubled the archbishop, who reminded the crowd that they were at a Mass and that Solidarity did not belong to any one political camp (Wprost 2009a; Katka et al. 2009; Sandecki and Katka 2009).

Following the Mass, the president spoke against the potential closing of the Gdańsk shipyard, which he described as a national monument, as unacceptable given the level of unemployment. He also used the occasion to encourage those present to participate in the upcoming elections for the European Parliament. He took a sideswipe at PO's campaign rhetoric in 2007 that spoke of a Polish economic miracle. President Kaczyński reminded those assembled that only God, not men, made miracles, and closed with the slogan, "there are no miracles; it's all lies" (which rhymes in Polish—*Cudów nie ma, wszystko ściema*) (Wprost 2009a; Katka et al. 2009).

Kraków: Tusk at Wawel

At the same time, Prime Minister Tusk was attending a commemorative ceremony at Wawel Castle in Kraków. Joining him were Presidents Lech Wałęsa, Aleksander Kwaśniewski, and Ryszard Kaczorowski (the last president of the Polish government-in-exile), as well as President Václav Havel of the Czech Republic and Chancellor Angela Merkel of Germany. In addition, the prime ministers of the Czech Republic, Hungary, Romania, Lithuania, and Ukraine also attended. Speeches were made by Cardinal Stanisław Dziwisz of Kraków, Tusk, Wałęsa, Merkel, and Havel. The overall tenor of the speeches was celebratory, with the foreign dignitaries acknowledging a debt of gratitude toward Poland for initiating the changes twenty years ago. Tusk went out of his way to thank the Catholic Church by remembering the contributions of both Pope John Paul II and Father Jerzy Popiełuszko, the murdered priest of the Stanisław Kostka Church in Warsaw. He also singled out Lech Wałęsa for praise and thanks, and thanked President Lech Kaczyński for helping Wałęsa in the rebuilding of Solidarity "in its most difficult moments" (Wprost 2009a; Tusk 2009; Katka et al. 2009). He also thanked a range of other important public figures, many anonymous heroes, and several important female activists, including Henryka Krzywonos, an opposition activist who played a crucial role in the 1980 strikes in Gdańsk; Anna Dymna, an activist on behalf of orphans and the disabled; and Janina Ochojska, another important humanitarian activist. Finally, he not only accepted the thanks of the neighboring countries of Eastern Europe but also thanked them for their contributions to the collective freedom of the region (Tusk 2009).

Gdańsk II: Tusk, Wałęsa, and Havel

After the conclusion of the festivities in Kraków, Tusk, Wałęsa, and Havel made their way to Gdańsk to attend a historical conference at Philharmonic Hall. The conference exhibition was opened by Bogdan Borusewicz, a leader of the Baltic opposition since the 1970s and at that moment the marshall of the Senate. He thanked the hundreds of thousands of Poles who risked their careers in the fight for Freedom. Wałęsa also spoke, and there was a video from President George H. W. Bush in which he thanked the Polish nation for its service to freedom (Katka et al. 2009). The commemoration of Lech Wałęsa's contribution came at the intermission in a celebratory concert that night in the city. He was featured in a "happening" where he knocked over an oversized domino labeled "Poland" which in turn took down several other dominoes labeled with the names of the other Soviet bloc countries (Picture 3.1).[12] The concert was the best-attended event of all, bringing 35,000 people together to listen a range of popular Polish and Western pop groups (Gazeta Wyborcza 2009b).

Katowice: The Union Celebration

Finally, on June 4 in Katowice there was a march of Solidarity trade unionists against "the ineffectiveness of the government in the struggle with the (economic) crisis and its disregard of social dialog." At least 5,000 people took part in a colorful and well-organized event. It included a marching band, drummers, and balloons, as well as a mocked-up copy of *Gazeta Wyborcza*, which was used as an informational handout. It also included comical effigies of a number of public figures and a large dragon (a symbol of Kraków) with the motto "Today I'd rather be with You than at Wawel with PO-liticians" (*Dzisiaj wolę być z Wami niż na Wawelu z POlitykami*). The prime minister, Stefan Niesiołowski, and Lech Wałęsa were particular targets of displeasure and ridicule (Katka et al. 2009; Gazeta Wyborcza 2009e).

In radio interviews the next day, both Kaczyński and Tusk commented on the divisive aspects of the commemoration. The president questioned the whole premise

PICTURE 3.1 Gdańsk, Poland, June 4, 2009. On the twentieth anniversary of the 1989 elections in Poland, Lech Wałęsa pushes over the first of nineteen oversized dominoes, symbolizing the impact of those elections on the fall of communism in other bloc countries.
Source: AP Photo/Alik Keplicz.

of celebrating in Kraków, given the importance of Gdańsk to the Polish struggle. He also blamed the media for the tension between himself and Prime Minister Tusk, as well as between PiS and PO. And while he expressed his thanks to Tusk for mentioning his role in Solidarity during his speech in Kraków, he suspected that this was a tactic suggested to him by political consultants. He also claimed that his departure from the events in Warsaw on June 3 was a product of Speaker Komorowski's invitation, which he understood was only to attend the exhibition and not the commemoration. He also acknowledged his antipathy to Lech Wałęsa, who had spoken badly about him in the past (Gazeta Wyborcza 2009j).

In his own interview on the radio, Tusk stressed that he worked hard to try to make sure that everyone invited to the government commemoration in Kraków attended. When asked specifically about President Kaczyński, he answered that "the President chose a different scenario for today, but he has the right to do so." Diminishing the significance of the dueling commemorations, the prime minister added, "one Poland celebrates in many places" (Gazeta Wyborcza 2009h).

The Politics of Memory

Poland was unique in the Soviet Bloc in that it had an organized and active opposition that resisted and challenged the party-state continuously, particularly over the last thirteen years of communist rule, 1976–1989 (Bernhard 1993; Ekiert 1996). It was the existence of this opposition that prompted the party-state authorities to seek Roundtable Negotiations and to hold the semi-competitive elections that eventually brought down the regime and set the ball rolling in the region. For the first sixteen years, politics in post-communist Poland was dominated by competition between ex-communist and post-Solidarity political forces. However, since 2005, the ex-communist part of the political spectrum has been in eclipse following massive corruption scandals, and Polish politics has been dominated by two post-Solidarity formations, the centrist Civic Platform and the Center-Right Law and Justice Party. Platform is currently (2007–2014) the stronger of the two—controlling both the government and the presidency.

Despite the fact that Poland had the most vibrant oppositional politics of the late communist period, and that its politics today are dominated by political forces descended from Solidarity, there is actually no consensus in the Polish memory field over the significance or meaning of the opposition's actions in 1989. Our analysis of the commemoration of the Roundtable Agreement shows the emergence of a fractured and fragmented memory regime with dominant post-Solidarity mnemonic actors taking four and one-half distinct positions during the 2009 commemorations.

On the other hand, ex-communist actors developed a coherent narrative in which the party reformist faction and its successors take credit for initiating the democratic reform process. In interviews conducted at the University of Michigan on the tenth anniversary of the Roundtable, several members of this group offered an account embedded in an "economic" discourse of necessity. In their reasoning, the economic system became so ineffectual in the late 1980s that drastic reforms were unavoidable. On the other hand, despite repression, "Solidarity" had survived the regime's efforts to destroy it and had become a permanent element in politics. Hence, there was no viable reform strategy that would not include it; the negotiations became necessary. Nevertheless, the communists claimed to be the leading force of the reform. Their story, in essence, may be rendered in a simple sentence: in *our* reform plans *we* had to find room for Solidarity, if *we* were to succeed together (Czyrek 1999; Gdula 1999; Orzechowski 1999).[13]

The basic logic of this "economic" story has remained constant; the ex-communists stick to it with discipline. It is clearly reflected in the way they positioned themselves for the celebrations of the twentieth anniversary in 2009: they were reasonable reformers, fully legitimate founding fathers of a democratic Poland embedded in Europe.

The post-Solidarity actors contributed to the memory regime on 1989 twenty years hence in a much more diverse fashion. The four post-Solidarity positions on the Roundtable are celebratory, mixed, negative, and silent. The remnants of the reformist faction from the period of the Mazowiecki government continued to think of the Roundtable as a fairly negotiated compromise that opened the way to a peaceful transformation to democracy. This was the group that commemorated with the SLD at the Sejm in February 2009. As revealed in a series of interviews conducted at the University of Michigan at the ten-year anniversary of the Roundtable (Kennedy and Porter 2000), most members of this group have stuck strongly to the narrative prevalent among Solidarity's negotiators. This narrative attributes far greater agency to society, the Solidarity movement and its leadership, as well as the Catholic Church (the pope and/or the Episcopate), than to the party-state. The existence and actions of Solidarity and its ability to turn the citizenry away from the party-state, challenging its legitimacy, are presented as the impetus for the reform process undertaken by the party (Wujec 1999; Bratkowski 1999). This narrative also acknowledges the imperfection of the Roundtable Agreement, but interprets it as a necessary step given the constraints posed by Poland's international position and the ambiguity about the expected Soviet response to radical change (Merkel 1999).

The negative interpretation of the Roundtable came from PiS but was also cultivated by a range of right-wing, clerical, and national forces. The Michigan project picked up some echoes of this orientation, but fewer of these activists were interviewed, as they were not included in the Roundtable process.[14] Activists from the Christian-national tradition complained about how they had been marginalized by the group around Wałęsa, who usurped the right to speak in the name of the entire society. Even in 1999, their belief was that they had been silenced, unrepresented, or only partially represented at the Roundtable (Chrzanowski 1999). Such logic was very strongly echoed in Roszkowski's presentation at the presidential debate on the Roundtable.

This interpretation of the Roundtable process continues even today (2014) in the narrative offered by many right-wing descendants of Solidarity, many of whom support PiS. It consists of five major points: (1) the compromise at the Roundtable went too far and/or the post-1989 governments failed to undo its damaging effects once the regime was defeated; (2) as a result, the ex-communists have retained too much (particularly economic) power; (3) public life has been corrupted by people tainted by collaboration with the old system; and (4) an unholy alliance of the reds and pinks (ex-communists and the reformist wing of the Solidarity movement) have continued to protect this rotten compromise. The fifth point focuses on Lech Wałęsa, who is excoriated for betraying the movement (perhaps as early as the 1970s) and being substantially responsible for the four failures listed above.

In the face of polarization between the more benign commemoration at the Sejm and more negative presentations at the presidential palace, the mixed positions of Lech Wałęsa and Lech Kaczyński and the silence of PO make political sense.

Wałęsa, as a focus of right-wing opprobrium as a sell-out, chose not to participate in anything they sponsored. At the same time, it was hard for him, also politically, to be seen celebrating the Roundtable with either the ex-communists or the reformists who sided with Mazowiecki. That would simply be further grist for the PiS mill. Lech Kaczyński was playing an ambiguous game. He backed off the most extreme negative positions that charged a conspiracy between Solidarity and the PZPR. But he nevertheless agreed that the Roundtable had nefarious consequences. Even if it was not a swindle, it was a bad compromise whose results require ex-post facto cleansing.

The silence of PO seems embedded in their understanding of the process of power transfer, initiated at the Roundtable, as built on an unwanted albeit necessary compromise. The nature of the bargain, given the guarantees for the communists and their allies, was not democratic, despite its eventual democratic outcome. It was the elections of June 1989 that moved the Polish reform process in a decidedly democratic direction. So, PO chose to focus on this moment, and with good reason given the way in which the Right bludgeoned anyone who defended the Roundtable and the whole process of power transfer.

The memory regime on the twentieth anniversary of 1989 continued to be fractured during the commemoration of the elections of June 1989 but became bifurcated, losing its multivocal, fragmented nature. For all the post-Solidarity actors, save PiS, the elections were the unambiguous beginning of Polish democratization and thus could bring them together despite differences on the significance of the Roundtable. A curious wrinkle in this shared belief about the June 1989 elections was the willingness of the SLD to take part, despite the fact that the elections thoroughly destroyed the limited reform strategy of the PZPR. That the SLD recovered by 1993 perhaps made the sting of that defeat inconsequential in retrospect, while the celebration of the democratizing nature of those elections marks their commitment to democracy. It also reinforced their foundational narrative in which the Roundtable figures as a keystone of *deliberate* democratic reforms.

For the mnemonic warriors of PiS, the original sin of the Roundtable continued to compromise the whole existence of the Third Republic, and literally required a re-foundation of Polish democracy. In a new, re-founded Poland (the Fourth Republic), the former communists would be completely purged from public life, their entrenched power broken, and those who had enabled and protected them punished. Effective as this was in mobilizing the political Right, this narrative did not become hegemonic in the public space of post-1989 Poland (for the polling and electoral data, see later discussion in this chapter).[15] This position continues to be challenged by a narrative that focuses on the successes of the 1989–2009 period and that emphasizes Solidarity's achievements.

Only one actor in Polish politics used the intense politicization of the Roundtable Agreement on its twentieth anniversary as a political strategy: PiS. Its leadership chose to engage in mnemonic warfare, as it offered an interpretation of the post-communist transformation of Poland as a Potemkin village that changed little. This political strategy paints everyone else in politics as compromised, and only PiS as pure enough to restore moral harmony. This is the stance of a quintessential *mnemonic warrior*.

Was this cultural-symbolic political strategy effective? Did it produce desired "political goods," such as popular support and thus power for the right-wing parties, in particular the Law and Justice Party, the most tenacious warrior? In a survey conducted in early October 2008, the leading polling organization, *CBOS*, found that Poles regarded the post-1989 period as the best period in the last hundred years of Polish history (49 percent of the respondents chose this option) (CBOS 2008). And in terms of what they have lived through in the recent period, Poles saw the fall of communism as the most important event (21 percent) of the recent past, just ahead of the selection of Karol Wojtyła as Pope (21 percent) and the regaining of independence in 1918 (20 percent). The creation of Solidarity in August 1980 was perceived as the most important event by only 11 percent of the respondents. These results do not support the idea that there is widespread dissatisfaction caused by a betrayal of the rank-and-file by Solidarity's leadership in 1989.

In early 2009 CBOS conducted a comprehensive survey, asking its respondents to assess the twenty years of post-communist development (CBOS 2009a). For a large plurality of the respondents (40 percent), the Roundtable Agreement was considered the most important breakthrough event that marked the end of communism. Their evaluation of the agreements was largely positive: 41 percent assessed them as "rather positive," 12 percent as "rather negative," 31 percent were "indifferent," and for 16 percent it was "hard to say." Importantly, 44 percent of the respondents saw the Roundtable Agreement as a "social contract," while 26 percent construed it as an "elite deal." For 30 percent it was "hard to say." The criticism of the Roundtable was most vividly reflected in the answer to the question of whether it was the best method of regime change in Poland: 30 percent of the respondents thought so, but 37 percent thought the "the compromise went too far." Only 8 percent claimed that it was "the wrong method, an unnecessary giving in to the communists." The 25 percent of the respondents who admitted that it was "hard to say" were mostly too young to remember the event personally.

The survey results reported above do not provide much evidence that the mnemonic wars of 2009 produced the outcome presumably desired by their instigator, the Law and Justice Party. It managed neither to impose its vision of history on the populace at large, nor to achieve tangible short-term political success. After winning a plurality of votes in the October 2005 Sejm (lower house) elections by a relatively slim margin (27 percent to Civic Platform's 24.1 percent), it decisively lost both the November 2007 (32.1 percent to Civic Platform's 41.5 percent) and October 2011 elections (29.89 percent to Civic Platform's 39.18 percent).

The immediate failure of PiS's political gambit was also confirmed by the results of the presidential elections in 2010 that followed the tragic plane crash in Smolensk on April 10, in which the president and ninety-five other prominent political and public figures died. It is hard to imagine a scenario that would play better into the mnemonic politics of PiS. President Lech Kaczyński was martyred on his way to a commemoration of a massacre of Polish officers by the Soviets in the Katyń forest during World War II. If his twin, Jarosław, could not win a presidential election in the face of such tragedy, could it be said that the Kaczyńskis' politics of mnemonic warfare had found a broad resonance among Polish voters? In the second round of the presidential elections, held on July 4, 2010, Jarosław Kaczyński, the dead president's twin brother, received 47 percent of the vote, losing to PO candidate Bronisław Komorowski, who was elected president on the basis of 53 percent. PO's stance of abnegation on the Roundtable and its pluralist engagement in the com-memorations of the June 4 elections proved to be winning strategies in this round of the PiS instigated mnemonic war.

PO's strategy in response to PiS's gambit was highly successful in the short term. Donald Tusk was the first Polish prime minister to win re-election, and President Bronisław Komorowski, appointed after the unfortunate demise of Lech Kaczyński, was elected to office in the next presidential election. This led to the longest period of cohabitation between a president and a prime minister from the same party in post-communist Poland. Political triumphs, however, are notoriously short-lived, and as of February 2014, PiS leads in the polls while PO's support hovers around the lowest point since its electoral success in 2011. PiS, at the moment, can count on the plurality of votes, but the composition of the next cabinet is quite uncertain.

Fractured Memory and the Quality of Democracy

Law and Justice's mnemonic warfare has, however, an effect on Polish politics; it has prevented the Poles from forging a standard discourse on the recent past. As a result of this fractured memory regime about the foundation of the Third Republic, Poland lacks a coherent *mnemonic field* that would help its citizens assess the com-munist past, commemorate Solidarity, and build a symbolic foundation for the new democratic order. PiS's promotion of its singular vision of the Roundtable and its ramifications for the assessment of Poland's post-1989 democracy has been the main factor preventing the country's political culture from fully gelling twenty-five years after transition.

First, no founding myth for the Third Republic has been proposed and popularly accepted. The Republic is a product of an agreement whose meaning continues to be a hotly contested political issue. Without agreement on the meaning of a founding political event, it is hard to imagine the formation of a commonly accepted, foundational narrative for the Third Republic. Given that Poles seem to be attached to historical traditions more than other nations (Domański 2004), it is peculiar that they can reach no consensus on the culmination of the heroic resistance of Solidarity through the peaceful negotiation of an end to communism.

Second, "co-memoration," a joint recalling of the collective past, is essential to generating a sense of community. The routinization of such occasions as national holidays has a very important function in generating a national identity. And in the generation of new identities, the establishment of a common symbolic frame of and for collective memory calls for the periodic staging of ceremonies to jointly mark consequential past events, on a regular basis, usually as anniversaries (Zerubavel 1996, 289). Yet, mnemonic synchronization—as Zerubavel calls it—of the Polish national community has not been built around any symbolic markers (events, personalities, or locations) related to Solidarity as late as the beginning of 2014. The founding events of the Third Republic made it into the ceremonial calendar of the new polity as state holidays only in July 2005, but even then not as a full-fledged holiday (a day without work). And, as our analysis shows, an attempt to celebrate the twentieth anniversary of the fall of communism in a unified national ceremony failed.

Paradoxically, however, the prolonged cultural indeterminacy and the periodic fracturing of the memory field have not impeded post-communist democratic consolidation, as some observers and theorists would predict. Most important, during the first twenty years of the post-communist period, a solid dose of pragmatism became firmly institutionalized in Poland and formed a normative barrier that no major political figure dared to cross, despite frequent "radical" rhetorical flourishes. Poles were increasingly satisfied with the post-communist transformations: in October 1991, 49 percent believed that after 1989 the situation in the country improved. In January 2009, the year of the twentieth anniversary celebrations, 80 percent held this view (Boguszewski, Kuźmicz, and Strzeszewski 2009, 67).[16] On the other hand, despite the empirically detected signs that early in the twenty-first century the public began losing interest in politicized historical debates (Szacka 2006, 219), the saliency of history as a political battleground was not fading away as late as 2014. What we learned, however, is that waging a memory war is a risky strategy. In 2009 the right-wing parties chose this strategy as their main political weapon and subsequently lost both the parliamentary and presidential elections.

Moreover, the long-term consequences of this choice go beyond electoral politics. PiS' mnemonic warrior stance is the main element of the fractured collective memory in Poland that continued to make it very difficult to unambiguously celebrate the achievements of Solidarity domestically, despite the fact they are acknowledged internationally. In this sense, the symbolic capital that the movement generated in the 1980s seems to have been wasted after the fall of communism.

NOTES

1. Not the original English, but a retranslation from Polish.

2. Historians from a range of perspectives participated, including: Andrzej Paczkowski, Andrzej Friszke, Andrzej Ajnenkel, Andrzej Nowak, Jan Skórzyński, Dariusz Stola, Janusz Kurtyka, Jan Żaryn, Andrzej Grajewski, Tadeusz Krawczak, Paweł Machcewicz, Andrzej Chojnowski, and Jan Kofman.

3. Roszkowski used the Polish word *Porozumenie* (agreement) and not the word *zmowa* (collusion), which is used in the more radical disavowals of the Roundtable.

4. See Głębocki (2008). The one point of the memo that addresses the Soviet Union reads as follows: "A difficult past weighs upon Polish-Russian relations. The threat of Soviet intervention, to which the Polish authorities appealed in moments of internal crisis, caused an increase in social mistrust. On the other hand the new Soviet policy of 'perestroika and glasnost' has aroused in broad circles of Polish public opinion general interest and sympathy, and also hopes for Poland's chances. This fact may have decisive meaning for Polish-Russian relations in the future. The inhibition of the current changes in Poland will hurt that process" (197–198).

5. According to Jan Skórzyński, who responded to Nowak at the commemorative panel, the only evidence of Gorbachev being the intended recipient comes from Irena Lasota, who found the letter in her personal papers. He also points out that Geremek is on the record as saying that the piece was authored by him but not meant for Gorbachev (Office of the President of the Polish Republic 2009, 20). The original French note is directed "A l'attention de George Soros." Janusz Kurtyka, responding to Skórzyński, claimed that the note was given to Soros, who was going to visit Moscow (34).

6. As opposed to the Polish *People's* Republic, the title of the country under communist rule, which was not a true republic like the pre-partition Polish Commonwealth or the Interwar Republic.

7. One conspicuous exception to this was Sejm deputy Antoni Mężydło, who gave an interview in which he spoke of the Roundtable in decidedly mixed terms and reflected on whether Poland could have made a cleaner break with communism if it had not initiated change in the region (Stróżyk and Mężydło 2009). Mężydło was one of a number of PO deputies who had been members of PiS and became disenchanted when Prime Minister Jarosław Kaczyński formed a coalition with Self-Defense and the League of Polish Families.

8. After their defeat in the elections of 1989, the leaders of the PZPR scrambled to form successor parties that could adapt to the new competitive democratic environment. The most successful of these, the SLD, presented itself as a modern European social democratic party, and by 1993 became the dominant political force in the country for several years. Its leader, Aleksander Kwaśniewski, served two consecutive terms as president (1995–2005).

9. The concept of the "third and fourth republics" was coined somewhat earlier by the political scientist Rafał Matyja. The term acquired force as political rhetoric in the electoral campaign of 2005, when the ruling SLD was rocked by several corruption scandals. Initially both PiS and PO used the rhetoric, but it was largely taken over by PiS when they abandoned the idea of coalition government with PO in 2005.

10. Palikot and Niesiołowski (the deputy marshall of the Sejm) have publicly suggested that former Prime Minister J. Kaczyński might be gay.

11. Previous post-1989 commemorations have been notable in the absence of important female public figures. This changed in 2009, when PO seems to have finally heard the message that had been repeatedly voiced by Poland's women's movements.

12. Wałęsa repeated this exercise in Berlin on November 11, 2009.

13. According to Gdula: "In 1980s, in our country's life, it was not unusual both for the authorities or the opposition to think that this state of the economy, the way it was managed, the whole organization of social life, that all this could not be continued, that it had run out, or, as they used to put it mildly, that the real socialism had run out of its developmental possibilities."

14. See Castle (2003) for a discussion of these groups.

15. Somewhat paradoxically, this political option included most leaders of the post-1989 Solidarity trade union. On this topic, see Brier (2009) and Ost (2005).

16. Since 2009 this very positive assessment of the post-1989 changes in the country declined, although still in June 2013 the plurality of Poles assessed these changes positively. See CBOS (2013).

4 Romania Twenty Years after 1989
THE BIZARRE ECHOES OF A CONTESTED REVOLUTION
Grigore Pop-Eleches

Introduction

The twentieth anniversary of the dramatic events that led to the fall of the Ceauşescu dictatorship was commemorated in a somewhat unusual fashion by Romanians. On the one hand, considering the scale of the protests and the human sacrifice in December 1989, the explicit commemorative events organized by both the Romanian state and civil society were surprisingly modest, and were largely limited to a commemorative symposium organized by the Institute of the Romanian Revolution of December 1989 on December 17, a small public march in Bucharest on December 21, a low-key official ceremony honoring the heroes of the revolution on December 22, and a parliamentary session on December 22. On the other hand, the political reverberations of the highly contested events of December 1989 were clearly visible during the presidential election contest that dominated the weeks prior to the twentieth anniversary of the Romanian revolution. In other words, Romania had a lot of electorally motivated mnemonic competition but very little reflective commemoration as it embarked on its third decade of its tumultuous post-communist path. Therefore, this chapter will focus on the interplay between political memory and electoral politics twenty years after December 1989, rather than on the fairly marginal commemorative events themselves.

If Romanians can agree on anything about the 1989 events, it is probably that many of the crucial details about what happened in those tumultuous days are still not known and may never be brought to light. While in theory one may expect such explicitly acknowledged uncertainty to promote mnemonic pluralism, in practice it has not hindered the politicization of the memory of 1989, nor has it reduced its political salience. Unlike in other ex-communist countries, however, the shortage of facts has blurred the lines of responsibility to the point at which, twenty years later, the symbols of 1989 had become a "free-for-all" resource for the electoral ambitions of politicians of all stripes. As this chapter will show in greater detail, this ambiguity led to the bizarre situation in which all the main political competitors engaged in the November/December 2009 presidential elections painted themselves as the true heirs of the 1989 revolution, while accusing their opponents of continuity with the communist regime. Nonetheless, the political reactions to some of these political maneuvers illustrated the limitations and risks inherent in such efforts to appropriate the memory of 1989. Moreover, the Romanian case highlights the important—but highly politicized, and hence contested—arbiter role of the participants in the 1989 revolution.

This chapter is organized as follows: the second section briefly describes the key commemorative events dedicated to the twentieth anniversary of the Romanian Revolution. The third section provides a broad historical background for understanding the commemoration of the 1989 revolution, and it briefly discusses the nature of the December 1989 events and the subsequent evolution of the political debates about the meaning and implications of the Romanian revolution. The fourth section focuses on the more immediate political context that framed the mnemonic politics on the twentieth anniversary of the revolution, with a particular emphasis on the 2009 presidential elections and the reverberations of the debates triggered by President Băsescu's decision to set up the Presidential Commission for the Study of the Communist Dictatorship in Romania in 2006. The fifth section recounts the debates and public statements about the 1989 revolution by the main political parties and leaders in the context of the presidential elections. The sixth section discusses the implications of the twentieth anniversary debates for the evolution of mnemonic politics in Romania and their impact on the broader political trajectory of the country. The final section concludes and briefly attempts to place the Romanian experience in a broader theoretical and comparative context.

Remembering 1989, Twenty Years Later

The commemoration of the twentieth anniversary of the 1989 revolution included a number of more or less politicized official events, which will be briefly discussed in this section. Chronologically, the first notable event took place on December 17,

2009: a symposium dedicated to the twentieth anniversary of the revolution organized by the Institute of the Romanian Revolution of December 1989 (IRRD).[1] During the session, which included an advance screening of a documentary about the Romanian revolution, the speech of former President Ion Iliescu was interrupted by Dumitru Dincă, a member of the Asociația 21 Decembrie, one of the most prominent revolutionary organizations, who sharply criticized both the film and Iliescu's speech for willfully ignoring the protests in Bucharest on December 21, 1989 (the day before Ceaușescu's departure). While Iliescu tried to dismiss Dincă as crazy, eventually both he and former Prime Minister Petre Roman acknowledged the film's shortcomings and promised that the oversights would be addressed in the final version of the film (*Adevărul* 2009).

The second event was a protest march organized in Bucharest on December 21, 2009, by the members of a civil society group called Noii Golani (the New Hooligans). The march, which had been approved by the local authorities and attracted only about 200 participants, was meant to commemorate the victims who died in Bucharest on December 21 (the day before the fall of the Ceaușescu regime). However, the protesters eventually switched course and started shouting "Romania—a police state," and some of the protesters attacked the police forces (Mediafax.ro 2009).

The last two events were directly organized by Romanian state institutions. One was a ceremony in which several public officials, including Mircea Geoană (as Senate president), with members of the armed forces, placed commemorative wreaths on the monument dedicated to the heroes of the 1989 revolution in Revolution Square in Bucharest on December 22, 2009. Finally, the Romanian Parliament hosted a commemorative session on the same day, which included speeches by several members of parliament who had participated in the 1989 protests (and which will be discussed in greater detail in a later section).

Historical Background

The Complicated Legacy of the Romanian Revolution

Romania was the only Eastern European country where the fall of communism triggered massive loss of human lives, with over 1,000 dead and many others wounded during the dramatic events of December 1989. What had started as a small protest among the parishioners of a reformed Hungarian priest, László Tőkés, quickly evolved into large anti-communist protests, which despite significant government repression quickly spread from the western city of Timișoara to several other cities and eventually led to the surprisingly rapid collapse of the Ceaușescu dictatorship.

From the outset, there was widespread confusion about many of the details surrounding the events of December 1989, including the number of victims (which was initially reported to be in the tens of thousands), the involvement of foreign secret services, and the identity of the "terrorists" responsible for the violent fighting, which continued well after Ceaușescu had fled Bucharest. Other than the number of victims, few of the questions were answered conclusively in the months and years after 1989, despite a large (and growing) list of studies published on the subject (e.g., Gabanyi 1990; Călinescu and Tismăneanu 1991; Gallagher, 1995).

What matters for the purpose of the present discussion is not what actually happened in 1989 but how the events were subsequently interpreted and incorporated into the post-communist political discourse. The first important feature, which sets Romania apart from the rest of post-communist Eastern Europe, is the significant and widely acknowledged uncertainty about many of the details of the December 1989 events. Remarkably, this sense of uncertainty was publicly expressed by both sides of the post-communist mnemonic debates, with anti-communist protesters repeatedly asking "cine-a tras în noiîn 16–22" (Who fired at us on [December]16–22), while former President Ion Iliescu reiterated in a recent interview that he still does not know who was responsible for much of the bloodshed during the revolution (România Libera 2009). However, as we will see below, this uncertainty about the facts has not triggered greater pluralism in the interpretations of the 1989 revolution, but may have given mnemonic warriors greater leeway in advancing their own versions of the events.

The second important peculiarity of the Romanian revolution is that it triggered fundamentally different interpretations about the very nature of the political events that occurred in December 1989. Whereas elsewhere in the region the debates center on the relative weight of opposition pressures and regime concessions in driving the democratic changes (e.g., Bruszt 1992), in Romania the main debate centered on the question of whether the December 1989 events that led to the downfall of the Ceaușescu dictatorship represented a revolution or a coup d'état. The reason for this fundamental disagreement is that the power vacuum left behind by Ceaușescu's hasty flight in the face of massive popular protests was rapidly filled by the National Salvation Front (FSN), which, in addition to a few prominent anti-communist dissidents, included a group of former high-ranking communist officials who had been side-lined in the final years of Ceaușescu's rule. While initially conceived as a broad anti-communist organization meant to stabilize the country's chaotic political situation, the Front very quickly became the focal point of profound ideological disagreements about the meaning of the revolution and the country's political future.

At the risk of oversimplification, there were two main political camps with two very different political interpretations of the 1989 events. One camp, which coalesced around Ion Iliescu and Petre Roman, regarded the Front as the embodiment of the

Romanian revolution and envisioned the National Salvation Front as the institutional vehicle for representing different political interests in what Iliescu hoped would become the basis of an "original democracy" that would transcend partisan divisions (Iliescu 1995, 61). For the FSN leadership and its many followers, the Romanian revolution had been victorious, and the FSN's overwhelming victory in the May 1990 elections represented the ultimate proof of its democratic legitimacy and the country's break with the communist past.

The second camp started to coalesce in early January 1990 around the recently refounded historical parties and the anti-communist dissidents, such as Mircea Dinescu and Doina Cornea, who quit the National Salvation Front in protest over what they considered the excessive influence of former communist officials. From their perspective, the Romanian revolution had been hijacked by a coup d'état organized by reformist communists, whose goal was to replace Ceaușescu's Stalinist dictatorship with a more reformist—but still inherently communist—regime modeled after Gorbachev's glasnost reforms. While some semantic differences existed within this broad current—with some observers avoiding the term "revolution" altogether and referring to the December 1989 events as a coup d'état, and others calling it a "hijacked revolution"—the general consensus was that the new regime broadly represented a continuation of the communist regime, albeit with a new top leadership.

A third—and closely related—peculiarity of Romania's post-1989 political system was that whereas elsewhere in the region the debates centered on the extent to which the communist successor parties had really experienced genuine transformations toward democratic socialist/social democratic parties, in Romania the main political contenders disagreed about the much more fundamental question about who the successors of the Communist Party were. While the Romanian Communist Party was officially outlawed a few days after the fall of the Ceaușescu regime, the anti-communist opposition viewed the National Salvation Front as the de facto heir of the Communist Party. In addition to the prominent presence of many former high-ranking communists in the Front's leadership, these critics pointed to the fact that prior to its transformation into a political party, the Front had taken over many of the state powers previously exercised by the Communist Party. They also pointed to Iliescu's lukewarm endorsement of multiparty democracy and market reforms, as well as to the new government's repeated reliance on force and intimidation tactics against its political opponents as symptoms of creeping "neo-communism."

Fractured Memory Politics in the Early 1990s

These fundamental disagreements about the nature of the 1989 revolution set the stage for a series of political confrontations, which fit squarely into the "us versus them" logic of the fractured memory regime. Thus, in March 1990 a group of former revolutionaries from Timişoara issued the so-called Proclamation of Timişoara, which notably included a proposal calling for the exclusion from public office for ten years of former high-ranking members of the Communist Party and the Securitate. The proposal, which would have banned the FSN's presidential candidate, Ion Iliescu, from running in the May 1990 elections, was embraced by the main anti-communist parties, the National Liberal Party (PNL) and the National Peasants' Party (PNT), and became one of the crucial demands of the anti-communist protests in University Square in Bucharest. The daily protests, which attracted tens of thousands of protesters from April 22 until their violent repression in June 13–15, became the focal point in the zero-sum struggle between two irreconcilable views about the meaning of the Romanian revolution, as well as about the country's political future. Thus, whereas the protesters declared University Square, which they occupied during the seven weeks of the protests, as the first neo-communism-free area in Romania and frequently chanted that "the only solution is another revolution," the FSN government painted them as extremist challengers to Romania's democracy, while President Iliescu famously called them "golani" (hooligans).

Perhaps not surprisingly, the terms of the "debate" did not lend themselves to compromise solutions, given that the core demands of the anti-communist opposition would have effectively excluded much of the FSN's top leadership from public office. Instead, the crisis was "resolved" in three main steps, which had, however, fairly little to do with deliberative democracy. In the first instance, the FSN leadership used its overwhelming majority in the interim national assembly to block any lustration provisions from being incorporated in the electoral law governing the May 1990 elections. As a second step, the FSN leadership used its clear victory in the May elections as a popular endorsement of the Front's democratic legitimacy and as further confirmation of the credibility of its version of the history of the Romanian revolution. When the opposition refused to back down, citing widespread electoral irregularities and manipulation, and the University Square protests continued even after the May elections, the new government moved to the third stage of its confrontation with its anti-communist opponents, which resulted in the violent repression of the protests, followed by three days of chaos in Bucharest during which Romanian security forces stood by as miners attacked not only protesters and opposition party offices but anyone suspected of harboring anti-FSN attitudes.

Thus ended the first stage of Romania's mnemonic politics, and its evolution confirms the potentially explosive nature of fractured memory regimes. What is less certain is whether the FSN's victory in this first round of the conflict was due primarily to its effective use of coercion and administrative resources in the fight against a poorly organized and splintered opposition, or because the opposition overestimated the Romanian public's willingness to reject the entire socioeconomic system of communism rather than its most dramatic aberrations, which had been embodied in Ceaușescu's personal dictatorship.

Gradual Rapprochement (1990–2005)

While a detailed analysis of the evolution of Romania's mnemonic regimes in the decade and a half after 1990 is beyond the scope of this chapter, it is worth mentioning a few broad developments during this time period. Following the electoral defeat in May 1990 and the repression in June 1990, the Romanian opposition was hardly persuaded by its opponent's version of the 1989 revolution—in fact, the events reinforced their fears about the dangers of a return to communist-era political tactics. While some of these fears were assuaged by the split of the National Salvation Front into two factions[2] and by the much cleaner elections of September 1992, the opposition parties maintained their principled resistance against the Iliescu regime, which largely explains their refusal to join a grand coalition with Iliescu's Party of Social Democracy (PDSR) in the aftermath of the 1992 elections. This refusal led Iliescu to seek allies among the more hard-line leftist and nationalist parties—some of which were much more unapologetic in highlighting their continuity with Ceaușescu's legacy—and thereby further delayed efforts to find common ground on dealing either with the communist past or with Romania's troubled transition (Pop-Eleches 1999).

Nonetheless, the intensity of the zero-sum logic of the memory regime was gradually reduced—not because the opposition completely abandoned the lustration efforts, but because its leaders rightly decided to focus their political efforts on issues with greater potential political payoffs, such as the growing economic costs of Romania's gradualist economic policies and the delays in Western integration caused by the slow progress of the country's economic and political reforms. Thus, the 1996 electoral campaign of the anti-communist opposition, which had largely succeeded in uniting under the banner of the Democratic Convention (CDR), focused primarily on the shortcomings of PDSR's post-communist governing record and on the promise of accelerated reforms and European integration, while toning down the earlier emphasis on the communist background of much of the FSN/PDSR leadership.

After narrowly defeating the PDSR in the November 1996 elections, the CDR did not pursue a vigorous anti-communist agenda, despite the fact that the CDR's backbone was the two historical parties (PNT and PNL) that had advocated lustration in 1990. While the Romanian Parliament eventually passed a lustration law in 1999, it was considerably watered down compared to the early demands of the Proclamation of Timișoara. Thus, even though the law provided access to the files of the Secret

Police (Securitate) and set up a Council for the Study of Securitate Archives to identify politicians and officials who had collaborated with the Securitate, the law did not require such officials to step down from their office, and it did not target high-ranking Communist Party officials (Stan 2002). Whatever the reasons for this surprisingly soft approach,[3] the CDR's failure to pursue the lustration issue vigorously during its time in office significantly defused the significant tension underlying the politics of memory vis-à-vis the communist period and the 1989 revolution.

After the elections of November 2000, Romania appeared to be set to leave completely behind the contentious memory regime of the early 1990s. Thus, the most consistent promoter of the maximalist anti-communist lustration agenda—the National Peasants' Party (PNȚCD)—failed to win representation in the new legislature, having borne the brunt of voter discontent for the country's protracted economic crisis in the late 1990s. The stunning defeat of the historic anti-communist parties, which was only partially mitigated by the National Liberal Party's (PNL) ability to squeeze into Parliament with 7 percent, effectively ensured that anti-communist lustration efforts were kept to a minimum in the 2000–2004 legislature. Meanwhile, the victorious Social Democratic Party (PSD) of President Iliescu had no interest in reviving the potentially divisive discussions about the communist past: after a campaign in which it had largely avoided earlier appeals to communist nostalgia and nationalism, the PSD tried and largely succeeded to recast itself as a pragmatic, competent, and moderate party, intent on promoting the country's NATO and EU integration efforts. This image makeover may have been facilitated by the contrast to the second-largest party in the new parliament, the Greater Romania Party (PRM), led by Corneliu Vadim Tudor, an outspoken apologist of Ceaușescu's nationalist communism. As a result, even though the 2000 elections did not really produce a resolution of the conflicting interpretations of the Romanian revolution, they effectively further reduced the political salience of the issue. This process was arguably reinforced by the fact that President Iliescu, who had been the most important target of the anti-communist lustration efforts, was barred by the Constitution from seeking an additional presidential term in 2004.

The Revival of Memory (2006–2010)

Despite the seeming inevitability that the Romanian revolution and its many unanswered questions would be relegated to the domain of historical inquiries, the period of 2006–2010 has marked a significant revival in the political salience of the communist past and the 1989 revolution. While Romania is not unique in the timing of this revival—Poland and Hungary experienced similar trends around the same time—the details of this mnemonic revolution bear the bizarre imprints of Romania's contested revolution and unusual party system.

To make a long story (somewhat) shorter, the main impetus for the revival of mnemonic debates came from a rather unexpected source: President Traian Băsescu. Băsescu hardly had the personal credentials of the earlier champions of the anti-communist cause (many of whom had been former political prisoners or dissidents): a former ship captain and Communist Party member, Băsescu served as a Transportation Minister in successive FSN governments in 1991–1992, and subsequently served two terms as a member of parliament on the lists of the Democratic Party (PD), the party that emerged from the reformist faction of the FSN after the 1992 split. While the PD entered into a governing coalition with the center-right Democratic Convention(CDR) in 1996, the party nevertheless maintained its Social Democratic platform and the party symbol of the former FSN (the Rose). Băsescu, who had managed to oust the former Prime Minister Petre Roman from the PD leadership after the party's modest performance in the 2000 elections, steered the party toward a coalition with the liberal PNL in the 2004 election. However, Băsescu's presidential campaign did not contain significant elements of anti-communist rhetoric and instead focused on the weak corruption record of the PSD. Indeed, during a televised debate with PSD's presidential candidate, Adrian Năstase, Băsescu joked about the bad fortune of Romanians who were forced to choose between two former communists. While this joke may have served primarily as a rhetorical device, at the time it captured the strange reality of Romanian politics whereby the two main presidential candidates came from parties that were both offshoots of the National Salvation Front.

The Romanian party system continued its strange contortions in 2005, when the PD abruptly announced that it would leave the Socialist International and instead join the European People's Party in a remarkably swift ideological conversion that raised surprisingly few eyebrows both within the party and from outside observers (Pop-Eleches 2008). While the conversion could be dismissed as yet another piece of evidence that ideology is irrelevant in Romanian politics, the subsequent political initiatives of the PD and President Băsescu suggest that the change was not simply cosmetic.[4] Perhaps most important for the purpose of the present discussion, President Băsescu decided in 2006 to set up the Presidential Commission for the Study of the Communist Dictatorship in Romania, chaired by Vladimir Tismăneanu, which published a 660-page report on the crimes of communism in Romania. This report, which received broad coverage both in Romania and abroad (e.g., King 2007; Tănăsoiu 2007), emphasized the responsibility of several leading FSN members and especially of Ion Iliescu, was presented by President Băsescu to the Romanian Parliament in a ceremony in which he declared that "as Romanian head of state, I condemn explicitly and categorically the communist system in Romania (…) and I declare with full responsibility: the communist regime in Romania was illegitimate and criminal."

While both the report and President Băsescu's speech were subjected to a number of more or less predictable criticisms,[5] the initiative, combined with the PNL's surprisingly lukewarm support for the report, established Băsescu and the PD as the main proponents of a renewed drive to revive the debates about the country's communist past.[6] Thus, in a strange reversal of roles, the traditionally anti-communist Liberal Party (PNL) was overtaken in its anti-communist stance by a party whose institutional origins were rooted in the National Salvation Front, which in turn was widely regarded as a communist successor party.

Over the course of the following three years, the personal conflicts between President Băsescu and the PNL leadership contributed to a deepening rift between the two erstwhile allies from the Orange coalition, ultimately resulting in an unexpected coalition between the PNL and its archenemies from Iliescu's PSD. While the full details of this unlikely cooperation are beyond the scope of this chapter, they included a joint effort to suspend President Băsescu from office in 2007, the PSD's parliamentary support for a PNL-led minority government in 2007–2008, and—despite their failure to form a coalition government after the 2008 elections— a remarkably close cooperation in the context of the 2009 presidential elections.

The 2009 presidential elections pitted three main candidates against each other: the incumbent president, Traian Băsescu, supported by the PD-L,[7] against the PSD candidate Mircea Geoană and the PNL candidate Crin Antonescu. Băsescu narrowly managed to outpoll Geoană in the first round (32.4 percent vs. 31.1 percent) but when the third-placed Antonescu (who polled 20 percent) announced that he was backing Geoană in the second round, it seemed all but inevitable that Geoană would win the second round. Despite a remarkably broad anti-Băsescu coalition, which also included the Hungarian Democratic Union (UDMR) and the remnants of the PNȚCD, and a mass media that was clearly favoring Geoană, Băsescu scored an unexpected (and very close) victory in the second round. What matters for the purpose of the present discussion, however, are not the circumstances of Băsescu's unexpected success but the fact that the electoral campaign and its aftermath provided the immediate political background against which the commemoration of the twentieth anniversary of the 1989 revolution took place.

Mnemonic Claims and Electoral Competition

While the official commemorative events discussed above offered a glimpse into the mnemonic contests that still dominate public discourse about December 1989, the most interesting and politically salient aspect was arguably how the memory of communism and its downfall were used in the heated electoral campaign for the Romanian presidency. As mentioned, one of the crucial moments in the 2009 presidential election campaign occurred when the third-place candidate from the first round, the liberal Crin Antonescu, announced that he would endorse the PSD candidate Mircea Geoană for the second round runoff, despite earlier calls by Băsescu to renew the center-right alliance, which had propelled him to victory five years earlier. Antonescu's endorsement was part of an agreement whereby the PSD, the PNL and the Hungarian minority party UDMR would back Klaus Johannis, the mayor of Sibiu and a member of the tiny German minority party, as the future prime minister.

While the announcement about Antonescu's endorsement should have propelled Geoană to an easy victory in the second round, the anti-Băsescu coalition decided to make a more dramatic statement by calling a massive public meeting in Timişoara on December 1 to announce the Partnership for Timişoara. Remarkably, this anti-Băsescu alliance brought together the ex-communist PSD and its two traditionally most important anti-communist challengers, the PNL and the PNŢCD, in what Crin Antonescu saw as "the end of the transition, of disorder, of confusion" and the establishment of "real political pluralism and a system in which the great ideological differences can be overcome for the construction of a common project" (*Ziare.com* 2009a).

At first glance, both the nature of the alliance between the main combatants of the mnemonic wars of the early 1990s and Antonescu's words suggest that the debate about the communist and revolutionary past in Romania may have moved in the direction of a pluralist memory regime. In fact, however, the event arguably represented an effort to establish a new interpretation of communism and the 1989 revolution in order to delegitimize the alternative vision of the past and to defeat President Băsescu and his political allies. In other words, Romania still had a fractured memory regime in 2009 but with a different—and much more complicated—fault line than in the early 1990s.

Before turning to the reactions from both Băsescu and third parties, it is worth briefly mentioning a few key elements of the political discourse of the proponents of the Partnership for Timişoara. First, the main meeting took place in Piaţa Operei, the square where the most important anti-communist protests in December 1989 had taken place. The message linking the two events was further reinforced by a large banner reading "1989–2009, in December, once every 20 years, Timişoara overthrows a tyrant." The banner reiterated one of the key arguments used by anti-Băsescu critics to link the avowedly anti-communist president to the communist past: his alleged authoritarian/dictatorial tendencies. Second, several of the politicians tried to establish the anti-communist credentials of an electoral alliance meant to elect a candidate from the communist successor party. Not surprisingly, the most important players in this respect were the leaders of the traditionally most intransigent anti-communist party, the PNȚCD, whose surprising endorsement of the alliance should have lent it greater anti-communist credibility, despite the party's political marginality after its electoral fiasco in the 2000 elections. Thus, Gheorghe Ciuhandu, the PNȚCD mayor of Timișoara, told the meeting participants that "if you see the hammer and the sickle, you should know that on its back is the image of Băsescu and who votes for Băsescu votes for the communists."[8] The leader of the PNȚCD, Radu Sârbu, even went so far as to claim that the unexpected partnership between his party and its erstwhile archrival, the PSD, would have had the blessing of the party's most important post-communist leader, Corneliu Coposu, a long-time political prisoner and well-known anti-communist advocate. Sârbu claimed that this support was justified by Geoană's contribution to the PSD's ideological reorientation toward modern social democracy. A third line of attack linking the 2009 elections to the anti-communist struggles of 1989–1990 was hinted at by the similarity between the "Partnership for Timișoara" banner of the 2009 alliance and the aforementioned "Proclamation of Timișoara" from March 1990. This argument was spelled out much more explicitly by Antonescu, who claimed that if the famous "point 8" lustration provision from the "Proclamation of Timișoara" would be applied to the contestants in the 2009 elections, it would affect neither him nor PSD candidate Mircea Geoană but only President Băsescu. While Antonescu did not spell out the basis for this claim during his speech, he probably alluded to unverified earlier claims that President Băsescu had been a Securitate informer (or even officer) during the communist period and, to a lesser extent, to the fact that Băsescu had been a member of the Communist Party before 1989.

Băsescu's defense and counteroffensive was also based on a number of different arguments. First, he denied any ties to the Securitate, and while he acknowledged his Communist Party membership, which he justified as having been driven by his desire to advance his career as a ship captain in the Romanian navy, he argued that, unlike his opponents, he had at least taken a public stand against the crimes of communism (see fn. 6). Second, he repeatedly emphasized the links of his opponents—particularly Mircea Geoană—to former President Iliescu, the symbol of Romania's stolen revolution in the eyes of most anti-communist critics, and to the "oligarchs," a group of businessmen with often dubious ties to the communist regime who had amassed large fortunes after 1990 and who controlled much of the Romanian mass media. Geoană's ties to one of these oligarchs, Sorin Ovidiu Vîntu,[9] arguably cost Geoană the election when he was forced to admit in the last televised election debate that he had visited Vîntu's house the prior evening. A third argument was Băsescu's reply to the repeated criticisms against his confrontational and divisive political leadership style. Rather than promising a more conciliatory approach, Băsescu pointed out that similar criticisms had been brought by Ceauşescu against the anti-communist protesters in Timişoara in December 1989.[10] He also explicitly highlighted the contrast between his own combative style and Iliescu's electoral motto in the 1990 elections—"A president for our peace of mind"—a slogan that many Romanians at the time had viewed as an attempt to avoid genuine debates about the revolution and the communist past. Finally, Băsescu's repeated references to having to fight against "sistemul ticăloşit" (the wicked system), by which he broadly meant the continuity of economic and political power between the communist and the post-communist power, contradicted the claims of the PSD-PNL alliance whereby Romania was ready to overcome the ideological conflicts of the early post-communist period through a newfound sense of national unity.

Given that much of political debates on the eve of the twentieth anniversary of the 1989 revolution in Romania consisted of mutual recriminations of ties to the communist past, the obvious question is which one of the claims was ultimately more credible and why. I will answer this question in two different ways: First, I will briefly focus on the role of third parties in adjudicating this contest over historical memory and the political uses of 1989, and then I will present some survey evidence that illustrates how the broader population responded to these competing claims.

In the Romanian context—and especially since the focal event was the Timişoara public rally discussed above—the unofficial role of arbiter fell to the organizations of former revolutionaries and more broadly to the residents of Timişoara. Judging by this standard, the mnemonic contest was clearly won *in absentia* by President Băsescu, or rather it was lost by his opponents. Thus, Timişoara residents reacted negatively to the launch of the Partnership for Timişoara, not so much because they were enthusiastic Băsescu supporters but because they felt that the use of the symbols of the 1989 revolution for electoral purposes was disrespectful, especially since the meeting was in favor of the PSD candidate, Mircea Geoană. In fact, several hundred Timişoara residents formed a counter-demonstration and interrupted the speeches of the official rally, which ended with the main speakers having to be escorted out the back door to avoid clashes with the protesters. While the PSD and PNL charged the local branch of Băsescu's PD-L with organizing the counter-protests, the media coverage of the protesters does not lend credence to this charge. Thus, one of the protesters said, "My father died in the center [in 1989] and now the communists have come here again." Another participant specifically objected to the use of the symbolically charged Piaţa Operei as the place for the pro-Geoană rally: "It is painful that, 20 years after the Revolution, the communists would gather here in Piaţa Operei. If they had gone to the Central Park instead, nobody would have minded" (*Monitorul de Cluj* 2009). Over the following days, similar protests against the electoral misuse of the memory of the 1989 revolution took place in Brasov, Cluj, and Bucharest (three other cities that had witnessed significant protests in December 1989).

The reactions to the Partnership for Timişoara rally also emphasized one of the unique features of the Romanian mnemonic landscape: the crucial role of the organizations of revolutionaries from 1989. Given the large scale of the December 1989 protests, there were revolution participants among the supporters of all political parties. Nonetheless, such organizations have maintained a certain visibility in Romanian public life, arguably due to the charisma of the courage inherent in participating in the very dangerous anti-communist protests (particularly in the early days of the revolution). Among these "guardians" of the Romanian revolution, the Timişoara rally provoked very similar types of criticism. Thus, Florian Mihalcea, the president of the Timişoara Association, said that "to compare the situation today with back then means to mock what Timişoara residents did during the revolution of December 1989." Moreover, the Timişoara Association, along with a number of other local civic organizations, sent an open letter to Timişoara's mayor, Gheorghe Ciuhandu, in which they accused him of selling symbols from the city's past, such as the Piaţa Operei and the Timişoara Proclamation, for the purpose of electoral gains (*Ziare.com* 2009). The important role of revolutionaries as arbiters was also highlighted during the debates of the IRRD symposium discussed in the second section of this chapter.

While the revolutionaries' organizations had traditionally taken a hard-line anti-communist stand, their reactions to the new mnemonic fault line highlighted by the 2009 elections are rather telling. Even though in their public statements the organizations of former revolutionaries did not endorse President Băsescu, they were clearly much more critical of the Geoană camp.[11] The greater dissonance in the mnemonic claims of the anti-Băsescu camp was also evident in the reactions from within the PNŢCD, the most recent addition to Mr. Geoană's "rainbow coalition." Thus, the Cluj branch of the PNŢCD criticized the party's leadership for entering into the Partnership for Timişoara alliance with the PSD and expressed its solidarity with the anti-communist protesters in Timişoara. Perhaps the most poignant reflection of this tension were the words of Ion Caramitru, a long-time prominent PNŢCD leader, who resigned from the party's leadership in protest against the "suicidal" and unnatural alliance with the PSD: "I don't believe in the promises, the acts and the origins of these people who are today leading the PSD. They are marked by their communist origins and I don't believe in the death of communism through communists" (*Revista 22* 2009).

To address the question about the broader reception of the competing mnemonic claims of the two presidential candidates, I will take advantage of the fortuitous timing of a panel public opinion survey, which interviewed respondents both before the first round (November 11–21, 2009) and between the two rounds of the presidential election (November 28–December 4 2009).[12] Given that the second wave of the panel happened after Antonescu endorsed Geoană and before the crucial TV debate between Băsescu and Geoană on the evening of December 4, I can analyze whether and how the events of December 1 affected the political preferences of average Romanian citizens. While none of the survey questions obviously asked about the Timişoara events (since the survey was already in the field), we can test how the attitudes toward the two main protagonists changed after December 1. To do so, I calculated the change between the two survey waves in how respondents evaluated the two candidates on a 0–10 barometer scale and then present the results separately for respondents who in the second round were interviewed before versus after the Timişoara events on December 1.

As a first cut, Figure 4.1 shows the overall support trends for the two candidates and reveals a rather clear reversal of fortunes: whereas before December 1 Geoană's favorability rating was growing by roughly twice as much as Băsescu, among respondents interviewed after the Timişoara Partnership events the pattern was almost an exact mirror image, which suggests that the negative reactions to the events had more than neutralized the initial popularity boost that Geoană received following Antonescu's endorsement. While it may be tempting to speculate whether this change affected the overall election outcome,[13] for the purpose of the present discussion, the more interesting question is how Geoană's relative losses were distributed as a function of how respondents viewed the communist past.

Since the survey unfortunately did not include any questions about evaluations of the communist regime, I will here focus on a question that asked respondents to rate the former dictator, Nicolae Ceauşescu, on the same 0–10 barometer scale

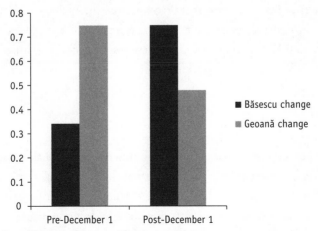

FIGURE 4.1 Overall Temporal Support Trends.

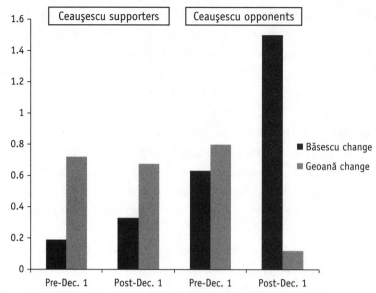

FIGURE 4.2 Temporal Support Trends (Attitudes toward Communism).

mentioned above. Based on responses to this question, I then divided respondents into two broad categories: Ceauşescu opponents, who rated him 5 or lower on this scale (and who make up a surprisingly low 38 percent of the sample) and Ceauşescu supporters/nostalgics, who rated him 6 or higher.

The survey evidence in Figure 4.2 confirms that the Partnership for Timişoara failed to win over the anti-communist voters, which Geoană's campaign was hoping to woo through its alliance with the traditional anti-communist parties and the symbolic choice of its launch. Instead the maneuver appears to have been highly counterproductive in that it erased Geoană's relative gains in the days following Antonescu's endorsement and instead gave Băsescu a large popularity boost (of 1.5 points on the 11-point scale) among anti-communist voters. Luckily for Geoană, his anti-communist message appears not to have been particularly credible for communist sympathizers: While support among these respondents also shifted away from Geoană toward Băsescu, the magnitude of the change was much smaller.[14]

Conclusion

This chapter has suggested that the most prominent feature of the mnemonic discourse surrounding the twentieth anniversary of the Romanian revolution was the creation—or at least the consolidation—of a new fault line regarding the interpretations of Romanian communism and its downfall. In doing so, it has arguably reignited some of the mnemonic wars of the early 1990s, albeit with two important differences. First, it has triggered a significant reorganization of the two warring camps: Whereas in the early 1990s the conflict was between the anti-communist PNL and PNŢCD, on the one hand, and the ex-communist PSD, on the other (with the Roman's PD somewhere in between but arguably closer to the PSD's position), by 2009 the main conflict was between the two offshoots of the National Salvation Front—the PD-L and the PSD—with the two historically anti-communist parties (PNL and PNŢCD) surprisingly siding with their traditional archenemy, the PSD. At the same time, the nature of the debate also shifted considerably: Whereas in the early 1990s the charges of neo-communist subversion against the ideals of the 1989 revolution were levied unidirectionally by the PNL and PNŢCD against the FSN (and later the PSD), by 2009 the two camps were each making competing claims of inheriting the mantle of the anti-communist resistance, while accusing their opponents of complicity and continuity with the communist regime.

At this point it is too early to tell whether this bizarre contest will continue, especially since the first round of this particular debate was arguably won by President Băsescu and the PD-L. While the political developments of the past three years suggest the likely continuation of the anti-Băsescu coalition between the traditionally anti-communist PNL and the ex-communist PSD—and the recent debates surrounding the suspension of President Băsescu by a parliamentary coalition of PSD and PNL have once again featured mutual accusations about ties to the communist past—it is possible that in future electoral contexts the alliance would downplay the question of a political issue that, for the time being, seems to be "owned" by President Băsescu. Some early signals of such an approach were already present during the debates of December 2009. Thus, when Băsescu accused Geoană of his ties to Ion Iliescu and the communist past, Geoană replied that Băsescu seemed intent on fighting with the ghosts of the past, while he "was a man of the future." If the PSD and its allies decide that they are better off lowering the salience of the communist continuity debate, then we may well see a renewed slide toward the pragmatic amnesia of the 2000–2005 period.

If (as is likely) this change in strategy is accompanied by the victory of the anti-Basescu coalition in the 2014 presidential elections (following their decisive victory in the November 2012 parliamentary elections), then Romania may well approach an (albeit perverted) version of mnemonic pluralism. A glimpse of what such a future may look like was offered by the speeches in the Romanian Parliament on the twentieth anniversary of the 1989 Revolution. Thus, Victor Socaciu, a well-known folk singer and PSD member of parliament, eulogized the long history of anti-communist resistance; while his list included a number of genuine dissidents like Ana Blandiana and Doinea Cornea, who were later vocal critics of the FSN, he also included Adrian Păunescu, a former court poet of Ceauşescu and later PSD senator, for his alleged dissident writings. Similarly, he praised a number of prominent politicians who emerged from the Romanian revolution, but singled out the early FSN leadership (Roman and Iliescu) along with two PNL leaders (Câmpeanu and Quintus). While Socaciu's speech is a step in the direction of a pluralist vision of the Romanian revolution by acknowledging the contributions of politicians from a broad spectrum of political backgrounds, it also illustrates the limitations of such pluralism: First, his speech included a glowing eulogy to former President Iliescu, whom he called a prominent and providential figure and whose alleged communist ties he brushed aside as much less important than the construction of Romania's democratic institutions under Iliescu's leadership; second, his inclusion on the same dissident list of Ceauşescu critics and former apologists reflects a significant degree of moral relativism; and, finally, his speech marks the continued use of the revolutionary past for partisan purposes, as is evident in both the choices and the omissions on the list of notable post-communist politicians.[15]

Overall, the political (mis)use of the memory of Romanian revolution of December 1989 after twenty years suggests a few potentially interesting conclusions. First, the unexpected reconfiguration of the entire political discourse about the communist past and its downfall after 2005 illustrates the extent to which the public memory of symbolically important historical episodes can be shaped by the short-term electoral priorities of political elites. Second, the "creative" reinterpretations of the past are underlined in the Romanian case by the bizarre situation in which both main protagonists in the debate were accusing each other of representing the dark sides of the communist past, while painting themselves as the solution to the country's unfinished communist legacy. Finally, however, the political blowback of the failed Partnership for Timişoara initiative suggests that, despite ambiguity surrounding many crucial aspects of the Romanian revolution, there still exist binding credibility constraints on efforts to rewrite historical memory (Kubik 1994; Müller 2002), and that those who transgress against certain "sacred" political symbols can end up paying a steep political price.

NOTES

1. The Institute was founded by President Iliescu during the final days of his last presidential term in December 2004 and its leadership, which Iliescu named, was composed largely from revolutionary participants who were close to Iliescu, whom they unanimously elected IRRD president (Wikipedia 2012).

2. Following months of personal and ideological conflicts between former Prime Minister Petre Roman (who had been deposed after yet another miners' riot in September 1991) and President Ion Iliescu, the Front split into a more reformist faction under Roman's leadership (which eventually changed its name to Partidul Democrat PD) and a more hard-line leftist faction under Iliescu, which changed its name to PDSR and eventually to Partidul Social Democrat PSD.

3. Possible reasons include the much greater urgency of jump-starting economic reforms to deal with the country's looming crisis in 1997, the CDR's dependence on the PD (the reformist faction of the FSN) for achieving the parliamentary majority, as well as the fact that in line with Nalepa's (2010) analysis of lustration, the CDR may have had a few skeletons in the closet (i.e., MPs who may have been affected by tough lustration laws).

4. It is, of course, quite possible that the maneuver simply represented a brilliant tactical move to fill the political vacuum left by the virtual demise of the PNȚCD, but this question is beyond the scope of this chapter.

5. Thus, MPs from the extreme nationalist PRM repeatedly interrupted Băsescu's parliamentary speech, while former President Iliescu criticized the report for downplaying the importance of the 1989 revolution and derided Băsescu for condemning communism in a context where "it no longer exists and no longer poses any threats" (cited in *Hotnews*, 2009).

6. This issue came up during one of the presidential campaign debates when Antonescu reminded Băsescu that he had been in both the Communist Party and the National Salvation Front with Iliescu. Băsescu replied that at least he had had the courage to condemn the crimes of communism, while Antonescu was laughing at him in Parliament together with Iliescu and Vadim Tudor.

7. In 2007 the PD changed names yet again to become the Democratic Liberal Party (PD-L), after merging with a breakaway faction of the PNL under the leadership of former PM Theodor Stolojan.

8. Cited on *Ziare.com*, 2009b.

9. Vîntu, who was convicted for his role in one of Romania's Ponzi schemes from the late 1990s, had been a Securitate agent before 1989 (*România Liberă*, 2010).

10. Geoană's uninspired reply to that remark was that he did not remember, since he was too young at the time.

11. Indeed, in one of the commemorative speeches in Parliament on the twentieth anniversary of Ceausescu's fall, the PNL MP, Raymond Luca, decried the fact that in the recent electoral campaign many of the revolutionary organizations had become electoral allies and tools of various political candidates, and even though he did not mention any names, the implications of the remark were fairly clear.

12. See Romanian Presidential Election Study (2009). I want to thank the authors for sharing their survey data.

13. Given Băsescu's razor-thin margin in the second round, and the fact that the magnitude of the change in Figure 4.1 was slightly larger than Geoană's initial popularity advantage, it is plausible that the Timişoara misstep could have cost Geoană the election.

14. I found similar patterns when using respondent's self-placement on a Left-Right ideological scale, but for that measure Geoană sustained significant losses compared to his rival among both Left and Right-leaning respondents, which suggests that his strategy may have succeeded in triggering bipartisan alienation.

15. Thus, except for members from the parties of the PSD-PNL alliance (Iliescu, Câmpeanu, and Quintus), Socaciu only mentions Petre Roman, Băsescu's predecessor and rival in the PD leadership, and he notably glosses over the more vigorously anti-communist PNȚCD leadership, especially Corneliu Coposu.

5 I Ignored *Your* Revolution, but You Forgot *My* Anniversary

PARTY COMPETITION IN SLOVAKIA AND THE CONSTRUCTION
OF RECOLLECTION

Carol Skalnik Leff, Kevin Deegan-Krause, and Sharon L. Wolchik

Introduction

When communism ended in Slovakia in 1989, Slovakia was part of a common state with the Czech Republic, Czechoslovakia. The launching point for the transition was itself a form of politicized historical memory. November 17 is international student day, commemorating the Nazi closure of Czech universities in 1939 and in particular the death of the Czech Jan Opletal as a result of student protests against the Nazi occupation of the Czech lands. Coming on the heels of regime upheavals in Hungary, Poland, East Germany, and Bulgaria, the commemorative "anti-fascist" marches in a number of Czech and Slovak cities were thinly disguised challenges to communist rule. When the communist regime retaliated against the students with massive force, a broader and peaceful popular mobilization sprang up and provoked a regime crisis. Responding to this upsurge and credentialed by widespread public support, the hastily organized opposition Czech Civic Forum and Slovak Public against Violence collaborated to negotiate an exit strategy with the Czechoslovak Communist Party (KSC) for a mixed interim government and free elections in June 1990.

This "Velvet Revolution" or "Gentle Revolution" produced dozens of memorable images of a society in near unanimous insistence on more freedom and a greater voice in its own future. The commemoration of the revolution's twentieth anniversary in the media and in public spaces in Slovakia emphasized those unifying images and sentiments. Television showed extensive documentary footage from 1989—usually grainy and black and white—and hosted panels featuring scholars and public officials discussing the period. Newspapers followed suit, and their online invitations to citizens to share their memories produced hundreds of postings on the anniversary, some of them touching, some quite scatological. Memories focused on the imagery of the era: a particular kind of cold-weather cap worn by Slovak leader Jan Budaj, the jangling of keys that were featured on a Slovak commemorative two-euro coin issued for the twentieth anniversary, the reconstruction in Bratislava of a 12-meter tall heart of barbed wire that artist Daniel Brunovský had erected in 1989 on the Slovak-Austrian border, where it stood until it was washed away in the flood of 2002.

But this rather comfortable and nostalgic veneer of consensus is profoundly misleading. Alongside the straightforward evocation of prominent events, the anniversary also produced a stream of highly combative recollections from Slovakia's political leaders. The politicians' recollections, while not supplanting the more consensual media presentation, reflected significant differences in political outlook and broke along the lines of Slovakia's political blocs. The approaches to the memory of 1989 thus differed significantly; it is useful to consider whether there is a discernible pattern to the recollections and, if so, what this says narrowly about the relationship between the events of 1989 and the political competition of 2009, and more broadly about the relationship between events, memories, and political outcomes. A comparison of the recollections of 1989 with those of other historical events, furthermore, suggests that leaders' choices to remember or forget do not reflect a broad preference for remembering or forgetting in general, but rather depend on a historical event's capacity to confer political gain or loss. It is also important to bear in mind that fractured histories can facilitate fractured historical memories. Here, as elsewhere in Eastern Europe, the frequency of twentieth-century regime and boundary change is fertile soil for the contestation of the past.

Memory and Political Competition

What role does the past play in present politics? Do memories of 1989 have a constraining effect on political leaders, or are they sufficiently malleable to serve as raw material for the interests of *any* political position? Political recollections of 1989 in

Slovakia suggest that at least some events do not benefit all parties equally and that the type of responses vary according to the likelihood that attention to the past will confer a political advantage or disadvantage.

No country's historical memory is ever truly banal, in Michael Billig's (1995) sense. There are always custody battles over the meaning of the past and the guardianship of identity and community. Memory wars are a recurrent feature of even the most established democratic regime (as the current US battle over "ownership" of the Constitution demonstrates nicely), but different groups and individuals play different roles in those struggles. The typology provided by Bernhard and Kubik offers useful categories for understanding the differences: mnemonic warriors who "tend to draw a sharp line between themselves, the proprietors of the 'true' vision of the past, and other actors who cultivate 'wrong' or 'false' versions of history," mnemonic pluralists "who accept that in addition to 'us' and our vision of history there are 'them' with their own legitimate visions of the past," and "mnemonic abnegators" who "avoid memory politics" altogether. The typology is extremely valuable for its classification of reactions to historical events based on scales of monolithic-to-pluralistic memory regimes and of low-to-high salience, but the case of Slovakia introduces several complications that profit from clarification.

In line with Bernhard and Kubik's framework, there were differences in the degree of pluralism and the degree of abnegation: parties of Slovakia's Right, which often had direct personal or partisan ties in terms of parties or leaders to the events of 1989, tended to follow the pattern of Bernhard and Kubik's "mnemonic warriors" in championing a positive view of a landmark democratic revolution and their central role in it. Others challenged the Right's exclusive claim to the revolution and the motives of the revolutionary leaders, and sought to provide an alternative vision of the value and consequence of the revolution itself, with a position that contained aspects of "mnemonic pluralism" and "mnemonic abnegation," though mixed and adapted in particular ways to fit the circumstances.

Those who used memory—either as warriors or as those defending themselves from warriors—tended to focus their energies according to identifiable patterns. They offered a vision of the past that corresponded to their own present strengths and called into question their opponents' weaknesses—quite often their perceived *moral* weaknesses. As Larson (2010) has shown in the context of the cultural elite, moral credentials appropriate for the post-communist engagement were constructed on the basis of one's real or imputed behavior in the socialist period and after; debates over the validity of those credentials for one's place in public life began immediately in late 1989. Elite biographies were instantly politicized—not only what one did or did not do at critical historical junctures of the recent past (late communism, 1989, 1992) but what larger historical passion plays one was associated with.

Accordingly, what is in question in the use of history is a debate over not only the meaning of the past, but also who has the moral right to participate in that discussion. Thus there are two interrelated ways in which historical memory becomes subject to political contestation: politicized battles over the meaning of the past, and political credentialing and de-credentialing of politicians because of their relationship—biographical or attitudinal—to the past. We see both in operation as the major Slovak political forces jostled for position around the memory of 1989. Indeed, claims to authentic interpretation of 1989 were frequently accompanied by charges that other actors were illegitimately "privatizing" what should have been a shared communal memory. A third strategy, perhaps unique to seemingly "teleological" events such as the revolutions of 1989, involved reference to the original goals of the revolution and the ability of the commemorator to achieve them, or even more frequently, the likelihood that opponents could derail or undo them.

The Context: Public Perceptions of 1989

We need to start with Kubik and Bernhard's caveat that the elite actors who possess agenda-setting power on how historical memory is mobilized are not working with infinitely malleable material. The perceptions of the broader public can limit and in some cases even supplant official and elite interpretations. For that reason, it is useful to be aware of the attitudes of those who receive and participate in commemorations. Slovak citizens expressed the third-highest approval rate of the change to democracy (70 percent) of the nine countries surveyed in the twentieth-anniversary PEW Global Attitudes Survey of 2009, after East Germans and Czechs. Interestingly, the age spread on this issue in Slovakia is the narrowest among the countries surveyed. Slovaks were fourth highest (66 percent) in approval of the change to capitalism, although here the age gap is among the widest in the region. Both Slovak responses are quite stable relative to the baseline attitudes expressed in 1991. In general, then, one might expect politicians to treat the 1989 milestone with some respect in terms of political freedoms, but there is equally clearly a bit more room to challenge its socioeconomic results. This is particularly true because, as in other countries, even those approving the change may nevertheless answer that they are not better off (18 percent) or are worse off (29 percent) than they were under communism.

In this context, November 1989 is important but not politically sacrosanct. A 2009 IVO/FOCUS poll asked Slovak citizens which postwar historical events they regarded positively or negatively. The Gentle Revolution is by far the most approved, but its 57 percent positive assessment is hardly consensual, and 14 percent of respondents regarded 1989 negatively (Bútorová 2010). There is ample room for contestation over its significance, and cross-national polling in 2009 suggests that this space was greater in Slovakia than in neighboring countries. The "need for political change in 1989" was embraced more emphatically in the Czech Republic (56 percent agreement) and Poland (65 percent) than in Slovakia (45 percent) (Bútorová 2010). Each combatant in the memory wars may thus appeal to a substantial niche audience.

The question of 1989 is complicated further by its relationship to national identity, and the awkward question of how (and if) to handle the fact that at the time of the revolution Slovakia was part of Czechoslovakia, and that the most prominent (if not the most important) public demonstrations in Czechoslovakia's revolution occurred in what is now the capital of another country. Although a few voices in 1989 emphasized a distinctly Slovak message, Czechoslovakia differed from other communist federal states in the lack of an essential connection between the downfall of the communist regime and the rise of demands for national independence. Democratization and the pulling apart of Yugoslavia and the Soviet Union developed in tandem, but Czechs and Slovaks mobilized against the regime together in 1989 before dissolving the state.

As a result, Slovakia celebrates an anniversary of an important event that occurred *before* its divorce from its partner and is intimately connected to the now-dissolved marriage. Slovakia, for example, shares with the Czech Republic the decision—unique in the region—to celebrate the political change of 1989 as an official public holiday in which people have the day off from work. But the date of the holiday—November 17—is specifically related to student demonstrations in Prague. As one Slovak blogger complained: "It is one of our historical mistakes that we celebrate only November 17, when Slovaks should be celebrating November 16 when the overthrow (*prevrat*) began with a large student demonstration in Bratislava, at which students also called for freedom of speech."[1]

Moreover, the protests of November 17, 1989, commemorated the 1939 Nazi crackdown on universities in Prague, which had no counterpart in Slovakia. The ambiguity extends even to one of the most resonant Slovak voices in the 1989 revolution: the Slovak heavy metal group Tublatanka's protest song "Pravda víťazí" ("The truth prevails"). Though the song became an unofficial rock anthem of revolution across Czechoslovakia, the title itself referred to the Czechoslovak national motto (1918–1992), which in turn derived from the proclamation of *Czech* religious reformer Jan Hus (ca. 1369–1415), and is still the official motto of the Czech Republic. Even the title of the revolution itself had national overtones, with some using the Slovak phrase "Gentle Revolution" (*nežná revolúcia*), while others opted for the better known Czech usage "Velvet Revolution" (*sametová revoluce*), and still others mixed the Czech adjective with the Slovak noun (*sametová revolúcia*).

Finally, in part for the economic and national reasons discussed above and in part by chance,[2] Slovakia's 1989 revolution produced no founding father figure. Whereas both the first and second presidents of the independent Czech Republic had emerged from the political crucible of the Velvet Revolution and the change that it launched, Slovaks cannot associate the November events with a dominant figure who continued to embody the period of transition. In 2009, when asked who they thought of in connection with the 1989 revolution, Slovak respondents gave top place to communist era dissidents: the popular Slovak actor Milan Kňažko, long-time Slovak regime challenger Ján Budaj, and the dissident Czech playwright Václav Havel, in that order, with significantly fewer naming independent sociologist and economist Fedor Gál and religious dissident Ján Čarnogurský (Bútorová 2010). Budaj exited the top level of politics after a collaboration scandal, Gál exited the country, Havel was a Czech, and while Kňažko and Čarnogurský continued to play important roles in government immediately after 1989, they found themselves pushed to the margins after the 1990s. None of them could be said to biographically embody the period of change in a way that set the course of transition, as Václav Havel and Václav Klaus did in the Czech Republic.[3]

A combination of historical circumstances thus weakened the possibility of a widespread political consensus regarding 1989, but what emerged was more than a mere difference of opinion; with a few specific exceptions, the differences of opinion related to 1989 mapped closely onto the deep political divisions of the later period of commemoration. But a public disagreement about the events of 1989 did not serve all political sides equally, and Slovakia's rival political blocs differed not only in their positions toward the period but in the resolution with which they expressed it.

The Warriors: The Communist Left and the Center Right

The commemoration of 1989 served as a touchstone for rival partisan readings of this event's significance and of the moral credentials that political rivals could claim from it. The clearest and most negative interpretations of 1989 came from the Left but were confined to the minor Communist Party. Slovakia's Center Right offered fairly clear views— positive ones—but there were differences in the means of expression and in the understanding of the scope and source of the revolution.

The Communist Left: Those Unambiguously Opposed

For many on the Left, 1989 came at great cost: an exchange of economic security for political freedoms. The most hostile response was that of the small Communist

Party of Slovakia (KSS), a party of those who sought to remain "unreconstructed" by splitting from the reformed communist successor party as it moved toward social democracy. The utter rejection of the November events marks the KSS as the only party actually to denounce 1989, and the KSS effort appears to be a deliberately chosen element of its political appeal. This party began calling attention to the anniversary of 1989 well before 2009. On November 17, 2007, it pronounced 1989 "a fraud on the citizenry," a carefully prepared coup, and argued that "the result of the socio-political change was criminal privatization, primitive theft of state property and the indebtedness of the whole society to foreign countries" (*Pravda* 2007). In 2009 the party assembled a few relatively small but sharply critical demonstrations. In the country's second-largest city, Košice, the KSS marked the anniversary with a small public rally that included a coffin inscribed "right to employment," ushered in with funereal music and the sardonic jangling of keys; placards announced the "crisis of capitalism," "the future belongs to socialism," "don't let us be impoverished," and "20 years, 7,300 days is enough" (*20. výročie* 2009). As memory warriors, KSS adherents accept 1989 as a watershed, but a disastrous one that destroyed an egalitarian communist system and defaced the historical memory of that system.

The Center Right: Defenders of the Revolution

While "Left" and "Right" have only a limited utility in describing Slovakia's political spectrum, the term "Right" has recently come to describe the parties that formed the country's 2002–2006 and 2010–2012 coalitions, ranging from Christian democratic to liberal, with participation from Hungarian minority parties. These parties—in parliamentary opposition at the time of the twentieth anniversary—tended to emphasize their own credentials as revolutionaries, to question the right of others to speak on the question, and to see the insufficiencies of the revolution primarily in terms of its insecurity and the possibility of a return to the previous situation. In short, the Center Right as memory warrior did not contest the meaning of 1989; rather, it contested the right of other parties to claim the guardianship of that meaning.

Center Right parties commemorated the revolution together at the Slovak National Theater under a twentieth anniversary banner that featured a hammer and sickle with a red bar through it.[4] Jointly, they celebrated 1989 as the collapse of a totalitarian regime that had "killed thousands" and as the launching of a path to Europe that had climaxed in accession to the European Union and NATO. Pointedly, they traced their own contributions to realizing the legacy of November: Slovakia's European integration, after all, had been accomplished on their watch.[5]

The central message of these parties, however, was contained not in the affirmation of the revolution's accomplishments, but in two challenges to the then-incumbent government led by Robert Fico and his party, Direction (Smer). The Fico government, they argued, was morally ineligible to credibly commemorate 1989 both because it undervalued the Gentle Revolution and because it continued to threaten the democratic legacy of that revolution.

The Center Right's effort to delegitimize its opponents is clear in its informal but quite explicit boycott of government commemorations. In a pattern widely reproduced across the region, the commemorations were celebrated separately by government and opposition—a telling indicator of a fractured memory regime. Also common to the region, the Slovak opposition explicitly couched this separation in terms of a univocal claim to legitimacy and moral authority. Mikuláš Dzurinda, former prime minister and then leader of the main opposition party, the Slovak Democratic and Christian Union (SDKÚ), said that to jointly observe the anniversary would be "similar to fascists organizing celebrations of the anniversary of the Slovak National Uprising" (*Pravda* 2009b), referencing Prime Minister Fico's previous membership in the Communist Party.[6] Slovakia's Christian Democrats took seriously their understanding of 1989 by refusing even to be present for interpretations of 1989 made by politicians close to the government who had held prominent positions during the period of Communist Party rule (*Pravda* 2009c).

Beyond symbol and metaphor, the opposition parties often went further, reminding citizens that Fico and many of his supporters had been closely tied to the communist regime. Pál Csáky, leader of the Party of the Hungarian Coalition (SMK), darkly commented that if the Velvet Revolution had not taken place, the Slovak prime minister of 2009 would likely have been "a young, hard-working communist, whose name would have been Robert Fico" (Vilikovská 2009).

Other comments (addressed in more detail below) directly attacked Fico for past public statements that showed his lack of interest in 1989 and its anniversary. They pounced in particular on Fico's statement in 2000 when, as an up-and-coming young politician who had deserted the dying Party of the Democratic Left (SDĽ) to found Smer, he told an interviewer from the magazine *Domino Forum*: "I didn't notice the revolution" (Hríb 2000). The Center Right brought this statement up repeatedly every November 17 to suggest Fico's lack of commitment to the post-1989 political regime (see Picture 5.1). Linking the Fico government with communism (and, by analogy, with fascism) was the strongest possible statement of the illegitimacy of any *other* parties' claim to the democratic legacy of November 17. Conversely, it was a claim to custodianship of that legacy.

But the Center Right's efforts did not only look backwa[rd] events of 1989 to look forward by suggesting th[

PICTURE 5.1 Bratislava, Slovakia, November 16, 2009. The youth affiliate of Slovakia's Christian Democratic Party offers Prime Minister Robert Fico a Russian-built crimson Zhiguli with the proviso that he use it to drive "back to Moscow." The car boasts the logo of Fico's party, Smer (Direction), with the wordplay "Direction toward decline," while the larger text reads "November '89, 'I didn't notice!' R. Fico."

Source: Photo/Christian Democratic Youth of Slovakia, https://www.facebook.com/zigulak.roba/photos.

revolution were not complete, and that they remained vulnerable to abuse, particularly by the Fico government (*Pravda* 2009d). Dzurinda of the SDKÚ argued that "November 17 has meaning only if we hold to its ideals today and tomorrow and in the future." Calls to restore the moral resonance of 1989 were coupled with denunciations of current demagogy and allusions to the corruption of the sitting government. Dzurinda darkly suggested that former Czech president Václav Havel's warnings of a new, more sophisticated totalitarianism in post-communist Europe were relevant "right h̶   ̶n Slovakia" (*Pravda* 2009d). The commemoration of November 1989 beca̶   ̶ restore the vision of a revolution that had been derailed in 2006 v̶   ̶n lost to Fico's Smer. Lest the political import of this message   ̶   ̶r, Pál Csáky of SMK capped his address to the audience by   ̶ks, looking toward the 2010 elections:

 ̶n of the journey (interrupted in 2006). And
 ̶ce together … the country will need in the
 ̶nd decent political parties. … And in
 ̶d political parties need is decent
 ̶rcent more. (*Nový Čas* 2009)

The decent political parties in question were, of course, those present in the theater to celebrate together: SDKÚ, KDH, and SMK, who, not at all coincidentally, had formed the previous coalition government and aspired to defeat the "indecent" Fico in 2010.

The Missing Warriors: Defenders in Absentia

Although the focus of this chapter is the domestic struggle over the memory of 1989 within Slovakia, it is important to reflect on the ambiguities of the commemoration of a Czech and Slovak event by noting that some of the most prominent and unambiguous calls to remember November 1989 came from Slovaks who chose to celebrate the revolution (and in some cases to spend their professional lives) elsewhere, memory warriors of the transition who left during the subsequent battle over the continuance or break-up of the Czechoslovak state. Here is a case of one memory regime at odds with another—1989 and the dissolution of the state in 1992.

Most striking is the case of sociologist Fedor Gál, a key figure in the foundation of VPN and the chair of its coordinating council in 1990–1991. Gál is emblematic of the ambivalences of November 1989. A Jew born in the Terezín concentration camp, his prominence in the Gentle Revolution gave way to a deluge of "grotesque anti-Semitic caricatures in the nationalist and communist media" (*Transitions Online* 2009) as he embraced a federalist position and continued to support joint statehood with the Czechs throughout the early 1990s.[7] Disillusioned by the impending Velvet Divorce and Mečiar's control of Slovak politics, he left Slovakia for the Czech Republic and established a successful career as part of the group that launched the private Czech television channel TV NOVA, which allowed him to engage in publishing and documentary work. In 2009, Gál gave numerous interviews to Slovak and Czech reporters. He presented his documentary on 1989 in Slovakia, but he celebrated November 17, 2009, in Prague.

Others with complicated relationships toward Slovakia and Czechoslovakia—including many so-called "federal" Slovaks of the communist era who lived in the Czech Republic after federalization of the state in 1969—sought balance in their celebration of the anniversary. Martin Bútora, a founding member of VPN who during the early 1990s split his time between Prague and Bratislava, remained in Slovakia after 1992. Bútora served as Slovak ambassador to the United States during the first post-Mečiar government and as president of the Bratislava-based Institute for Public Affairs, but he maintained strong ties to the Czech Republic. On November 17, 1989, Bútora divided his day between Prague and Bratislava, participating in a roundtable at Charles University with Polish and Russian dissidents and then returning to

Bratislava to speak at the Slovak National Theater. Memory actors such as Gál and Bútora point to a special aspect of mnemonic contestation—part of that contestation is the definition of the boundaries of the group for which a given past is salient. Who shares the past? Can Slovaks celebrate 1989 by airbrushing Czechs from the picture? Some of the *relativizers,* to whom we now turn, framed 1989 in precisely this way.

The Relativizers: Slovak Nationalists and the Center Left

The events of 1989 produced enough ambiguity in memory and public perception to put certain limits on the number of unambiguous voices. Even the regime divide was not unambiguous in Slovakia. The partisan expression of the regime divide was somewhat blurred in the 1990s by the more resonant divide over Prime Minister Vladimír Mečiar's authoritarian tendencies in office; in that period, the communist successor Party of the Democratic Left (SDĽ) aligned uneasily with the Center Right parties against Mečiar's Movement for a Democratic Slovakia (HZDS), both in opposition and, after Mečiar's departure, in government. By 2009 the regime divide had re-emerged, if in somewhat different form, as Robert Fico positioned his new party, Smer, as both a social democratic party and a claimant to the role of a communist successor party. The most important nationalist voice among mnemonic actors has been the Slovak National Party (SNS). What the SNS shares with other actors analyzed in this section is a mnemonic approach that relativizes the importance of 1989.

The Slovak Nationalists: Revolution as a Prelude to Independence

For many of those deeply committed to the cause of the ethnic *Slovak* nation, 1989 presents a challenge: the most visible figures of the revolution did not endorse (and in many cases criticized) the independence of Slovakia in 1992, for nationalists the central historical watershed of modern history. Yet without the end of the Communist Party's leading role and the political pluralism permitted by revolution, Slovakia's independence is difficult to imagine. Indeed, the nationalist take on 1989 has consistently been one in which the democratic significance of the regime change is subordinate to its significance for the national question.

The dominant force in Slovakia's politics during the 1990s, Mečiar's HZDS portrayed itself as the true heir of 1989 and actively criticized other leaders of 1989 as having unfairly stolen the mantle for themselves and then misused it for their own benefit. Although the party did not hold a formal celebration of the anniversary,

Mečiar's once dominant but now foundering HZDS, which would fail to return to parliament in 2010, did take the occasion of the twentieth anniversary to lay claim to 1989. With a notable degree of defensiveness, an HZDS official said that the party felt itself to be carrying on the *positive* legacies of 1989, reminding the public that HZDS had originated as a platform within VPN and insisting that their aim had been to restore the original VPN program. Mečiar also argued that the gains of freedom had come at the cost of social insecurity (*Pravda* 2009a).

The most national of the major party formations, the Slovak National Party (SNS), views *all* commemorations through the lens of the twin logics of statehood and national identity. Indicative are its logo and website, which insist on its continuity with the nineteenth-century Slovak National Party. The "masthead" of its website proclaims itself to be "the oldest political party of Slovaks from 1871," and the SNS eagle logo surmounts the Slovak cross, with the 1871 date emblazoned below (Slovak National Party 2011). Thus, while SNS vice president Anna Belousovová emphasized the necessity of change in 1989, she and other leaders predictably emphasized its importance in laying the foundations for Slovak independence, reminding the public that SNS had been, from its (re)founding, committed to Slovak statehood (*Pravda* 2009a). After staking the SNS claim to 1989, Belousovová challenged the credentials of Center Right parties in particular, asserting that 1989 belonged to the whole nation, not just to a small group of "ideological privatizers" who used the occasion to act as supreme arbiters of democracy (*Pravda* 2009b).

Both HZDS and SNS expressed a distinctive position on the meaning of the revolution, acknowledging democracy and the market but emphasizing its importance as a necessary precondition for Slovakia's independent nationhood. They emphasized the unfinished business of the revolution as Slovakia's national independence, which the leaders of the revolution itself and their successors in the Slovak Right were not suited to handle.

Direction (Smer): Commemoration as Political Threat and Opportunity

Whereas the narrative of the nationalists was relatively simple—praise for anything that forwarded Slovak statehood and scorn for anything else—the position of Robert Fico and his party Smer was significantly more complicated. Fico used the opportunity to respond to the efforts of the Center Right to question his authority to speak on 1989 and to characterize him as an active threat to the legacy of November. Fico's rebuttal, as we will see, was equally complex: he and his party countered opposition criticism by suggesting alternative standards by which to judge the revolution, both as it transpired in 1989 and the legacies that it left in 2009.

Fico's biggest immediate problem was how to commemorate an event that he did not appear to care about (even while it was happening). By the time he took office as premier in 2006, Fico's *non*-recollection of 1989 was already well known, and he had compounded the impression by his absence during subsequent anniversaries of November 17. In 2007 he was in Prague for government meetings (none of which involved commemoration of 1989) and in 2008 he inspected a new stretch of highway away from Bratislava. In October 2009, Fico's office announced that he would be even further afield: on the eve of the anniversary he would be in Moscow, and on November 17 itself he would fly to London before returning home for evening commemorations. Although his itinerary promised remarks on 1989, these would take place before a British audience in London at University College, not in Slovakia. The Internet response ranged from indignation at the "apparatchik's" behavior to agreement that there was nothing really to celebrate (*TA3* 2009), but it was hard to mistake the message that he was not interested in over-emphasizing a turning point in which he himself, then a newly minted young Communist Party member of twenty-five, had not participated.

Although Fico's travels away from Slovakia suggested a form of abnegation, his speech in London reflected an effort to weigh parts of the past, not so much as pluralism but as a single, coherent narrative that sought to put the strengths and weaknesses of communism in a relative framework. Fico framed his London talk with an anecdotal preface in which he balanced the pros and cons of the changes of 1989: under communism, he recalled having to get permission to go on honeymoon from the authorities and standing in line all night at the travel agency. However, he had no trouble paying for it with the "generous student grants" of the time. He remembered the persecution of Charter 77, but also noted that he and other law students successfully sued their university for restitution of thefts from the student dormitory. He acknowledged the benefits of democracy but called for respect for people who had lived under communism. In short, he spoke to the 33 percent of the public, especially older people, who believed they had been better off under communism, reading 1989 through that prism. The speech thus served as an indirect challenge to a conception of the regime divide posited by his opponents and offered a very direct message of redemption to those for whom 1989 had proved disappointing or threatening.

Having presented this rather tepid vision of the need for regime change in 1989, Fico then sought to undermine the credibility of his political opponents with regard to 1989 and to strip away some of the opposition's claims to moral righteousness by suggesting that it was motivated primarily by economic greed and that it lacked national sentiment. With periodic bows to the political and civil rights provided by the revolution, Fico presented the revolution as hijacked by a narrow socioeconomic elite that used political means to gain financial resources (a broadly expressed theme that could have applied both to Mečiar's clientelistic privatization during the mid-1990s and to the neoliberalism of the Dzurinda governments that succeeded Mečiar after 1998). He spoke directly to some who had "stood on the podium" in 1989 and subsequently dirtied their hands by manipulating the marketplace.

To the extent that revolution was necessary, Fico suggested, it needed to maintain or even deepen the efforts toward ameliorating socioeconomic inequality and building the Slovak state. He argued that what was needed to fulfill the Gentle Revolution was not the shoring up of political democracy, as his opposition had suggested, but rather the strengthening of social justice, a legacy his opponents had devalued. He also emphasized that the revolution laid the groundwork for national independence and hinted at the need for all citizens of Slovakia to reaffirm their commitment to their country, controversially recommending that Hungarians in Slovakia "learn to speak perfect Slovak."

Whether intentional or not, Fico's November 16–17 travel odyssey offers an apt metaphor: Moscow (a reference to his communist past and the social protection of that era), London (a reference to democracy and his rightful place as a defender of it), and Bratislava (a reference to his commitment to an independent Slovakia). The destinations (though not necessarily in the same order) reflect his defense against those who questioned his qualifications to evaluate 1989, and his effort in turn to de-legitimate his opponents by emphasizing their lack of commitment to Slovakia's welfare protections and its national sovereignty.

Comparative Anniversaries: Warriors Everywhere (But Not All the Time)

The anniversary of 1989 is a particularly prominent example of the use of memory, but it is not the only one, and it must be put into broader perspective. An understanding of the nature of memory regimes writ large requires a look at other circumstances: first at the anniversary of 1989 in different circumstances, particularly those one year later, at the twenty-first anniversary, and second at the treatment of other anniversaries, both by the Fico government and its successors. What this concluding review will illuminate is the extent to which the past can be quite incoherent, with each mnemonic actor stitching together a different patchwork of historical mileposts as emblematic of Slovak identity.

Same Anniversary, Different Governments

Just over half a year after the twentieth anniversary of 1989 commemorations, Slovakia's voters brought about a political change that would have been difficult to predict (though not impossible to imagine) from the political configuration of November 2009: Robert Fico's coalition fell from a clear majority in public opinion polls to a minority position in parliament, though Fico's party itself remained the single largest party in Slovakia. The new governing coalition, led by SDKÚ's Iveta Radičová, was composed of the three opposition forces that in 2009 had celebrated together at the National Theater: the SDKÚ, the KDH, and the Hungarian minority (although the latter was represented by a new party). One of the changes brought about by this reversal of fortunes was a clear difference in the treatment of 1989. Indeed, as if making up for lost opportunities, the coalition spent as much time on the "twenty-first anniversary of 1989" commemorations in November 2010 as other governments in the region had spent in 2009 on the twentieth. This rapid and significant shift sets aside any notion that government status might have caused Fico's government to take its muted and ambiguous position and also reaffirms the conclusion that 1989 works asymmetrically to provide more political advantage to the parties of the Center Right than to those of the 2006–2010 Fico government.

Also notable are signs that the government treated November 17, 2010, not only as the twenty-first anniversary of 1989 but also as the first anniversary of November 17, 2009, as the anniversary itself became the source of political contest. The twenty-first anniversary not only allowed the new government the chance to revisit the historical events, but also provided the opportunity to revisit and criticize the treatment of the twentieth anniversary by the Fico government, through the greater size and visibility of its own celebrations. Commenting on the twenty-first anniversary celebrations, the *Slovak Spectator* noted that "[u]nlike in 2009, events this year were fully embraced and supported by leading officials of the Slovak government" (Terenzani-Stanková 2010). The members of Radičová's coalition used their newly gained governmental podium to remember publicly the fact that Fico himself did *not* remember.

Same Government, Different Anniversaries

The game of "who forgot what" can have many players, however, and Fico joined the fray in September 2010 by arguing that the new government's leaders—the same leaders who had criticized him for his lack of attention to 1989—were themselves lax in the commemoration of other anniversaries (*Pravda* 2010a). In particular, Fico noted the government's lack of interest in the anniversary of the Slovak National Uprising of 1944 (August 29) and the Day of the Slovak Constitution (September 15), on which Fico and his political allies held a brief commemorative service in front of Bratislava castle (at the site of a controversial Smer-sponsored statue of Svätopluk, identified a bit anachronistically on the statue as the "King of Ancient Slovaks").

Fico's reminder of the need to recognize other anniversaries suggests that the difference in commemoration of 1989 came not from a party's reluctance to look to the past but rather from a reluctance to emphasize historical events at odds with its own self-identity and political interest.

Fico's emphasis on the anniversaries of the uprising and the constitution reflect a different set of priorities: the uprising of 1944 against Germans and their Slovak allies is one of the most positively regarded historical events associated with Slovakia's communist past, while Constitution Day calls attention to Slovakia's move toward independence (the *actual* anniversary date of independence, January 1, is overshadowed by the non-political celebrations of the New Year). In citing these particular days, Fico's statement thus emphasized the recollection of dates associated with his own party's ties to (the positive aspects of) the communist past and national independence.

So active, in fact, was Fico's participation in celebrations of the sixty-fifth anniversary of the uprising that it provoked critical comments by the newspaper *Pravda*, which described Smer as "privatizing the uprising" (Schnierová and Milan 2009). One year before, SDKÚ deputy Milan Hort made the same comment about Smer's "privatization" of the eighty-ninth anniversary of the death of early twentieth-century Slovak leader Milan Rastislav Štefánik, and *Pravda* described the celebration of the one hundred sixtieth anniversary of the "Petition of the Slovak Nation" to the Hungarian Diet as having "the feeling of a party rally" (Kostelanský 2008).

A review of all major anniversary celebrations underscores the fact that Slovakia's fractured twentieth-century history makes it impossible for any one political orientation to assimilate and embrace all of it. Those, like the SNS, who understand the World War II Slovak state as the template for later independence cannot also acclaim the Slovak National Uprising. Thus a chronicle of other anniversary commemorations yields a pattern of fairly sharp divides between the commemoration choices of Slovakia's political forces that corresponds almost precisely to the country's underlying dimensions of political competition (national, economic, religious), although not always with its government/opposition alignments:

- Slovak nationalists and Smer overlapped on many national anniversaries, including the Petition of the Slovak Nation, the 1907 killing of Slovaks by Hungarian troops in Černová, and events related to the creation of independent Slovakia in 1992–1993.
- Slovak nationalists and Christian Democrats overlapped on some anniversaries where religious and national themes intertwined, particularly the death of Slovak Nationalist leader (and Roman Catholic priest) Andrej Hlinka.[8]
- Christian Democrats (KDH) and the Slovak Democratic and Christian Union (SDKÚ) overlapped on anti-communist anniversaries and those

related to the founding of Czechoslovakia. The Christian Democrats and SDKÚ actively commemorated the anniversary of the creation of Czechoslovakia in 1918, linking it explicitly to the revolution of 1989.

Certain parties were also alone in certain kinds of commemorations:

- Smer was particularly strong in its commemoration of the Slovak National Uprising of 1944, a challenge to "clerico-fascism" that had been highlighted in the communist period as a safer historical reference point because of its communist participation and rejection of religious leadership.
- The Slovak National Party (SNS) alone made strong positive statements about anniversaries related to the independent Slovak state of World War II and its president, Josef Tiso. Only SNS, furthermore, suggested that the country should officially commemorate the October 27 anniversary of the 1907 Černová killings under Hungarian rule as the national holiday instead of the October 28 anniversary of the creation of Czechoslovakia, and linked the founders of Czechoslovakia to the death of Štefánik (*Pravda* 2010b). The party also made a direct connection between this tragedy and the current behavior of the Hungarian government and the "great Magyar chauvinism" of Slovakia's minority party SMK (Slovak National Party 2009). Unlike other parties, SNS also celebrated the anniversary of the 1920 Trianon Treaty, which transferred huge swaths of territory from Hungary to other countries (and did so quite controversially by erecting plaques to the event in predominantly Hungarian areas).
- The Christian Democrats alone drew significant attention to the anniversary of the 1988 "Good Friday" march for religious freedom.
- The SDKÚ alone called for a holiday to commemorate the entry of Slovakia into the EU (though the suggested date—the first of May—was already a state holiday).
- The Party of the Hungarian Coalition was alone in avoiding commemoration of the creation of the Slovak National Council in 1848.

This preliminary review suggests that while parties may have differed on the margins in their tendency to embrace anniversaries and commemorations, the overall differences were in theme rather than the relevance of the past as a whole. Each party found in the past the themes that corresponded best with its present positions and those of its present voters. Abnegation does not appear to be a generalized approach so much as an effort to avoid the negative associations of specific historical landmark events.

Assessing the Results

Fico drew fire by arguing that 1989 made little difference for his life (at least at the time), but the ultimate question for this chapter is whether the memories of 1989 made any difference to Slovakia's political environment. Since the recollections were split largely along party and coalition lines, it is possible that they were simply a reflection of larger processes with no independent force of their own. There are, however, some indications that the 1989 anniversary forced some parties and leaders into more awkward positions than others and thereby played an asymmetric role.

Bernhard and Kubik focus on the emergence of three types of mnemonic regimes—the (rare) unified type, the contentious (and dangerous) fractious type, and the equally fractious but less dangerous pillarized type.[9] The example of Slovakia suggests that the categories apply well but only in a more complicated manner that links parties and other interested groups to particular types of approaches for specific remembered events rather than to memory as a whole. As with parties' "issue ownership," furthermore, parties tend to adopt "warrior" positions on memories in which they gain support from encouraging the dominant public memory or, at least, the memory resonating with its putative electorates, while on others they engage in abnegation—"it doesn't matter"—to avoid losses from memories that are "owned" by other parties. This is not at all to say that memory warriors are necessarily insincere. Just as identities are not infinitely malleable, neither is one's positioning toward the past, and even more important, to the existing cultural framing of the past.

The one approach that does not appear often from any political actor is the "pluralist" notion that "there are many ways to see it." Even when parties do acknowledge ambiguity, they are more likely to do so by offering a hegemonic position of ambiguity—"we argue some things were good and some things were bad" than by accepting the possibility that "other people (perhaps correctly) see it differently."

In Slovakia, at least, the parties that benefit from some commemorations of the past are hurt by others, and the asymmetries tend not to be enduring or system-wide. Likewise the differences among parties regarding anniversaries and memories in general tend to refer to specific events rather than to overall approaches. The impact of memory in Slovak politics has depended far more on the political advantage (either in terms of electoral support or moral certainty) that a particular event provides to a political actor than an overall interpretation of history itself. In this sense, everybody is sometimes a warrior and sometimes an abnegator. Moreover, in Slovakia, the broader public does not usually receive coherent competing visions of the past; instead, there is a more episodic competition of memory fragments and shifting reference points. It is a bit ironic, therefore, that even though parties themselves do not engage in pluralist recognition of multiple viewpoints, Slovakia's citizens who attend to political questions have little choice but to sift through multiple, politically motivated visions of what events mean and which ones are truly important.

NOTES

1. The Bratislava student demonstration of November 16 started as an observance of International Student's Day and escalated into a protest demonstration. In this instance the police monitored the demonstration, but there was no crackdown like that in Prague the following day. Žatkuliak (2009, 115–116) designates this as the "introductory act" of the Gentle Revolution. In his speech at the University of London, Fico also noted this in passing.

2. Alexander Dubček's death in an automobile accident in 1992 deprived the country of perhaps the only plausible candidate for a "founding father" in 1989, though even this would have been complicated since he was most closely associated with the changes of 1968, which sought to create not democracy, but "socialism with a human face."

3. Even some of the "jointness" of the commemoration has fallen into obscurity, along with some key figures and organizational structures. The Slovak Public against Violence (VPN) that emerged in November is still a central part of the memory narrative, but Krapfl (2009) documents the emergence of competition between branches of VPN and those of the (Czech) Civic Forum in the same municipalities in Slovakia in November 1989, a competition that ended with the dominance of VPN branches.

4. The Center Right parties included the Hungarian minority party Slovak Magyar Coalition (SMK), and two Christian Democratic Parties, the Slovak Democratic and Christian Union (SDKÚ) led by former prime minister Mikuláš Dzurinda, and the dissident-spawned Christian Democratic Movement, originally led by Ján Čarnogurský.

5. VPN had immediately invoked the need for a "return to Europe" in the 1990 elections, with its slogan "A Chance for Slovakia" superimposed on a map of Europe in its election posters.

6. The Slovak National Uprising of 1944 was a failed but heroic challenge by a coalition of communist and non-communist resistance groupings to the wartime Slovak state aligned with Nazi Germany. Under communism, the regime appropriated the uprising to celebrate it as an essentially communist undertaking. Hence the uprising's commemoration was politically charged, but certainly it would have been highly incongruous for fascists to embrace the occasion.

7. See, for example, his interview in the autumn of 1992, when the breakup of the state was assured. In that interview he declared his homeland to be Czechoslovakia, not Slovakia (*Kultúrny život*, 1992).

8. One of the most prominent Slovak politicians of interwar Czechoslovakia, Andrej Hlinka led the autonomist Hlinka Slovak People's Party until his death in 1938. Critics, especially those with a "Czechoslovak" outlook, questioned his loyalty to the Czechoslovak state; hence celebrating his memory tended to be divisive. See, for example, Slovak National Party 2007.

9. "A Theory of the Politics of Memory," Chapter 1 of this volume.

6 Remembering the Revolution

CONTESTED PASTS IN THE BALTIC COUNTRIES

Daina S. Eglitis and Laura Ardava

Introduction

In the mid-1980s, oppositional social movements arose in the Baltic republics of Latvia, Lithuania, and Estonia to challenge the Soviet order and, eventually, pursue full independence from the USSR. In the post-communist period, oppositional social movement activities and goals of the 1986–1991 period have been subject to a contentious politics of memory, creating deeply fractured memory regimes. This chapter examines the signal events of the opposition period in the Baltic republics and their commemoration in the decades that followed the restoration of Baltic independence in 1991. We pay particular attention to the Baltic Way of 1989, the Latvian and Lithuanian barricades of January 1991, and the final de facto re-establishment of independence in the late summer of 1991, showing that different commemorations have produced different articulations of and contests about the meaning of the past.

On August 23, 1989, several years of growing activity in Baltic civil societies culminated in a powerful display of opposition and unity: On that day, an estimated 2 million people joined hands in a human chain that stretched from Tallinn in the north, through Riga, and south to Vilnius. The Baltic Way of 1989 itself was deeply enmeshed in the politics of memory, as it marked the fiftieth anniversary of the Molotov-Ribbentrop Pact, the secret protocols of which had divided the

Baltics and parts of Poland into spheres of influence and, in the eyes of many Balts, sealed their fate as occupied republics of the Soviet Union. The Baltic opposition's counter-hegemonic narrative of history characterized the dominant Soviet story of the past as illegitimate, positing that Baltic entry into the USSR in 1940 was not "voluntary," but rather that the countries had been occupied illegally and brutally. Further, the Baltic narrative categorically rejected the central Soviet historical tenet that the Red Army "liberated" the Baltics after World War II. Brüggemann and Kasekamp note that "[the Baltic's] own hidden history was a popular and effective weapon, because reconstructing an amputated national memory was meant to mobilize anti-Soviet protest, create solidarity and eventually, after the break-up of the USSR, even [to] gain international support" (2008, 426).

In the field of Soviet-era memory politics, central and republic-level Soviet institutions continued to articulate the historical narrative that had been in place since the 1940s, highlighting the story of Baltic "liberation" and "national brotherhood" that formed the foundation of legitimacy claims (Lehti, Jutila, and Jokisipila 2008, 403). In a period in which this legitimacy was broadly questioned, Soviet institutional actors backed their position with coercion, which was manifested in the January 1991 killings of civilians by Soviet troops in Vilnius and Riga. On January 12, armed Soviet forces seeking to repress the independence movement in Lithuania mounted an attack on the television tower and demonstrators in Vilnius, killing 14 and injuring 110 civilians. On January 13, an estimated half-million people from across Latvia gathered at the barricades constructed by protesters to speak out against the violence in Lithuania and to protect Latvia's own nascent political institutions, including the Supreme Council, Council of Ministers, and the television building. Though the demonstration was peaceful, Soviet forces took the lives of six people in Riga (Bleiere 2005, 399–400). The events of January 1991 and the barricades themselves would later become important objects of remembrance and commemoration in Latvia and Lithuania.

Later that year, the Baltic opposition achieved its crown objective, full de facto independence. While all three republics had earlier issued parliamentary declarations of independence, they remained tethered to the USSR institutionally, economically, and militarily. The transformation of declarations into political reality came about on August 24, 1991, as President Boris Yeltsin signed, on behalf of the Russian Federation, a declaration recognizing the Baltics as independent entities. Not long after, the Soviet era came to a close as the union dissolved into fifteen independent entities. Contested narratives of both the recent and distant past, however, would continue to haunt Baltic societies and politics into the first decades of independence.

In this chapter, we look at the commemoration of these three socially and politically significant moments of anti-Soviet and pro-independence opposition in the

Baltics at the twentieth anniversary of each, following with an analysis of the politics of memory, the contests, and the actors in these post-communist commemorations. We conclude with a brief discussion of social and political effects and consequences of memory politics in the Baltic countries.

The Fractured Past: The Layered Politics of Memory in the Baltic Countries

James Mark has called post-communism "a culture of historical reinvention, in which political parties, state-sponsored historical institutions, cultural sites and individuals [package] the meanings and memories of dictatorship to meet the needs of a new political system" (2010, 215). The fractured memory regimes in the Baltics suggest that this "historical reinvention" has been subject to contestation between ethnically and economically stratified communities of mnemonic warriors. In this chapter, we examine these contests through the lens of contemporary commemorations of events of the opposition period.

Anniversaries, a central object of commemorations, "thrust the past into the present" (Burch 2008, 452). Commemorations offer a venue for the enactment of memory, a collective ritual of mourning or celebration constructed on the foundation of a community or country's dominant narrative of history. They are, at least theoretically, a key part of building collective national identity. Commemorative ritual serves the function of socialization within a particular community, but in the case of memory conflict, it potentially sets communities against one another, undermining social unity and even political development (Ardava 2011, 365).

In the Baltic countries, commemoration of the signal events of the period of opposition to Soviet rule has been, in some instances, intertwined with the memory politics of World War II. While titular Baltic populations have embraced a narrative of the mid-twentieth century that elevates a story of occupation, victimization, and struggle against the Soviet order, Russian-speaking minority communities have been more inclined to embrace the Soviet-era historical narrative of the heroic Soviet army liberation of Europe. Beyond this split in memory politics, there are detectable fissures within titular ethnic communities over the significance and meaning of the recent past, that is, 1989 to 1991. Below we explore problems and practices of commemoration in the Baltics twenty years after the period of opposition.

The story of contested memories begins with the evolution of three mnemonic narratives that compose the fractured memory regimes of the Baltic countries after communism. The three ideal-typical narratives, which will be discussed in the context of several commemorative anniversaries, include, first, the *ethnic elite political narrative*. We suggest that this narrative, which emanated from dominant political elites of the titular ethnicities, was characterized by efforts to euphorically paint the opposition-era past as the triumphant and inevitable path to "progress" and "freedom." These terms, while clearly representative of the Soviet-era opposition's efforts, were often left loosely defined: In Latvia, for instance, mass public disenchantment with economic development and political corruption created a problem of legitimacy for the iteration of a triumphant narrative of the recent past. Second, the *political and economic alienation narrative* recognized the legitimacy of the anti-Soviet opposition's goals of independence, democracy, and markets, but problematized recent history with a critical position. This narrative projected onto the past a patina of bitterness born of the political and economic crisis of post-communism, representing a widely shared sense that power and resources passed from one elite to another without reflecting or meeting the needs of the masses. Third, the *ethnic alienation narrative*, embraced in particular by Russophone populations in Latvia and Estonia, was characterized by discontent with the political and economic evolution of post-communism, particularly the fate of Russophone minorities. In some instances, this narrative assumed a position on World War II history that overtly rejected the Baltic characterization of mid-century events as an occupation in favor of a Soviet-era story that depicted the actions of the USSR and its army as "liberation." In contrast to the politics of memory in Central Europe, the Baltic politics of memory at the twenty-year mark was more deeply layered, weaving together mnemonic contests about the recent past with battles over the memory of the World War II era.

Remembering the Baltic Way After 1989

In the memory politics surrounding the post-communist commemoration of the Baltic Way of 1989, there was a continuing articulation on the part of many commentators of the pre-war history that precipitated the original Baltic Way action. As the Baltic Way of 1989 was itself an object of memory politics, an assertion of the illegality and tragic consequences of the Molotov-Ribbentrop Pact of 1939, a commentator in the Latvian press put pre-war history at the center of his ten-year retrospective, writing that:

> The Latvian nation was not permitted to determine its own fate. It is important to remember the history of the occupation because it constitutes the greater part of our history in this century. It was a serious [endurance] test, complete with efforts to eradicate nations and their cultural values. Not for nothing is it said that for Latvia the Second World War ended only in 1991 when, with the collapse of the Soviet empire, independence was regained. (Lācis 1999, 2)

Rather than treating 1989 (or the period around it) as the only object of commemoration (or contestation), this layered politics of memory melded mnemonic
struggles surrounding the World War II era with those of the opposition era, replay-
ing in part the narrative contest between Baltic and Soviet histories that animated
the opposition in the 1980s and early 1990s.

The commemoration of the Baltic Way at the ten-year mark elevated the collective memory of an event that represented both the apex of Baltic cooperation
in the face of Soviet power and a key step toward the realization of independence.
The ex-president of Lithuania, Valdas Adamkus, suggested in a television discussion
devoted to the fifteenth anniversary of the Latvian People's Front that the "day of the
Baltic Way was the day of our victory" (Latvian Television 2003). The elite political
narrative across the Baltics emphasized the Baltic Way as the euphoric and historic
commencement of the road to independence and the inevitable linear progression
toward Europe and European institutions like the European Union and the North
Atlantic Treaty Organization (NATO).

Commemoration in the elite political narrative articulated the Baltic Way as an
unqualified moment of unifying triumph for Balts and cast it as emblematic of a
progressive road forward. At a conference devoted to the tenth anniversary of the
Baltic Way, Latvian Minister of Foreign Affairs Indulis Bērziņš proclaimed, "Today
the Baltic Way is no more the call for freedom and the demonstration of physical
unity. Today the Baltic Way is the road of dynamic advancement, development and
the road of cooperation for the Europe's common future" (1999, 60). Where critique
was part of the narrative, it was aimed primarily at a public whose patriotism seemed
to be flagging. As Latvian Prime Minister Andris Šķēle declared, "It might sound
naive but at the moment there is a disastrous lack of people with high principles. We
have to learn to believe again and again. To believe in our strength, in our nation,
in our future. We have to go back to school and learn to love our state" ("Baltijas
vienotība gadu tūkstošu mijā" 1999, 2).

Comments of those outside the political elite who organized and participated
in the Baltic Way were more critical, stepping back from a triumphalist vision of
the past to one more circumspect about the direction that the Baltic Way and the
unity it symbolized had taken. On the tenth anniversary, the weakening of solidarity
between the Baltic States was an important theme in press accounts: as one Latvian
commentator lamented, "Time has passed, independence has been re-established,
but the former feeling of [unity] is considerably diminished. Unity is invoked in
speeches; to a lesser extent it is visible in genuine practices... [consider the] Baltic
wars over herrings, eggs, [and] pigs..." (Upleja 1999, 2).[1]

A cleavage also opened around the significance of the Baltic Way as a signpost
on the road to independent governance and positive social, economic, and political

change. In Latvia, early post-communist discourse around the memory of 1989 was characterized in the ethnic Latvian community by both a shared historical narrative of the Baltic Way as a representation of the opposition's rejection of the Soviet story of World War II and a political narrative that split those who achieved political and economic power after post-communism and those who bore its more dire consequences. The history and memory of *victimhood* (of which 1939 and the Soviet occupation were emblematic) were united, while, paradoxically, the history and memory of *victory* (which the Baltic Way represented) were divided, as not all of the "victors" were winners in the contentious (and often corrupt) politics and competitive capitalist markets of post-communism.

This discontent, we suggest, became the foundation of a political and economic alienation narrative, embraced by some segments of the titular ethnic population. In an interview with the Russian-language newspaper *Vesti Segodnya* on the fifteenth anniversary of the Baltic Way, Dainis Īvāns, a leader of the pro-independence movement in the 1980s, noted his deep disappointment with developments in post-communism: "You know, when the government of Repše [the prime minister] was in power, I even started to wonder, was it really worth fighting then for the establishment of this state..." (Elkin and Fal'kov 2004, 1, 4).

This narrative of unfulfilled hopes cast a pall on the memory of the Baltic Way that, while not challenging the historical narrative on which it was founded, projected onto the memory a bitter story of millions of Balts standing together in order to realize a transfer of power to a new political elite, which was broadly perceived as failing again to represent the needs and wishes of the people. A Latvian participant in the Baltic Way wrote at the fifteen-year anniversary, "We fought for a more honorable Latvia and hoped that the government would be more responsive and understanding of their people" (Kabuce 2004, 1). Letters to the press reflected this bitterness: "Now there is a little disappointment because the living conditions have not improved; patriotism has the undertone of sadness" (Ivanova 2004, 2). A retired history teacher suggested that "[p]eople who joined hands in the Baltic Way expected another Latvia." Articulating the sense that a transfer of power to a new elite rather than to the people had occurred under the cover of the opposition movement, one letter writer offered the following: "Today I see that society has not changed much, but those who hold the power have" (Kabuce 2004, 1). Indeed, this narrative highlighted the more precarious aspects of the road to Europe, which was strewn with the waste of lost economic industries and low living standards for populations like the elderly and rural-dwellers, and was characterized by the dominance of new elites more disposed to realizing their own economic and political interests than those of the nation.

On the one hand, the ethnic Latvian political elite was able to elevate a triumphant narrative of 1989 through its access to the levers of political power and associated political capital. On the other hand, the political and economic alienation narrative found its most potent expression in the media, that is, in the writings of sympathetic journalists, letters to the editor, and, increasingly, new media forms such as Internet comments. Clearly, a media voice is a form of capital in the field of historical memory, though it may be less durable and more ephemeral than the capital exercised by those who hold political and economic power. The elite, importantly, also have a media voice, which can be deployed in opposition to competing narratives of the past or present.

In the layered politics of Baltic memory, the mnemonic contest over the meanings and consequences of August 1939, which was the object of the original Baltic Way demonstration of 1989, was more acute. This contest over the past was waged most visibly by mnemonic warriors split largely along ethnic lines, with titular Baltic populations on one side and ethnic Russians (or Russian-speakers), whose narrative was capitalized with the support of the Russian state, on the other. This deeply fractured memory regime can be articulated with the elaboration of a third key narrative in Baltic memory politics after 1989, that is, the ethnic alienation narrative.

The Baltic opposition of the late 1980s was composed of majorities of titular Baltic populations, as well as sympathetic segments of the Baltic Russian-speaking minority and other ethnic minority groups. Just as some Balts were loyal to the ideas of the Soviet Union, some of the Russian-speaking population actively supported independence, taking part in demonstrations such as the Baltic Way. The failure of many in the Russophone community to gain expected national citizenship after the re-establishment of independence, together with a realization of the loss of political power and status, initiated the reorganization of collective memory on the basis of historical resentment. This drew together Russian-speakers who had thrown in their lot with the pro-independence Balts with the segment of the minority Russophone population who rejected the pursuit of independence and did not welcome independence.

One of the unifying aspects of the ethnic alienation narrative has been its broad rejection of Baltic commemorative practices. While scholars have highlighted the function of commemorative practices in forming and reaffirming a collective conscience in communities (Zerubavel 2003), in the Baltics they have contributed to the deepening of a fundamental ethnic divide. Looking at the case of Latvia, Zepa and colleagues point out that "[it is clear that] Russian-speakers often see [Latvian] national holidays though a negative prism, seeing those as political holidays that are most likely to contribute to societal cleavages" (Zepa et al. 2008, 6). Commemorations are, as Evans points out, more than just the marking of historical events: "At a fundamental level…commemoration is about politics and ideology. It is about identity formation…" (2006, 323). The rejection of commemorative practices highlights a deeply skeptical perspective on the dominant post-communist narrative of Baltic history.

Commemorations of events of the opposition movement of 1986–1991, such as the Baltic Way, evoked a negative reaction that united the Russian-speaking communities and separated them from Baltic political elites. For instance, some of the most scorching public discourse on the Baltic Way appeared in the first decade after the historical action, a period characterized by bitter political battles over issues like citizenship, property rights, and the right to education in the Russian language, and, as the following quote suggests, a deepening stratification of the population along economic lines. In an interview with the Russian-language newspaper *SM Segodnja,* a Russian-speaking pensioner in Latvia suggested that "[a]t the moment, the unemployed persons, homeless persons, [and] pensioners dying of hunger could create a chain of the same length [as the Baltic Way].... This chain would serve as a public rebuke to those [in] power..." (Elkin 1998, 1, 3).

Heartbeats for the Baltics: Memory Politics in 2009

The twentieth-anniversary of the Baltic Way of 1989 was most visibly commemorated by a mass athletic event, "Heartbeats for the Baltics."[2] Adhering to the historical route of the Baltic Way, the 31-hour long unity run, completed like a relay in segments, took place on August 22–23, 2009 (Picture 6.1). It began in the south with an introduction by Lithuanian president Dalia Grybauskaitė in Vilnius and in the north with an introduction by Estonian president Toomas Hendrik Ilves in Tallinn, and culminated at the Freedom Monument in Riga with Latvian president Valdis Zatlers's participation in the last kilometer of the run. Perhaps consistent with the unity theme, Riga's mayor, Nil Ushakov, an ethnic Russian, ran the last kilometer with President Zatlers and addressed the gathering at the Freedom Monument.[3] As the initiative for the unity run came from Latvia's president, the public relations campaign was realized most broadly there. The event assembled more than 60,000 people from the three Baltic States (notably, about 50,000 of those were from Latvia).

The President's Chancery and the Latvian Orienteering Federation commissioned the public relations agency, Deep White, which, collaborating with public relations agencies in Estonia (Alfa–Omega Communications) and Lithuania (KPMS), worked out an appealing and powerful public relations campaign.[4] Three weeks before the unity run, preparatory activities were underway, including online registration for the run at the homepage (www.baltijascelam20.lv), a publicity campaign, and the creation and distribution of logo T-shirts. The first participant registered

PICTURE 6.1 Riga, Latvia, August 23, 2009. Runners participate in the Latvian leg of the Baltic unity run, "Heartbeats for the Baltics."
Source: Photo/Ints Kalniņš.

after the press conference was the president of Latvia. He was joined by a group of popular celebrities and twenty-year-olds born on the historical day. Similar press conferences and public relations activities took place in Lithuania and Estonia.

Arguably, the elite's political capital that might have been invested in the construction of a specific version of the common past was not extensive due to widespread disillusionment in society, including not only the Russian-speaking minority, but also a segment of ethnic Latvians disgruntled with corruption in politics, the deep downturn in the economic fortunes of the middle class, widespread poverty among the elderly and children, and the accelerating loss of population to migration (in Latvia and Lithuania, in particular). That is, the exercise of political elite power via the definition and legitimation of a particular vision of the past was compromised by their own diminished legitimacy in society.

Social discontent and disunity created a memory climate inimical to an elite-centered articulation of a Baltic Way historical narrative. On the one hand, Balts shared a fundamentally well-defined narrative of World War II occupation and oppression. On the other hand, there was a widely shared sense in 2009 that the promises and values of 1989 and the Baltic Way had been undermined by the political elite. As such, we suggest, political elites (particularly in Latvia, which was the primary organizer of "Heartbeats for the Baltics") attempted less to construct a grand narrative as to imbue the past, specifically the cultural vessel of the Baltic Way, with ambiguity. "Heartbeats for the Baltics" was a *commemoration spectacle* untethered from the burdens of the "grand narratives" of history (Lyotard 1979). Rather, it subsumed struggles over memory and meaning in a time of crisis and disunity beneath a glossy, well-planned and executed event that elevated form over meaning and substituted a "show" of unity for authentic societal (or Baltic) unity.

Though it appeared to resist mnemonic conflict, "Heartbeats for the Baltics" did not represent mnemonic abnegation. Indeed, it clearly sought a narrative link to the Baltic Way of 1989: An editorial published five days before the run in the English-language *Baltic Times*, prepared in cooperation with the Latvian Foreign Ministry, called the run a "living history lesson for those who were born after the Baltic Way or do not remember it because they were too young..." ("Baltics Run for Unity" 2009). If the Baltic Way was, as the website for the run suggested, "a historical symbol which lives in humanity's collective memory, fostering understanding of solidarity and the meaning of free expression and the values of freedom," then there was little discussion of those values or the aspirations and hopes that had compelled 2 million Baltic inhabitants to join the human chain. The "mini-narratives" around the run, instead, were fragmented, ranging from discussions of running practices and health to modest (or banal) political calls for a "new Baltic Way" that would "confirm unity" (articulated by Zatlers), which was described by Grybauskaitė as useful for "[reducing] the negative consequences of the recession, undertaking greater responsibilities and [being] more courageous in dealing with the challenges of our age," though no substantive steps toward such an end were offered ("Baltic Presidents Urge Citizens to Remember 'Baltic Way'" 2009).

The unity run earned mixed reviews from the press and public. On the one hand, support was voiced for the event and its efforts to revive the unity and hope of 1989. Pauls Raudseps, a commentator from the Latvian daily newspaper *Diena,* noted, "Sunday demonstrated that irrespective of all difficulties, there still are huge resources of goodness that are being broadened for the formation of a brighter future" (2009, 2). Some newspaper readers and participants also characterized the unity run in glowing terms. An inhabitant of Riga called the editorial office of the newspaper *Latvijas Avīze* to express her pleasure: "I experienced inexpressible gladness and excitement to tears watching the marathon of unity. I was glad that the action was successful, that so many young people, [and] young families with small children took part in it" (Geida 2009, 24).

On the other hand, many people expressed skepticism about the event and its intentions. A commentator from the Latvian daily national newspaper *Neatkarīgā Rīta Avīze*, Viktors Avotiņš, characterized the "unity run" as a "façade" of unity:

Of course, patriotic events are needed...I am also in favor of unity. Alas—for a unity which is demonstrated not in concert with the appeals and invitations of some "ministry of propaganda," but for [a unity] which does not have to be specially planned, [and] which emanates from current practices (of society, of power structures)....In the Soviet period, it was common to demonstrate for that which did not exist. But for that [unity] which at this time is absent, I will not run...I see as deceptive such official or semi-official actions that do not represent existing circumstances, but are used as a curtain to obscure those circumstances. (2009, 2)

His comments drew on a bitterness founded not least in his recent observations about the widespread and dramatic out-migration of Latvians, particularly from rural areas, seeking to escape the country's difficult economic conditions, and he sarcastically added, "...I have been helpless to influence this scenario...but at least I can participate in a unity run. That will definitely help."

Interestingly, Avotiņš's observation that in the Soviet period "it was common to demonstrate for that which did not exist" recalls Burawoy and Lukacs's observation about socialist "painting rituals" like centrally planned and obligatory workers' demonstrations in pre-1989 Hungary: "Precisely because workers have to act out the virtues of socialism, they become conscious of its failings. In painting socialism as just and rational they become critical of its irrationality and injustice" (1992, 147). While forced participation in Soviet rituals, arguably, made the juxtaposition of reality and representation particularly acute, Avotiņš's point that the run—a "shell" of unity, in his words—drew attention to the *lack of unity* in society, in particular between the goals and interests of the political elite and society, was echoed in other comments as well. His skepticism was broadly reflected in Internet news portal comments, which included points like the following:

- "...does [President] Zatlers have no shame[?] In order to divert attention from the [troubles] that he and other politicians have cooked up, he intends to manipulate people's emotions with an event to commemorate the Baltic Way. Leave this amazing historical event alone!" ("Skolotajs," August 3, 2009, on the *Diena* news portal)
- "Kudos to [Mayor Ushakov] for running and for his speech at the Freedom Monument....Maybe this unity will fulfill those dreams from twenty years ago. Yes—unity between Latvians, Russians, Jews, Belarusians, and all ethnic groups in Latvia for the purpose of improving social welfare and culture and not [just] the unity between the oligarchs...." ("Sandis," August 23, 2009, on the *Diena* news portal)

- "I hurt for my nation, today I cried, I watched TV, remembered how unified we were 20 years ago, but today it seemed to me that the event [Heartbeats for the Baltics] was devoted to burnishing the image of [President] Zatlers, and I wait with trepidation about what tomorrow will bring, what new taxes await us, how many people will be left unemployed, how many hungry children will not be able to go to school on the first of September." ("Zuze," August 23, 2009, on the *Delfi* news portal)

Ritualized commemorative practices act in modern societies as vehicles for the development, sustenance, and dissemination of collective memory. In 2009, the Baltic Way was "commemorated" by a striking media event, which substituted public relations–centered unity *in form* for unity *in practice* and the gloss of a commemorative spectacle for a reflection on the past, largely pushing to the margins efforts by social actors to engage in a mnemonic contest over the meaning of this event. This entailed, arguably, a transference of meaning, with the substitution of new memories for old memories, rather than a targeted commemoration of the Baltic Way of 1989. As one press account noted, "Just as [people] remembered where they stood in the Baltic Way, now [they] will remember the section which they ran [in the relay] ("Sirdspuksti savienojas Rīgā" 2009, 1, 3).

Organizers hailed "Heartbeats for the Baltics" as a stunning success, noting that it set a record for the number of participants in comparable marathons in the Baltic countries. Clearly, the public relations campaign was successful, assembling more than 60,000 active participants—in addition to spectators—for the event (though there was, notably, a lack of *Baltic* unity in the unity run, which was apparent in the low Lithuanian and Estonian participation). But an examination of the objectives and ideals once embedded in the chain of 2 million, as well as their relationship to the stark realities of the current situation, was left out. As such, the unity run, "Heartbeats for the Baltics," reproduced the Baltic Way in form but drained it of larger meaning, leaving in its place a platform for the articulation of "mini-narratives" that disengaged from the politics of memory of 1989, elevating instead a (successful) commemoration spectacle that may have functioned, paradoxically, to both obscure and illuminate disunity and distrust in contemporary politics, as well as in the articulation of the meaning of the past.

The Past Is Not Past: Layered Memory Politics in 2009

In 2009, because of the seventieth anniversary of the Molotov-Ribbentrop Pact, the clash between historical narratives surrounding World War II was conspicuous in society and the press. For instance, a discussion devoted to the anniversary of the pact was organized at the "Moscow House," a cultural center for Russian-speakers, in Riga. The Russian-language newspaper *Vesti Segodnya* offered a lengthy report on the discussion. A historian from Russia, Aleksandr Dyukov, and Latvian historian Kaspars Zellis were invited as "expert speakers." At the discussion, Dyukov declared that the Baltic States and Poland were accessories to the outbreak of World War II and, as such, to their own occupation. According to the Dyukov, the fact that in 1939 Latvia and Estonia signed non-aggression pacts with Germany convinced Russia that Germany wanted to consolidate its power in the Baltics. As such, the Soviet Union had two possibilities: it could either negotiate or go to war with Germany. The Russian historian asserted that the Molotov-Ribbentrop Pact was signed to avoid the outbreak of World War II. A press report on the discussion emphasized that the Latvian historian was representing the "contrary ground": "The audience was listening carefully, but if to Dyukov by obvious favor, then to Zellis rather by demonstrative correctness" (Slyusareva 2009, 6).

These irreconcilable narratives of mid-century history, which were evoked by 1989 and the Baltic Way but went beyond it, are significant for social and political life in Latvia and Estonia in particular, as both are home to large Russophone populations, many of whom migrated during the Soviet period. Brüggemann and Kasekamp point out that "[in] the case of the post-Soviet Baltic States, the politics of memory created a 'real' history that was based upon a common understanding of collective victimhood under Soviet rule, thus excluding the Russian-speaking minority from the state-building memory community. This selective approach to the past was prone to create borders against those who did not share the alleged common experience" (2008, 426).

On the one hand, the official post-Soviet commemorative calendar is entwined with a dominant narrative that elevates a historical story representing part of the Baltic population, but that may be experienced by others as a "state-sponsored policy of exclusion" (Onken 2010, 278). On the other hand, the contesting narrative coming from the Russian-speaking community is experienced by many ethnic Latvians, Lithuanians, and Estonians as a failure to acknowledge their experience and memory of repression and occupation.

In the field of memory politics, mnemonic agents engaged in the contest over who will tell the "legitimate" story of World War II remain locked in an irreconcilable debate. Balts, while split in some instances on the meaning and memories of the opposition period, remain unified behind the titular ethnic narratives of World War II history, the reclamation of which was a key goal of the opposition period. The weight of the state, the dominant educational institutions, and, importantly, the individual living memories of older generations of ethnic Balts lend powerful capital to the story of occupation and repression, which is linked, at the point of inception, to the Molotov-Ribbentrop Pact of 1939.

More than half a century of Soviet historical writings underpin the legacy of the Baltic Russophone historical narrative and, notably, are a key aspect of Russian and Baltic Russian identities, which derive from the narrative of the Soviet army construed as "liberator" of Europe (Ehala 2009). This narrative also draws on the capital of individual memory, certainly to the degree that Red Army veterans both inside and outside the Baltics see themselves as the liberators of Europe and the conquerors of fascism. The Russian state itself offers powerful supporting capital to this narrative, as was apparent in the Bronze Soldier incident in Estonia in 2007.[5] The tight linkage of identity and memory has deepened the intractability of tensions over history's telling and commemoration. As Lehti, Jutila, and Jokisipila note, "the heroes of one story are the villains of the other" (2008, 411).

To the Barricades: Remembering January 1991 in Lithuania and Latvia

In January 2011, Lithuania and Latvia hosted commemorative activities that highlighted the lost lives and the heady combination of fear and anticipation that had permeated the opposition's construction of barricades in 1991. The barricades were erected to thwart the efforts of conservative Soviet forces to place obstacles in the path of Baltic independence and represented Baltic resistance in the wake of the killings of Baltic civilians by Soviet forces in Vilnius and Riga. In Lithuania, President Dalia Grybauskaitė participated in a commemoration at the cemetery where victims were buried. An honor guard of young men born in the years of opposition stood watch nearby. In memory of the events, a 200-meter-long flag was carried through Vilnius from the main cathedral to the parliamentary building, where a special session marked the occasion (Bos 2011).

Visiting in Vilnius, Solvita Āboltiņa, chairwoman of the Latvian parliament, noted that she was grateful for the opportunity to participate in the commemorative event together with Lithuanians. Her speech, a portion of which was in Lithuanian, emphasized the heroic character of the Baltic struggle for freedom, the political resonance of those events, and their historical significance: "We remember the events that changed the course of history twenty years ago not only in the Baltic States, but also, possibly, the entire world. The Baltic States were not only a part of the fall of the Iron Curtain, but also the ones that started these global changes" ("Bonfires for Freedom" 2011).

Commemorative events dedicated to the twentieth anniversary of the barricades also took place across Latvia. The Dom Cathedral in Riga hosted an exhibition, and the Ministry of Foreign Affairs offered a traveling exhibition of historical photographs. Commemorative bonfires were kindled in Zaķusala and other symbolic locations, offering the public the opportunity to share their memories. Officials and representatives of the cultural intelligentsia spoke at commemorative events. The events of the commemorative week also included special school lessons, a concert devoted to the builders and protectors of the barricades, and the screening of historical documentaries at the Barricades Museum and the Museum of the Occupation of Latvia, as well as a conference at the Latvian Academy of Sciences. On January 20, the Latvian parliament held a ceremonial meeting, which including the laying of flowers at the Monument of Freedom and other commemorative sites ("Sākas barikāžu divdesmitgades piemiņas pasākumi" 2011).

Two decades later, the public remembering of the barricades of January 1991 could be characterized as acutely romanticized. Lithuanian president Grybauskaitė declared in an address to parliament, "Freedom was not given as a gift," and while the country had to fight for it, Lithuania "passed the test of history and courage with blazing bonfires and resounding songs of hope…" (Bos 2011). Well-known Latvian political journalist Ināra Egle described the historical days of January 1991 in similarly emotional terms, writing that:

> Probably the smell of smoke from the barricades has remained deepest in the senses of many people. It [the smell of smoke] has been preserved in the heavy jackets, in the mittens of barricade's keepers, and in the walls of Old Riga's houses. There have never afterwards been so many bonfires as there were in January 1991, when people from across Latvia protected the capital city…. The keepers of the barricades were warmed with the tea and sandwiches brought by anonymous people, songs performed by musicians of Riga, and the voices of radio announcers. […] The atmosphere of the barricades was dispersed across Latvia…" (2011, 11–12).

In contrast to the more atomized discourse of the Baltic Way and Molotov-Ribbentrop events of August 2009, the dominating discourse of the commemoration of the barricades of January 1991 was more optimistic. Many Latvians indicated that they would fight again against threats to Latvian independence. Singer Ieva Akurātere, a key cultural figure of the opposition period in Latvia, said, "I think that people at any moment would be ready to fight for Latvia. Certainly, some are disappointed in this state, some others feel tired of it, some [feel] crushed, but new reserves [of strength] always arise. Life is not a suit that fits perfectly. You have to try and try it again" (Puisāne 2011, 16). A similar sentiment was echoed in the words of a young Lithuanian who had been with the opposition in Vilnius: Two decades later, Ruslanas Iržikevičius said, "I hope that neither me, nor my children will ever have to be in such a situation again in the future. But if the worst came to the worst, I know where I would be" (Scott 2011).

Commemorations also evoked some critical reflections, as they had at the anniversary of the Baltic Way. In Latvia, historian Ilga Kreituse pointed out in an interview with the daily newspaper *Neatkarīgā Rīta Avīze* that the "losses engendered by the leaders of the Latvian People's Front are greater than the gains. People have seen that their ideals were used as a platform for providing a good life for some people." Notably, Kreituse articulated this narrative of unfulfilled expectations using the language of a powerful slogan of the Latvian opposition, "Even in *pastalas* [peasant slippers], but in a free Latvia." In contemporary Latvia, she noted pointedly, "the slogan has become the reality. Part of society really continues to walk in *pastalas,* but some have patent leather shoes" (Mediņa 2011, 1, 4). Lithuanian Alfredas Girdziušas, who was working as a photojournalist for the newspaper *Lietuvos aidas* at the time of the barricades, also expressed a frustration with the change—or its lack—in the intervening years: "Oligarchs with a post-Soviet mentality are in our government, they made their fortune when others were freezing on the barricades. The rural areas are devoid of young people and education is not affordable. After 20 years, we got this, we never expected this 20 years ago" (Scott 2011).

Commemorations intended to remind Balts of their shared history also exposed transnational divisions. In Lithuania, President Grybauskaitė called not only for remembrance, but for justice and the prosecution of those responsible for killing civilians in January 1991: "there is no limitation for crimes against humanity and freedom of a nation." Prime Minister Andrius Kubilius echoed her sentiment, suggesting that Russia should be held to account and asking for compensation to the families of the fourteen civilians killed by Soviet troops. The Russian embassy in Vilnius roundly rejected the suggestion that Russia should be held responsible for the events of 1991 (Bos 2011).

Interestingly, several months later, the split between mnemonic actors who sought to remember (and punish) and those who preferred to forget was more fully exposed when Austrian officials arrested Mikhail Golovatov, a retired KGB officer wanted in Lithuania for crimes linked to the Soviet troops under his command in January 1991, and then released him less than a day later, ostensibly on technical grounds. While an Austrian official acknowledged "old wounds," the country's reaction was broadly judged by Lithuanians as dismissive of their history and pursuit of historical justice (Davoliute 2011). In the politics of memory, the events of January 1991 took on international dimensions, pitting Lithuania (and the other Baltic countries, which supported it) against both a Russian state that rejected responsibility for Soviet-era crimes in the Baltics and a European Union country that elevated bureaucratic rationality over what Lithuanians perceived as recognition of historical victimhood.

On the one hand, the commemoration of the barricades in Lithuania and Latvia did not evoke acute mnemonic conflict. Commemorations sparked more romantic than critical reflection, evoking a time of unity and courage in the face of danger. On the other hand, the memory of the barricades *as a response to a crime* committed by Soviet forces was more contentious, pitting the painful memories and desire for justice of Lithuania, in particular, against the negation of the past apparent in both Russian and, later, Austrian actions. While Russia refused to recognize complicity in the crimes of its political forebear, Austria elevated a formal rationality over Lithuania's attempts to use legal means to engage in a reckoning with the past.

Twenty Years of de facto Independence: The Commemorations of 2011 in Estonia and Latvia

The twentieth anniversary of de facto independence was commemorated broadly in Estonia and Latvia. [6] The Estonian state organized a massive song festival, "The Song of Freedom," which took place on August 20, 2011, and gathered a crowd of tens of thousands ("Baltics Celebrate 20 Years of Independence" 2011). The Estonian singer Chalise, also known as Jarek Kasar, commented on the massive commemorative event, noting that "[f]reedom is having the opportunity to [have such an event]— true freedom is being able to enjoy it" (Boyce 2011). Many of Estonia's top musicians, as well as Latvia's most popular music group, Brainstorm, joined a group of international cultural figures for the events. "In order to celebrate it memorably and show Estonia's gratitude to the countries that recognized Estonia regaining its independence 20 years ago,...The Song of Freedom will be held on the 20th of August [on the] Tallinn Song Festival Grounds," noted an official website devoted to the twentieth anniversary of Estonia's independence (The Song of Freedom 2011). The event was addressed by Estonian president Toomas Hendrick Ilves, who declared, "In these twenty years we have walked a way that many other states and people have spent a lifetime on." US secretary of state Hillary Clinton made an appearance by video, noting that "[t]oday Estonia is a shining example for countries around the world yearning for democracy and economic opportunity" ("Baltics Celebrate 20 Years of Independence" 2011).

Reflecting the complexities of the recent past, Ilves also added that, "There are a lot of heroes in our story of freedom—more than a million of them, who yearned for a free state.... Many people whom fate had led from the farthest reaches of the Soviet Union to Estonia came with us—with the Estonian state. Some remained stuck in the past; and it has been our complicated task to lead them from there into the future" (www.president.ee). In his words was a subtle assertion of the mnemonic dominance of an Estonian (and Baltic) vision of both history and progress and the sense that this narrative position could and should be transferable to those, presumably Russophone residents, who remained locked in a mnemonic embrace with the Soviet past and practices.

It is notable that Estonia has, by most accounts, weathered economic and political crises more successfully than its neighbors. While all three Baltic countries were hit hard by the economic crisis that commenced in 2008, Estonia recovered relatively rapidly, forging a path forward with technological innovation and more transparent governance. Estonia has also lost a far smaller proportion of its population to labor migration. While the Bronze Soldier incident of 2007 highlighted a powerful mnemonic fissure in Estonia between ethnic Estonians and Russian-speakers, it is arguably the case that within ethnic Estonian society there has been less of a cleavage centered on class stratification and resentment, and this has made commemoration of the recent past less contentious.

Latvia's commemoration of the definitive beginning of Baltic independence from the USSR was ambiguous. In late August 2011, the capital city of Riga organized three days of events in honor of its eight hundred tenth anniversary. On August 20, while Estonia was celebrating independence, Latvia hosted the Elite Aerobatic Formula (EAF), a competition of pilots engaged in complicated "air acrobatic and aerobatic tricks...in the sky above the Daugava river" (Logger 2011). The TriatelX Race, which gathered participants for a race through the narrow streets of Old Riga, took place on the same day. The city celebration culminated in a jubilee concert.

Commemorative events focused on the twenty-year anniversary were less elaborate and more exclusive, including the public in only a fraction of the organized events, which were oriented primarily toward cultural and political elites. The commemorations commenced on the morning of August 21 with an ecumenical service in the Dom Church and the ceremonial laying of flowers at the Monument of Freedom. Later, local musicians performed Latvian classical music at a concert in the Latvian National Theatre. Members of the Supreme Council of the Republic of Latvia and members of the former Congress of People's Deputies of the Soviet Union, who supported the restoration of Latvia's independence in 1991, as well as officials and foreign diplomats, were invited. For the broader audience, the concert was broadcast by television and radio. Afterward, the speakers of the Baltic and Nordic countries' parliaments, along with members of the Supreme Council, planted young trees in Jēkabs Square by the main Saeima building (BNS 2011).

Māris Antonevičs, a commentator for the Latvian national daily newspaper *Latvijas Avīze*, pointed to the Latvian-Estonian contrast in an August 2011 column, writing that:

Over the weekend, the [Riga] city jubilee was celebrated....The program was really multiform—knights, aviation shows, food, singing and dancing. The most popular Latvian pop group "Brainstorm" did not take part in the celebration; it performed at a no less important event titled, "Song of Freedom" in...Tallinn. There the celebration, which had a different character, also took place over these [same] days. It was devoted to the twentieth anniversary of the restoration of *de facto* independence. Actually, this anniversary is not less important for Latvians...however, it can be asserted that it remained in the shadow of the city jubilee. Only a few, so to speak, elite activities were scheduled....So, why do Estonians celebrate extensively but Latvians commemorate bashfully?...An Estonian journalist Anvar Samost notes that in Estonia the attitude towards August 20 has changed [positively] during the past six years and it is to the credit of the president, Toomas Hendrik Ilves....It is clear that henceforth Estonia will not let pass the opportunity to accent and celebrate historical moments involving national independence. I am not sure about Latvia. (2011, 3)

Earlier, we suggested that the Baltic Way commemoration, "Heartbeats for the Baltic," represented a commemoration spectacle. In particular, we argued, the commemorative activities emphasized the reproduction of the Baltic Way in form, while freeing it from grand narratives. As even the romanticized remembering of the barricades showed, social atomization, born of both ethnic and class alienation from political elites, has remained a threat to political elites. Like "Heartbeats for the Baltic," the celebration of the past—in this instance, Riga's eight hundred tenth anniversary—could take place without a broad critical reflection on the past. A distant and uncontested anniversary commemoration stood in for a potentially more divisive and unsettling reflection on how Latvia had evolved politically and economically in the twenty years following the end of Soviet communism.

Division endured however, manifesting, for instance, in continuing sharp commentary in the Russophone press. For instance, a commentator in Latvia's Russian-language newspaper *Chas* chastised the ethnic politics of the post-communist period, pointedly noting, "When the job was done, the [opposition era] Latvian People's Front abandoned the banner 'Latvia—our common home!' and started to implement *de facto* the slogan 'Latvia—for Latvians!'...Only their efforts to turn history back, to establish a heaven for Latvians in a multinational state went on not only for two days, but more than twenty years. And despite the obvious failure, [they] are not going to give up on their pursuit…" (Vatolin 2011, 2).

In Estonia, a common and unifying historical narrative emerged around the commemoration of the de facto re-establishment of independence. In Latvia, commemoration again took on an unreflective quality, reserved primarily for elites and wedged between the events of Riga's eight hundred tenth birthday, an anniversary that engaged public interest with spectacle rather than history. What, then, was the quality of these memory regimes in 2011? On the one hand, we might argue that they were, at least within ethnic communities, largely unified, albeit not in the same way. In Estonia, the twenty-year anniversary prompted broad public celebration focused on the memory of Estonians' pursuit of freedom. In Latvia, unity was forged more fully around a substitute anniversary that was largely free from the contest and critique that might have been invited by broader attention to the twentieth anniversary.

On the other hand, memory regimes in the Baltics are, as noted earlier, layered, and memories and commemorations of the events of the opposition period have often been wrapped up with contested memories and anniversaries of the World War II period, which array mnemonic warriors on each side of an ethnic divide. While this fissure was not central to the public narratives of August 2011, it is interesting that some Russophone commentators pointedly noted the exclusion of Russia's (and Russian president Yeltsin's) contributions to the realization of de facto independence. Characterizing this position, the Latvian national daily newspaper *Diena* published the remark: "Why does [Latvia] avoid giving real weight to the events of August in the history of Latvia? That entails recognizing the role of contemporary Russia in the restoration of the real independence of Latvia. The image of an enemy has been necessary for the politics of Latvia and [the events of August 1991 are] incongruous to it. Stalin's Russia occupied Latvia in 1940, but Yeltsin's Russia in 1991 accepted the independence of Latvia. It seems invalid for many [people] in the politics of Latvia—they need exclusively the Russia that is, was, and remains the occupier" ("Pučs beidzies" 2011, 2).

Conclusion: The Politics of Memory and the Quality of Post-Communist Democracies in the Baltics

The foundational layer of historical narratives in the Baltics is deeply fractured. Social actors are split by ethnicity around irreconcilable World War II narratives of "occupation" and "liberation." While there is broad unity in each ethnic (or linguistic) community around the narratives of the World War II era, the memory of the recent past is less unified within titular ethnic communities, where memories are colored by different perspectives on the post-communist present. Research published by the Advanced Social and Political Institute (ASPRI) of the University of Latvia, for instance, indicates that only 32.2 percent of all respondents[7] and just 45.7 percent of Latvians are proud of the period of opposition (including the Baltic Way, the Barricades, etc.) (Ijabs and Rozenvalds 2009, 197). This "dissatisfaction" with the past reflects, arguably, a broad discontent with contemporary political, social, and economic developments.

What are the implications of memory politics more than twenty years after the signal events of the Baltic Way, the barricades, and the de facto re-establishment of independence? In our conclusion, we consider this question briefly in terms of institutional legitimacy, the party system and party politics, and civic peace.

First, while the politics of memory undergirds a fractured historical narrative, there is considerable stability in the institutional framework. Basic legitimacy claims are bolstered by membership in European institutions like the European Union and the North Atlantic Treaty Organization. Notably as well, institutional legitimacy is supported by the consistency of dominant historical narratives in the Baltics with Western narratives of World War II, which recognized the illegitimacy of Soviet occupation.

Second, the politics of memory has had an effect on the party system and party politics, as well as democratic consolidation more generally. While electoral politics has been characterized by frequent changes in party platforms, composition, and names (Eglitis 2011a), it has been relatively consistent in the explicit or implied division of parties by ethnicity, with some parties known as "Russian parties" and others recognized as representing the positions of the titular ethnic group (though some party members, of course, cross ethnic lines, and politics within the dominant ethnic groups is still highly contentious) (Auers and Ikstens 2005). In Lithuania, with a far smaller Russophone population, ethnic politics has been dominated by a Polish-Lithuanian cleavage. Voting across ethnic lines has not been commonplace in national elections.[8]

Another characteristic of the political environment is the theme of existential threat, with fears that accession to power of one group threatens the survival of the language, culture, and community of the other. While the politics of memory does not constitute the entirety of this problem, the fractured remembrance of the past lends itself to a political climate that is inimical to compromise and easier for elites to manipulate for their own political purposes. Writing on the Latvian case, Pridham points out that "[democratic] consolidation takes longer to achieve, as it is a deeper process than democratic transition" (2009, 468). No less critically, he notes, "a basic problem facing Latvian democracy" is "the conflict and tension between traditional elements and modernizing tendencies." Among the former he counts "difficult historical memories, which have continued up to the present day to remain powerful…and focused on the question of the Soviet experience" (487).

Third, contestation over narratives of the past can be linked to individual episodes of civil disorder, as was the case in Estonia around the Bronze Soldier incident. However, ethnic tensions around irreconcilable positions on history and memory have, arguably, been balanced by other factors in society, including long-standing sites of integration like the workplace and family (in Latvia, for instance, rates of ethnic intermarriage are high). Arguably, the halting, but still notable, rise of a middle class has also contributed to social stability. However, as demonstrated by the Latvian referendum in February 2102 on making Russian a second official language, ethnic tensions continue to be part of the Baltic context. The failed effort to establish a second national language, which garnered only about a quarter of the vote, reflected a political and social environment still deeply permeated by both historical and contemporary divisions.

Shaped by the forces of history, as well as contemporary politics, economics, and social processes, mnemonic actors have brought to Baltic commemorations differing visions of the past, underpinning the opening of battle fronts over memories, particularly of World War II. In addition, as Latvia's case highlights, memory politics has fostered the evolution of the commemorative spectacle, which brings the past into the present in form while emptying it of substance. Between these extremes, the Baltics have seen commemorations that evoked both euphoria and critique. Commemorations in the Baltics carry the burdens of fractured contemporary politics and societies. Whether the politics of memory, in which these commemorations are rooted, carries the seeds of continued ethnic, economic, and political atomization or the potential for broader societal reconciliation remains to be seen, perhaps in the next twenty years.

NOTES

This work was supported in part by the European Social Fund via its "Support for Doctoral Studies at University of Latvia" program, as well as by the Latvian National Research Program's "National Identity" subproject "Latvian Social Memory and Identity."

1. This refers to trade wars over commodities in post-communist Baltic markets.

2. Other shared events included the flights of powered paragliders, which took to the air and crossed the three countries between August 17 and August 22, 2009. The only shared event that was organized exclusively by civil society was the Baltic Chain Run, a two-day motorcycle tour of the route organized by the Estonian Motorcycle Club.

3. Ushakov's participation earned a mixed reception from Latvians. On the one hand, his participation and the fact that he laid flowers at the Freedom Monument were positively noted. On the other hand, it was pointed out that his party, Saskaņas centrs (Harmony Center Party), has

been among the Russian-oriented political organizations unwilling to recognize and condemn the 1940 occupation of the Baltics.

4. Deep White earned the "Best international communications campaign for 2009" award for the Heartbeats project at the Baltic PR Awards 2010 (Deep White Public Relations 2010).

5. The Bronze Soldier statue in Tallinn (known in the Soviet period as the "Monument to the Liberators of Tallinn" and sometimes referred to by the Russian-speaking population as *Alyosha*) has become the object of intense conflict, which is the product of acutely different understandings of what the statue represents historically. From the viewpoint of many ethnic Estonians, the Bronze Soldier is a symbol of Soviet occupation and repression, but from the viewpoint of Estonia's Russian-speaking community and the Russian state, it is a symbol of Soviet victory over Nazi Germany in World War II and also, at least recently, a symbol of equal rights in Estonia. In April 2007, the Estonian government undertook preparations for the relocation of the statue from the city center of Tallinn to the Military Cemetery on the outskirts of the city. Disagreement over this action led to two nights of riots that resulted in one death and multiple injuries. The relocation also earned the condemnation of the Russian government. At an emergency meeting, the Estonian government opted to relocate the statue immediately because of security concerns. On April 30, the statue was placed at the Cemetery of the Estonian Defense Forces in Tallinn, where it continues to be the object of commemorations on May 9, Soviet Victory Day (Brüggemann and Kasekamp 2008; Lehti, Jutila, and Jokisipila 2008; Kattago 2008; Smith 2008).

6. This section does not include a discussion of Lithuania because that country emphasized the anniversary of March 11, 1990, the day when Lithuania's semi-autonomous parliament became the first in the USSR to declare independence (though this was not recognized by Soviet authorities in Moscow). On that day, a special session of parliament recognized Soviet-era dissident leader Vytautas Landsbergis, who later became independent Lithuania's first president.

7. Survey respondents included 1,000 inhabitants of Latvia, 623 of whom were Latvians.

8. The pattern of ethnically divided voting shifted somewhat in Latvia in the 2009 local election of Nil Ushakov, a member of the Russian-dominated Harmony Center Party, to the post of mayor in Riga. In research done by the Marketing and Public Opinion Center (SKDS) in 2011, Ushakov earned positive ratings from 81.7 percent of Russian and 58 percent of Latvian residents of Riga (Stankēviča 2009). Ethnically split voting, however, remains characteristic of national elections, as the 2011 parliamentary election demonstrated.

7 Memories of the Past and Visions of the Future

REMEMBERING THE SOVIET ERA AND ITS END IN UKRAINE

Oxana Shevel

Independence in 1991: Gained, Gifted, or a Bit of Both?

August 2011 marked the twentieth anniversary of the historic vote for state independence in the parliament of the former Ukrainian Soviet Socialist Republic. On August 24, 1991, days after the failure of the conservative coup in Moscow, the Ukrainian republic's legislature voted 346 to 1 for the Declaration of Independence. A referendum to confirm the vote for national independence took place on December 1, 1991, when a hugely impressive 90.3 percent voted "yes" with a high turnout of 84 percent. Every region (*oblast*) of Ukraine voted "yes," even a majority in the ethnically Russian Crimean peninsula (54 percent).[1] On the basis of these figures alone, one might conclude that the 1991 independence was overwhelmingly supported by both the Ukrainian political elite and the citizenry, and that the twentieth anniversary of this event therefore must have been a broadly celebrated national holiday marking the historical realization of popular will. In reality, however, the events of 1991 were a more complicated story, and commemoration of these events twenty years later could therefore range from celebration, to mourning, to various reactions in between.

Several contentious issues surrounded the attainment of state independence and the end of the communist era in Ukraine. From the time the Soviet regime was consolidated across Ukraine after World War II, following the suppression of pro-independence and anti-communist armed insurrection in western Ukraine by the late 1940s to early 1950s, and until Gorbachev came to power and introduced the new electoral politics in 1989–1990, only a small group of Ukrainian dissidents dared to dream of Ukrainian state independence.[2] Even within the dissident movement, the main preoccupation was Ukrainian cultural and linguistic preservation and survival in the face of the increasing predominance of the Russian language and the Soviet-Russian culture, especially in large cities in central and southeastern Ukraine. The mainstream of Ukrainian dissent in the 1960s and the 1970s pursued a "legalistic approach"—working within the system (rather than seeking to overthrow it), with the goal of forcing the Soviet state to abide by its declared commitments to individual and national rights (Kuzio and Wilson 1994, 54–55).[3]

The rise of Mikhail Gorbachev to the post of general secretary of the Soviet Communist Party in 1985 brought fundamental changes to the power and politics at the center and in the republics, changing the realm of the possible, especially between 1989 and 1990, when events accelerated enormously and Ukrainian state independence ultimately became a reality. As Gorbachev slowly loosened the constraints on political discourse, the notoriously conservative Ukrainian Communist Party found itself challenged by the national opposition movement, Rukh. Rukh, or the Ukrainian Popular Movement in Support of Perestroika, was formed in 1989 by former dissidents and Kyiv-based Ukrainian cultural elites. Conceived originally as a popular movement in support of Gorbachev's perestroika, in 1990 Rukh dropped the words "in Support of Perestroika" from its name and became the main social and political force advocating the independence of the Ukrainian state. In the March 1990 elections to the Ukrainian Supreme Soviet pro-independence candidates won between 25 and 30 percent of the seats; for the first time, the Ukrainian Supreme Soviet became a real parliament where the Communist majority had to contend with a small[4] but not inconsequential, and increasingly vocal, "national-democratic" opposition.

Until the end of the Soviet era, attitudes toward Soviet rule and Ukraine's political status (continued membership in the union or independence) remained ambiguous, and Ukraine in general lacked the clear trajectory of the Baltic republics toward separation from the USSR. Rukh's base of support was regionally skewed. In the 1990 elections Rukh-supported candidates won almost every seat in Galicia in western Ukraine, and did well in another western region with a shorter history of Soviet rule, Volhynia. It also had strong showing in the capital, Kyiv, and in some other urban centers in central Ukraine, but not in the south or in the east.[5] The ambiguity of popular attitudes toward independence was also evident during the March 1991 referendum called by Gorbachev to help gather support for his proposed new

PICTURE 7.1 Kyiv, Ukraine, August 1991. Ukrainians cheer the declaration of independence by the parliament (Verkhovna Rada of Ukraine).
Source: Photo/Ukrinform.

version of a union treaty to preserve the USSR. In this referendum, Ukrainian voters declared themselves to be in favor of both Ukrainian sovereignty and continued membership in the Soviet Union.[6]

The overwhelming votes for independence just a few months later—legislative in August 1991 (Picture 7.1) and popular in December 1991—was not caused by a dramatic growth of "national" sentiment in the population or the growth of political power of national-democrats in the Ukrainian parliament. Rukh did not have the strength to win independence on its own, and the Ukrainian communist elite remained entrenched. However, responding to the new electoral politics introduced by the 1990 elections, by the end of 1990, the Ukrainian communist elite effectively split into Soviet loyalists and national communists. As many scholars of Ukraine observed, it was the collapse of central authority in Moscow, following the abortive August 1991 coup, and the subsequent decision of the national communists (such as the chairman of the parliament, Leonid Kravchuk) to cast their lot with pro-independence forces that made Ukrainian state independence a reality (D'Anieri 2007; Wilson 2000). Popular vote for independence during a referendum on December 1, 1991, was massive, with 90.3 percent in favor and 84.2 percent turnout, but for many, if not most, the main motivation was hope for economic improvement, not national or cultural rebirth. Rukh skillfully campaigned with the message that Ukraine was economically exploited by the union center and would

НІ – НОВОМУ СОЮЗНОМУ ДОГОВОРУ!

Всі, хто не хоче,
щоб Україна
була колонією,

ГОЛОСУЙТЕ ПРОТИ
ІМПЕРСЬКОЇ
ФЕДЕРАТИВНОЇ
СОЮЗНОЇ УГОДИ!

Тільки НЕЗАЛЕЖНА
УКРАЇНСЬКА ДЕРЖАВА
забезпечить життя та безсмертя
НАРОДУ УКРАЇНИ.
Голосуйте за це!
Голосуйте за співдружність
незалежних держав!

PICTURE 7.2 Ukraine, February 1991. "No to the Union Treaty!" Rukh leaflet against Gorbachev's referendum on preservation of the USSR.

Source: Photo/Vakhtang Kipiani.

become "a second France" once it was free to decide its own affairs, and transmitted this message, backed by economic statistics, in its campaign leaflets (Picture 7.2).[7]

Polls conducted one month before the referendum found that 79 percent of voters saw "escape from economic crisis" as the top priority, 63 percent "stabilization of the economy and better standards of living," while only 21 percent listed "the cultural rebirth of Ukraine" and 18 percent "the securing of political sovereignty of the republic."[8]

Given the messy combination of factors behind the attainment of independence in 1991, coupled with the economic collapse that followed independence and the continued poverty, social inequality, and corruption, it is hardly surprising that a number of different narratives of the independence of 1991 have been constructed. Was Ukrainian state independence, gained in 1991, a culmination of decades (or even centuries) of a "national-liberation" struggle by Ukrainian patriots? Or was it merely a present to Ukraine granted by largely external events and persons? Was it liberation from the Soviet-Russian yoke and the attainment of "natural" nation-state status for an objectively existing distinct Ukrainian nation, or was it a historical tragedy, "the greatest geopolitical catastrophe of the 20th century," to quote Russia's President Putin (Kuchins 2005), because it separated not just a single communist state but tore apart an "authentic" Slavic nation composed of Russians, Ukrainians, and Belarussians? Are Ukrainians better off now, in an independent but poor and corrupt state, or were they better off during the "golden age" of Brezhnev-era stagnation and state-guaranteed social protections? In no small part the politics of memory in Ukraine centers on such alternative interpretations of the Soviet past, and there is no consensus either at the societal or the elite level on these issues. Alternative interpretations of the Soviet era—and by extension different attitudes to the events of 1991 (is it an anniversary to be celebrated or to be mourned?)—were evident in the 1991 commemorations.

The Twentieth Anniversary of Independence: Celebration or Mourning?

The twentieth anniversary of independence was celebrated in August 2011, shortly after a tectonic political shift in Ukraine—the victory of Viktor Yanukovych in the 2010 presidential elections. After losing his bid for presidency in 2004 following the Orange revolution, he narrowly defeated Yulia Tymoshenko, the former ally (turned bitter rival) of outgoing president Viktor Yushchenko. In September 2010, the Constitutional Court had boosted the powers of the president and had turned Ukraine back into a presidential republic by reversing a reform introduced in 2004 that curbed presidential powers in favor of parliament, and Tymoshenko and a number of other high-ranking government officials from the "Orange period" were in jail awaiting trial on politically motivated charges of corruption and abuse of office.

The political climate of power grab by president Yanukovych and the opposition's scrambling to resist it directly affected the twentieth anniversary of independence celebrations. While the government arranged for street festivities and concerts to mark the anniversary, courts in Kyiv, Donetsk, and other cities banned the opposition from holding alternative public marches to commemorate independence. In Kyiv, several thousand supporters of the opposition were barred by police at the eleventh hour from walking along one of the main streets, and clashes between police and the marchers ensued. The opposition-organized march was headed by members of the competitively elected Ukrainian parliament that voted for independence in 1991. The fact that the riot police prevented these "fathers" of independence from peacefully marching through the capital city on the twentieth anniversary of independence was decried by the opposition as a manifestation of cynicism and the anti-Ukrainian nature of the Yanukovych government.[9]

In addition to the public festivities and clashes, the marking of the twentieth anniversary of independence was also prominent in the media, where assessments were, not unsurprisingly, mixed. In its issue dedicated to the twentieth anniversary of

Ukraine's independence in August 2011, the lead article in *Dzerkalo Tyzhnia (Mirror Weekly)*, the most respected Ukrainian weekly, consisted of nothing but a list of dry facts: Twenty years since it became an independent state, Ukraine ranked first in the world in child alcoholism; first in Europe in HIV-AIDS infection rate among adults; second in the world in the amount of debt owed to the IMF; 69th in the world in the Human Development Index (HDI); 110th out of 177 states in level of wealth; 131st out of 180 in freedom of speech; 134th out of 180 in level of corruption; and the list went on and on (Kotliar 2011b). Another popular news portal, *Zahid. net*, illustrated its articles dedicated to the twentieth anniversary of independence with a picture of rakes under the Ukrainian flag, alluding to a common saying about repeatedly stepping on a rake (*Zahid.net* 2011).

Needless to say, the message was pessimistic—there is little to celebrate. After twenty years as an independent state, Ukraine had little to show. To drive the point home, *Dzerkalo Tyzhnia* also published a selection of leaflets distributed by Rukh on the eve of the 1991 independence referendum. The leaflets promised that independence will bring economic prosperity: "We produce at the level of European states, but earn five to seven times less than the Europeans"; "Ukraine is a European country on the basis of its capacity, Moscow's colony in reality"; and "We are poor because we are not free. To be rich we have to be independent."

Given the unfulfilled hopes and expectations and grim socioeconomic reality twenty years after independence, the twentieth anniversary was more of a somber milestone than a cause for celebration. This was the message emphasized in many commentaries on August 1991, but it was not the only message. Commentary in the media also highlighted some achievements of independence, while sociologists released opinion polls that showed solid, and by some accounts growing, support for independence among Ukrainian citizens. Among its achievements as an independent state, Ukraine can count the maintenance of interethnic peace in a regionally, ethnically, linguistically, and religiously divided society that many expected to become the second Yugoslavia at the time independence was declared. Preservation of territorial integrity and state independence itself was another oft-cited achievement, as well as peaceful changes in political leadership. Ukraine was the first non-Baltic post-Soviet state where an incumbent president lost and stepped down in competitive elections in 1994 (Kravchuk); since then, three more elections for the top office took place, with two more incumbents, Kuchma and Yushchenko, peacefully leaving office (albeit not without a political crisis at the end of Kuchma's second term in 2004). Polls conducted on the eve of the twentieth anniversary registered substantial support for independence—the highest in twenty years, according to the Razumkov Center poll,[10] and also an increase in the number of people who are proud of being Ukrainian and whose main identity is as a citizen of Ukraine.[11]

Growing nationwide acceptance of state symbols, in particular the blue and yellow national flag demonized in the Soviet period as a symbol of anti-Soviet Ukrainian nationalism, is also an important trend. As one commentator remarked, "not only in Lviv, but also in Donetsk and Crimea people are cheering for the national team with the blue and yellow flag. At the beginning of the 1990s this would have been nonsense" (Fesenko 2011).

The twentieth anniversary commemorations show clearly that the Soviet period and its end in Ukraine were remembered very ambiguously. This is due not only to the mixed record of twenty years of independence but also to historically formed regional divisions, with the Russian-speaking southeast of the country and Ukrainian-speaking center-west diverging in attitude on a number of issues, including the Soviet past. This arguably makes creation of a *national* mnemonic field more complicated in Ukraine than in many other post-communist states. Memory politics is particularly contentious in Ukraine due to the fact that many of the competing mnemonic actors at the elite level fit the definition of *mnemonic warriors* (to use Kubik and Bernhard's typology from Chapter 1) who see the content of collective memory as non-negotiable, and who see themselves as the proprietors of the "true" vision of the past.

Given that mnemonic actors among the political elite construct visions of the past to legitimize their efforts to gain and hold power, the response of the public to elite offerings is a fundamental component of the memory regime. This chapter will thus analyze memory politics and the menmonic field in Ukraine at two levels—the state level, where political elites engage in memory construction, and the societal level, where the public reacts to the elites' mnemonic proposals. In democratic societies, social organizations often offer alternatives to the constructs of the state-sponsored memory regimes on a variety of issues. In Ukraine to date, the public has been largely on the receiving end, although in the years following the 2004 Orange revolution a group of Ukrainian historians did organize and offer an alternative vision of history that will be discussed later in this chapter.

At the state level, mnemonic warriors dominate the political action in the field of memory regimes construction, and each group of warriors is striving to establish a unified mnemonic field where their view of the past will be the hegemonic one. However, given the attitudes to the past displayed by the Ukrainian citizens, the efforts of mnemonic warriors cannot be characterized as successful. Instead of a *unified/hegemonic* mnemonic field that each group of mnemonic warriors has aspired to create, the mnemonic field in post-independence Ukraine has instead been *fractured and contentious*, with each version of history offered by the elites resonating with some but being rejected by other Ukrainian citizens. Examination of popular attitudes suggests, however, that *pillarized* memory regimes may be possible in Ukraine, even on the most contentious issues. As will be discussed later, public attitudes may support the emergence of a mnemonic field where different views of the past and visions of history are perceived as legitimate, and holders of views opposite to one's own are not demonized and delegitimized in the public space but by contrast are engaged in dialogue. According to Kubik and Bernhard, *mnemonic pluralists* are the type of (usually elite) political actors who foster this kind of mnemonic field, but in Ukraine such actors are largely absent. At the same time, opinion polls show that a substantial part of the population is *ambivalent* about the contested historical past (rather than siding up firmly with one or another camp of mnemonic warriors). The last section of this chapter will discuss how this state of popular mnemonic ambivalence offers possibilities for the potential future emergence of pillarized memory regimes.

Mnemonic Actors and Elite-Level Memory Politics

As Kubik and Bernhard point out, memory regimes around particular historical events are products of struggles between politically relevant actors who formulate and propagate a specific vision of the past. In democracies the key politically relevant actors are political parties, but in the post-Soviet context, where parties are weak and the party system highly fluid, scholars have conceptualized politically relevant actors in terms of political camps rather than political parties as such. In Ukraine, the three main political camps have been the Left, dominated by the unreformed communists; the nationalist and national-democratic Right; and the amorphous Center, dominated by former apparatchiks and the succession of parties of power they have formed.[12] The constructed views of the Soviet past in general, and of the independence in particular, by these actors could not be more different.

The main political actor within the Ukrainian Left has been the orthodox Communist Party of Ukraine (KPU). The KPU has not evolved much ideologically since the Soviet era and continues to oppose market capitalism and Western-oriented foreign policy. A monograph on the Ukrainian Left published in 2000 concluded that "KPU evolution in the ideological sphere is not very noticeable" (Haran and Maiboroda 2000, 65). Another analysis has noted how KPU "has remained completely loyal to the Soviet past" (Wilson 2002, 31), has shown "precious little loyalty to the new Ukraine" (ibid., 33).[13] Its leaders also describe themselves as "Soviet patriots."[14] Seeing the Ukrainian nation as constituent members of the "Slavic-Orthodox civilization" and/or a component of the single "Soviet people," the KPU laments both the collapse of the unified Soviet state and of state socialism. The KPU thus juxtaposes the Soviet era as an unambiguously positive period and Ukrainian independence as an unambiguously negative period. This attitude is clearly evident in statements by Petro Symonenko, the KPU leader. Symonenko has argued that the real independence day for Ukraine is not August 24, 1991 when the Ukrainian parliament declared independence, but November 7, 1917, the day of the Bolshevik revolution. November 7, Symonenko contends, is "the main holiday" for Ukraine, "essentially the independence day," and that "there is no other day that marks the beginning of Ukrainian state independence" (*Novynar.com.ua* 2010).[15] By contrast, August 24, the official Independence Day, can be celebrated, according to the leader of the Ukrainian communists, "only by representatives of big oligarchic capital and their lobbyists in government organs for whom these two decades [since independence] were marked by successful appropriation (*prykhvatyzatsia*) of people's property," as well as by "national-fascist clowns of different varieties" who "for twenty years are slobbering essentially a fascist slogan—'Ukraine for the Ukrainians,' and under this slogan robbing the motherland and sowing antagonism and xenophobia" (*Komunist* 2011). The message of the Left is clear and unambiguous—thumbs up for the Soviet era, thumbs down for independence. This message could not be more different from the one expressed by the Right.

Within the Ukrainian Right, the political party Rukh, the successor of the perestroika-era pro-independence popular movement, was the main actor in the 1990s. Its breakup led to the emergence of several Right and Center-Right parties, of which the Our Ukraine party has been most significant in the second decade of independence. Ideologically, the Ukrainian Right has been the polar opposite of the Ukrainian Left on virtually every issue, from economic reforms to foreign policy, and this opposition is reflected in its position toward the Soviet past. At the heart of the Right's view on the Ukrainian nation and the Ukrainian state is, first and foremost, the emphasis on the distinctiveness of Ukraine and Ukrainians from Russia and the Russians. Russia is presented as the main "other" against which Ukrainian identity is defined, an occupying empire (Tsarist and later Soviet) from which Ukraine's independence was finally regained in 1991.[16] The Right's vision of Ukrainian history is that of a centuries-old national-liberation struggle from various occupiers (Poles, Tatars, and above all, Russians) that brought only brief periods of independence in the past (the Kievan Rus', the Cossack republic of the seventeenth century, the Ukrainian Republic of 1917–1921). In 1991 the dream of independent statehood was eventually realized.

With Ukrainian state independence being a sacred value for the Right, the twentieth anniversary of this independence was indisputably a milestone to welcome and to celebrate. The holiday, however, was bittersweet, since the realities of independent Ukraine turned out to be quite different from what the Right had desired when Rukh spearheaded the drive for autonomy and eventually independence in the late

1980s and the early 1990s. This mix of celebration and disappointment is evident in the statements issued by political actors of the Right on the occasion of the twentieth anniversary of August 1991. For example, a letter signed by the leaders of a number of right of center political groups and parties lauds the fact that independence declared on August 24, 1991, lasted, and that "Ukraine has been recognized by the world community as an independent state with borders, national symbols, its own body of laws, Constitution, and armed forces" (*Volyn'* 2011). At the same time, the statement qualified those sentiments. Ukrainian independence, for which the signatories, including Rukh's founders, had fought, was meant to be "Ukrainian in substance, socially just, and democratic, with the subordination in practice of the members of parliament, the Presidents, and the government as a whole to the Ukrainian voters." This, however, did not happen, and the reason for this, as far as the Right is concerned, is the continued dominance by Soviet-era elites who have controlled the top echelons of Ukraine's leadership during the post-independence period. These "products of the Soviet party-nomenklatura system...only manipulated the principles of statehood, without any intention to implement them. Instead, they robbed and appropriated communal property and created a clan-oligarchic system" (*Volyn'* 2011).

The above quotes make it clear that in the early twenty-first century the Left and the Right in Ukraine are antagonists who hold diametrically opposed positions on the Soviet past and who advocate diametrically opposite versions of historical memory. Each sees history in black and white terms, and each sees itself as the proprietor of the "true" vision of the past that needs to be transmitted and accepted by others. As such, the Left and the Right are clearly mnemonic warriors.

The third group of political elites in Ukraine is the amorphous centrists, dominated by the former apparatchiks, often referred to as the party of power. A defining feature of the "party of power" is ideological amorphousness. As Wilson put it, "the center...never had much of an identity of its own, [and] has been occupied by virtual politics, a shifting kaleidoscope of clan groups, shadowy business and old *nomenklatura* interests" (Wilson 2000, 185).

In terms of Kubik and Bernhard's typology, Ukrainian centrist elites are *mnemonic abnegators*—actors who avoid memory politics either because they are uninterested or see no advantage in engaging in them. Ukrainian "centrists" fit this definition because the old apparatchiks and the new businessmen who dominate political parties comprising the center are indeed uninterested in thinking in terms of mythical time and instead focus on the present. As mnemonic abnegators, the centrist elites have never offered any original approach to historical memory or its own vision of the country's past. Nevertheless, the centrists participate in cultural and mnemonic wars instrumentally. In their approach to historical memory, the centrist elites lean toward either the Left's or the Right's versions of history, depending on the political and electoral environment at the time. The Center could not afford to act as a true mnemonic abnegator in the post-independence period because, even though the party of power has been a dominant force in the political arena, it was not quite strong enough to command a parliamentary majority on its own.[17] The centrist elites therefore had to make alliances either with the communists and the Left, or with national-democrats and the Right. In electoral terms, it was equivalent to seeking voter support either in the southeast or the center-west of the country. Given that among the centrist political parties there has never been much differentiation on programmatic issues—all claim to support a market economy with high social standards, democracy, European values, and constructive friendly relations with Russia[18]—centrist political elites had no qualms about using and abusing historical and cultural hot button issues to mobilize supporters and reap political and electoral profits. In sum, in their view of the Soviet past, the centrists tend to avoid controversy when they can and act instrumentally when they cannot. Thus, President Yanukovych's article in the issue of *Mirror Weekly* on the eve of the twentieth anniversary of Ukrainian independence was full of clichés, self-praise, and attempts to convey optimism. Pretentiously titled "Ukraine Is 20 Years Old: Our Path Is Just Beginning," the article is peppered with clichéd references to "European values," "European choice," the goal of a "democratic and prosperous Ukraine," and "the unifying force of the independence idea" (Yanukovych 2011). It talks about society's "ongoing struggle to overcome Soviet legacy," and asserts that "romantic fascination" with the fact of independence (presumably by the national-democrats) had to give way to "concrete steps and pragmatic approach" (with the capable pragmatics being the centrist elites). There is neither explicit condemnation of the Soviet past (beyond a reference to unspecified "legacies" to be overcome), nor praising of the Soviet era.

The wholesale rejection of the Soviet past, its wholesale embrace, and the "centrist" neither-nor position without any coherent message of its own have been and remain the three main memory regime options for the remembering of the Soviet era in Ukraine. In the 1990s and the early 2000s, these three options were clearly associated with, respectively, Rukh, the communist party, and the oligarchic parties of power. In the subsequent period—from the time of the 2004 Orange revolution and beyond—the three memory regime offerings have remained unchanged and continue to be the only three options offered by the political elites, but the association of each option with the Right or Left opposition or the power-holding center, respectively, has changed.

One of the main changes brought about by the Orange revolution and the election of Viktor Yushchenko as president in 2004 was that, for the first time, the power-holding group in the country was not the ideologically amorphous "centrist"

Soviet-era nomenklatura that had only an instrumental interest in the questions of historical memory. Instead, from 2004 to 2010, much (although not all) of the ruling elite group—most notably the president himself—subscribed to the version of the past advocated by the Right, and made historical memory central to their political agenda. Yushchenko personally saw the inculcation of the nation into the "proper" version of collective memory as a priority. He remarked in a television appearance: "What is Ukraine if it has different views even on history?" (*President. gov.ua* 2008).

The mnemonic agenda of Yushchenko's presidency included a campaign to recognize the 1932–1933 killer famine unleashed by Stalin on Ukraine as a genocide of the Ukrainian nation (an interpretation vehemently opposed by Russia and by the Ukrainian communists), as well as attempts to revise the Soviet-era interpretations of World War II, in particular the assessment of the Ukrainian nationalist organizations such as the Organization of Ukrainian Nationalists (OUN) and its military wing, the Ukrainian Insurgent Army (UPA).[19] In what was arguably the most controversial decision of his presidency, during its final weeks, Yushchenko awarded posthumously the Hero of Ukraine title, the highest state honor, to the leader of the OUN, Stepan Bandera. Earlier he had conferred the same honor on the UPA commander-in-chief Roman Shukhevych. The OUN and UPA fought for an independent Ukrainian state against the Soviet forces well into the 1950s, and the award was conferred for "defending national ideas and battling for an independent Ukrainian state." The move was controversial and drew condemnation internationally because many members of the OUN and the UPA were also implicated in the Holocaust and the murder of Polish and Ukrainian civilians in western Ukraine.[20] Within Ukraine, anger at Yushchenko's decrees and rejection of the OUN and the UPA generally had rather different roots. In the Soviet era, the Jewish victims of the Holocaust were subsumed in the category of "peaceful Soviet citizens" in the official discourse, and the Ukrainian-Polish conflict of the war period and UPA's role in it was also a blank spot in the official narrative of the war. Instead, it was the OUN and the UPA's fight against Soviet forces and history of violent resistance to Soviet control of Ukraine in the 1940s and 1950s that alienated those attached to the Soviet narrative of the war, concentrated in the south and east of the country. Yushchenko did little to integrate these regions into his vision of Ukrainian identity on this and many other issues as well.[21]

The embrace of the Right's position by those in power following the 2004 Orange revolution was something new in Ukraine. Moreover, the new mnemonic position of the president and pro-presidential political elites played a role in the collapse of the "Orange" coalition and the bitter rivalry that emerged between president Yushchenko and his one-time ally and former prime minister Yulia

Tymoshenko. While their rivalry revolved around a struggle for political power, memory issues were also salient, as Yushchenko and his supporters on the Right viewed Tymoshenko and her party as not "pro-Ukrainian" enough on national and cultural issues (which in part also explains her narrow loss to Yanukovych in the 2010 presidential race).[22] Tymoshenko and those around her, however, never articulated any alternative conception of the past. Instead, for her, just as for the quasi-centrists of the Kuchma era, historical memory issues were of secondary importance—something to be mindful of only inasmuch as they affected their electoral fortunes and the first-order concerns of maintaining and increasing political and economic power.

When Victor Yanukovych assumed the presidency in 2010, the ideology of the power-holding class swung sharply to the Left. As far as its attitude toward the Soviet era, the Yanukovych regime is a return to amorphous centrism, compared to Yushchenko. Yanukovych's twentieth anniversary speech discussed earlier is a case in point. At the same time, rather than returning to Kuchma's role as the main arbiter between clans and groups, including the interpretation of the past, Yanukovch embraced the "Russian-Soviet-East Slavonic identity" to a greater extent than had either Kuchma or his predecessor Leonid Kravchuk (Riabchuk 2012, 445). While Yanukovych personally demonstrates much less interest in the politics of memory than did Yushchenko, instead of striking the familiar "centrist" tune of maintaining social stability, advancing modernization, and "improving livelihood today," he occasionally engages in memory politics. For example, he spoke against Yushchenko's honoring of Bandera and Shukhevych, and the decrees were repealed in court shortly after Yanukovych became president, although the stated rationale was juridical rather than political or moral.[23] Yanukovych also spoke against the interpretation of the 1932–1933 famine as a genocide of Ukrainians, recasting it instead as a "common tragedy of the people of the USSR" (BBC, 2010)—this characterization has long been Russia's position—and signed a law authorizing the official use of the Soviet flag in Ukraine during Victory Day celebrations (May 9). Active revision of the official history and its teaching in schools has also taken place during Yanukovych's tenure following the appointment of a notorious Ukrainophobe, Dmytro Tabachnyk, as Minister of Education (Kapliuk, 2010).

Given that two of the three main elite actors in Ukraine are clearly mnemonic warriors (the Left and the Right), the memory regimes produced at the elite level are best characterized as fractured/contentious. This has been the case throughout the independence period. The period after the Orange revolution was different inasmuch as the governing elites were not "centrists" but a mixture of Right and Center, but the nature of the mnemonic field produced by state policies was still divisive and contentious. Even if one could argue that during Yushchenko's tenure the national mnemonic field was particularly contentious, during all periods (pre-Orange revolution, the Orange period, and post-Orange revolution) the mnemonic field was fractured and contentious due to the consistent articulation of two distinct, coherent, and contradictory historical narratives by elite actors who saw themselves as proprietors of the "true" vision of Ukraine's past. The mnemonic warriors of the Left and the Right have sought to convince others, including society at large, to accept their vision of the "true" past, but it has proven difficult to do. The "centrists" have tried to cast themselves as moderates, but their message has been both muddled and unconvincing. Ultimately, each of the three main actors in memory politics in Ukraine has been repeatedly criticized by opponents, as well as by more neutral commentators, for espousing exclusionary versions of the past, and/or for being downright hypocritical.

For example, the communists' criticism of the "oligarchs" and praise of the Soviet system as an embodiment of popular interest does not square with either the well-known realities of the Soviet system, when the nomenklatura enjoyed perks and privileges inaccessible to the majority of the people, or the current lavish lifestyle of the KPU leaders, or the KPU's position vis-à-vis the "oligarchic" parties. KPU leader Petro Symonenko reportedly lives in a luxurious mansion with a marble balustrade and an underground garage (Gomon 2010), and his party has been a reliable ally of the "oligarchic" parties in the Ukrainian parliament.

The version of the past championed by the Ukrainian Right—demonizing all things Soviet and stressing Ukrainian/Russian distinction and historical opposition—is also of limited appeal in contemporary Ukrainian society. Perpetual economic crisis and the collapse of living standards and the social safety net following independence can create nostalgia for the late Soviet era, not only for supporters of the KPU but for ideologically non-committed citizens as well. This yearning for the social safety of the Soviet era is indeed shared by many Ukrainians, especially, but not exclusively, older citizens.

In a society where many are bilingual and bicultural, a weariness of the Right's vision of Ukraine and Russia as "others" has set in. The cultural image of Ukraine espoused by the Right, "a romantic, essentially peasant, and premodern Ukraine—white cottages, embroidered shirts, 'beetles buzzing above the cherry trees,' one Ukrainian language, etc." (Dutsyk 2011) has a limited appeal in contemporary society, among both the bicultural plurality and Ukraine's smaller ethnic minorities.

The self-proclaimed centrists have not done much better than the Left and the Right as far as winning over society with their vision of the "true" past. For one, the Center has not articulated any distinct image of the past, while the attempts of the elites from the parties of power to speak of the Soviet past in "centrist" terms have for the most part rung hollow. In a caustic response to President Yanukovych's article on the twentieth anniversary of independence, one public intellectual spelled out just how the ruling elite's message is unconvincing:

> From the president's article we learn, that "the harsh reality ruined hopes for the fast improvement of living conditions, and for rapid construction of free and prosperous society and law-based democratic state." But the president, naturally, does not mention who was and remains the main creator of this mythically impersonal "reality." Moreover, he does not mention that this mysterious 'reality' ruined the hopes of his fellow citizens quite selectively: for some reason neither Viktor Fedorovych himself, nor all of his buddies who successively appropriated Ukraine during the last twenty years, have suffered one bit from this wretched "reality." Quite the opposite in fact—thanks to independence, all of their "hopes for the fast improvement in living conditions" were realized to the fullest measure. We also learn from the president's article that "for several decades now our society is struggling to overcome the Soviet legacy." The president again is shyly quiet about his own role in the overcoming of this "legacy." He does not mention either his own signature under the decree returning the red Soviet flags to the official use, or progressive re-Sovietization of school textbooks by the Ukrainophobic [education] minister, or the remaking of the so-called "Ukrainian Security Service" into a de-facto KGB, or the continued existence of numerous monuments to the Bolshevik vampires and places and streets named after them. (Riabchuk 2011)

The next section will consider to what extent the memory regimes articulated by the Ukrainian political elites resonate with the Ukrainian public, and how the elites' failure to impose any one memory regime on the public may in fact enable pillarized memory regime in Ukraine.

Popular Reception of Elite Offerings: Ambivalent Society and the Prospects for a Pillarized Mnemonic Field

With key elite mnemonic actors in Ukraine composed of two sets of mnemonic warriors (communist and nationalist) and a power-holding Center that prefers strategic abnegation, a fractured and contentious memory field has been consistent throughout the twenty years of independence. Because of the more pluralistic nature of Ukrainian politics (in comparison to Russia and Belarus), its ethnolinguistic and regional diversity, and the presence of strong political opposition (no matter whether the party of power rules in alliance with the Right or the Left), mnemonic warriors have not been able to establish mnemonic hegemony.[24] The oscillation of political power has resulted in the rotation of mnemonic warriors, each trying but ultimately failing to firmly establish their vision of the past throughout the society at large.

Ukraine may not be doomed, however, to perpetual memory wars, but might be able to move toward a pillarized mnemonic field where, Kubik and Bernhard assert, "competing visions of the past 'peacefully coexist'" and where "[m]nemonic actors either accept this state of affairs or engage in a dialogue whose goal is a compromise in the form of a mnemonic reconciliation." Such a mnemonic field is not only more conducive to political pluralism and democracy; it is arguably the only sustainable one in a society such as Ukraine that features multiple historical, ethnic, linguistic, and cultural experiences and identities. One way for such a pillarized mnemonic field to emerge is for mnemonic actors to become mnemonic pluralists who recognize that others can have their own legitimate visions of the past and who believe that the others are entitled to their visions. At the moment (2013), none of the Ukrainian political actors active in memory politics is a mnemonic pluralist. Still, at the level of society there are foundations for a pillarized mnemonic field—an environment where a large share of the population is not committed to a singular vision of the "true" past and thus is potentially open to a dialogue to discover "the areas of overlap among the competing visions and to articulate a set of common *mnemonic fundamentals*"—de facto already exists.[25]

The share of mnemonic pluralists in the society can be estimated from opinion polls on contested historical events and personalities. Studies of Ukraine usually emphasize the east-west divide, which is a real, important, and persistent feature of the country (Arel 2011; Katchanovski 2006). At the same time, many scholars have cautioned against the oversimplified image of Ukraine divided in two monolithic opposing camps—Russian-speaking pro-Russian east and Ukrainina-speaking pro-Western west—by drawing attention to fractured and multilayered local, regional, and borderline identities that exist within each of the two camps (Hrytsak 2004; Portnov 2010; Richardson 2004; Zakharchenko 2013; Zhurzhenko 2002). Furthermore, even if the east and the west have strong and often opposite opinions on a variety of issues, there is also a sizable center of the country that is distinct from both the east and the west by its ambivalent attitudes and that is often overlooked by analysts of Ukraine. As opinion polls show, on virtually any hot-button contentious issue, a trifold rather than a twofold division exists in Ukraine, with the extreme west and east of the country holding for the most part opposite opinions, while the numerically large and strategically important center of the country remains ambivalent on many issues, including historical memory and the Soviet past.

One good illustration of this trifold division and ambiguity in attitudes in the geographical center is a poll that asked Ukrainians whether they support granting the fighters of the UPA the status of participants in the national-liberation struggle. The "correct" way to remember the UPA may be the single most contested issue in memory politics in post-independence Ukraine. As a nationalist anti-Soviet resistance movement, the UPA and the OUN were demonized during the Soviet period as an embodiment of anti-Soviet Ukrainian nationalism and traitors from the point of view of "Soviet motherland." Since independence, the Right has wanted to elevate the UPA and the OUN and their leaders into the pantheon of Ukrainian heroes for fighting for Ukraine's independence.

The narratives of the "OUN-UPA" issue advanced by the political elites do not give Ukrainians a choice other than "heroes and freedom fighters" or "traitors and murderers" when it comes to remembering these groups. At the same time, even on this arguably most divisive historical issue in today's Ukraine, there appears to be some room for compromise in society. A December 2007 poll asking Ukrainians if they support granting the UPA fighters the status of participants in the national-liberation struggle showed, predictably, that the east and the west sharply disagreed on the matter: in the western regions, 77 percent supported the idea, while in Donetsk and Crimea just 13 percent did.[26] The center, however, was not nearly as polarized. According to the poll, voters in central Ukraine were equally divided, with 38 percent opposing recognition while 38 percent supporting it partly or fully.

The poll gave an option not only to express support or opposition to the UPA veteran status, but to answer "difficult to say" or to answer "I support recognition [of UPA fighters as veterans] as long as the government does not impose its view on the citizens and everyone can decide whether or not to honor UPA fighters." Nationwide, these two responses gathered 18 percent and 16 percent, respectively, which can be interpreted to mean that over one-third of the population was (in 2007) potentially open to a compromised solution to the "OUN-UPA problem" and accepted the existence and the legitimacy of different memories of the OUN and the UPA. Central Ukraine again stood out as the region most open to a memory compromise, given that it had the largest share of undecided (25 percent, compared to 18 percent in Ukraine as a whole).

More research needs to be done to tap into versions of popular memory on divisive historical topics to ascertain the presence and the size of the reservoir of popular receptivity to pluralistic ways of remembering the past, how this reservoir has varied by region and perhaps by age, education, or other criteria, and what kinds of pillarized memory regimes on particular issues the public may be willing to support. Based on the data discussed in this section and on the growing body of research that highlights the layered and multidimensional identities held by many Ukrainians,[27] even if they are forced (or chose) to embrace more exclusive identities at election times, a general hypothesis can nevertheless be advanced that just as regional societal divisions have been shown to enable political "pluralism by default" in Ukraine and a more competitive politics that would not have existed otherwise (Way 2005; Brudny and Finkel 2011), these divisions also have the potential to lead to pillarized memory regimes on variety of issues. Importantly, popular mnemonic pluralism exists at the level of society by default—not because of state policies or the actions of elite actors. Whether "official" pillarized memory regimes will emerge in Ukraine remains to be seen. For such regimes to emerge, one of the two things would need to happen. First, elite action: the Ukrainian elites would have to start acting as mnemonic pluralists—something they were unable and unwilling to do so far, not least because manipulating "memory wars" is a quick shortcut to electoral mobilization when political parties are unable to differentiate themselves on other programmatic issues. Yet, if the political elites were to start acting like mnemonic pluralists, they would meet a rather receptive audience at the popular level, especially in the geographic center of the country.

As of 2014 there is no indication that any elite group is prepared to act as mnemonic pluralists. Moreover, the situation arguably became more pessimistic at the end of 2012, when in the October 2012 legislative elections, the first national-level elections since Yanukovych ascended to presidency, the ultra-nationalist Svoboda (Freedom) party had a surprisingly strong showing and became one of the two new parties in the Ukrainian parliament, capturing 37 out of 450 seats. The Euromaidan protests that began in November 2013 further polarized Ukrainian society and raised the profile of Svoboda as one of the key forces of the protest movement. The outcome of the Euromaidan protests are unknown, but it is likely that in the next election cycle historical memory will again be manipulated by political elites eager to mobilize their base.

Still, even if elites do not start acting as mnemonic pluralists, a pillarized memory regime conducive to dialogue and mutual tolerance could still emerge. This would be a second conceivable path: the elites acting as abnegators, staying off the topic of memory politics, and letting the society sort it out. If this were to happen, the benefits of a pillarized memory regime could accrue spontaneously. Without elites engaging in memory wars, the east and the west may feel less threatened that the current or prospective government will assail their "historical truth" with state power and institutions. In the absence of siege mentality in the east and the west, the live-and-let-live attitude currently characteristic of the center may begin to radiate out, as it were. Such a memory regime would not end east-west disagreements overnight, but it will enable a search for common "mnemonic fundamentals" in the society through discovering the areas of overlap among the competing visions.

So far there have not been any discernible initiatives from civil society organizations to solve memory disputes via compromise, although research in anthropology and sociology shows that at the societal level such a search for compromise is often going on spontaneously, and/or is guided by individuals such as schoolteachers.[28] That said, there has been one societal-level initiative worth mentioning. From 2007 through 2009, twelve professional historians from different regions of Ukraine held a series of meetings in which they reviewed the history textbooks used to teach history in grades seven through twelve and proposed a radically new concept for a basic history textbook. The commission put forth a detailed proposal for the content of history textbooks that was finalized in March 2010, just after Yanukovych was elected president. The proposal centered on the idea that to present a version of historical memory, which can form the basis of national unity, a textbook needs to take a fundamentally different approach to history. It needs to be narrated not through the prism of historic ethnic nations but through the prism of individuals and groups inhabiting the territory of today's states.[29] This new conception of history teaching would effectively deconstruct both the "Soviet" and the "national" approaches to the country's past. Interestingly, the project was sponsored and paid for by the state under the guise of the National Memory Institute during the tenure of President Yushchenko, who personally embraced a much different view of Ukraine's past.[30] Yushchenko departed from office before the historians finished their work, and under Yanukovych the commission, in the words of its head Natalia Yakovenko, "died a quiet death."[31]

The historians' initiative is now defunct, but even if it is resurrected in the future and provokes a nationwide discussion about how to approach the past in a way that serves to unite rather than to divide,[32] the process is sure to be lengthy and torturous. Nevertheless, it would be preferable to constant memory wars that have accompanied Ukrainian independence. Ukrainian political elites of all persuasions may eventually come to see it as preferable to the evidently futile struggle to establish a hegemonic mnemonic field in Ukraine. If this were to happen, Ukraine could become a (rare) example of a state with weak democratic traditions and divided society that nevertheless establishes a pillarized rather than fractured/contentious mnemonic field.

NOTES

1. Results of the referendum vote by region are reproduced in Kuzio and Wilson (1994, 189).

2. The dissident movement arose during the Khrushchev's "thaw" and became known as *shestydesiatnyky* (the generation of the 1960s).

3. The Brezhnev-era Ukrainian dissident movement was not large in absolute terms (one survey put the number at exactly 942 in the early 1970s [Krawchenko and Carter 1983, 85]), but it was

probably the largest in the USSR and also the most severely repressed by the KGB. According to the Moscow Helsinki Group, by the early 1980s Ukrainian dissidents constituted the largest single group of political prisoners in the USSR, while another study estimated that Ukrainians accounted for between 60 and 70 percent of political prisoners in the Gulag camps of Mordovia (estimates as cited in Kuzio and Wilson 1994, 58). For a comprehensive analysis of the Ukrainian dissident movement in the last two decades of the Soviet period, see Kasianov (1995).

4. By comparison, similar popular fronts in the Baltic republics, Transcaucasia and Moldova won up to 80 percent of seats in the same elections.

5. Regional variations in the 1990 vote for Rukh-supported candidates are reproduced and analyzed in Kuzio and Wilson (1994, 124–125).

6. The Gorbachev's ballot question was "Do you consider it necessary to preserve the USSR as a renewed federation of equal sovereign republics, in which human rights and the freedom of all nationalities will be fully guaranteed," to which 70.5 percent of Ukrainians voted "yes." Leonid Kravchuk, chairman of the Ukrainian parliament, inserted an additional question on the ballot throughout Ukraine: "Do you agree that Ukraine should be a part of the Union of Sovereign States on the basis of the Declaration of State Sovereignty of Ukraine [passed in July 1990]", to which 80.2 percent said "yes." March 1991 referendum results for Ukraine, including breakdown by region, in Kuzio and Wilson (1994, 161).

7. Rukh campaign leaflets from the 1991 referendum are reproduced in *Ukrains'ka Pravda* (2013).

8. Poll results in November 1, 1991, issue of *Holos Ukrainy*, as reproduced in Kuzio and Wilson (1994, 190).

9. See the commentary of opposition leaders on the events of August 24, 2011, in *Radio Svoboda* (2011).

10. The Razumkov Center poll showed that 62.8 percent of respondents supported independence. While this is substantially lower than the 1991 referendum results, when over 90 percent of Ukrainians voted for independence, it is an increase from previous years and the highest support recorded since 1991 (*Razumkov Center* 2011).

11. In 1992, 46 percent of respondents chose "citizen of Ukraine" as their primary identity; in 2010 this percentage rose to 51 percent. At the same time, the percentage of those primarily self-identifying as citizens of the former USSR dropped from 13 percent in 1992 to 7 percent in 2010. Polling data by the Institute of Sociology of the Ukrainian Academy of Sciences, as reported in Fesenko (2011).

12. On this threefold division of the political spectrum in Ukraine, see Wilson (2000), especially chapter 9.

13. Communist member of parliament Yurii Solomatin, as quoted in Wilson (2002, 33).

14. The communist position on Ukrainian national and state independence as articulated by the party head, Petro Symomenko, can be found in Symonenko (1996). It is also analyzed in Haran' and Maiboroda (2000, 72–75), and in Wilson (2002). These studies note how, by the late 1990s, Ukrainian communists began to supplement their nostalgic Soviet nationalism with East Slavic nationalism that emphasizes the unity of Russians, Ukrainians, and Belarussians in particular, rather than all Soviet nationalities in general.

15. It was the Bolsheviks and Lenin personally, Symonenko reasoned, who enabled Ukrainian independence, since in 1917, following the fall of tsarism, the Bolsheviks in the Russian State Duma supported the first Universal of the Central Council of Ukraine (*Ukrains'ka Tsentral'na Rada*)

that proclaimed the autonomy of Ukraine within the Russian empire. Lenin's nationality policies in the Soviet period also enabled Ukrainian state independence, according to Symonenko.

16. For the history of Rukh and its ideology, see Honcharuk and Shanovs'ka (2004); also Kulyk (1999).

17. In the post-independence period, the center controlled about 40 percent of parliamentary seats most of the time. For the share of seats held by the Left, Right, and Center in the Ukrainian parliament (Verkhovna Rada) by convocation since 1991, see Shevel (2011, Table 4.1).

18. On this lack of programmatic differentiation, see, for example, Osipian and Osipian (2012).

19. This was not the first time the "OUN-UPA" question was put on the government agenda, as back in 1997 President Leonid Kuchma created a government commission to study the activities of the OUN and the UPA. However, it was during Yushchenko's presidency that the government began to push for a legal recognition of the OUN and the UPA members as war veterans in earnest. The first government legislative initiative to this effect was sent to the parliament in 2005 (www.kmu.gov.ua, 2005). All in all during 2005, the first year of Yushchenko's presidency, seven draft laws to this effect were registered in the parliament by pro-presidential deputies (Shevel 2001, Table 1, 152).

20. The many aspects of the controversial past and the memory of Bandera specifically and of the OUN and the UPA generally are covered in Amar et al. (2011). For a summary of Bandera's political past, Yushchenko's decision to grant him hero status, and international condemnation of this decision, see also Snyder (2010).

21. According to one study that tracked Yushchenko's visits, statements, and participations in commemorative events, during the entire period of his presidency he took part in official historical and cultural commemorations only in the "Orange" regions of the country (the center and the west of Ukraine), essentially "ignoring the places of memory of the south-east" (Osipian and Osipian 2012, 634–635).

22. Yushchenko and a number of prominent Ukrainian cultural intelligentsia figures called for an "against all" vote in the second round, on the argument that Tymoshenko and Yanukovych are equally unsuitable to represent a pro-Ukrainian position in the cultural and foreign policy spheres in particular.

23. In April 2010, a court in the eastern Ukrainian city of Donetsk ruled that Yushchenko's decrees granting Bandera and Shukhevych the Hero of Ukraine awards were illegal, not because of Bandera's and Shukhevych's actions, but because neither was a citizen of Ukraine (*Ukrains'ka Pravda*, 2010). The rationale behind the court's reasoning has been questioned given that a dozen other holders of the Hero of Ukraine status also died before 1991 when the Ukrainian citizenship law entered into force, and therefore are also not citizens of Ukraine, but there has been no motion to annul these awards as well (Hudyma 2010).

24. As Portnov puts it, "the presence of several regional centers with their versions of history contributes to the preservation of pluralism in public sphere and does not allow any one narrative to become dominant on the whole territory of Ukraine" (Portnov 2010, 14).

25. Kubik and Bernhard, "A Theory of the Politics of Memory," Chapter 1 of this volume.

26. Poll by the Democratic Initiatives Foundation conducted in December 2007, results as reported in *Ukrains'ka Pravda* (2008).

27. Hrytsak (2004), Portnov (2010), Richardson (2004), Zakharchenko (2013), and Zhurzhenko (2002) are all examples of such studies.

28. For example, social anthropologist Tanya Richardson, who studied how history is taught and received by high school students in different regions of Ukraine, questioned the effectiveness of history education in inculcating ideas about the nation and its history contained in history textbooks. Instead, Richardson observed that "personal and family memoirs, Ukrainian historical narratives, and Soviet official history all contest each other in the classroom, often leading to ambivalence among young people" (Richardson 2004, 130).

29. For details on the historians' proposal and justifications, see lecture by Natalia Yakovenko, the head of the historians' working group (Polit.ru 2010). All documents produced by the working group are available at the website of the National Memory Institute (Ukrains'kyi instytut natsional'noi pamiati 2009).

30. Although, as I have discussed elsewhere, the initiative came from historians rather than from the state and the approval of the historian's final proposal by Yushchenko's government was also not certain (Shevel 2011, 157–164, especially fn. 96).

31. Yakovenko as quoted in Trehub (2011).

32. In January 2011, for example, a group of 28 historians from different regions of Ukraine launched a civic movement to promote historical reconciliation. The historians warned against deepening memory wars and political elites' use of historical memory as an instrument of electoral mobilization, and argued that historical reconciliation has to be based on European democratic principles in the field of history teaching and that societal initiatives from below, rather than elite and state level policies, need to play "important, if not the leading role in task of historical reconciliation" (*Ukrains'ka Pravda* 2011).

2 Pillarized Memory Regimes

Remembering, Not Commemorating, 1989

THE TWENTY-YEAR ANNIVERSARY OF THE VELVET
REVOLUTION IN THE CZECH REPUBLIC

Conor O'Dwyer

> Since we can no longer assume any single historical event, no matter how recent, to be
> common knowledge, I must treat events dating back only a few years as if they were a
> thousand years old.
>
> —MILAN KUNDERA, *The Book of Laughter and Forgetting*

Introduction

Observing the Velvet Revolution in November 1989, Timothy Garton Ash predicted, "In Poland it took ten years, in Hungary ten months, in East Germany ten weeks: perhaps in Czechoslovakia it will take ten days" (1993, 78). The Velvet Revolution stood out not only for its swiftness but also for its sharp break with the old regime. It exemplified a compressed, intense narrative of regime replacement, as compared to the slower negotiated transitions or reshuffling of the ex-communist guard evident in its neighbors. The only parallel for such swift and radical regime replacement was East Germany.[1]

Czechoslovakia and East Germany's revolutions were unusually photogenic, and therefore it is tempting to speculate that they would be easier to remember, and easier to commemorate, than those in which events, outcomes, and interpretations were more fluid. In both, the old regimes' death throes had been accompanied by mass demonstrations and, especially in Czechoslovakia, the triumphant ascendancy of long-suffering dissidents. "Havel to the castle!" cried the demonstrators massed in Prague's streets, while with their outstretched hands they shook thousands of key chains in unison. In both countries the crowds marched, the cameras rolled, and in very short order, the communists capitulated. Free elections brought crushing defeats for the old guard. Both countries then led the region in the rapidity and extensiveness of their lustration of communists in public office. In short, the revolution had a clear-cut beginning and end, and the enemies—clearly demarcated throughout the process—were swept away. By contrast, for their neighbors regime change was more drawn out and, at least in the minds of some, murkier.[2]

But were these clear victories in fact so memorable twenty years later? Or did the more clear-cut break with the old regime have precisely the opposite effect, that of making the past seem somehow more distant and inaccessible? One theme running through the Czechs' 2009 commemoration of the Velvet Revolution would seem to be a desire to recall the revolution through reliving, or at least restaging, it—as if for fear that it was in danger of becoming a forgotten, lost world. As I will describe in this chapter, the anniversary occasioned surprisingly deep and committed efforts, mostly by students, first, to reconstruct what daily life had been like before 1989 and, second, to redeploy a version of the anti-politics that dissidents such as Havel had used twenty-plus years earlier.

Newly founded student groups created all manner of art installations and happenings to rediscover what life was like under "totalitarianism," often in seemingly obsessive detail (I use quotes because this was their term). In part, this reflected simple demography; the student groups comprised members who were children during the revolution, or had not yet been born. The new groups felt a deep sense of frustration with official politics in the Czech Republic in 2009. They drew inspiration from the dissidents' earlier moral critique of politics, even if their updated version of anti-politics was directed explicitly at politicians in a way that the original anti-politics limited itself from doing. A constant refrain in the groups' mission statements was the need for education, and one senses that the dissidents' moral example was something the students sought to relearn.

Strikingly, the grass-roots mobilization of younger people in commemorating the Velvet Revolution was counterbalanced by a general apathy on the part of national-level political institutions—the government, state offices, and political parties. Following the impressions of outside observers such as James Krapfl (2010) and Susan Pearce (2010), I argue that this lopsidedness was a defining feature of the Czech commemorations.[3] In sharp contrast to the picture that Bernhard and Kubik paint of the Polish commemorations, the Czech memory regime in 2009 was not constructed in partisan terms: it was not defined by debates among representatives of the major political parties. In fact, as I describe below, the major parties and political figures did not become much involved in the commemorations—certainly not to the degree that they did in Poland. The major commemorative events were organized by newly established NGOs and citizens' groups, not by institutions of the national state or political parties.

Instead, the defining axis of the Czech memory regime was between society and politicians as a whole, that is, between an idealized civil sphere and a putatively corrupted political system. In an odd way, then, the 2009 commemorations re-enacted the logic of the anti-politics mode so characteristic of the Czech opposition *during* the Velvet Revolution itself. The commemoration became a form of protest against politics as usual—and the desensitized, unreflective, egoistic style of living that it enables. The debate was not, as in Poland, whether 1989 had been a real revolution, but whether the ideals of the Velvet Revolution had been forgotten in the transition. To recover these ideals, they had to relived, not just commemorated.

My aim in this chapter is to portray and compare the official and unofficial (i.e., civil societal) marking of the twenty-year anniversary of 1989 in the Czech Republic. In doing so, I focus primarily on the events occurring on November 17, which in contrast to most of the rest of post-communist Europe is an official holiday commemorating 1989 in the Czech Republic. My sources are drawn mostly from the descriptive accounts and photographs published in Czech newspapers—especially *Mladá fronta dnes*, which I chose because it is the largest Czech daily and, while generally considered Center-Right in tone, is mainstream enough to be at least relatively unbiased. Where possible, I supplement these sources with the manifestos and reports of the civil societal groups that I cover, many of which are available on the Internet. Finally, though I was not present for the commemorations myself, I was fortunate enough to have attended conference presentations by American academics who were, and these offered very useful insights and impressions (Krapfl 2010; Pearce 2010). After contextualizing and then contrasting the official and civil societal responses to the anniversary, I turn in the last part of this chapter to the significance of the mismatch between the two.

The Political and Social Context of the Anniversary

In order to place the 2009 anniversary in its proper context, this section will first (very briefly) describe the Czech political system leading up to 2009 and the general mood of society at that time. In describing the political and social field, I will characterize the main actors and conflicts in terms of Kubik and Bernhard's theoretical framework.

The 2009 Czech commemorations centered around November 17, the day on which, twenty years earlier, police had used force to break up a peaceful demonstration of students in Prague. Within a day, Czech university students began organizing a grass-roots opposition, bringing news of the crackdown to the rest of the country, formulating demands, and organizing a national student strike. By the night of November 20, hundreds of thousands of Czechs had taken to the streets of Prague. The numbers grew each night, quickly reaching half a million. A nationwide general strike on November 27 brought the regime to its knees, and on the 29th the Communist Party formally relinquished its "leading role," paving the way for a multi-party government and the election of Václav Havel as president. Timothy Garton Ash called it "the most delightful" of the 1989 revolutions (quoted in Stokes 1993, 157).

Skipping ahead to 2009, the political and social field on which these events would be remembered was shaped by three key post-1989 developments: the generally successful transition to a market economy and multiparty political system, the remarkable stability of the party system up to that point, and the perceived shortcomings of the political class and Czech democracy more generally.[4] The first two of these generally depoliticized the Czech memory regime, at least in partisan terms. Among political parties, the Czech memory regime came very close to the unified type described by Bernhard and Kubik. The last of these—the perceived shortcomings of post-communist democracy—had the opposite effect, destabilizing and fragmenting the memory regime. Significantly, however, this line of cleavage was not political; unlike Poland and other examples in this volume, it ran between political parties as a group and civil society.

Overall, this produced a uniquely complex mnemonic field. On the one side, the absence of major conflict among political parties—or more accurately, their near unanimous abnegation of 1989—placed this field within Bernhard and Kubik's "unified memory regime" category. Civil societal groups, by contrast, did debate and engage the legacy of 1989; however, they did so in the anti-political mode of 1989 itself. This anti-political critique of the broader political class was, in comparison to the mnemonic conflict presented elsewhere in the book, less sharp-edged and less personal. As was the case before 1989, anti-politics was fully capable of coexisting with the very political authorities whom it critiqued. Its critique was more about the disconnect between the "spirit of 1989" and the disappointments of Czech democracy in 2009; it was not about settling political scores based on dueling narratives of 1989. It implicated the political class collectively and called for its reform, but it also allowed coexistence with it. The closest description of this mnemonic field is Bernhard and Kubik's notion of "pillarization." In 2009, as before, the anti-politics ideal of "living in truth" could be thought of as a kind of pillarized coexistence of civil and political society. To show the architecture of this mnemonic field, I describe now the three overarching features of post-communist Czech development mentioned earlier.

Turning first to the post-communist transition, roughly a week before the 2009 commemorations, the Czech public opinion polling agency STEM released the results of a poll about attitudes toward democracy and the transition.[5] In general, people's evaluations were positive. The poll showed strong support (around 90 percent) for the political liberalization brought by 1989: the opening of borders, the possibility to express one's opinion and found organizations and civic groups, and so on. Likewise, around 80 percent of respondents positively rated new economic freedoms like the greater choice of goods and the possibility to own property. Even the basic structural economic reforms of the transition period, which can be more polarizing in post-communist societies, had wide support: around 75 percent supported the introduction of a market economy, and about two-thirds rated positively the influx of foreign capital. Not surprisingly, some aspects of the economic transition received less favorable ratings: two-thirds of the respondents negatively rated the increased differences in wages and wealth. Ratings of the situation of pensioners and health care were also strongly negative. But, in terms of overall quality of life compared with the pre-1989 period, 63 percent saw an improvement. In broad brushstrokes, then, the poll suggested a rather positive picture of democracy and the market on the eve of the twenty-year anniversary of the Velvet Revolution. This generally positive consensus on the basic changes in people's lives suggests why questioning the significance or authenticity of the 1989 revolution would have little payoff for most political parties—with the exception of the Communist Party of Bohemia and Moravia (KSČM), which disproportionately draws the votes of pensioners.[6]

The second relevant feature of Czech post-communist development for understanding the memory regime in 2009 was the party system, which at that time remained one of the most stable in the region (Deegan-Krause and Haughton 2010).[7] On the eve of the commemoration, Czech politics was populated by the same handful of political parties that had been established between 1990 and 1993. In the last elections before 2009, the top four of these parties—the Civic Democratic Party (ODS), the Social Democrats (ČSSD), the Communists (KSČM), and the Christian Democratic Union-People's Party (KDU-ČSL)—had collectively polled 87.7 percent of the vote.[8] The primary line of cleavage was socioeconomic, anchored on one end by the pro-market liberals of ODS and on the other by the economically leftist Social Democrats. The Communist Party (KSČM), one of the few unreformed communist successor parties in the region, maintained a stable electorate but was permanently excluded from political influence. Since 1989, all other political parties have refused to consider it as a coalition partner, freezing it out of government.

The unusual stability of Czech party politics had two important consequences for the 2009 commemorations. First, the permanent exclusion of the KSČM from power at the national level effectively quarantined the communist past from post-1989 politics. Moreover, Czechs undertook the earliest and most radical lustration of ex-communist officials in the region, purging them from public office and the state. In contrast to Poland, where the specter of continuing crypto-communist infiltration of politics—the infamous *układ*—has been used by political parties such as Law and Justice to discredit their competitors, in the Czech Republic this political weapon was less useful. The ex-communists were visible, and they were political outsiders. The argument that the 1989 revolution had been on some level a backroom deal strained credulity.

To use Bernhard and Kubik's theoretical framework, the memory regime of 1989 was neither fractured nor contentious, at least when it came to political parties. The third section of this chapter will describe the parties' behavior during the commemoration, but for now I will describe the overall dynamics of the political field. With the communists vanquished and excluded, none of the established parties could be characterized as mnemonic warriors. Instead, the Czech political parties were best described as abnegators, with a very small smattering of pluralists. Abnegators predominated, as most parties subscribed to a broadly shared vision of 1989 as a successful break with a nightmarish communist past. Absent any alternative interpretations of the revolution, parties did not politicize it, leaving individuals to commemorate 1989 as they saw fit. Some abnegators, notably the Social Democrats, chose the path of abnegation as staying away from the field of memory politics altogether.[9] The only true pluralists, ironically, were to be found in the Communist Party, some members of which defended the former regime's achievements even while acknowledging the legitimacy of the new democratic order. Another voice in the KSČM also acknowledged the legitimacy of 1989 but contended that the ideals of the revolution had been betrayed in the transition (see the following section). This last view closely echoed the real cleavage in the Czech memory regime, that between civil society and the political class, to which I turn now.

Student groups and the young, the prime movers during the events of 1989, took the 2009 anniversary as an opportunity to publicly indict political parties as a group for failing to live up to the ideals of 1989. While parties presented 1989 as the end of a nightmare, these civil society groups argued that the Velvet Revolution's very success ended the engaged, moral philosophy of public life that had made it possible. Setting aside for a moment the substance of their indictment, I would argue that this development represented a second, less favorable, consequence of the Czech party system's stability—that familiarity breeds contempt. The unchanging cast of Czech politics created the impression that the public sphere had become the preserve of career politicians concerned primarily with enlarging their own privileges. To the student groups, the entire political system seemed rigid, out of touch, and hypocritical. Václav Klaus, an iconic leader in the early 1990s and, in 2009, president of the country, epitomized this staleness—especially as he shifted his inflexible neoliberalism to new issues like global warming and the European Union. On both issues, his doctrinaire views appeared like quackery. Václav Havel, the other icon of the early 1990s and, in 2009, a private citizen, fared much better in the anniversary's events, as we shall see.

The sense that the country's political elite were driven by partisan power considerations rather than the public interest was exacerbated by a series of high-profile embarrassments in the first part of 2009. In May 2009, the ODS-led government of Mirek Topolánek fell halfway through the country's presidency of the European Union. Topolánek's government had itself been the product of a protracted and very difficult process of forming a coalition after the 2006 elections, in which the Czech Left and Right stalemated. The timing of the government's collapse was embarrassing, coming as it did during the country's rotation in the EU presidency and its ratification of the Lisbon Treaty. Replacing Topolánek, Jan Fischer led an independent caretaker government until June 2010. To many Czechs, the political system seemed fragile and the established political parties incapable of exercising leadership. It certainly did not help that at the same time the Czech Republic, along with most of the rest of Europe, was in the grips of a financial crisis. And it most certainly did not help that, during the summer, photographs of then Prime Minister Topolánek cavorting in the nude with topless sunbathers at one of Silvio Berlusconi's villas had been leaked to newspapers around Europe. Going into the twenty-year anniversary then, the political class was certainly not in top form.

The Official Commemoration of 1989: Abnegation All Around

In the official sphere of national politics, the twentieth anniversary commemoration of 1989 was muted, even absent. The only significant event was an international conference organized by the Czech Senate, "The Path from Shackles," which brought together the parliamentary leaders of post-communist countries and also included historical and artistic exhibitions at the National Museum.[10] But this was more an international than a Czech event, and in my reading, its program suggested the bland tone of international summits more than that of critical reflection. Aside from this event, the Czech state, in the summary of the newspaper *Mladá fronta dnes*, "left the 20-year commemorations to the people" rather than taking an active role in organizing them (Wirnitzer 2009). The press reported that the dearth of official commemorative events resulted from political bickering—mainly over the collapse of the government, as mentioned above—which left no time for event planning. In the words of the government's spokesman, Roman Prorok, "Considering the turbulence of the last year here, unfortunately, we weren't successful in organizing in anything [major]; there wasn't time." He then (rather unconvincingly for a twenty-year anniversary) explained, "We have to consider that public events such as these must be organized a year ahead of time—certainly not half a year or a month before" (Wirnitzer 2009).

Given the series of embarrassments endured by Czech politicians on the European stage—the "turbulence of the last year"—one cannot help but suspect that Czech politicians wanted nothing more than to retreat from the public limelight to lick their wounds. While such proximate causes no doubt played a role in the elites' collective abnegation, at a deeper level the near absence of official commemoration reflected the shared historical memory of the mainstream political parties, none of whom questioned the narrative of regime change as an unqualified change for the better. As noted above, only the communists questioned this narrative, but did so from a pluralist position of accepting the overall legitimacy of 1989. True, the communists' position provoked a hint of mnemonic conflict on the part of the conservative ODS party, as will be described later, but it was halfhearted at best. It was strongly outweighed by the party's overall stance that there were more pressing practical concerns to be dealt with and that 1989 was best left to citizens to commemorate themselves. From the point of view of political grandstanding, the 1989 anniversary was rather a let down.

The Right focused on 1989 as the repudiation of communist rule, emphasizing 1989 as a historical rupture. But attempts by the Right to lay claim to 1989 were both halfhearted and tended to backfire. For example, on November 17, Mirek Topolánek, the leader of ODS and recent prime minister, visited a former communist concentration camp for political prisoners (Kopecký 2009). "There is no better place to talk about freedom than here, which signified the absence of freedom," he said. He also used the occasion to make a political jab at the Left, making reference to one perhaps surprising result in the public opinion survey mentioned earlier. Despite their generally positive views of the political and economic reforms since 1989, less than half of the respondents placed the 1989–2009 period as "among the best in Czech history" (Kopecký 2009). Shrugging aside the difficulties of interpreting such an open-ended survey question, Topolánek found a moral for the Right. "Sheep are locked up in a pen," he said, "but every day they can go out to the pasture and have something to eat. And there are also people, who will always prefer the pasture over the chance to run free outside of the pen" (Kopecký 2009). As described in the fourth section of this chapter, this comment, which was more or less ignored by other parties, provoked a strong outcry from the civil societal groups that emerged during the commemorations, who turned it around to publicly mock political officials.

Another indication of the Right's failure to claim 1989 was President Václav Klaus's participation in one of the few official commemorations on November 17. Klaus's role as the father of Czech conservatism and the public face of ODS proved inextricable from his role as head of state, and the commemoration event went far from smoothly. At around 11 a.m., he came to Národní třída in Prague to lay a wreath at the memorial to the demonstrators attacked in 1989. He arrived with heavy police protection and immediately was met with loud jeers from the assembled crowd and then cries of support from others in the crowd. The detractors yelled "Don't embarrass us!" Some held up signs saying, "Klaus is not our president—Students of '89" (Kratochvíl 2009). (A second contingent called out "Long live Klaus!," though according to Krapfl [2010], at least some of these were yelling "Long live Klaus...somewhere else!") Klaus himself shook a few hands and left. Later he commented in a television interview, "I expected far worse. The overwhelming majority were on my side. I hope you could see that. It's a natural thing for a democracy and a huge victory that one can shout at the president or mayor, and the police don't move in with clubs. It's a victory that not everyone appreciates" (Kratochvíl 2009).

For the most part, though, the political Right elevated the lackluster public commemoration to a sort of principled inaction: ODS leaders suggested they thought it best to leave it to individuals to accomplish in whatever manner they saw fit. Speaking on behalf of Václav Klaus, a presidential spokesman commented, "The President is of the opinion that, rather than celebrate by taking part in some spectacular public event, it is better to remember and commemorate this day among people and with people, just as it was in the events themselves 20 years ago and since" (Wirnitzer 2009). Klaus's calendar also included plans to attend a signing of his book, *Where Tomorrow Begins* (So much for commemorating history!). For his part, ODS chief Mirek Topolánek acknowledged the dearth of official commemoration, but he blamed the European Union—or at least the problems the Czechs had faced during the presidency of it: "I read it like this: in the past year we as Czechs caused so many problems [in the EU] that it kind of blocked out the fact of this twenty-year anniversary" (Wirnitzer 2009). Echoing Klaus, in the days before November 17, Topolánek stated: "[November 17th] deserves to be celebrated just as much as the majority of citizens think that there is something to celebrate.... On the other hand, it's possible that it's better for civil society alone to determine how the commemorations proceed. It's a better indication of society here than some kind of '1st of May' holiday organized by the state" (Wirnitzer 2009).

As elsewhere in post-communist Europe, the anniversary of 1989 presented the Left with the more difficult tactical position. For the Czech Social Democrats, the safest strategy was to avoid getting drawn into any kind of identification with the old regime. The abnegation of the Czech Right—"We've been too busy with other more important things to organize a commemoration"—presented them a nice opportunity to avoid drawing attention to themselves. This is abnegation of the sort that Bernhard and Kubik characterize as staying away from memory politics (Chapter 1 of this volume). This stance was nowhere better illustrated than in an interview with Jiří Paroubek, the chief of the Social Democrats. A newspaper was interviewing the leaders of the major Czech political parties, asking them what they had been doing on November 17th, 1989. While the leaders of most parties described the emotion that they had felt on that day, Paroubek recalled it as a normal workday: "I can't recall the whole day. I was, I think, at work as usual. In the afternoon, I met with friends in one Prague hotel. On the one hand, it was a pleasant, friendly meeting; on the other hand, it was also a working meeting because I had to help them prepare the budget for the next year" (Němcová 2009b).

Ironically, only the Communists refused to take refuge in abnegation. They engaged the commemoration by training their rhetoric on the unfulfilled promise of the 1989 revolution: democratic ideals had been betrayed. Consider the following symbolic protest by Martin Herzán, a Communist Party politician. Herzán created a memorial medal for the November 17th anniversary. It showed the image from the revolution of two fingers held up in a sign of peace, and on it was inscribed the following text, "The 20th anniversary of frustrated expectations that truth and love will triumph over lies and hate" (Laudin 2009). Rather than award the medal to anyone in particular, he took it to the Charles Bridge—probably the central point of historic Prague—and threw it into the Vltava. In doing so, he wanted to "draw attention to the fact that so many of the noble ideals of the Velvet Revolution had been drowned" (Laudin 2009).

Miloš Jakeš, the last general secretary of the Communist Party before 1989, now an 87-year-old pensioner, offered the following unapologetic thoughts about the revolution: "For what happened to us here, there were no timeless reasons. The economy worked here; living standards were on an incomparably good level. There was a good standard of life then" (PŘEHLEDNĚ 2009; Musil and Vocelka 2009). But such comparisons were far afield from those of currently active politicians, including the leadership of the Communist Party. In the words of the latter's vice-chairwoman Věra Žežulková, "Now after 20 years, it's the others' [former regime functionaries] turn to apologize for what they caused" (PŘEHLEDNĚ 2009). Even the communists did not really question the 1989 revolution; their position came closest to a kind of mnemonic pluralism.

In sum, my survey of the anniversary commemorations indicates that national political institutions—the government, state offices, and political parties—remained mostly on the sidelines. If anything, the political Right, namely ODS, came out the worse for the attempts of its leaders Topolánek and Klaus to speak out on the occasion. The national institutions' curious absence was made only the more conspicuous by the more successful anniversary events organized by municipal-level institutions, such as the Prague city government's (*Pražský magistrát*) event on the Old Town Square on November 17. Since this event was planned by a public office, I include it with the official commemorations. However, in tone, content, and partisan organization, it had much more in common with the civil societal events that will be described in the next section. This is hardly surprising, as local government tends always to be less ideological and partisan than that at the national level.

On November 17, Prague's Old Town Square was the site of an extensive and rather lighthearted commemoration, recalling and re-enacting day-to-day life before the revolution.[11] As a kind of living museum of the era, the square was filled with various stands recreating (and spoofing) such staples of "real existing socialist" life as Tuzex, the state-owned stores where using vouchers (*bony*) purchased for hard currency, people could buy "luxury" goods from the West. The recreated Tuzex store sold such communist-era extravagances as Barbie dolls, Kinder chocolate eggs, and gumballs. Perhaps more wittily, to buy these things one had to procure *bony* from black-market money-changers (*veksláci*) lurking around the square in their obligatory and infamous jean jackets. Better still, to procure *bony* from the money-changers, one had to first best them in a shell game—a detail that recreated the typical person's experience of being ripped off by the *veksláci* while buying *bony* on the black market under communism. Also recalling the communist-era grocery, people queued before greengrocer stands to buy bananas from white-coated "staff." Just as in communist times, "customers" could also request to register a complaint or even compliment in the *Kniha přání a stížností* (book of suggestions and complaints). Draped around the square were banners with slogans from the old regime: "Together with the Soviet Union for All Time!" and "Whoever Won't Work Won't Eat." Mocking these slogans, there were also banners with unofficial mottos from communism, such as "Who Doesn't Steal, Steals from His Family." With their informal and carnivalesque atmosphere, the events on the Old Town Square showed much in common with the civil societal events described in the following section.

Civil Society's Remembrance of 1989: Anti-politics Relived

If the official commemoration of the November 17 anniversary was modest to lackluster, that of civil societal groups stood in sharp contrast. Czech student groups,

NGOs, and cultural figures were extremely active in the 1989 anniversary. According to James Krapfl's (2010) impressions from observing the commemorations across much of Central and Eastern Europe, Czech society's response was matched only by that in East Germany in terms of vibrancy and scope. But even here there were contrasts, as the German state took a much more visible, active role in the anniversary than the Czech one. This lopsidedness between the official and civil societal marking of 1989 revealed a deeper cleavage in the Czech memory regime, between civil society and the political class.

Uncannily echoing the epigraph from Milan Kundera's depiction of Czechoslovakia's "normalization" following the Soviet invasion in 1968, the grass-roots commemorators of 2009 were preoccupied with remembering life before and during the Velvet Revolution. Remembering the past is not the same as commemorating it, though. Commemoration sanctifies and thereby distances the past. By contrast, through remembering the past, these groups sought to discover continuities with the present, both good and bad. As I will describe below, by remembering and, in fact, restaging the experience of life under communism, these groups argued that many of the failings of communist society were still present after 1989: political passivity, weak civil society, and failure to hold politicians to moral standards.

Reliving the Velvet Revolution uncovered not only a critique of the present, but a political model for reshaping it. That model was anti-politics, the self-described non-political model of opposition exemplified by such pre-1989 groups as Charter 77 in Czechoslovakia and the Committee for the Defense of Workers (KOR) in Poland. The anti-politics model had focused on moral resistance to political authority. It had used non-political tactics, such as "living in truth," cultural criticism (typically in the form of self-published *samizdat*), and public letters to carve out a sphere of individual freedom in a political world dominated by ideology. During the Velvet Revolution, the anti-communist opposition had also adopted the anti-politics mode, elevating Charter 77's figurehead Václav Havel as its leader and coalescing into an umbrella group, Civic Forum, which refused the label of political party (Carnahan and Corley 1992, 123). When, in 1990, Civic Forum did run as a party in the first free elections, its campaign was marked by self-mockery, irony, and willful amateurism. As one observer wrote, "Having long endured a politics imposed from above, full of insufferably wooden rhetoric, elaborate ceremony, and self-important men in cheap suits and slicked-back hair, they [Civic Forum] decided the only antidote was to make this campaign into a carnival" (Horn 1990, 11). In 2009, carnival and mockery would again be deployed against the political class.

By re-adapting anti-politics for 2009, these groups formed a moral critique of post-communist Czech democracy and, in particular, the political class, regardless of party affiliation. Czech politicians were, in this view, hypocritical, self-serving, and untruthful—in short, unworthy of the ideals of the revolution. In this way, these civil societal groups attempted to use the past as a tool to change the political present.

These civil societal efforts were embodied, and to a large degree coordinated, by two recently founded, mostly student-based, nonprofit groups, Opona (Curtain) and Inventura demokracie, or Democracy Czech-Up, the group's own translation of its name into English.[12] Given the critical role of students in the Velvet Revolution itself, this continuity was significant. Both groups had branches in the larger cities across the country, and so before describing their activities in specific locales, I will describe their overarching visions.

Opona is a nonprofit nongovernmental organization (NGO) established in 2007 "to develop free, publicly accessible commemorations of the 20th anniversary of the fall of the Iron Curtain."[13] As with Inventura demockracie, it was founded by young people, most of whom were too young to have played an active part in the events of 1989. Also like Inventura, this group was grass-roots based, and (quite emphatically) was not organized by the state or political parties. It received funding from a wide variety of public, EU, and private associations, though because of the European (and Czech) financial crisis far less than the sums originally promised (Opona 2009, 4). Opona stressed that its primary target audience was "young people, the so-called first free generation." Like Inventura, it announced its desire to engage with and understand the pre-1989 past, not to distance itself from it. As it stated in its 2009 Annual Report:

> Our projects focused especially on the latter group [the young generation], emphasizing interesting, nontraditional and modern approaches which would capture one's attention at first sight and also communicate in a comprehensive form the fundamental information and ideas. Another important goal of our projects was to stimulate an intergenerational dialogue, motivating young people to have conversations with older generations, and at the same time show them that the era of Communist Czechoslovakia cannot be seen only in black and white, suggesting how difficult were the choices their parents and grandparents had to make in their lives. (Opona 2009, 4)

During the course of the 2009 calendar year, the group organized events such as "The Totalitarian Circus," which combined art, theater, and educational seminars to present personal stories of those who lived under communism.[14] It also organized a traveling exhibition, the "Totalitarian Calendarium," as well as a large-scale art and multimedia installation called the "Totalitarian Simulator." On the more academic/

public-policy side, it hosted an international conference on the role of EU accession in post-1989 democratic development.[15] However, the largest, most visible, and probably most resonant commemorative event organized by Opona was the 17th of November march in Prague. This retraced the steps of the student demonstration that twenty years earlier had initiated the Velvet Revolution and which I will describe in more detail.

Inventura demokracie was founded approximately a year in advance of the 2009 commemorations to, in its own words, "connect [the] celebration of twenty years of Czech democracy with a critical reflection of the post-revolution development of society and politics" (Inventura demokracie 2009a). A student initiative, its leadership was drawn largely from Charles University in Prague but also included members from a host of other Czech universities such as the Czech Technical University in Prague and Masaryk University in Brno. Inventura's mission statement is worth quoting at some length because it best encapsulates the kind of politically engaged anti-politics practiced by the group:

> We are the first student generation of whom it is often said that we're not marked by Communism. Insofar as we did not experience the time before November 1989 and know nothing about it, then it is thought that we have escaped its influence. The truth is the opposite; the less we know about the past, the more we are in thrall to it. A whole twenty years has gone by—and a proper reflection on our Communist past has not even been started. And we believe that's why we're in such a mess....
>
> Once we begin to know what it was that made our pre-November '89 society unfree, we will have a better chance of recognising similar risks today....Even today we have to expose new and stealthy forms of totalitarianism and react to them appropriately....
>
> Insofar as our generation is distinctive in any way, it is exactly in that it isn't distinctive in any way, least of all as far as values are concerned. We're not very interested in public affairs and politics angers us—and mainly we simply don't understand it....We're no different in that from all the older people around us....Those who should be our authorities and teachers are accustomed to ignoring the public sphere and living their own private life. That's been picked up by us easily. We too unhesitatingly value our own private interest higher than the common interest, and it seems perfectly natural. It never occurs to us that it could be otherwise.
>
> In this way an unobtrusive process sets itself in motion: participation in the public sector becomes more and more distasteful, the feeling grows that we have no influence on public activities, and we think ourselves all the more

justified in not participating. It becomes more and more difficult to enter the public space, and soon it will be completely closed to a decent person. That is the point when our freedom will be directly threatened—but by then it will be too late for us to do anything.

To put it bluntly: our democracy is fragile and easily lost. If it functions at all, it is not because it is guided by some invisible hand of historically inevitable democratic principles. Democracy is built on the concrete efforts of specific individuals. It only has a chance if we take it on, urgently, as our own personal concern. (Inventura demokracie 2009b)

In my reading, this text strongly recalls the anti-politics mode of the 1989-era dissidents, in particular the seminal essay of Czech dissident Václav Havel, "The Power of the Powerless."

Like Havel's essay, this manifesto is at its core a *moral* critique of politics. Like "Power of the Powerless," Inventura's critique aims first to expose the oppressive structure of conventional, that is, conformist thinking, which enables ordinary people to live within ideological confines without noticing them. The worst sin in this view is group-think, the unquestioning acceptance of an ideological, and therefore imprisoning, narrative of history. The failure to question, to oppose group-think, strengthens the ideological power structure while corrupting both the individual and society. What differs, however, is the solution. For Havel, it was to "live in truth," to withdraw from the official lie into a private sphere. In his allegory, the greengrocer resists the lie by taking down the signs with communist slogans posted in his shop window. For the members of Inventura, such withdrawal is in fact the problem. They face the dilemma of exposing publicly the political lies around them without become tainted by politics in the process. Moreover, exposing political lies now is not as simple as not doing something (e.g., not posting the revolutionary slogan in the shop window); it requires the very political act of organizing collectively and engaging politicians in debate. But, of course, a strong distaste for politics pervades the text; thus the students' dilemma, how to combine anti-politics' moral clarity with political engagement?

Inventura's activities were an admixture of sometimes jarring elements. They organized public meetings with politicians during the year before the commemorations, during which they demanded four core reforms of the legislative system: (1) limits on immunity for members of parliament, (2) stricter regulation of lobbying activities, (3) changes to the method of election of public media councils, and (4) banning the use of "wild-riders," that is, legislative amendments having little to do with the base legislative proposal (Horáková 2009). The group videotaped these meetings and later released them on a DVD. As this list of demands suggests, Inventura demokracie was harshly critical of contemporary Czech politics and political parties. In addition to these legislative efforts, Inventura staged a multitude of "happenings," using agitprop techniques intended to startle Czechs into political reflection. Since the anniversary's events, the group continued the goal of promoting "inventories" of public institutions, such as Czech Radio.

Opona and Inventura captured, and largely set, the tone of Czech society's commemoration of 1989: youthful, grass-roots, countercultural, and critical. To give a sense of this atmosphere, the next two sections describe some of the main society-initiated events in Prague and Brno, the country's two largest cities.

In Prague

In Prague, as in other bigger Czech cities such as Brno and Ostrava, the marking of 1989 was centered around November 17, an official holiday of commemoration. Speaking to the strength of civil society's engagement with the anniversary, however, there was considerable activity before and after the 17th as well. As mentioned above, Inventura demokracie had initiated its town-hall meetings for legislative reform a year in advance. One week before the 17th, Inventura unveiled a monument in front of the Malostránská náměstí Metro station, which, lying between Prague Castle and Charles Bridge, is one of the most visible and photogenic locations in the city. The culmination of the group's year-long campaign for legislative reform, the monument depicted the "result" of the group's appeal to Czech politicians to "Give us a present for our 20th birthday." It was a giant gift box tied in a big red ribbon and topped with a giant, crude but unmistakable replica of a turd (see Picture 8.1). The humor was decidedly puerile, but the symbolism nonetheless pithily communicated Inventura's willingness to confront the political establishment, albeit with nontraditional techniques.

Following the unveiling of their "present," Inventura staged daily happenings, conferences, and protests—"Days of Inventory" as they called them—leading up to November 17. These continued, perhaps even escalated, the group's rhetorical confrontation with the Czech political establishment. On the 17th itself, Inventura organized another provocative happening on Václavské náměstí, Prague's central square and staging ground for many of its most significant historic events, including the Velvet Revolution. In this one, participants held up masks with sheep's faces, charging Czech society with conformism and passivity, using a symbolism that Orwell would have appreciated (see Picture 8.2). Beyond the more general critique of Czech society's passivity, however, the symbolism of the sheep was a pointed and direct mockery of the ODS leader and former Prime Minister Mirek Topolánek. As described earlier, Topolánek had during the course of his visit earlier that day to

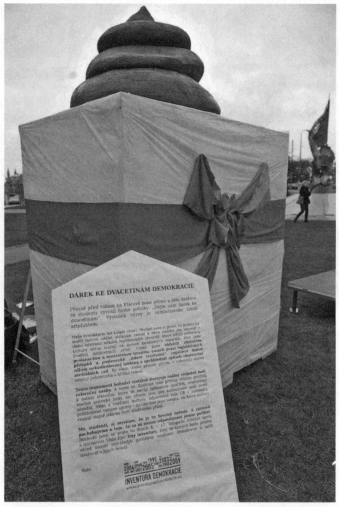

PICTURE 8.1 Prague, The Czech Republic, November 8, 2009. Inventura demokracie presents Czech politicians a gift on the twentieth anniversary of the Velvet Revolution.
Source: ČTK Photo/Roman Vondrouš.

the former political prison Vojna u Příbrami made some choice observations about those who did not consider the last twenty years among the best in Czech history. Clearly, Topolánek had in mind the stereotypical old-age pensioner orphaned in the transition from communism to the market economy when he made his comments. What was interesting, and jarring, about these protestors with sheep's masks was that they came from a completely different demographic—the young, the educated, the "beautiful people," those presumed to be more at home in this new post-communist world (Zlámalová 2009). The students' identification with the "sheep" so offhand-edly dismissed by Topolánek resonated with their message that they were not so different from the previous generation, that the revolution had not swept away

PICTURE 8.2   Prague, The Czech Republic, November 17, 2009. Inventura demokracie stages a happening on Václavské náměstí.
Source: Lidové noviny Photo/Tomáš Krist.

communism's social legacy, that society was still passive. The sheep's masks were a call for society to participate in Czech democracy.

In terms of sheer numbers, the biggest event on the November 17th anniversary was a march organized by Opona. It retraced the steps of the student demonstration twenty years earlier that, when attacked by the police, had set off the chain of ever larger demonstrations that led to the regime's capitulation.[16] Beginning in the afternoon, the march slowly wound its way to the place, Národní třída, where the police had attacked twenty years earlier. Following the march, at around 6 p.m., a grand "Happening" of experimental theater, performance art, and music was staged on Národní třída. An estimated 7,000 people took part in the march itself; and around 25,000 took part in the events on Národní třída (Opona 2009). The sight of thousands marching through Prague re-staged the revolution, albeit on a smaller scale. According to media accounts, the majority of the marchers were young people, too young to have participated in the 1989 events themselves (Kratochvíl and Bezr 2009). Various accounts stress the carnivalesque atmosphere of the occasion. Accompanying the march were vehicles giving out "velvet tea" and "velvet grog." The carnivalesque atmosphere was marred briefly at one point when the march crossed paths with a few dozen supporters of the neo-nazi group National Resistance (Národní odpor) and far-right Workers' Party (Dělnická strana). But the police quickly contained any conflict, and the march proceeded without incident.[17]

As an additional indication of the civil-societal—as opposed to party-political or state-directed character—of the event, the tone of the marchers' placards and chants recalled the anti-politics of dissidents in and before 1989. One placard read, "Red [for the Communist Party], orange [for the Social Democrats], blue [for the Civic Democratic Party], all good for corrupt people" (Kratochvíl and Bezr 2009).[18] Compare this with Civic Forum's slogan twenty years previous: "Parties are for [Communist] Party members. Civic Forum is for everybody" (Carnahan and Corley 1992, 123). Václav Klaus, the European Union, and the communists all were repeatedly singled out for criticism in the slogans of the marchers, while dissident hero Václav Havel received loud acclaim. In the musical-theatrical program that followed the march, politicians were conspicuously absent.

Again, Havel was the exception. He delivered a brief speech before the program and was presented by the organizers with a hand-knit white scarf. Like the march, the concert was strongly infused with the countercultural feel of the dissident circles of twenty years earlier, including songs and appearances from the likes of the Plastic People of the Universe (whose arrest in 1976 sparked the founding of Charter 77), Lou Reed (whose band the Velvet Underground was the inspiration for the Plastic People), Pražský výběr (whose leader Michael Kocáb was elected to parliament in the first free elections of 1990), and Joan Baez (who first met Havel in a 1989 visit to Czechoslovakia, allowing him to carry her guitar to escape arrest) (Kratochvíl and Bezr 2009).

In Brno

In Brno, Inventura demockracie organized a parade of lanterns that, reflecting the group's student core, ended at Masaryk University. There the university's rector addressed the crowd (Závodná 2009). Originally planned for 200 participants, an estimated 800 took part in the parade. As with the march in Prague, the occasion had a spontaneous and homespun feel.[19] Following the parade, leaders from Inventura demokracie discussed the group's year-long—and, in terms of actual policy change, unsuccessful—campaign for legislative reform. The discussion strongly suggested that the group was poised to take on a more directly political role: in the words of the group's chairman Jan Skalík, "This past year's contact with politicians has awoken in us the feeling that we cannot rely on them only. This proclamation is formulated therefore as an exhortation to us all" (Závodná 2009).

In short, as in Prague, civic groups composed primarily of students took the lead in Brno's commemorations.[20] As Havel noted during his visit to Brno, "I see hope in how this twenty-year anniversary is being commemorated. I had expected that the occasion would be a distant-seeming holiday, one day in the weekend that everyone would use as an extended half-day off and treat as a traditional ritual. That's not what happened. For a week already, I've been going from one setting to another, and everywhere there are calls for the future, for the outlook ahead. Everywhere people are reflecting on the present in all of its ambiguity, and this is hugely encouraging" (Mareček 2009).

Conclusion: What Is the Significance of the Disparity Between the Official and Societal Markings of 1989?

There was a striking lopsidedness between the official and civil-societal markings of the Velvet Revolution in the Czech Republic in 2009. Civil society's remembrance of the anniversary empathized and connected with the dissident legacy of 1989, while at the same time critically reflecting on current-day politics. Surprisingly, the political class seemed content to abnegate commemoration, to bow out of the discussion of the anniversary's significance. When pressed on this, they argued that it was more fitting that civil society celebrate 1989 than the state. In this, they were more right than they would probably have liked because civil society groups took the anniversary to rediscover and redeploy the revolution's anti-political opposition mode against them as representatives of an unaccountable and self-serving power structure.

I have characterized the memory regime revealed by these dynamics as pillarized. The anniversary did not occasion a big partisan clash, but it did reveal a rift between the political class writ large and elements of civil society over the practice of democratic politics. The latter accentuated the divide between themselves and the politicians, but their narrative of 1989 and its aftermath was closer to critique than repudiation. Thus, the anniversary highlighted a disagreement about the proper role of civil society in Czech democracy, and on this theme, politicians were neither entirely quiet nor all so enchanted with civil societal groups. Unsurprisingly, Václav Klaus bemoaned what he described as a creeping "Havlismus" in Czech society, which he defined as the de-ideologization of politics (Buchert 2009). Klaus's complaint in fact only reinforces the overall picture described here.

This unusual memory regime deserves reflection. Is it a good thing that so many Czechs took 1989 as a reason to re-examine (and criticize) the quality of democracy in the Czech Republic? What is the significance of the new "politically engaged anti-politics?" Does it suggest a crisis of faith in democratic politics that the politicians did not engage in developing rival narratives of the 1989 revolution? Or is this willingness to scrutinize the past and present it without loud partisan battles a sign that, really and truly, the transition is over, that Czech politics has reached post–post-communism?

A more definitive answer to these questions will require more historical perspective and is beyond the scope of this chapter, but my instinct is that these developments are more positive than negative. First, the rediscovery of anti-politics was, in some sense, the most sincere form of marking 1989, remembering it as the carnival that it was. Second, while students' scrutiny of the practice of Czech democracy employed a confrontational and accusatory tone, at least the substance of the critique was profoundly democratic and prospective. If 2009 served to force the realization that civil society is weaker than it should be, well then, the very messengers bringing this news were new civil society groups. Of course, "politically engaged anti-politics" is even more a contradiction in terms than anti-politics was. Even during the commemorations themselves, it was easy to speculate that the critique of politicians would for some soon become a reason for entering politics. Far from being a crisis of faith in democracy, though, this would be a sign of its further consolidation, and 2009 was a challenge to the form of post-communist Czech democracy that reaffirmed its basic legitimacy.

NOTES

1. See Stokes (1993) for a good comparison of the three paths of regime change—regime replacement, negotiated transition, and palace revolutions—in 1989.

2. I am thinking here of the Kaczyńskis' critique of the Polish Roundtable, as described in Chapter 3 on Poland in this volume (Bernhard and Kubik), but one could also point to Romania's messy regime change, or even to Hungary's negotiated transition, which reflected the efforts of reform communists as much as it did an opposition movement.

3. Interestingly, to judge by the impressions of Krapfl (2010), the only possible parallel in the region was, again, the former East Germany. Krapfl, in fact, distinguishes between "aristocratic" and "democratic" commemorations in 2009. The aristocratic sort are stage-managed by the state and do not draw on civil society; examples include Poland and Hungary. East Germany and the Czech Republic exemplify the "democratic," or civil society-based, type.

4. Paradoxically, the last of these was a symptom of the first two.

5. The poll was conducted between October 31 and November 9, 2009, and had 1,278 respondents. My summary of the results is based on Němcová (2009a).

6. KSČM is the direct and only successor party to the pre-1989 Communist Party of Czechoslovakia (KSČ). The Czech Republic is anomolous among its neighbors for preserving a largely unreformed ex-communist party in politics.

7. It should be noted that, in retrospect, 2009 may prove to have been the end of an era in Czech party politics. After 2010 and the onset of the European financial crisis, the Czech party system has looked increasingly fragile (cf. Haughton, Novotná, and Deegan-Krause 2011).

8. To put this in perspective, the vote share of the first post-transition parties in Poland in its 2007 elections was 9.1 percent!

9. Kubik and Bernhard, "A Theory of the Politics of Memory," Chapter 1 in this volume.

10. For a summary of the event, see Ministerstvo vnitra *České republiky* (2009).

11. This description is based on "Staroměstské náměstí ovládla socialistická hesla a veksláci" (2009).

12. See Inventura demokracie 2009a. "Czech-Up" is a play of words on the phrase "checkup" (as in "inventory"). The institution of inventory was a quintessential institution of state socialism. State-run stores would be closed, often for extended periods of time, as state inspectors took inventory of all items to determine whether store assistants were cheating. This institutional practice caused irritation and was the subject of innumerable jokes.

13. The group's website can be found at http://www.oponaops.eu/opona/cs/uvod. Accessed January 10, 2011.

14. For a full list of Opona's events during the year see its Annual Report (2009).

15. The title was "From the Fall of the Iron Curtain in 1989 to the Enlargement of the European Union in 2004: The Role of Civil Society and the Idea of Europe in the Process of Democratic Transformation of the Central and Eastern European Countries," and it was held on May 1, 2009.

16. Interestingly, the 1989 march had commemorated *student* resistance to Nazi occupation during World War II.

17. For a full description of the Far-Right protestors' march, see Eichler (2009). As a brief summary, the Far-Right groups, which had been banned from demonstrating, assembled near the National Theater (*Národní divadlo*) and scuffled with heavily armed police. Forty-nine were detained. Those extremists who met up with the march were fleeing from the confrontation.

18. In Czech, the slogan had more of a ring, rhyming as follows: "Červená, oranžová, modrá, pro neřády dobrá!"

19. Krapfl (2010), who was present as a participant-observer, also strongly emphasized the amateur quality of the Brno commemorations in his account.

20. On this point, see also Krapfl (2010).

3 Unified Memory Regimes

9 Making Room for November 9, 1989?
THE FALL OF THE BERLIN WALL IN GERMAN POLITICS AND MEMORY
David Art

Introduction

The year 2009 was marked with anniversaries in a country where history, memory, and politics have long been more deeply interconnected than perhaps anywhere else. Germans commemorated the sixtieth anniversary of the founding of the Federal Republic on May 23 and the seventieth anniversary of the invasion of Poland on September 1 before turning to the year's major event: the twentieth anniversary of the fall of the Berlin Wall on November 9. But as every observer of German politics knows, the peculiarities of German history ensured that even that ostensibly happy date would not be reserved solely for celebration. On November 9, 1918, the ill-fated Weimar Republic was born from the ashes of World War I. Five years later, on the same date, Hitler launched his infamous Beer Hall Putsch, an act of treason that could have resulted in the death penalty, but which instead netted him a six-month stay in Landsberg and time to write *Mein Kampf.* On November 9, 1938, the Nazis orchestrated a nation-wide pogrom, euphemistically known as "the Night of the Broken Glass," that marked a major step toward the Final Solution.[1] Perhaps the Germans should have waited a day longer to rush the Wall so that the anniversary of its fall would not have to compete for space with memories of the birth of an unpopular democracy, a botched coup that could have changed the course of German history had the judges not found Hitler to be acting patriotically, and the precursor to the Holocaust.

Given these complications, the twentieth anniversary commemoration of the fall of the Berlin Wall went off smoothly. World leaders gathered to give speeches. Lech Walesa tipped over the first of 1,000 8-feet tall styrofoam dominoes that then cascaded for 1.5 kilometers along a central stretch of the old Wall. Although the German dailies were not without some laments, the criticisms were more muted than those directed toward most previous attempts at state-managed commemorations. The left-wing *Tageszeitung* called the domino ceremony childish (*Tageszeitung* 2009), while the right-leaning *Frankfurter Allgemeine Zeitung* pointed out that some of the predecessors of the international leaders in attendance—particularly Margaret Thatcher and François Mitterrand—had not welcomed German unification at all, and decried the fact that "it's become almost trendy to compete over who was the most supportive of German reunification" (*Frankfurter Allgemeine Zeitung* 2009). Chancellor Angela Merkel (CDU) praised the courage of the East Germans who had challenged the dictatorship first in Leipzig, and later in Berlin, before dismantling the Wall. At the same time, she tempered her remarks by noting that November 9th was also the night of Pogromnacht, and that German unification was still far from complete. Merkel and President Horst Köhler (CDU), who also reminded Germans that "November 9th 1989 was inseparable from November 9, 1938," managed to avoid the numerous pitfalls that await German politicians who engage, voluntarily or not, in the politics of memory. November 9, 2009, may not go down as important a day for the construction of memory as May 8, 1985, when Richard von Weizsäcker's speech commemorating the fortieth anniversary of the end of World War II reframed the debate about the role of the Nazi past in the present. Yet it was certainly no Bitburg.

When one takes a broader view of the memory of 1989, however, things appear more problematic. The year 2009 was marked by numerous debates about the past—and particularly the past of the German Democratic Republic (GDR)—that intruded dramatically into contemporary partisan politics. In this chapter, I would like to point out three separate issues that the twentieth anniversary raised, and locate the political stakes of those debates.

The first was the relationship of the particular *memory regime* surrounding the fall of the Wall to the broader *field of memory* in the Federal Republic. I will argue that the field of memory in contemporary Germany has been so deeply structured by a unified memory regime about the Nazi past that it is difficult for other types of memory regimes to become salient parts of the mnemonic field at all. Moreover, since the memory regime of the Nazi past has also become the *official memory regime* of contemporary Germany, any potential memory regimes that undercut or challenge its core elements are unlikely to find broad acceptance. Karl Wilds originally termed this unified memory regime the *culture of contrition* (Wilds 2000), while others have termed it Holocaust-centered memory or the Bonn memory regime (Langenbacher 2010). But whatever term one uses (and I use the terms interchangeably in this chapter), this narrative stresses Holocaust commemoration as a permanent duty for Germans.

This Holocaust-centered memory regime was constructed through political battles, some of which I will trace, in West Germany. In the immediate aftermath of German unification, many politicians and intellectuals feared—and many others hoped—that the culture of contrition would be replaced by either a "normal" memory regime, one in which the Holocaust would not assume the central role, a reconsideration of German suffering during World War II and its aftermath, or partial displacement by memory of the crimes of the communist regime that had just collapsed. Put another way, there was a concern that the Holocaust-centered memory regime would fracture and play less of a role in shaping the entire field of memory.

This not only failed to occur, but the Holocaust-centered memory regime has only become more salient and more of a structuring force in the field of memory since 1989. This interpretation of the development of memory politics in Germany—one which I will flesh out more in the following text—provides one answer to the central puzzle that frames this chapter. To restate, the key question is why 1989 has failed to become part of a resonant founding myth of a unified, democratic Germany. At the tenth anniversary of the fall of the Wall, Ralf Dahrendorf noted that "1989 is not the decisive event in German intellectual consciousness that it is in the rest of Europe, and it is certainly not a sigh of relief for the triumph of an open society" (*Die Zeit* 2009a). Ten years on, the Germans have not come any closer in recasting 1989 as the equivalent of 1776 in the United States or 1789 in France. The dominance of a unified Holocaust-centered memory regime in the mnemonic field in Germany, I argue, has prevented a more heroic memory regime surrounding 1989 from becoming salient.

The persistence of the culture of contrition offers one explanation for why celebrations of 1989 were so muted twenty years after. But so too does a second issue—the trajectory that unification has taken since the fall of the Berlin Wall. The failure of unification to deliver the "flourishing landscapes" that Helmut Kohl notoriously promised was a major part of the commemorations. The twenty-year anniversary provided an opportunity to reflect on developments, preventable or inevitable, that have produced a region of economic malaise within the most economically powerful country in Europe. In addition to the economic divisions, there was ample opportunity in 2009 to offer further reflections on "the wall in the head." Given that most predictions for economic convergence are not particularly encouraging, and given that most studies show a wide gulf between East and West German political attitudes in a variety of issue areas, it is perhaps not that surprising that 1989 has not achieved a more glorious place in Germany's collective consciousness.

A third issue that tempered the celebration of the collapse of the Wall was the eruption of a debate about the nature of the regime that had built it. To be sure, the process of "working through" the communist past began nearly immediately after reunification, and none of the issues that surfaced in 2009 was really new. Yet much as debates about the Nazi past have come in waves, 2009 marked a crest in the political significance of the historical memory of the GDR. The key issue was whether the Left Party's ambiguous relationship to the GDR past rendered it an illegitimate political actor. If so, then the SPD was locked into a policy of *Ausgrenzung* (exclusion) toward it. If not, then the Social Democrats had more options. While these political stakes were important, the fact that the memory of the GDR continues to be a point of dispute also makes it difficult to come up with anything approaching a common interpretation of the fall of the Wall. Simply put, if a large percentage of German citizens continue to believe that the GDR not only had many positive sides, but also was in many ways preferable to the current Federal Republic, it is difficult for November 9, 1989, to become an unambiguous day of celebration.

In sum, to understand why November 9, 1989, has not assumed the significance that Dahrendorf and others hoped it would, we need to analyze preexisting memory regimes and their place in the broader field of memory, the balance sheet of unification, and the historical memory of the GDR. The rest of this chapter looks at each of these issues in turn.

Memory Regimes in the German Field of Memory

Germany's process of coming to terms with the Nazi past has become a scholarly obsession over the last twenty years. Rather than attempting the nearly impossible task of saying anything novel about the subject, I would like to use the framework developed in the introduction of this chapter to summarize the major developments in memory regimes since 1989, and to demonstrate how the preexisting culture of contrition (which, again, refers to the unified memory regime of the Holocaust) has constrained attempts to introduce a more heroic founding myth into the broader field of memory in the Federal Republic.

One can say that there have been very few mnemonic abnegators in postwar Germany. Even during the first several postwar decades, when discussion of the

Nazi past was muted, German politicians regularly invoked the past for a variety of ends. As Jeffrey Herf has shown, politicians like President Theodor Heuss (FDP) and Kurt Schumacher (SPD) began speaking about German responsibility and the duty to remember the victims of the Holocaust only a few years after the end of the war (Herf 1997). To be sure, one can find statements from Konrad Adenauer that cast him as an abnegator, such as his famous complaint in 1946 that the Allies "finally" stop punishing ordinary Germans who had been first seduced, and later victimized, by the Nazi regime. At the same time, it was also Adenauer who forced the Luxembourg Restitution Agreement, which committed West Germany to pay reparations to Israel, through stiff resistance in his own party. While the early literature on memory politics in the Adenauer era suggested that the Nazi past was largely forgotten, more recent works have painted a more nuanced picture (Langenbacher 2010). One can say, however, that the dominant memory regime concerning the Nazi past in the early Federal Republic was one that privileged German suffering over German complicity. The most significant day in West Germany's commemorative calendar was not May 8 or November 9, but rather Volkstrauertag (National Day of Mourning), which was observed two Sundays before the Advent and is largely devoted to Germany's own military and civilian casualties.

In East Germany, mnemonic abnegation was impossible. The GDR's self-definition as an anti-fascist state required a memory regime about the Nazi past to support this myth. The heroes in the struggle against the Nazis were the German communists and members of the proletariat who had liberated themselves from their capitalist oppressors. This narrative "externalized" the Nazi past by placing the entire blame on the West Germans who, as GDR politicians never tired of pointing out, had welcomed former Nazis back into politics and society. The non-political victims of the Nazi regime—Jews, homosexuals, Sinti and Roma, Poles, the mentally and physically disabled, religious leaders—were completely left out of what, not surprisingly given the nature of the regime, became a unified/hegemonic memory regime.

While the GDR's field of memory would change only slightly before 1989, West Germany's underwent major shifts. Contrary to conventional wisdom, the "generation of '68" did not turn the Holocaust into a central point of reference. The memory entrepreneurs of the student movement did use the Nazi past as a weapon against the political establishment, but their narratives of World War II were not terribly more nuanced than those that preceded them. Accusing parents, professors, and politicians of Nazi sympathies did not lead to a transformative debate about the significance of the Holocaust for contemporary politics: Indeed, the victims of the Nazis were once again largely left out of the story. Willy Brandt's historic gesture of atonement in Warsaw may now seem like a critical juncture in the history of memory politics, but it was in fact an isolated, spontaneous act that did little to reshape Germany's remembrance of World War II.

The real changes came in the 1980s, and they were the product of what at first blush seemed like an attempt at mnemonic abnegation. Chancellor Helmut Kohl (CDU) has long talked about "normalizing" the Nazi past, and he made several attempts at this in the mid-1980s. The most famous was Bitburg, in which he and Reagan stood over the graves of German soldiers killed during World War II. The fact that members of the Waffen-SS were buried in Bitburg did not lead to a change of plans, and was the first in a series of memory battles between those who "wanted the Nazi past to pass away," and those who believed in what I and others have called "a culture of contrition." Yet to cast Kohl and the conservative historians who took what has been deemed a "revisionist" position in the famed "historian's debate" as mnemonic abnegators misses the point: They were not uninterested in memory, but in fact were deeply interested in it. Their fundamental position was that memory of German crimes had crowded out other possible, and far more glorious, historical narratives that could become a basis for a "healthy" national identity (Maier 1988). Put another way, the dominance of the Holocaust-centered memory regime had so structured the entire field of memory that more heroic formulations of German nationalism were not possible. It is worth pointing out that none of these memory entrepreneurs sought to deny or forget the Holocaust, although some, like Ernst Nolte, did seek to limit its hold over Germany's collective consciousness by comparing it with Stalinist crimes (Nolte 1985).

Yet efforts at normalization failed, and developments of memory politics in the 1980s demonstrate that "mnemonic contests are difficult to settle and often produce unintended consequences...for their instigators."[2] The winners were the advocates of the culture of contrition, and they succeeded in creating a bipartisan memory regime before unification. One could characterize these memory entrepreneurs as mnemonic warriors, in that they insisted on a number of non-negotiable historical interpretations. These include the view that the Holocaust was singular and cannot be compared to other atrocities, that May 8 represented a liberation rather than a defeat, that one cannot commemorate German suffering without noting that it followed from German complicity, and that the Nazi past can never be allowed to "pass away." Politicians violated these points of what I have called "political correctness, German style" at the cost of their careers (Art 2006).

Unification threatened to overturn the culture of contrition, for several reasons. First, the euphoria led to a surge of patriotic feelings that were hitherto muted, or denied entirely, in the Federal Republic. Second, the East Germans had marginalized the Holocaust in their memory regime of the Nazi past over the last forty years, so the Holocaust-centered memory regime that West Germans had constructed was quite foreign to them. Third, unification implied a "normalization" of the German question, and the new Germany would be expected to take its role as a responsible European power. Indeed, the United States had long been indirectly calling for the Germans to take on a greater military role in the world (this was one of the motivations for Reagan's ill-fated visit to Bitburg), which was not possible so long as Germans considered perpetual pacifism as the only possible lesson from World War II and the Holocaust.

Yet as in the 1980s, the decade of the 1990s saw not the diminishing of the Nazi past in contemporary politics, but rather a series of memory events that succeeded in institutionalizing the culture of contrition in reunified Germany. The debates are familiar to observers of German politics: the decade-long discussion about the look and location of Germany's central monument to the Holocaust; the exhibit about the crimes of the German army; Daniel Goldhagen's (author of *Hitler's Willing Executioners*) book tour in Germany; the exchange between Martin Walser and Ignaz Bubis; the invocation of "Nie Wieder Auschwitz" to first preclude, and then demand, the use of German military power in the Balkans; the long-delayed payment for German slave labor, and the admission of historical responsibility by a number of Germany's best-known companies (Wüstenberg and Art 2008). The winners in every single one of these debates were those who wanted more memory, more responsibility, more contrition for the Holocaust. Surely, the revival of right-wing extremism in unified Germany made it very difficult for any politician to take a strong position against the importance of remembering Nazi crimes: to even suggest such a thing risked receiving the endorsement of neo-Nazis. But the persistence of the culture of contrition demonstrates that memory construction is highly path dependent. The debates of the 1980s did produce clear winners and losers, and the latter—mostly conservative politicians—largely modified their positions. The result of these battles was that there was not only a smaller constituency of potential mnemonic abnegators, but also a running list of historical controversies that had—at least in the realm of politics—been pretty much settled. No serious person would try to deny the singularity of the Holocaust again, for that battle had been lost long ago.

For a brief period after the end of the millennium, it appeared that old battles *could* be reopened, and potentially be won. When none other than Günther Grass, one of the most prominent defenders of the culture of contrition, published a novel that highlighted German suffering (*Im Krebsgang*, Crabwalk), Germany's memory regime appeared to be morphing into a pillarized one in which multiple narratives of the same past could coexist (Grass 2002). Other publications, as well as the German government's decision to open the Zentrum gegen Vertreibungen (Center against Expulsions) in Berlin, appeared to confirm this trend. Yet the culture of contrition once again proved remarkably resilient (see Langenbacher 2010). As Ruth Wittlinger (2008) notes, Angela Merkel's approach to the Nazi past has been characterized by three key features:

1. An unambiguous acknowledgement of German historical responsibility arising from its Nazi past, without any attempts to "normalize" the German past;
2. A clear appreciation of German suffering, coupled with an unambiguous acknowledgement that this happened as a *consequence* of Nazi Germany's aggressive expansionism;
3. The creation of a link between past, present, and future, signifying the impact of Germany's historical responsibility on discourse *and* policy.

Of these three points, only the second one represents a slight change in Germany's hegemonic culture of contrition, as German suffering is explicitly acknowledged. Yet by drawing a direct causal link between German actions and German suffering, Merkel avoids the relativizing discourse that derailed conservative politicians in the past.

What does all this mean for the memory of 1989? In a land in which memory politics has become so institutionalized, the fall of the Berlin Wall does not only have the misfortune (if one could call it that) of falling on the same day as Pogromnacht, but *any* attempt to highlight a heroic narrative runs up against the culture of contrition. The twenty years since unification have neither unraveled nor undermined this memory regime's power in structuring both contemporary political issues and the larger field of collective memory. Rather, memory politics has broadened and deepened the culture of contrition. So when a German politician discusses the courage of those East Germans who demonstrated in Leipzig, Berlin, and elsewhere in the summer and fall of 1989, it is all too easy to contrast this heroism with the lack of "civil courage" of the millions of Germans on Pogromnacht, which made it abundantly clear to Hitler that further measures against Jews would not be met with any societal resistance. This is the first reason that the fall of the Berlin Wall has not become a more important part of Germany's memory regime.

Flourishing Landscapes and the Wall in the Head

On October 2, 2010, the twentieth anniversary of German unification, the German weekly *Die Zeit* published a piece titled "Twenty Things That We'll Do Better at the Next Unification" (*Die Zeit* 2010). Twenty journalists each identified a major error at unification whose legacy continued to shape Germany's economic, political, and social landscape. Below I focus on three in particular. While not necessarily endorsing these suggestions, they are useful in framing the problematic of unification.

The first helpful suggestion for next time was to set the exchange rate of the weaker to the stronger currency at four and half to one. Of all the errors of unification, Kohl's decision that East and West German marks be traded at parity appears to have been one of the gravest. At the time, there was enormous pressure for "one to one." East German demonstrators held signs with slogans like "Kommt die D-Mark, bleiben wir, kommt sie nicht, gehn wir zu ihr (If the Deutschmark comes, we'll stay, if not, we're coming to you)," and there was genuine fear of a mass emigration from East to West. Many East Germans also argued that real unification demanded setting the exchange rate at parity: "Eins zu eins, sonst werden wir niemals eins (One for one, otherwise we'll never be one)."

In the event, massively overvaluing the East German mark prevented neither of these developments. Many East Germans left anyway: nearly 6.5 percent of the former East German population has emigrated to West Germany since 1991. The brain drain has left many small towns in the East starved of young people, particularly women. Unification also obviously did not lead to the "flourishing landscapes" in the East that Kohl predicted, and economic convergence appears to be at least decades away. The basic figures are well known: despite receiving 1.3 trillion euro in direct transfers from the federal government, labor productivity in the East is only 70 percent of that in West Germany, and unemployment is twice as high (Anderson 2010). Despite a few clusters of strength (mostly high-tech) in some urban areas in the southeast of the country, there are good reasons to fear that the East is becoming a German Mezzogiorno—a region of intractable economic underdevelopment that drains the rest of an advanced industrial economy.

It is debatable whether setting the currency rate at 4.5:1—or even at 7:1, as was being discussed at the time—would have radically altered this situation. Given forty years of separate development, rapid economic convergence was unlikely, and any policy decision could have produced a host of unintended consequences. Yet the consensus is that setting the currencies to parity led to the immediate bankruptcy of many East German firms that could no longer compete when their currency, in effect, became massively overvalued. Setting the currency exchange differently would have slowed down this process, and perhaps given some of the more competitive firms a chance to adapt to the new environment. Once unemployment skyrocketed in the early 1990s, it became difficult to bring under control, as the well-known "unemployment trap" (whereby long bouts of joblessness makes workers increasingly less employable) kicked in (Merkl and Snower 2008). Whether persistent economic divisions were the inevitable product of forty years of separate development, or whether they could have been ameliorated by sounder policies, the fact remains that no German politician can give a speech about the significance of 1989 without at least alluding to the unfinished nature of unification.

A second suggestion was for former dissidents to play a larger political role in the reunified country. The author of this lament (Alexander Cammann) calls it a "scandal of our political culture that today a former IM is far more likely than a former political detainee to become a Minister" (*Die Zeit* 2010).[3] A. James McAdams makes a similar point in a recent essay, noting that "the GDR's former dissidents and regime critics, who had the wherewithal to question their government's authority when opposition of any kind seemed pointless" quickly became "among the most politically marginalized segments of the eastern German population" (McAdams 2010, 35). How this came to pass lies outside the scope of this chapter, and a convincing explanation would certainly be deeper than the common observation that the uncompromising character of dissidents is not well suited for the messy compromises of democracy.

Whatever the causes, the marginalization of the dissidents has implications for the memory regime concerning 1989. As McAdams points out, it has "prevented Berlin from taking full advantage of an opportunity to incorporate the dissidents' actions into the Federal Republic's legitimating mythology" (McAdams 2010, 40). As an example, he cites a speech by Chancellor Merkel commemorating the twentieth anniversary of what turned out to be the last municipal elections in the GDR, during which dissidents identified voting fraud and generated momentum for the demonstrations throughout the summer and fall of 1989. On the face of it, Merkel's remarks look laudatory: "Without May 7 . . . no November 9 and no October 3. Without the civil courage of these independent groups of citizens on the day of local elections and without the protests, the Wall would not have fallen and there would have been no reunification." But McAdams suggests that the Chancellor's remarks signified a broader trend:

> Although she advised in her speech that Germany as a whole owes the oppositionists a debt of respect for making national unity possible, she treated the protests in the GDR as though they had little relevance to West Germany before 1990. At the risk of exaggeration, it is as if the mass demonstrations and cries of "We are the people" had taken place on another planet. Hence, only when the dissidents had finished their work was Bonn prepared to transmit to the region the legal, political, and economic institutions that were required for reunification. (40)

A third suggestion was to have a national discussion over a new constitution, rather than in effect making West Germany's Basic Law the law of the new land.

The idea was that such a debate would have given East Germans a stronger connection to the Federal Republic, and perhaps overcome the feeling that they had been colonized by the West. Countless public opinion polls suggest that the "wall in the head" endures. To cherry-pick a couple of examples, in 2010 only 25 percent of East Germans felt like "real citizens" in unified Germany, and 59 percent claimed they didn't "feel so well" in it. Whereas 28 percent of West Germans were either unsatisfied or very unsatisfied with democracy, the figure in East Germany was 46 percent. While 82 percent of West Germans considered democracy to be important or very important, only 69 of East Germans did (*Spiegel Online* 2010).

One could find encouraging signals from public opinion polls as well. In 2009 there were signs, for example, that generational change might slowly erode the wall in the head. Whereas 36 percent of Germans between the ages of 40 and 49 defined themselves as either Ossis or Wessis, only 11 percent of those between 14 and 19 did (*New York Times* 2009). Still, the preponderance of evidence points to an attitudinal cleavage between East and West that is now reflected in the German party system (Kopstein and Ziblatt 2006). As with the economic question, it is debatable whether politics could have led to a more rapid convergence of political attitudes. Certainly, a softer economic landing from socialism would have led to less dissatisfaction with democracy. But whatever the magnitude and causes of the "wall in the head," it remains impossible to commemorate unification without making mention of it.

The Unrechtsstaat and the "Kleine DDR"

One of the major attitudinal differences between East and West Germans concerns the memory of the GDR. According to a survey conducted twenty years after the fall of the Wall, nearly half (49 percent) of East Germans agreed with the statement that the GDR had "more good than bad sides," whereas 8 percent agreed with the statement that it "had almost only good sides" (*Die Zeit* 2009b). These attitudes are symptomatic of an "Ostalgie" that has been perceptible since the early 1990s. Some of the manifestations of this syndrome, such as specialized markets carrying familiar products from the GDR to cater to the tastes of East German pensioners, are politically harmless. Others, such as the growth of kitschy exhibits around symbols of Germany's division, are deeply offensive to those who suffered under communist oppression. But the most important questions revolve around the nature of the GDR, the crimes committed under it, and—crucially—whether those perpetrators should be allowed to hold political office.

The persistence of nostalgic attitudes toward the GDR is not the result of a failure to examine the communist past. In light of the perceived failure to turn to a critical examination of the Nazi past in the immediate postwar decades, Germans were hardly going to make the same mistake twice. As Norbert Frei notes, "the political class of the Bundesrepublik was willing to supply the necessary resources for a thorough scientific investigation of East German history," a readiness that was notably lacking during the first decades of the West German regime (*Zeit Online* 2009). By the mid-1990s, historical works on the GDR could fill a small library and, according to Frei, the "East German dictatorship was being researched in an exemplary manner." Part of this had to do with the fact that East Germans, upon seeing smoke rising from Stasi buildings, stormed them and ensured that the millions of files contained within them would not be lost to history. Wolfgang Schäuble (CDU) was one of the very few historical abnegators in the debate about what to do with the files (he maintained that they should be destroyed), and the surviving documents have proven to be a treasure trove for historians.

Of course, the existence of the Stasi files also means that the legacy of the GDR is constantly threatening to intrude in the daily partisan politics of the Federal Republic. In 2009, this happened twice—both times in dramatic fashion.

The first episode occurred in March 2009, when Erwin Sellering (SPD), the minister-president of Mecklenburg West Pomerania, stated in an interview: "I reject the condemnation of the GDR as an *Unrechtsstaat* in which there was nothing good at all about it," adding that "the former West Germany also had its weaknesses just as East Germany had its strengths" (*Reuters* 2009). This added fuel to a long running debate over the use of the term "Unrechtsstaat" as an accurate designation for the GDR. The term translates poorly, but it describes a state that is not based on the rule of law and is thus both lawless and unjust. Germans have a particularly rich history of launching national debates that seem to turn on semantic distinctions—the flaps over such terms as "Leitkultur" (leading culture) and "national Stolz" (national pride) are two relatively recent examples (Art 2006)—and an outside observer could be forgiven for believing that disputes about whether the GDR was an "Unrechtsstaat" or a "Rechtsstaat" (state based on the rule of law) would best be left to legal scholars. But as Sellering's remarks make clear, the controversy about the Unrechtsstaat was less about semantic and juridical distinctions, and more about whether there were any positive sides to the former East Germany.

From a historian's perspective, this was a rather inane debate. Of course, there were some things that the GDR did reasonably well, aside from crushing dissent and keeping tabs on its population. And it is understandable that those who lived the majority of their lives in the GDR would want to remember positive experiences. As Mary Fulbrook demonstrated in her detailed study of the GDR, these two strands come together: the strong and common desire to claim that one had lived a "perfectly normal life" in East Germany does not rest entirely on historical amnesia

(Fulbrook 2005). For every Stasi IM, there was a bureaucrat who worked hard to find a pensioner the garden she had been promised years before, or arrange for a flat for a young couple. Simply put, the realities of the GDR were more complex than a term like Unrechtsstaat can hope to capture.

But history and historical memory are, of course, two different things, as are scholarly versus political debates. It is worth recalling once again the famous historians' debate, which turned on the question of whether the Holocaust was roughly equivalent to the crimes of Stalinism. For scholars of comparative politics, the question of comparability is puzzling: of course one can compare and contrast events—even the most terrible ones—in order to bring out their similarities and differences. But in political discourse, the "singularity" thesis became identified with the contrition position, and the comparability thesis with the "normalization" camp. With the fault lines drawn so clearly, it was impossible—and politically costly—to try to straddle these two positions.

This is what Gesine Schwan learned when she entered the Unrechtsstaat debate. A former professor of political science who had written a book on coming to terms with the Nazi past, Schwan was the SPD's presidential candidate and the primary challenger to President Horst Köhler, who was seeking a second term. Schwan refused to describe the former GDR as an Unrechtsstaat in an interview with the *Tagespiegal* in May, just in time for the commemoration of the sixtieth anniversary of the founding of the Federal Republic. Although she also noted in her remarks that the GDR was certainly not a Rechtsstaat, as it was "not a state based on the rule of law, there was no system of checks and balances on the use of power, and arbitrariness reigned," she was quickly cast as an apologist for the former regime. Some members of the Greens and the SPD withdrew their support for her, and Köhler was elected to a second term.

While it is debatable whether Schwan's position in the Unrechtsstaat controversy cost her the presidency, the point is that one could begin to speak of a politics of the GDR past that, like those surrounding the Nazi past, were now intruding into contemporary partisan politics. To some extent, this had been occurring since the mid-1990s, and usually revolved around the Party of Democratic Socialism (PDS), which was the official successor to the East German communist party. In 1994, for example, the CDU injected what would become known as the "red socks" campaign into the national parliamentary elections. The CDU poster showed a red sock pinned to a clothesline with the caption "into the future…but not in red socks." This was a deliberate reference to the fact that the SPD and the Greens had formed a minority government in Saxony-Anhalt that relied on the support of the PDS. The central message—and one that the CDU repeated during its 1998 "red hands" campaign—was that the PDS's failure to distance itself from the crimes of the GDR rendered it an illegitimate player in the German party system.

The second episode was born out of an attempt to overcome what had become a highly effective argument for the CDU, and a tactical problem for the SPD. Despite predictions to the contrary, the PDS did not wither away but continued to expand its vote share in state and national elections in the former East. The party continued to appeal to those who felt that socialism was a good idea, if badly carried out. At the same time, it turned to populism (Hough and Koss 2009). In 2005, it merged with a leftist splinter group of the SPD (the WASG) and was renamed Die Linke (the Left Party). The growing success of this new party, and particularly the possibility that it could draw significant votes in the West, represented a huge problem for the SPD. Should the SPD form state governments with the Left Party? Or should it take an adversarial strategy toward it and refuse to work with it? Combining these strategies was not possible, as the SPD leader in Hessen, Andrea Ypsilanti, learned in November 2008. After ruling out cooperation with the Left Party before the election, Ypsilanti tried to renege on this promise and form a minority SPD-Green government with the toleration of the Left Party. But this provoked a rebellion from within the SPD, and ultimately led to the dissolution of the Hessen state parliament and new elections in January 2009, in which the SPD was trounced. Ypsilanti resigned as party chairman shortly thereafter.

This was precisely the type of outcome that Matthias Platzeck (SPD), the Prime Minister of Brandenburg, tried to avoid in November 2009. In an essay that appeared in *Der Spiegel* under the title "Versöhnung Ernst Nehmen" (Taking Reconciliation Seriously), Platzeck argued that forming a Red-Red (SPD-Left Party) coalition in Brandenburg would help to overcome "an unhealthy rift" (ein ungesunder Ris) that had formed in East German society (*Der Spiegel* 2009). He compared this act of reconciliation to the integrating gestures of Kurt Schumacher toward former members of the Waffen-SS in the early years of the Federal Republic. He closed the essay with the following argument:

> Drawing the right lessons from history has less to do with a ritualized mastering of the past than with our daily readiness for a new beginning. Those who are ready for that must be welcomed by Democrats. That was true in the decades after 1945 in West Germany, and it must finally prevail twenty years after unification.

Like so many past attempts to put history to rest, this one only succeeded in stirring it up.

Politicians from all parties—including his own SPD—criticized Platzeck for, among other things, "eingeschraenkte Gesichtswahrnemung" (a limited historical view/perspective) and for trivializing the Nazi past. Yet Platzeck followed through on his article by forming a coalition with the Left Party in November of 2009, just several days before the twentieth anniversary of the fall of the Wall.

Platzeck had succeeded Manfred Stolpe as prime minister of Brandenburg in 2002. Stolpe's admission that he had worked with the Stasi did not derail his political career. He took it as a point of pride that Brandenburg was called "the little DDR" in the Federal Republic. Other politicians, particularly those from the Left Party, were also not overly hampered by their communist pasts. The leader of Brandenburg's Left Party, Kerstin Kaiser, admitted and apologized for her role as a Stasi IM, and one can find a self-critical portrait of her biography on her website. Yet having a former IM as the second-in-command of Brandenburg—even if it was the little DDR—was viewed as too much, and Kaiser agreed to not be part of Platzeck's cabinet.

Yet it turned out that Kaiser was only part of a much larger problem: the upper-ranks of the Left Party contained many individuals who had not come clean about their Stasi pasts. Within the first week of the coalition, four members from the Left Party in the new cabinet were outed as former IMs or as full-time members of the Stasi. Another four, including Kaiser, who had revealed their pasts, received a thorough public inspection. The four who had covered up their pasts ended up resigning their posts, but the affair cast into sharp relief what was perceived to be a failing to deal with the DDR past, particularly in Brandenburg.

The affair clearly raised important issues for the Left Party. Could it continue to appeal to those who were nostalgic for the GDR without isolating other potential voters who are attracted more by its populism than its core ideology? Just how deep were the links with the old regime? Does being a former IM disqualify one from holding high political office?

Yet the problems in Brandenburg also had major implications for the SPD. The national party has appeared to endorse, or at least not criticize, local and state alliances with the Left Party. This had led many to speculate that party leaders were beginning to rethink their strategy of ruling out a coalition with the Left Party at the national level. In March 2009, for example, SPD leader Franz Müntefering stated that the Left Party should no longer be measured solely in terms of its relationship to the GDR past. Although he ruled out a coalition at the national level, it did appear to many observers that the SPD's position toward the Left Party was softening. Had the Brandenburg experiment not attracted so much negative attention, it could have provided another argument for those who were in favor of strategic flexibility. The first red-red (SPD-Left Party) government had been doing reasonably well in Berlin, and success in Brandenburg would have furthered the case that the Left Party was not threatening to erode democracy or bring back the GDR. Yet this was obviously not to be, and the SPD has since tried to distance itself from the Left. In the presidential elections of 2010, the SPD chose Joachim Gauck as its candidate. Since Gauck had been an anti-communist activist and the first Federal Commissioner for the Stasi Archives, many interpreted this as a clear signal that the SPD was going to continue with the national level policy of *Ausgrenzung* (marginalization) of the ex-GDR Left.

Conclusion

The twentieth anniversary of the fall of the Berlin Wall forced Germans to take positions on the meaning of that world-historical event in the context of partisan political calculations and a preexisting memory regime. To a far greater degree than anywhere else in Central and Eastern Europe, this Holocaust-centered memory regime determined what other memory regimes could become salient in Germany's field of collective memory. As I have argued, this political-cultural construction—combined with the enduring social and economic divide between East and West—made it difficult for Germans from across the political spectrum to cast November 9, 1989, as an unambiguously heroic day in German history. Perhaps things will be different in 2019 or 2029, but for the foreseeable future it is difficult to imagine Germans coming to the type of national consensus that would allow them to unabashedly celebrate their only successful democratic revolution.

In part this is because both the Left Party and its political competitors will no doubt continue to try to profit from memory politics. It may seem counterproductive for a Left Party politician like Ulla Jelpke to praise former members of the Stasi for their "courageous mission [Einsatz] for peace," but so long as such sentiments are widely shared among the party's core voters, she and others will search for opportunities to tap into East Germans' indignation that their history is being written by the ultimate victors (colonizers to many) in the Cold War (*Spiegel Online* 2010b). Christian Democratic politicians will predictably take such revisionist readings of history as undisputable evidence of the Left Party's extremism and will raise the issue whenever the SPD looks to be contemplating any type of cooperation with it. With the rise of the Pirate Party and the mounting internal conflicts within the Left Party at the time of this writing, it may be that the SPD will have more coalition options if support for the Left Party continues to hemorrhage. But given that the Left Party has been written off several times before, it is difficult to imagine that the dynamics I have outlined here do not continue.

Moreover, the election of Joachim Gauck to the federal presidency in March 2012 has only reinforced the political salience of East German history. Gauck lost out to Merkel's favored candidate Christian Wulff in the presidential elections of 2010, but after Wulff was forced to resign following a financial scandal, Gauck became the consensus candidate of all parties except the Left. By nominating Beate Klarsfeld, best known for her relentless and successful efforts at bringing former Nazis to justice, the Left Party pitted a "Nazi hunter" against the "Stasi hunter" Gauck. Of course, the Left Party's nomination was purely symbolic, as Klarsfeld had no hope of beating a cross-party candidate like Gauck. Yet the fact that the two candidates for president could not only be easily separated from memory politics, but were in large part defined by it, should give pause to anyone who believes that the past in Germany—either the Nazi Past or the DDR past—will be allowed to pass away.

One could nevertheless interpret the selection of Gauck over Klarsfeld as a sign that Germany is moving away from a Holocaust-centered memory regime. Gauck's signing of the Prague Declaration on European Conscience and Communism in 2008, which calls for Europe to recognize the crimes of both communism and Nazism, has raised criticism from those who view it as a repetition of the Historians' Debate of the mid-1980s (*Times of Israel* 2012). Like all German presidents before him, Gauck will be expected to visit Israel, Poland, and other historically sensitive places and to make regular statements on the meaning of the Holocaust, and it is possible that he may depart somewhat from the ritualized discourse that I have summarized here. Yet is it worth recalling that while President Wulff was forced to step down over a financial scandal, the president before him (Horst Köhler) got into considerable trouble for violating the culture of contrition. During a visit to Afghanistan, Köhler stated that German troops might be called upon to preserve trade routes in the future, and that such deployments would be in Germany's national interest. Such a remark would be uncontroversial in most countries, but Köhler was accused of favoring gunboat diplomacy and was linked to the aggressive nationalism of the past. Gauck's biography may give him more room for maneuver in the perilous field of German memory politics, but it is unlikely that he, or any other German politician, would try to take on the culture of contrition head-on.

Stepping back from the intricacies of German memory politics and adopting a comparative perspective, one obvious yet nonetheless critical difference from other post-communist transitions is worth emphasizing in closing: East Germany was the only state to disappear entirely and to be absorbed by another. As I have argued, this meant that mnemonic warriors faced cultural constraints in the form of West Germany's preexisting memory regime. And these constraints were particularly strong because West Germany represents a rare case of a nearly unified memory regime organized around the culture of contrition. Yet at the same time, the nature of unification (some would say "colonization") provided opportunities for mnemonic warriors operating in the East to link memories of communism to an emerging political cleavage in a very powerful way. By salvaging some redeeming qualities from the DDR past, memory entrepreneurs helped reinforce an East

German political identity that has endured for two decades despite frequent pre-dictions that it would disappear within a matter of years. Since the DDR was a prototypical hard-line regime in which only a vanishingly small percentage of the population could lay claim to a dissident heritage, this memory regime was bound to be based on nostalgia, apologia, and a lingering sense that unification, for all its positive sides, involved a heavy dose of "victor's justice" that turned ordinary East Germans into victims once again. It is probably impossible to put this proposition to a social scientific test, but it may very well be that it is precisely this type of indignant memory regime—as opposed to a memory regime based on heroism or momentous achievements—that ends up casting the longest shadow on contemporary politics. After all, perhaps the most well-known observation on the role of memory comes from the muse of a post–Civil War American south that could not move beyond its defeat. "In the South," William Faulkner wrote, "the past is never dead; it's not even past."

NOTES

1. The term Pogromnacht is now viewed as preferable to the older "Kristallnacht"; the latter can be conceived as trivializing the event as it refers directly to the broken glass outside Jewish busi-nesses but not to the deaths, suicides, and imprisonments that resulted from it.

2. Kubik and Bernhard, "A Theory of the Politics of Memory," Chapter 1 of this volume.

3. IM is short for Inoffizieller mitarbeiter (literally, "unofficial work colleague") and is the des-ignation given to Stasi informers.

10 The Inescapable Past
THE POLITICS OF MEMORY IN POST-COMMUNIST BULGARIA
Venelin I. Ganev

IF POLITICS IS construed in terms of the strategies of identifiable elites who manipulate historical narratives and cultural symbols in their pursuit of power, then it would be justified to argue that the twentieth anniversary of November 10, 1989— the day when long-serving communist dictator Todor Zhivkov was deposed and the one-party regime began to unravel—did not have a significant impact on Bulgarian politics. Many of the politicians who found themselves in influential positions in 2009 were apparently uninterested in taking advantage of the occasion; many of those who wished to exploit it had already lost much of their political influence. But if politics is defined in broader terms, as a set of practices that center on fundamentally important notions such as the meaning of collective life and good governance, then it would be fair to say that 1989 is an inescapable point of reference in any intellectually relevant conversation about the nation's political experiences. The end of communist rule is routinely construed as the decisive scission that split history into two distinct periods—"before" and "after"—and the juxtaposition of "what was then" and "what is now" continues to form the background against which political actors of all stripes must craft their strategies for outmaneuvering opponents as well as their messages to the citizenry. In that sense, the politics of memory is a phenomenon in comparison with which any other type of politics in the country fades into insignificance.

Commemorating 1989: "Let's Congratulate Ourselves on the Transition!"

The official celebration marking Zhivkov's ouster was a low-key affair. The only public event was the opening of a photo exhibition called "20 years in 60 pictures" in the charming garden in front of the Bulgarian National Theater. The main sponsor of the event was not the Bulgarian government, but the European Union (as a part of an initiative called "Europe, United and Free")—which raises the question of whether in the absence of outside funding Bulgarian political elites would have bothered to make plans for any festivities at all. And the main organizer was the non-political and non-partisan Bulgarian Telegraph Agency (*24 Chasa* 2009). The very manner in which the ceremony was managed limited its potential to generate political controversies. An open invitation was extended to all who wished to attend, which meant that there were no clearly identifiable hosts and guests—the former enjoying the privilege to determine who should be invited and who should be snubbed, and the latter relishing the opportunity to publicly refuse to attend and thus casting doubts on the political legitimacy and worthiness of the event.

A closer scrutiny of the political profile of the self-selected participants warrants the conclusion that "former" is the most appropriate adjective to attach to descriptions of those in attendance: barring miraculous comebacks—and there have been very few of those in Bulgaria after 1989—their political careers appear to be over. More prominent among them were former President Zhelyu Zhelev, former Prime Minister Simeon Saxkoburggotski, former Deputy Prime Ministers Evgeni Bakurdzhiev and Nikolai Vassilev, former Ministers Milen Velchev and Iordan Sokolov, former Speaker of Parliament Georgi Pirinski. In contrast, political celebrities who currently enjoy power and command the attention of the media did not honor the celebration. Apart from then-Prime Minister Boyko Borissov, almost none of the well-known figures in GERB, the ruling party at the time, showed up.[1] The leaders of the two largest opposition factions, Sergei Stanishev (BSP) and Ahmed Dogan (MRF), did not take part, and neither did other highly visible parliamentarians like Volen Siderov and Yane Yanev (representing Ataka and Order, Legality, Justice, respectively). To the extent that the event generated a controversy at all, that happened when an attempt was made to herd all participants for a photograph. While most responded positively, some (most notably, former Prime Minister Ivan Kostov) refused to join in. But even that mini-controversy failed to dispel the overall impression that there was not much at stake in what transpired in front of the magnificent National Theater.

The ceremony ended with a short speech delivered by Prime Minister Borissov. For the most part, it consisted of clichés about Bulgaria's successful bid to join the

European Union and the ongoing progress toward a "European standard of living and European mentality." One particular phrase that the speaker used, however, stood out as a colorful patch on a gray piece of cloth: "Let us congratulate ourselves on the transition!" (Trud 2009a). This phrase sounds awkward in Bulgarian. The expression "let us congratulate ourselves on" is typically used with reference to specific dates, events, or anniversaries rather than protracted, ongoing, open-ended processes like "the transition." On the other hand, this expression is indelibly etched in the memory of every Bulgarian citizen born before 1980, because it was always used by communist dictator Todor Zhivkov at the end of his annual New Year's Eve messages broadcast on both channels of the Bulgarian National Television on December 31 at 11:50 p.m. ("Let us congratulate ourselves on the New Year!"). Thus the very act of celebrating the end of the communist era conjured up a rhetorical idiom that confirmed this era's continuing relevance to post-communist political mores. As I will argue in this chapter, the Bulgarian prime minister's choice of words is not coincidental: Borissov's mnemonic hint attests to the fact that for all important actors in the country the past remains an important political resource. How this past should be remembered, and how it should be related to the present, are still among the basic issues that ruling elites and partisan opinion-makers evoke as they endeavor to manipulate the Bulgarian political landscape to their advantage.

Hermeneutic Wars: Interpreting 1989

In the absence of grand political dramas to cover, Bulgarian media entrepreneurs marked the twentieth anniversary with a series of interviews featuring two kinds of politicians: surviving high-ranking officials of the old regime and anti-communist activists who burst onto the political scene in the 1990s. These interviews revealed two important facts. First, the question of what exactly happened is no longer exploited for opportunistic political purposes and has ceased to spawn conspiracy theories. The events of November 1989 have been stitched together into a straightforward narrative—about how Zhivkov's ouster was the culmination of the intraparty factional struggle that unfolded in the absence of popular anti-regime mobilization—whose veracity no one finds it necessary to challenge. Second, the *meaning* of this narrative—its significance for understanding quintessential Bulgarian political experiences—is aggressively contested. What follows from the fact that November 10 happened as it did? Behind the varying answers given to this question loom irreconcilable political differences and radically diverging normative commitments. Here, then, is one of the interesting characteristics of the politics of memory in Bulgaria: Factual peace has emerged; yet hermeneutic wars have been unleashed.

Former Politburo members opined that it is only natural that their party was the driving force behind the changes—and that the Bulgarian people's quiescence was an expression of loyalty to the regime. From their vantage point atop the pyramid of power, the legitimacy of the communist regime was never seriously questioned. Regardless of certain feelings of frustration and disgruntlement, the population remained devoted to the communist project and was therefore entitled to expect that the Party would do what it had been doing since 1944—lead a united nation to a better future. Notably, the former comrades do not proffer identical interpretations of the motivation and strategies of the two groups that became involved in the drama, the pro-Zhivkov and the anti-Zhivkov factions.[2] According to Iordan Yotov, the clash pitted those who, like himself, were interested in pressing forward with "the struggle for socialism" against the forces of "counterrevolution."[3] The former group was still committed to the emancipatory Marxist experiment; in contrast, the faction that succeeded Zhivkov in power "broke up with the great ideals." The reins of power thus passed into the hands of "traitors" who turned their backs not just on the socialist system, but also on "the people, on the working class which was the dominant power in Bulgaria." He ends his interview with the following lament: "Hardly anyone writes about the dictatorship of the proletariat anymore...." (Trud 2009d).

It is worth underscoring that Yotov's insistence that, as a result of the replacement of dictatorial methods with democratic practices of governance, the quality of life in Bulgaria has deteriorated dramatically is far from outlandish in a Bulgarian context. In fact, the two-pronged argument that comparisons between the pre- and post-1989 era should be construed in terms of the benefits of socialism and the evils of capitalism, and that the abandonment of "the great ideals" has generated catastrophic consequences, constitutes the cornerstone of the hegemonic political discourse in contemporary Bulgaria. Why and how this discourse—which relentlessly valorizes the pre-1989 era and thoroughly repudiates the post-1989 period—became entrenched in the Bulgarian political sphere is a question that cannot be fully answered here.[4] But one specific factor should be mentioned—the media in the country, and particularly the crucially important print media, are owned and controlled by former officers from the communist secret services.[5] Despite the fact that they amassed considerable personal wealth after 1989, these individuals apparently consider their affiliation with the power structures of the communist dictatorship as the highlight of their professional careers and seem to have a personal stake in perpetuating the positive depictions of the communist era that they internalized while serving Zhivkov's regime.

Yotov's nostalgia for the dictatorship of the proletariat, therefore, is rather typical. That does not mean, however, that his former comrades share all his views. In what was by far the most interesting material on November 10 to appear in the Bulgarian press in 2009, Georgi Atanassov, Zhivkov's last prime minister, expressed somewhat different opinions.[6] He defended the behavior of the anti-Zhivkov faction of which he was one of the most prominent leaders: "We believed that the change will produce positive results. And we fought to make things better." More generally, while somewhat vague on the question of the coup's long-term objectives—a Soviet-type perestroika or a Polish-type embrace of liberal democracy—Atanassov refrained from using the rhetoric associated with the Marxist revolutionary project. In two key respects, however, his account of 1989 is similar to Yotov's. First, he insists that Zhivkov's ouster was an internal party affair, "a normal change within the party," which proved that responsive communist leaders were committed to leading the country out of the crises that confronted it. Second, he reiterated the point that public pressure "from below" was not a factor that played any role during the November events. Asked whether he was concerned that "the opposition" might bring about the collapse of the regime, Atanassov responded: "The opposition? What opposition? Some discontent had accumulated in society, but in Bulgaria there was no such thing as a serious, organized opposition" (Trud 2009b; see also Trud 2009c). Far from being the culmination of a legitimacy crisis, the November 10 plenum was a spectacle that routinely transpires in one-party regimes stricken by internal factional bickering—a spectacle that, according to this interpretation, played itself out in front of a population whose passivity reflected not fearful submission but enduring trust in the system.

The contention that November 10 was a plot concocted and carried out by party cadres is not disputed by former leaders of the opposition. Former President Zhelyu Zhelev[7] unambiguously asserted that "November 10th was an intra-party coup." Attempts to portray Zhivkov's removal as a response to societal pressures are misguided because "the way in which it was carried out—as a result of behind-the-scenes machinations...conforms to the classical scenario of a conspiracy within the framework of the party itself" (Trifonova 2009). Former President Petar Stoyanov expressed similar views.[8] The change at the top, he argued, "was conceived as a party intrigue rather than the regime's reaction to growing public indignation" (Stoyanov 2010). Along the same lines, another former UDF luminary, Petko Simeonov, pointed out that "the Bulgarian dissident movement did not have any hierarchy and did not enjoy massive support" (Simeonov 2010). That November 10 was a plot featuring party leaders trying to fortify their power rather than accommodate an assertive public is thus a consensually embraced proposition in various discourses on the past.

An analytical distinction is necessary in order to situate this consensus into a broader interpretive framework that might help us understand the politics of memory in post-communist Bulgaria: the distinction between factual wars and hermeneutic wars. Factual wars are usually triggered by, and often focus on, empirical questions such as who did what when and why. Typically, warriors concerned about "getting the facts straight" would proffer diverging views on issues related to the politically relevant actors, the most important decision-making sites, and the agendas pursued by actors who had the power to shape the course of events. Are political elites who participated in discussions more influential than those who allegedly pulled the strings behind the scenes? Are public forums like the Roundtable Talks and the formal agreements that they institutionalized more significant than secretive decision-making locations where informal private deals were struck? To what extent did political priorities informing post-1989 transformations reflect an officially announced agenda, and to what extent were they shaped by assiduously concealed conspiracies? These are the kinds of questions around which factual wars revolve—and their ultimate objective is to present the definitive "empirical" proof that specific historical junctures should be remembered in a particular way.

The nature of hermeneutic wars is somewhat different. Such conflicts unfold in a political environment marked by consensus regarding the essential facts. The focal point of raging controversies is *the interpretation* of such facts—or, put differently, the hermeneutic accounts put forward by rival political factions. Hermeneutics, authoritatively described by Hans-Georg Gadamer as "the art of understanding texts," is arguably an indispensable, if not necessarily widely noticed, component of any significant form of political engagement. But this art is particularly important when a narrative that constitutes the focal point of a political community's obsessions and aspirations is "no longer immediately situated in a world" and therefore "is estranged from its original meaning and depends on the unlocking and mediating spirit that we, like the Greeks, name after Hermes, the messenger of the gods" (Gadamer 1989, 164–165). The distinguishing characteristic of hermeneutic wars, therefore, is that they are not set off primarily by ongoing disagreements about the empirical content of a narrative "text"—they begin because an unquestioned empirical narrative is *not* embedded in a shared universe of meaning and therefore readily lends itself to competing interpretations, all of them invoking higher truths. The ultimate objective of hermeneutic warriors is not to reveal unknown facts or to debate the empirical basis of historical narratives, but to articulate a rhetoric that seeks to persuade a nation that its paradigmatic experiences have a particular meaning (Khan 2011).

It is my contention that the 1989-focused exchanges that took place in Bulgaria in 2009 should be considered a form of hermeneutic warfare. To the extent that the views espoused by former communists and anti-communist activists differed, it is with regard to *the interpretation* of the events surrounding November 10, 1989, and particularly the fact that anti-regime mobilization was largely absent. What does this fact tell us about Bulgarians' political mentality? And how is it related to the country's post-1989 transformations? It is such broader issues, not just concerns about who did what and why, that propel the politics of memory in Bulgaria. Admittedly, it was not the words of gods that Bulgarian hermeneutic warriors who wanted to play the role of "unlocking and mediating spirits" invoked—but they did assert, quite explicitly, that what is at stake in the controversies regarding the proper interpretation of 1989 are essential characteristics of the Bulgarian political tradition as well as the nation's place in the modern world.

As we already saw, from the vantage point of former Politburo members like Yotov and Atanassov, the fact that in 1989 Bulgarians did not rally behind causes like democracy and freedom is fairly easy to comprehend. What this fact means is that the institutionalized practices of the one-party regime provided essential material benefits that the population deeply appreciated—and that the reigning Marxist-Leninist ideology satisfied its spiritual and cultural cravings. For the leaders of the opposition, to the contrary, the absence of grass-roots activism reveals a troubling aspect of Bulgarian political culture. According to their interpretation, a modern political community can realize its aspirations only if it has the determination to confront oppressive rulers with demands for more rights and freedoms, the courage to make sacrifices in the pursuit of democracy, and the spiritual strength to envisage for itself a better future—and what the events of November 1989 showed is that Bulgarian society was not determined, courageous, or strong enough. Stoyanov opined that it is this regrettable dearth of idealism, civic mindedness, and hope that sets Bulgaria apart from other Eastern European nations. His answer to the question of whether he would celebrate the twentieth anniversary of November 10, 1989, was "No. What happened on that day should inspire neither exultation, nor a sense of national pride. In fact, this is the only date in contemporary East European history that has nothing to do with the massive civic mobilization against communism" (Stoyanov 2010). Far from bespeaking allegiance to normative principles, popular quiescence revealed a widespread willingness to forgo idealistic aspirations in order to enjoy the simple pleasures of a bearable everyday life.

As already pointed out, the conversation about 1989 was more or less confined to the ranks of former politicians. But there were exceptions—and the most remarkable feature of non-politicians' contributions to this exchange is that they belabored precisely the theme regarding the population's passivity in 1989. Georgi Gospodinov, a popular writer, argued that those who wish to celebrate the collapse of communism in Bulgaria should consider dates other than November 10: "on November 10th we were told on television that we were free. The passive voice in this sentence is really important. We were told.... It is as if we received an award for our extraordinary patience." It would be more appropriate, Gospodinov pointed out, to celebrate November 3, not November 10. On November 3, a week before the anti-Zhivkov coup, an anti-government rally was held in Sofia for the first time since the late 1940s. Several thousand people gathered in front of the National Cathedral, walked the short distance to the National Assembly and, amidst chants of "Democracy!" and "Freedom!," delivered to the all-communist parliament a petition against several ecologically disastrous industrial projects in the Rila Mountain. Gospodinov acknowledged that the number of those involved was small—between 5,000 and 10,000 citizens.[9] Nevertheless, he points out, "on November 3rd there was a daring…attempt to break through the unfreedom encrusting our bodies" (2009). Since it is not changes at the top, but the political awakening and civic involvement of the people that should turn specific dates into important thresholds of a country's history, November 3 might conceivably be enchanted as such a threshold. November 10, in contrast, should serve as a reminder that something essential was missing in the Bulgarian 1989—a nation's desire to be free.

In an interview broadcast during an evening news program on November 10, 2009, Kiril Marichkov, the Bulgarian "Paul McCartney" (he plays bass, sings and writes songs for *The Crickets*, the most successful Bulgarian rock band, and had a brief career as a UDF politician in the early 1990s), went even further. What 1989 exemplifies, he asserted, was the idealistic aspirations and the democratic power of liberty-loving people. Hence the truly commemoration-worthy date was not November 10, but November 9, the day when Berliners forced their rulers to open the Wall. Compared to the German November, the Bulgarian November was nothing more than "a coup carried out under pressure from KGB." The behavior of the majority of Bulgarians should not be interpreted as a commitment to social ideals, communist or other. It simply demonstrated that the prevalent mentality in the Bulgarian political community is such that fear and pragmatic acceptance of the status quo will always trump the desire for a better life in freedom. Hence, Marichkov concluded, there is no such thing as a "Bulgarian 1989" that is worth remembering (*BTV Novinite* 2009).

It would be warranted to assume, then, that at present both political elites and the citizenry as a whole appear confident that they know what happened on November 10, 1989—*wie es ist eigentlich gewesen*. Zhivkov was pushed out as a result of a coup, and the Bulgarian people were not involved in the process. Some political actors—like the leaders of GERB, the ruling party in 2009—obviously did not find this story interesting enough and refrained from pushing it in a particular direction. For those who dominated the political arena in the 1990s, however, the declaration of peace on the facts was simply a way to continue political wars by other means. First and foremost, these wars focus on what happened in the 1990s, and in that context November 10 is invariably construed as nothing more than the inconspicuous beginning of a process that almost everyone in Bulgaria wants to forswear. According to the former rulers, the decline experienced during the first decade of post-communist transformations should be attributed to the abandonment of Marxist ideas and the end of the Party's benevolent and visionary leadership. According to the leaders of the opposition, the decline transpired because even after 1989 the country continued to be governed by Zhivkov's comrades, whose predatory behavior a passive population indifferent to democratic values and civic virtues could not effectively resist (Ganev 2007). Hermeneutic wars take place, then, at least in part because, in an effort to blame each other for the turbulent 1990s, Bulgarian political elites seem determined to distance themselves from, rather than strategically appropriate, the events of 1989. But such conflicts are also fueled by irreconcilable interpretations of the pre-1989 period. What is the truth about the socialist past? This question is still centrally important for the politics of memory in post-communist Bulgaria; it is also a *casus belli* frequently invoked by the country's mnemonic warriors. In the next two sections, I will analyze two flare-ups of mnemonic confrontation. The first one was set off by an attempt to institutionalize a particular vision of the period of communist hegemony, and the second one revolved around what might be called national mnemonic basics. What these confrontations suggest is that while the question of what happened on November 10, 1989, does not elicit opposing views, the memory field in Bulgaria with regard to what transpired before that date is fractured—and that amidst the ebbs and flows of democratic politics, no political group or coalition is in a position to permanently officialize their historical interpretations. That does not mean that all participants in the mnemonic wars wield equal power—as will become clear, political and media actors who praise the socialist era are in a much better position to disseminate their messages than their rivals. But it does mean that the politics of memory in Bulgaria will continue to be marked by fluidity and volatility in the foreseeable future.

Legislative Battles and Memory Regimes: What Happened Between September 9 and September 12, 1944?

In their introduction to this volume, Michael Bernhard and Jan Kubik formulate a two-pronged hypothesis: mnemonic warriors will use various means to entrench what they consider to be the truth about the past—but such campaigns will almost never create stable equilibriums and will therefore fail to put such "truths" beyond and above the flux of democratic politics. What transpired during the passage of key amendments to "The Law on Political and Civil Rehabilitation of Repressed Citizens" in the Bulgarian Parliament confirms this hypothesis. The clash that this event triggered had all the trappings of a mnemonic war that culminated in a parliamentary majority's effort to legislate about the correct interpretation of the nation's history. What it also demonstrated is that such efforts invariably encounter resistance—and are liable to be reversed when the circumstances change.

The amendments were drafted by the BSP-dominated government in 2008 when it was clear that the party of the ex-communists was losing influence and would almost certainly be defeated in the upcoming general elections. The only controversial issue was what should be considered the beginning of unlawful repressions in Bulgaria. The two proposed dates were September 9, 1944 and September 12, 1944—and, as students of Eastern European politics and history can imagine, there was a lot at stake in this seemingly trivial controversy. September 9 is the date when, as a result of a successful coup, the Communist Party won control over the state's repressive apparatus—and instantly unleashed the first wave of Red Terror. September 12, on the other hand, is nothing more than an arbitrarily chosen later date, which is significant solely because it is not September 9.

BSP's parliamentary faction rallied behind the view that the Law should refer to September 12, not September 9—and this position is consistent with the party's relentlessly propagated vision of the past, a vision centered on the notion that Bulgarian communists had a legitimate claim on power because they led the nation's struggle against "the fascist enemy." While it is true that during the communist era innocent people did suffer and some repressions did occur, the argument underpinning this vision goes, most of the violence that took place in the mid-1940s was in fact justified; and after the late 1940s, violence played a marginal role in Bulgarian politics and most Bulgarians did not even notice it (Baeva and Kalinova 2010). In 1944–1945 the repressive measures targeted primarily "enemies of the people" implicated in crimes against the resistance. Hence what transpired between September 9 and September 12 was "just retribution" meted out to fascist murderers, an understandable reaction driven by anti-fascist anger and the noble desire to win the war against Nazism. Clearly, then, the choice of September 12 was an attempt to re-legitimize one of the foundational myths upon which the legitimacy of Bulgarian communism was built, namely that the Communist Party's rise to power should be attributed to the justness and righteousness of the causes it defended (Bulgarian Parliament 2008).

Predictably, this choice was criticized by the opposition—and the critics articulated their own version of history, one that accentuated the fact that between September 9 and September 12 several hundred people—including journalists, teachers, and priests—were murdered throughout the country. More generally, BSP's opponents argued that the historical record is undisputed: while the Red Terror did not peak until October, when the number of victims reached thousands per week, summary executions were carried out *en masse* immediately after the communist coup (Troanski 2004). Hence to claim that there was a kind of virtuous interlude during which communists were entitled to kill in the name of justice would be a travesty—and therefore the Law should begin to "tick" on September 9, the day the killings started. Professional historians quickly joined the debate—in effect endorsing the opposition's views. And the general public did not remain indifferent—in some newspapers and various websites the contention that the communist system was essentially non-repressive and only liquidated fascists was subject to withering criticism, often articulated by victims of the old regime (Mediapool 2008).

How the controversy ended is also instructive—because it suggests that the very notion of an "end" may be inapplicable to such controversies. In the BSP-dominated parliament the ruling coalition outvoted the opposition—and apparently succeeded in its effort to officialize its version of history. As it turned out, the vote provided only a temporary closure. After the ex-communists lost the next elections, the new ruling party, GERB, voted to replace September 12 with September 9 as the date when unlawful repressions began in Bulgaria in 1944 (*Durzhaven vestnik* 2009). It should be pointed out that GERB's decision to revisit this issue is somewhat of a puzzle: the party—which was not represented in the legislature in 2008 and did not take part in the parliamentary debates discussed above—had not taken any particular position in the public controversy surrounding the BSP's draft, never referred to this issue during its electoral campaign, and, generally speaking, tried to practice mnemonic abnegation by bracketing questions related to the communist period (I will defend this claim more fully later). So to argue that GERB had a democratic mandate to "set the historical record straight" or that it sought to impose a "truth" that was an essential component of its political identity would be misguided. Much more plausibly, GERB's political operatives—who, as we saw, did not have a strategy for exploiting the twentieth anniversary of 1989 for their partisan purposes—craftily identified the September 9 versus September 12 debate as an opportunity to score against BSP, the political force they still considered their most formidable opponent, and proceeded to do so.

The main conclusion to which the mnemonic war surrounding the amendments to "The Law on Political and Civil Rehabilitation of Repressed Citizens" lends credence is easy to sum up: analyses of memory regimes and mnemonic fields, and particularly how such regimes and fields are formalized, situated in institutional settings, and sanctioned politically, should fully recognize the centrality of political agency. Of course, the impact of popular attitudes and sentiments should not be completely discarded; but when it comes to the essential questions about the past—who can hear what, when, how and why—the paramount significance of partisan actors should serve as point of departure for any meaningful conversation. To be sure, in any democracy these actors are bound to appear a motley bunch. For authentic mnemonic warriors—like the BSP and its opponents in the Bulgarian parliament in 2008—how memories can be built into overarching cultural and political archetypes will always be a consideration more important than the effort to understand specific historical events (Schudson 1992, 127). Others, like GERB, will favor mnemonic instrumentalism: They will enter controversies about the past only if they deem that to be important for winning the next political duel. But the essential fact remains: What a mnemonic regime looks like is a question that cannot be fully answered with reference to holistically embraced cultural symbols, popularly shared attitudes, or majority-endorsed perceptions of the past. Such regimes are the outcome—the tentative, reversible, shifting outcome—of a variety of strategies pursued by a multiplicity of actors at different times.

Mnemonic Basics in Bulgarian Politics: The Simple Uses of the Past

In an intriguing essay on collective memory and commemorative practices in the United States, Sheldon S. Wolin argues that societies that place greater value on change and seek constantly for ways to promote it will be relatively indifferent or purely ritualistic toward the past (1989, 32). One might contend that the opposite is also true: Societies that refuse to accept change would tend to assign a positive value to the past. Post-communist Bulgaria might serve as a perfect example in that regard. A crucial aspect of the politics of memory in the country might be depicted in the following way: The "mnemonic basics" of the country are permeated by an attitude that I have called "the valorization of nostalgia."[10] In a Bulgarian context, the notion of "mnemonic basics" encompasses neither past-oriented propositions that everyone takes for granted nor the public pronouncements of compromise-seeking pluralists who try to demarcate a common ground that rival political forces might share, but refers to a fairly stable distribution of preferences and opinions regarding the past, which create the matrix of opportunities and constraints that define the mnemonic field and shape the behavior of political elites. These preferences and opinions, in turn, are shaped by a hegemonic discourse that not only exemplifies and justifies nostalgia, but also posits it as an ethical stance that distinguishes the morally commendable individuals who embrace it from the morally unhinged ones who do not. Nostalgia is singled out as the litmus test that highlights the differences between moral positions: one marked by a clear grasp of what is right and what is wrong, and inspired by the affirmation of forms of collective life that recognize human dignity; and the other marred by individualistic postures revealing ethical shallowness and insufficient respect for the set of values that constitute the bases of shared life. A fuller explication of the notion of the "valorization of nostalgia" cannot be pursued here.[11] What is important for the purposes of this chapter is that the prevalence of this attitude in Bulgaria rendered possible the coalescence of mnemonic basics into what Eviatar Zerubavel calls a "zig-zag rise-and-fall" narrative: "an essentially tragic scenario in which, following some unfortunate event…a story of success suddenly turns into one of decline" (2003a, 18–19). These basics are thus grounded in the understanding that the moral, economic, and social accomplishments of the pre-1989 regime are overwhelming, whereas the post-1989 age brought about nothing but misfortunes.

Two opinion polls conducted at the end of 2009 are particularly revealing in that regard. Both polls were initiated by Bulgarian National Television (BNT), which asked viewers to select the country's "most important construction project" and "most important political event" since 1878—the year when Bulgaria emerged as an autonomous political entity. In "the most important construction project" contest a crushing majority of the audience, 60.69 percent, voted for Dimitrovgrad (Dimitrov-town), a city built from scratch in the late 1940s and early 1950s.[12] What Dimitrovgrad stands for in the Bulgarian political imagination is the great accomplishments of the communist era. The city is named after Georgi Dimitrov, the only Bulgarian communist leader to attain the status of an internationally recognized celebrity. Outside Bulgaria, Dimitrov is known primarily because he courageously defended himself during the Nazi-orchestrated Reichstag Fire Trial (notably, his behavior earned him an honorable mention in Hannah Arendt's *Eichmann in Jerusalem* [1997, 188]) and also because as a chairman of the Komintern he sanctioned the massacre of tens of thousands of non-Soviet communists during Stalin's purges in the late 1930s. In Bulgaria itself, Dimitrov is remembered as the politician who presided over the communists' ascent to power, spearheaded the destruction of the non-communist opposition, and consolidated the one-party "dictatorship of the proletariat." Throughout the entire socialist period, the building of Dimitrovgrad was relentlessly celebrated as the archetypical communist success story: Inspired by the Marxist vision of a perfect future, youthful enthusiasts under the guidance of the Party created a new urban environment where technologically advanced factories manufactured first-rate industrial products and where the pursuit of a great revolutionary project lent meaning and value to the communal life of dedicated and idealistic workers. To be sure, not everyone in the country shares the romantic depiction of Dimitrovgrad as a model town: Dissenters argued that the industrial units there constantly generated losses and had to be subsidized; that the equipment fairly quickly became obsolete and came to symbolize, if anything, the communist regime's failure to embrace and foster technological change; that life in the city was actually hard and workers stayed there only because they were not allowed to move elsewhere. As the results of the poll indicate, however, such voices had no demonstrable impact on Bulgarian mnemonic basics. In the memories of BNT's viewers—the vast majority of whom have never seen the geographically remote and touristically unattractive place—Dimitrovgrad exists exactly as depicted by the communist propaganda machine.

The results of the second poll, about the most important political event in modern Bulgarian history, confirmed that the socialist past is considered praiseworthy. A plurality of the votes, 24.29 percent, was cast for September 9, 1944, a date already discussed in the previous section. In contrast, November 10, 1989, did not even make it to the top five.[13]

The debates that the release of the polls' results set off brought into sharp relief another characteristic feature of the politics of memory in post-communist Bulgaria: Mnemonic basics are almost always weaponized by mnemonic warriors who seek "to draw a sharp line between themselves, the proprietors of the 'true' vision of the past, and other actors who cultivate 'wrong' or 'false' versions of history."[14] The debate that began when the selection of September 9 was announced might serve as a case in point.

The most influential expert invited to comment on the BNT poll was Iskra Baeva, an avowed BSP supporter who is also a history professor, a highly visible pundit interviewed practically every week by the mass media, and, perhaps most importantly, one of the authors of the history textbook that will mold the thinking of several generations of Bulgarian high-school students. According to Baeva, the results of the poll reveal, first and foremost, "deep disappointment with the politico-economic system established after November 10th." But they also show something else: The Bulgarian people are mature enough to reject various lies about the socialist past. These lies began to pollute the Bulgarian public sphere in late 1989, when the anti-communist opposition organized "the first democratic rallies" and tried to mobilize popular support behind "the rejection of everything that took place between September 9th and November 10th." The purveyors of falsehoods deliberately turned themes like "the repressions during the early years of socialism, the economic failures, the shortages, the ban on foreign travel and the censorship" into staples for their propaganda efforts and generally sought to portray the socialist era as "the worst in our modern history." The poll should therefore be construed as "public protest against the imposition of such 'new truths.'" What it made clear is that both older generations who can remember life "back then" and younger cohorts of citizens who have no firsthand knowledge of communism but still voted for September 9 can easily discern socialism's undeniable virtues: "as socialism recedes into our memories, it is easier to grasp the positive social characteristics of that system. Whatever one's ultimate judgment about socialism, it cannot be denied that it made it possible for everyone to get free medical care and education—and that the pensions back then ensured a much higher standard of living." The very fact that such attitudes prevail can only mean one thing: Collective memories in Bulgaria are not contaminated by anti-communist lies and obfuscations. BNT's viewers thus endorsed the *old* and *only* truth, namely that 1944 marks the moment when, under the leadership of its Communist Party, Bulgaria embarked upon a remarkably successful journey toward progress (Baeva 2010).

Professor Baeva's views did not go unchallenged. The same issue of the widely read tabloid where her article was published also featured an essay by Kalina Androlova on the brutality of the communist regime (Androlova 2010). But this media battle was rather lopsided: What it attests to is that communism's admirers come from the academic, cultural, and political establishment, whereas its critics mostly speak from the margins. Androlova, for example, is a journalist whose résumé suggests that the only time when she actually had any power to speak of was during her tenure as an editor-in-chief of a small-circulation weekly—a position from which she was fairly quickly dismissed (*Kultura* 2011). Unlike Baeva, she has no access to academic institutions or major political players like BSP—and most definitely she is not among those who have the power to decide what Bulgarian students will be taught about the 1944–1989 period.

In view of this asymmetry of influence, it is not surprising that, in addition to being lopsided, the debate about Bulgaria's mnemonic givens is also a limited one— many of the claims advanced by the more powerful faction are in fact not questioned at all. To refer to Androlova once again, the only line of criticism pursued in her essay is that the communist regime was repressive and violent; she does not dispute Baeva's claim that under that same regime remarkable social and economic progress was also made. Thus one of the central propositions bandied about in the Bulgarian mnemonic wars—namely that the Communist Party transformed a backward country into a modern, industrialized, technologically advanced society where virtually every family enjoyed a lifestyle not altogether different from that of Western European middle classes—is tacitly confirmed. The only question open for debate is whether the loss of freedom is an acceptable price to pay for all the good things the communists provided. In other words, those who want to understand what was wrong with communism should think in terms of a grand Faustian bargain in which the value of liberty is weighed against the comforts of life under a government that takes good care of the citizens' essential needs—and should consequently forget about the chronic shortages, the long queues, the tiny government-built apartments with crooked walls and windows that refused to shut in January, the fantastically dirty city buses that never arrived on time, the Trabants and Ladas that fell apart and could never be properly fixed, the twelve years it took to get a phone number, and also about the fact that everything the middle classes really coveted, from toilet paper to decent shoes to Bulgakov's *The Master and Margarita*, could only be obtained not from the government but through *blat* or on the black market.

A comparison of prevalent attitudes toward the post-1989 period in Bulgaria and Poland would suggest that the two countries are not dissimilar: In both, discussions of the current situation are dominated by "domestic critics [who] bemoan the pitiable state of...political culture and zero in on the unresolved dilemmas that plague the *performance* of...democracy" (Kubik and Linch 2006, 10). But important differences are also easily noticeable. In Poland, these discussions follow unpredictable trajectories that veer in various directions and draw on an array of narrative genres, from the paranoiac story of deceit to the rational account that invokes the politics of the possible. In Bulgaria, similar conversations are confined to the reiteration of a simple proposition: Under the *ancient regime* everyone enjoyed a high standard of living, whereas now the people live in misery. J. H. Plumb once observed that "the more literate and sophisticated the society becomes, the more complex and powerful become the uses to which the past is put" (2004, 11). The case of post-communist Bulgaria does not offer much evidence in support of this hypothesis. Despite the fact that the country proved to be democratically literate as well as sophisticated enough to join the European Union, the past is still put to fairly simple uses: Influential opinion-makers argue that the communist era was great; dissidents object that the communists have blood on their hands. The politics of memory follows a script unburdened by distractive complications.

In sum, the Bulgarian mnemonic field circa 2009 appears less fragmented than elsewhere in Eastern Europe. It *is* fractured—but the size of the pieces is rather different. Compared to the celebratory accounts of communism's accomplishments, the memory of its failures is like a Madagascar lingering in obscurity next to the imposing vastness of Africa. To be sure, this might change. In a sense, mnemonic warriors like Professor Baeva find themselves in a paradoxical situation insightfully analyzed by Benedict Anderson in his remarks on Ernst Renan. Renan famously argued that all French citizens have the duty to "have already forgotten" the Saint Bartholomew Massacre (the French is *doit avoir oublié*, an injunction that is stronger than simply *doit oublier*, must forget). The paradox, Anderson points out, is that Renan did not bother to explain the term "Saint Bartholomew Massacre"—thus assuming that everyone who considers themselves to be French would understand the reference (1983, 199–200). A similar paradox might subvert the efforts of mnemonic warriors to distinguish between "imposed new truths" to be forgotten and "old truths" to be remembered forever. Baeva does not have to explain what expressions like "the repressions during the early years of socialism, the economic failures, the shortages, the ban on foreign travel and the censorship" stand for, because she assumes, correctly, that her readers would have no problem comprehending them. But what that means is that such "truths" are not imposed—they were readily within the grasp of anyone who considered himself or herself to be a Bulgarian adult in 2009.

That any national bag of recollections contains diverse pieces of mnemonic candy is a truism. But it is important to remember that which memories will be designated worth keeping and which will be considered worth being silent about is not simply a personal decision; it is also a social process whose aggregate outcome is crucially affected by the messages with which individuals are bombarded in a relentlessly aggressive media environment—which in turn means that for the content of mnemonic basics to change, power shifts must occur.

Conclusion: The Arrival of the Abnegators?

Students of Bulgarian politics might be tempted to argue that 2009 is the year when such a power shift transpired. The July parliamentary elections swept into power GERB, a newly formed party whose candidates for office displayed utter indifference toward issues related to the pre-1989 era, and whose campaign promises were entirely oriented toward the country's "European future." Moreover, ever since the beginning of his political career in the early 2000s, Boyko Borissov, GERB's charismatic leader who was sworn in as a prime minister, behaved as a mnemonic abnegator: he avoided memory politics, made it clear that he considered protracted conversations about communism and its legacies a waste of time, and persistently sought to portray his policies as solutions to present problems.[15] It is rather tempting therefore to link the rise of Borissov's GERB and the twentieth anniversary of 1989 into an argument about how the politics of memory is becoming obsolete in Bulgaria.

Such a conclusion would be premature. To the contrary, the facts, and particularly Borissov's comments on communism, suggest that for a variety of reasons, abnegators may find themselves drawn into the unending debates about the past. During his celebratory speech after the elections, GERB's leader announced that he dedicated his victory to the memory of a grandfather murdered by the communists in 1944. Why he decided to make this unexpected statement is unclear; uncharacteristically for a politician who exemplifies the notion of macho sangfroid, he might have been overwhelmed by pent-up emotions, or he may have been guided by tactical considerations in the context of the ongoing struggles with BSP. Either way, the reference to communist atrocities on the night of elections won by abnegators simply confirmed that in Bulgarian politics the past is inescapable: It still affects the behavior of key actors, and it is still recognized as a valuable resource by competing political elites.

More than a year later, when the twenty-first anniversary of 1989 was marked, the prime minister revisited the question of the communist past—and again his intervention carried an element of surprise. In a widely publicized interview, Borissov explained why even though he deems his own government to be successful, it would be incorrect to compare it to Zhivkov's governments: "Even if we build one percent of what Zhivkov built for Bulgaria, even if we do one percent of what he did during his rule…that would be an enormous success, for us or for any other government.… The fact that 20 years after his ouster no one has forgotten him shows that he did lots of things. For 20 years we've been merely privatizing what was in fact created back then" (*Mediapool* 2010). That the same politician who complained about communist repressions would also sing paeans to Zhivkov would be a problem only for those who insist, against all the evidence to the contrary, that consistency is beneficial in politics. In fact, to characterize Borissov's actions as erratic would be too simplistic—because they shed light on two important aspects of the way in which mnemonic abnegators are positioned in the political field. First, strategic decisions regarding non-participation notwithstanding, these political actors will find it very difficult to avoid getting involved in mnemonic wars. Observers who raise the question of why Borissov would be willing to play on both sides of the barricade separating communism's opponents from its admirers will miss the truly important point—which is that he *had* to be on the barricade. Second, when abnegators do get involved, they behave not as entrepreneurs, but as bricoleurs. As we know from Joseph Schumpeter, the distinct feature of entrepreneurial conduct is doing things that are "outside of the range of existing practice" (1991, 411). Neither the reference to communist crimes in the 1940s nor the praise of Zhivkov fit this description, and therefore describing what abnegators like Borissov do as entrepreneurship is unjustified. In contrast, their behavior bears a close resemblance to that of the "bricoleurs" analyzed by Claude Levy-Strauss. The bricoleur does not seek to disrupt existing practices or invent new ones: "his universe of instruments is closed and the rules of his game are always to make do with 'whatever is at hand'" (Levy-Strauss 1966, 17). Arguably, it is precisely because mnemonic abnegators are not interested in history that they will be forced to rely on mnemonic warriors' articulations of the past. More generally, one might hypothesize that the abnegators' forays into the battlefields of memory will not be inspired by original ideas or creative re-envisioning of historical symbols, meanings, or images. Of course, this does not mean that such forays will be unsuccessful; but it does mean that as long as mnemonic wars rage on, the abnegators will not enjoy the power to unilaterally set a society's agenda.

I submit that to generalize about mnemonic abnegators based on Borissov's declarations is a suspiciously speculative endeavor. But his rhetorical choices do reveal an important truth about Bulgarian democracy: In order to succeed, those who compete on the national political scene must project the image of someone who can articulate a compelling, if not necessarily coherent, interpretation of the past. Sometime ago, Stephen Vaughn pointed out that "we do not have to believe Santayana when he said that those who fail to remember the past are doomed to repeat it. Still, those who do not remember are in jeopardy of suffering at the hand of those who do" (1985, 11). Boyko Borissov, a mnemonic abnegator with sharp political instincts, seems to have instinctively grasped that in order not to be outflanked by those who claim to possess a better knowledge of history, he must establish for himself the reputation of a politician who has reflected on the past and can sum up its important lessons. And that is the ultimate proof that Bulgaria's present is crucially shaped by the insuppressible politics of memory.

NOTES

1. Hereafter, political parties in Bulgaria will be identified by means of the following abbreviations: GERB (Citizens for European Development of Bulgaria), ruling party; BSP (Bulgarian Socialist party), former communist party; UDF (Union of Democratic Forces), main anti-communist coalition in the 1990s whose influence declined dramatically in the 2000s; MRF (Movement for Rights and Freedoms), a political party supported mostly by ethnic Turks.

2. The leaders of the victorious anti-Zhivkov faction were Defense Minister Dobri Dzhurov, Foreign Minister Petar Mladenov, Prime Minister Georgi Atanassov, Minister of Foreign Economic Relations Andrei Lukanov, and former Poliburo member Alexander Lilov.

3. Iordan Yotov was a member of Politburo (1984–1989) and editor-in-chief of *Rabotnichesko delo*, the Party's newspaper (1979–1989).

4. For more on the hegemonic political discourse in Bulgaria, see Ganev (2012).

5. This fact was revealed by the Committee on Dossiers, an institution established by Parliament in the mid-2000s. The sole function of this Committee is to disclose information about Bulgarian citizens who have collaborated with repressive apparatuses before 1989 and who currently occupy important public positions. Since 2007 the Committee has been publishing lists of such former agents, and the names of virtually all owners and editors-in-chief of nationally important newspapers have appeared on these lists.

6. Georgi Atanassov served as a prime minister from 1986 to 1990. For the first time since 1989 he disclosed unknown details about the coup itself. Discussing the well-known fact that the general secretary was persuaded to resign after a meeting with his old comrades from the early 1940s armed communist resistance, Atanassov revealed that the initial outcome of this meeting (which he did not attend) was that Zhivkov vowed to step down not *immediately*, but "at a future plenum of the Central Committee of the Communist Party." Grasping the danger of this ambiguous formulation, the prime minister pressured his co-conspirators to demand a second meeting, and it was during that second meeting, held on November 9, that Zhivkov finally agreed to step down the next day. Atanassov also recalled that during the afternoon session of the historical November 10 plenum, Zhivkov demanded the floor in an apparent attempt to rally his supporters and stage a comeback, but Atanassov refused to give him the floor and pressed forward with the conspirators' plan.

7. Before 1989 Zhelyu Zhelev was an influential dissident whose book *Fascism* was banned; in December 1989 he became chairman of the newly formed Union of Democratic Forces (UDF), a coalition of anti-communist organizations. He was elected president by the Great National Assembly, and subsequently won the first popular vote for the presidency in January 1992. He lost his bid for the UDF nomination in the 1996 primaries and stepped down when his presidential term expired in 1997.

8. Petar Stoyanov began his career as a UDF activist; he won the UDF presidential primaries in 1996 and subsequently defeated the BSP candidate in the presidential elections. He was president from 1997 until 2002.

9. Other dissidents mention the number 3,000; the figure given by the communist media at the time was 1,000. I would like to thank Emilia Zankina for reminding me of this controversy.

10. On the notion of "mnemonic basics" see Bernhard and Kubik, "A Theory of the Politics of Memory," Chapter 1 of this volume.

11. For a fuller explication of the idea of "valorization of nostalgia," see Ganev 2012, 3–15.

12. The second largest number of votes, 7.98 percent, was cast for Kozlodui, Bulgaria's only nuclear power station, built during the Zhivkov era. The highest ranked non-communist project was the magnificent building of Sofia University, which received 5.5 percent of the votes (Novinar 2009).

13. According to those who cared to cast votes, the second and third most important events were the rescue of Bulgarian Jews during World War II, 22.03 percent, and the declaration of independence in 1908, 13.87 percent (Web Café 2010).

14. Cf. Bernhard and Kubik, "A Theory of the Politics of Memory," Chapter 1 of this volume.

15. On mnemonic abnegators, see Bernhard and Kubik, Chapter 1 of this volume.

11 It Happened Elsewhere
REMEMBERING 1989 IN THE FORMER YUGOSLAVIA
Aida A. Hozić

IN THE POLITICAL space(s) of the former Yugoslavia, torn apart by battles over collective memory as much as over territory (Ugrešić 1996; Čolović 2002), it is truly surprising how similar—albeit not uniform—were commemorations and recollections of 1989. The further one moved from west to east—from Slovenia, where discussions about 1989 touched upon the break with communism, to Macedonia, where 1989 was hardly mentioned except in official speeches, the more it became clear that mnemonic wars in this corner of the post-communist world were not being fought over memories of the previous regime or of its end. Instead, ex-Yugoslav mnemonic warriors used the anniversary to chase ghosts of their old and new wars, count their bodies, mobilize their offspring, and debate the pros and cons of Europeanization, initiated—in their view—by the fall of the Berlin Wall.

The shift in focus was probably understandable. As in many other communist countries, 1989 in Yugoslavia marked the formation of the first non-communist political parties. However, unlike in the countries behind the Iron Curtain, 1989 in Yugoslavia did not mark the beginning of a political transition but the end of a country "for many decades considered *the* communist country most likely to evolve in the direction of democratization." (Vujačić, 2004). At the time when most Eastern European countries said their good-byes to communism with waves of political protests, Slobodan Milošević, leader of the Serbian Communist party, solidified his power by riding a wave of "spontaneous" popular gatherings organized by his minions in Serbia, Kosovo, Vojvodina, and Montenegro. The culmination of Milošević's "happenings of the people" and "undoubtedly the moment of his greatest triumph as a leader" (Vujačić, 2006), was the commemoration of the six hundredth anniversary of the Battle of Kosovo in June of 1389. The anniversary of the Serbs' battlefield confrontation with the invading Ottoman army attracted more than a million attendees (including the entire political leadership of the former Yugoslavia) and many more television viewers. Milošević used the occasion "to present himself as the true leader of Yugoslavia" (Jović 2009) and gave a rousing speech about the continued importance of fights and battles, including armed ones, which would later be used as evidence against him in the International War Crime Tribunal in The Hague (Radio-televizija Srbije 2009b).

Thus, in November 1989, when the Berlin Wall came down, newspapers in Serbia devoted almost equal attention to this extraordinary (geo)political event and the contemporaneous election of Slobodan Milošević as the president of the Presidency in Serbia (Čolović 2009; Media Centar Sarajevo 2009). But the situation was not really much different in the rest of Yugoslavia, where the majority of republican communist leaders, correctly reading the tea leaves from Eastern Europe, rushed to erase the word "communist" from the names of their parties, quickly paid lip-service to political and party pluralism, and/or embraced nationalism as ways to retain power. In Yugoslavia, the fall of the Berlin Wall was quickly overshadowed by the emergence of nationalism as the most powerful political force and, shortly thereafter, led straight to war.

Consequently, over the next two decades, neither successor parties to the former Yugoslav communist party nor their opponents had much interest in revisiting the common socialist past. Memories of communism—and of coexistence—were, in the words of exiled writer Dubravka Ugresić (1996), *confiscated* by the new regimes. They were replaced with conflicting narratives of World War II crimes and strategies for national reconciliation, or buried behind denials of crimes from the new wars and layers of myths and legends from the ancient past. As far as the Yugoslavs were concerned, the events of 1989 happened elsewhere.

This chapter reviews the way in which the anniversary of 1989 was *publicly* marked in six Yugoslav republics—Slovenia, Croatia, Bosnia and Herzegovina, Serbia, Montenegro, and Macedonia. It has a structure similar to other chapters in this volume. Each section about an individual republic starts with a synopsis of events of 1989 and then proceeds to describe the commemorations in 2009. The last part of the chapter is devoted to analysis of the politics of commemoration in the former Yugoslavia, which, as we shall see, confirms many of the editors' expectations about the relationship between *mnemonic actors, 1989/2009 mnemonic regimes,* and *mnemonic fields* but especially about the role of the former communist parties in mnemonic confrontations with their communist legacy.

But discussions about 1989 in the former Yugoslavia also serve as interesting counterpoints to the internationally accepted narrative of 1989 as the year of regime change and European unification. Political and discursive ambiguities over the European status of the Balkans and ex-Yugoslav states after 1989 (Todorova 1997; Lindstrom 2003; Subotić, 2001; Petrović 2012a) problematize self-satisfied visions of Europe such as the one promoted in 2009 by the German Konrad Adenauer Stiftung—a "dream come true" united Europe that "guarantees freedom and peace" and is prepared to defend its "European and Christian values against intolerance and the intolerants" (Kunze 2010). And yet, the politics of memory in ex-Yugoslav states also curiously dovetails with the trend to create a "common European memory," pushed for by a broad coalition of political parties (with the notable exception of socialists) in the European Parliament. Thus, in the following pages, I follow both threads of analysis; while domestic political variables provide us with a helpful framework to analyze debates about 1989 in the countries that were once Yugoslavia, the international dimension acts as a useful reminder that *mnemonic practices* and *fields*—particularly in Europe—are no longer properties of nation-states alone.

Slovenia

In comparison with its former neighbors to the south and the southeast, Slovenia had a relatively painless exit from communism and from Yugoslavia. Liberalization of political life had begun in 1986, when the more dogmatic wing of the Communist Party of Slovenia stepped aside and gave way to the more liberal leadership of Milan Kučan (Ramet 2008). The key actors in the process of democratization were two former pillars of the regime—the Alliance of the Socialist Youth of Slovenia and the Socialist Alliance of Slovenia—and an increasingly vibrant and mobilized civil society (Fink-Hafner 2006).

Two events were particularly important in pushing Slovenia toward independence and democracy. In 1987, the Slovenian art group Neue Slowenische Kunst (NSK) participated in a federal competition to design a poster celebrating Tito's birthday and the national Day of Youth (Monroe 2005). The holiday had a spectral dimension; it was the perfect example of the way in which the empty seat of power exerts its influence. Although Tito had died in 1980, the celebration of his birthday—also known as the Day of Youth—continued. Each year, the festivities included a baton relay throughout the country (symbol of the "brotherhood and unity") and a massive choreographed performance by thousands of people at the Yugoslav Army Stadium in Belgrade (Videkanić 2010). After NSK won the competition, the art group revealed that the poster was a replica of a Nazi poster. A major political scandal ensued, but the provocation brought to light the NSK's thesis that Yugoslav communism was no different than other totalitarian regimes.

A year later, in 1988, one of the leaders of the opposition, Janez Janša—a candidate for the president of the increasingly vocal Alliance of the Socialist Youth—was arrested in Ljubljana with three other men. They were charged with treason for an alleged leak of secret documents of the Yugoslav Army. In a military trial, conducted in Serbo-Croatian rather than Slovenian, Janša was sentenced to eighteen months of prison. His arrest and the trial galvanized Slovenian opposition in events known as the Slovenian Spring and precipitated its move toward secession from Yugoslavia.

In September 1989, the Slovenian Parliament adopted amendments to the Constitution, which enabled the creation of a new electoral law as well as the formation of new political parties and multiparty elections. The first free elections were held in April 1990. Milan Kučan, leader of the former Communist Party of Slovenia, was elected president of the Presidency (at that time still a collective body), while the large opposition coalition called DEMOS won 55 percent of the seats in the Parliament. Alojz Peterle, a Christian-Democrat and member of this coalition, became the prime minister. Janša was appointed Minister of Defense. In 1991, Slovenia declared independence from Yugoslavia, and after a 10-day war with the Yugoslav Army, it became a de facto independent country. Unaffected by the wars in the former Yugoslavia, which raged between 1991 and 1999, Slovenia joined the European Union in 2004 and the Eurozone in 2007.

In the years since 1989, Slovenia has oscillated between Center-Left coalitions (led by Liberal Democrats) and, after 2004, Center-Right coalitions led by Janša's Slovenian Democratic Party. Kučan remained president of the country for more than 10 years, ending his term(s) only in 2002. Appearing as uneventful, especially to the outsiders, Slovenian politics has generally been assessed as the model of a consolidated democracy and successful transition (Rizman 2006).

Seemingly civilized alterations in power obscure the depth of Slovenian mnemonic wars, which have been flaring since the 1980s, when it became publicly known that Tito's partisans and the Communist Party killed thousands of Slovenian Home Guard members—anti-communist and, presumably, Nazi collaborators—at the end of World War II (Bevc 2008). In the mid-1980s it also surfaced that some thirty-three survivors of Dachau and Buchenwald concentration camps had been put on trial in Slovenia in 1948 under the assumption that only Nazi collaborators could have exited the camps alive (Krivokapić 1986). Throughout the 1980s, Slovenian opposition, particularly intellectuals around the journal *Nova Revija* who would later constitute the core of DEMOS, promoted the platform of "national reconciliation" (Dragović-Soso 2002). The platform was used to de-legitimize the Communist Party and its hitherto impeccable record of heroic struggle against the

Nazis. Following the first free elections in Slovenia, the newly elected government, led by President Kučan, held the first reconciliation ceremony on July 8, 1990, at Kočevski Rog—the site of Slovenian Partisans' headquarters during World War II and some of the worst massacres of the withdrawing Nazi collaborators. The ceremony has since become traditional, and it is usually officiated by the Archbishop of Ljubljana and is attended by key state officials, including—if the specific office demands—former communist politicians. A small chapel erected at the site symbolically represents all the mass graves around Slovenia, while the ceremony includes prayers for all deceased Slovenians and asks for reconciliation and forgiveness among the living (Štor 2009).

However, no communist leaders have been put on trial for the summary executions at the end of World War II (Černič 2009; Janša 2009). In 2005, Janša's government filed charges of genocide against a former communist politician, Mitja Ribičić, for his alleged participation in the execution of 217 people in 1945, at the end of World War II. But the Higher Court halted the process, citing lack of evidence (Fink-Hafner 2010). And so graves and dead bodies continue to haunt Slovenian politics. As an anthropologist, Svetlana Slapšak (2009) wrote in her comments on the 1989 anniversary, Slovenia has developed an entirely new "archeology of unmarked graves, the principal site of battles for prestige among new historians, who rely on powerful media effects of excavated skulls and weeping old men and women in front of television cameras." The battle over revisionist history is, of course, the battle for political power—and it sharply divides Slovenian Center-Right parties and their controversial leader, Janez Janša, from the Center-Left successors of the Communist Party and Slovenian Left-leaning intellectuals who have resisted the temptation to participate in the nationalist project, including feminists such as Slapšak. The post–World War II crimes have become a personal fixation for Janša, who has never forgiven the Slovenian communists for their role in his 1988 arrest and military trial (Janša 1995; Meier 1999; Janša 2009). His opponents, on the other hand, view the hunt for dead bodies as vengeful political manipulation and a populist cover for Janša's own corruption scandals, intolerance toward minorities, and authoritarian tendencies (Rizman 2006).

Thus, it may not have been a coincidence that in early 2009, just as the rest of Eastern Europe was gearing to celebrate the twentieth anniversary of its transition to democracy and shortly after Janša's government had been replaced by Social Democrats (successors of the Communist Party), the Slovenian Commission on Concealed Mass Graves announced the discovery of a cave with some 300 bodies from the immediate post–World War II period. The Commission itself was formed in 2005, during the reign of Janša's Center-Right coalition. Its findings were included in the Reports and Proceedings of the 8th of April European Public Hearing on Crimes Committed by

Totalitarian Regimes organized by the Slovenian Presidency of the Council of the European Union (January–June 2008) and the European Commission (2010).

Huda Jama, as the cave discovered in 2009 is known, quickly became a hot political topic. Members of the commission claimed that more than 15,000 bodies could still be found in graves around Slovenia and compared the numbers and the crimes to the more recent genocide in Srebrenica. "The killings that took place here have no comparisons in Europe," said Jože Dežman, head of the commission (Štor 2009). Meanwhile, Danilo Türk, Slovenian president and an independent politician, refused to comment on the cave and angered the Slovenian Right by making an unfortunate comment that he did not wish to discuss "second-class issues." When Janša's party called for the president's resignation, he explained that he did not mean that mass graves were "second-class issues" but that political manipulations of dead bodies were not worthy of the president's attention (Štor 2009).

The Commission on Concealed Mass Graves presented its report to the Slovenian Parliament in October 2009. The report (Jambrek 2008) served as a backdrop to the anniversary of 1989 and as an occasion for Janša to accuse the Social Democratic leadership and Slovenian Left of not doing enough to commemorate the fall of the Berlin Wall. At an international conference about 1989 in November 2009, sponsored by the Konrad Adenauer Stiftung and organized by the Institute Jože Pučnik, the intellectual arm of his own political party, former Prime Minister Janša said that "the spirit of totalitarianism continues to live in Moscow and Ljubljana" (Potič 2009). In Janša's view, Slovenia and Russia were the only two post-communist countries that did not properly mark the fall of the Iron Curtain because they both lacked pre-conditions for the complete dismantling of totalitarianism in their states. According to Janša, there was nothing surprising in the Slovenian lackluster acknowledgment of the events of 1989—the number of politicians who were ready to make the full transition to democracy was very small in Slovenia and "the arms of secret services very long." He reminded the audience at the conference of the difficult debates in the Slovenian Parliament about the European Declaration on the Victims of Totalitarianism, which his own government had proposed during its term of EU presidency, and equated the governing coalition's inadequate response to 1989 with their lack of official support for the observance of August 23, Day of Remembrance of Victims of All Totalitarian Regimes (Potič 2009; Planetsiol.net 2009).

In December 2009, as the anniversary year came to its end, President Türk made another controversial decision. He gave the Silver Order for Services to Tomaž Ertl, communist-era Minister of Interior, for his role in the so-called Operation North. In 1989, Ertl had prevented the staging of one of the pro-Milošević "happenings of the people" in Ljubljana. Under Ertl's leadership, Slovenian secret services intercepted the trains bound for Ljubljana and prevented Milošević's rally organizers from ever reaching the Slovenian capital. But in Slovenia, Ertl was also known for his role in the repression and persecution of Slovenian opposition and the media through-out the 1980s. Even more important, Ertl personally approved the investigation (and eventual arrest) of Janez Janša in 1988 (Nežmah 2009a, 2009b). Expressing the frustration of many who cannot find a place for themselves in Slovenian mne-monic wars, Slovenian philosopher Slavoj Žižek—known in the rest of the world as a leftist—blamed the Slovenian Left for refusing to address the killings at the end of World War II and Danilo Türk for giving the award to Ertl. To award Ertl for just one deed and neglect the rest of his biography, said Žižek at an event celebrating the twentieth anniversary of Slovenian independence, was like awarding Hitler for the building of motorways (*Slovenia Times* 2011).

To sum up, despite democratization and prized EU membership, Slovenian mne-monic politics in 2009 seemed to be running in old circles. The Slovenian Left was proud of the relatively peaceful and successful transition from communism and exit from Yugoslavia, in which even police officials such as Ertel had played a positive role. The Slovenian Right, and Janša in particular, viewed reformed communists (and those on the Left who had made peace with them) as unreconstructed totali-tarians. "Certain remnants of the communist era," wrote Janša (2009), hinting at Yugoslav secret services, "are much more persistent in the ruins of the small empire than they are in the countries that were once a part of the Large Red Empire."

The absence of public commemorations of 1989 exposed the depth of the partisan rift between Slovenian political parties, in which memories of World War II crimes—collaborationist and communist—play a critical role. The quest for Slovenian sover-eignty in 1989–1991 masked some of those differences through the explicit pursuit of a "national reconciliation strategy" in the early transition period. But the lack of closure on both sides of the spectrum—the unwillingness of the Left to seriously investigate any of the possible communist war crimes from World War II and the unwillingness of the Center-Right to give up on the charges of genocide against the former communist leaders—keeps mnemonic warfare at the heart of Slovenian politics. And what the Slovenian Center-Right, under the leadership of Janez Janša, could not achieve at home it has exported abroad, joining the pan-European quest for "harmonization of memory" and equalization of communist and Nazi crimes in the name of victims of "all totalitarian regimes" (European Parliament 2009).

Croatia

Unlike Slovenia, Croatia has not had an easy transition to democracy; it has had two regime changes since 1989 (1990 and 2000), a major war on its territory

(1991–1995), and significant involvement in the war in Bosnia and Herzegovina (1992–1995). Croatia has also had a historical legacy even more difficult than that of Slovenia. In 1941, the Croatian Ustashe—a fascist revolutionary movement— established an independent state, which closely collaborated with the Germans and whose territorial ambitions engulfed most of Bosnia and Herzegovina and extended all the way to Belgrade. Among numerous crimes committed by Ustashe, the most contentious over the years has become Jasenovac—a concentration camp ran by Ustashe—where hundreds of thousands of Serbs, Jews, and Roma perished in World War II.

Croatia's transition to democracy and independence from Yugoslavia was thus complicated by the existence of the legacy of this World War II state. The first multiparty elections were held in April 1990 and were easily won by the party of Croatian Democratic Unity, led by Franjo Tudjman—a partisan, a former Yugoslav general, and then, subsequently, a fairly low-key nationalist dissident in Tito's Yugoslavia. Tudjman's winning coalition, which had significant financial backing from the Croatian diaspora, included Croatian nationalists, some with direct links to World War II Ustashe, a number of turn-coat communists, and some key figures of the former Yugoslav military, police, and secret services (Hockenos 2003). This unlikely alliance was kept together for ten years (from 1990 to 2000) by fervent nationalism, vocal anti-communism, and the mobilizing power of the wars—against the Serbs and Serbian aggression in Croatia proper and in defense of Croat national interests in Bosnia and Herzegovina. The wars brought new charges of atrocities against the Croatian nationalists, most significantly for the operation Oluja (the Storm)—a blitzkrieg action in 1995 in which the Croat military regained control over the territories occupied by Croatian Serbs and expelled some 150,000 civilians from their homes. Since the official narrative portrays the Homeland War "as a clean series of battles waged against an external enemy and a crucial step in consolidation of an independent Croatian state" (Peskin and Boduszyński 2003), indictments of Croatian generals for war crimes by ICTY in the Hague provide a constant source of potential mobilization for Croatian nationalists—even after their electoral and political defeat in 2000.

The other rallying symbol of the Croatian nationalists has become Bleiburg, an Austrian town where partisans—in a similar fashion to Slovenian Kočevski Rog— allegedly executed an unknown number of defeated Germans and Nazi collaborators (Croatian Ustashas and members of the Croatian Home Guard, but also Serb Chetniks and the members of a Muslim Handžar Division) at the end of World War II. Throughout the 1990s, Tudjman used Jasenovac and Bleiburg to promote his own vision of "national reconciliation" between Ustashe, their victims, and Tito's Partisans. On several occasions he suggested that the remains of those who were killed in Bleiburg should be brought to and buried in Jasenovac. He rescinded that request only after an international outcry (Biondich 2004; Radonić 2012).

Instead, what has become institutionalized is the Croatian Parliament's 1995 decision to sponsor an official commemoration in Bleiburg each year on May 15. The commemoration is usually attended by state officials, including representatives of the Croatian Social Democratic Party, successor to the Communist Party. Over the years, however, the ceremony has also become a gathering ground for ultra-nationalists, Croatian black-shirts, and politicians and/or intellectuals who insist upon the continuity between the Croatian World War II state and the newly formed independent Croatia.

In May 2009, Croatian president Stipe Mesić—whose electoral victory in 2000 was seen as the marker of Croatia's second regime change—stirred up a controversy by condemning Bleiburg commemoration as an "Ustasha party paid for by the Croatian parliament." Mesić warned that statements by Croatian politicians that Tito was a war criminal led to relativization of the crimes in Jasenovac. Those who were killed in Bleiburg, argued Mesić, were not killed because they were Croats, Serbs, or Muslims but because they were Nazi collaborators. "Fifteen hundred guards in Jasenovac, who continued to resist surrender even after the end of the war, were not exactly innocent," said Mesić (*Večernji List* 2009).

And so, just as in Slovenia, the counting of dead bodies and the different positioning of political actors toward state crimes in different historical periods served as the backdrop to discussions about 1989. It was a difficult year to celebrate in Croatia. Croatian prime minister Ivo Sanader resigned in the summer of 2009 because of damning charges of corruption. The country was riveted by battles between different organized crime groups, reflective of the depth of the intra-elite power struggles. Not surprisingly, most political actors and commentators chose to ignore mnemonic wars on this anniversary of 1989 and to take stock of the transition instead. Croatian newspapers assessed the economic "before" and "after" of 1989. Much space was given to the Pew Research Center's (2009) findings of declining support for the transition to democracy and capitalism in post-communist states.[1] Croatian politicians reminisced about the formation of the first non-communist political parties in 1989 (Butković 2009). Several intellectuals, referring to the notorious shortages of the 1980s, concluded that things were better because bananas—one of the sorely missed items in the "then" times—were now plentiful (Tomić 2009). A glance through the headlines of *Jutarnji List*, Zagreb's most popular daily newspaper, illustrates the state of the commemorative mind: "Even 49 percent of East Germans Believes That They Lived Better under Communism" (*Jutarnji List* 2009a); "They Live Five Years Longer Now but They are Still Dissatisfied" (*Jutarnji List* 2009d);" "Zizek: The Reds Are Still in Power but Now They Are Dressed as

Managers" (*Jutarnji List* 2009e); "Drakulić: West Germans Still Treat East Germans as Second-Class Citizens" (*Jutarnji List* 2009c); "Did Jan Palach Set Himself on Fire for the Sake of McDonald's?" (Tomić 2009).

It is, therefore, possible to argue that the most important *political* message about 1989 was contained in the official statement of Croatian president Stjepan Mesić. "The war is over," said Mesić, "but the walls in our heads are still there." "Fortunately," he added, "there is a way to destroy these walls. Guilt should be individualized and we should cooperate with our neighbors. That is the way to fulfill European conditions and join the most elite club in the world—European Union" (Ured Predsjednika 2009). In other words, Mesić saw Croatia's ability to come to terms with its own crimes, deliver war criminals to The Hague, and normalize relations with Serbia as ways to abolish mental walls and achieve the most important political and civilizational goal—entry into the European Union.

The absence of public commemorations—and even controversies over the meaning—of 1989 should not be interpreted as a sign that the Croatian *mnemonic field* is unified and/or hegemonic. Rather, the way in which 1989 was addressed (assessing transition, evading open confrontations with difficult issues in the past, subordinating mnemonic warfare to the prospects of EU membership) is indicative of the way Croatian politicians, of both Left and Right, have been dealing with the Yugoslav communist past since the late 1980s. For the Croat successors of the Yugoslav communist party—the Social Democratic Party—Tito's era has been an inconvenient burden and a potential challenge to their patriotism; for the Croat nationalists, HDZ in particular, rhetorical identification of Serb aggression in the recent war and the partisans' crimes in Bleiburg have worked as a charm in silencing their political opponents. But it has also created the problem of how to deal with the fact that numerous Croats had embraced communism and prospered for forty-five years in the former Yugoslavia. Forgetting communism—or actively confiscating the communist past—has thus been seen as the precondition for the construction of a national memory and, increasingly, for Croatia's Europeanization.

Bosnia and Herzegovina

All throughout Yugoslavia, the 1980s were the years of great countercultural mobilization against the regime—in theater, film, and, particularly, in rock music (Gordy 1999; Levi 2007). In Bosnia and Herzegovina, the youthful democratization impulses coalesced around a band called Zabranjeno Pušenje (No-Smoking Band) and the "New Primitives" movement that they inspired. The movement drew attention to people on the margins of life—forgotten working class heroes, petty thieves, miners, truck drivers, young women turned prostitutes—as most vulnerable and as fundamentally betrayed by Communism. After initial frictions with local political authorities, the "New Primitives" became the most recognized face of Sarajevo's opposition to communist apparatchiks, budding nationalists, and politics as usual (Levi 2007). By 1989, they had a television program, *Top List of the Surrealists*, that drew millions of viewers across Yugoslavia. A few weeks after the fall of the Berlin Wall, the program featured a skit about a garbage men war along the wall dividing Eastern and Western Sarajevo, with piles of waste intentionally thrown from one side to another. The skit echoed discussions about a "unified Europe" and "six little Yugoslavias," which permeated political discourse at the time. The show's director, Miroslav Mandić, explained the origins of the skit in 2006: "We knew that the fall of the Berlin Wall was a momentous event but we did not know what it had to do with us. So we translated the event into a context that seemed closer to our political reality" (2006). With Sarajevo divided in the aftermath of the Bosnian war, the skit is now viewed as one of the most prophetic artifacts created in Yugoslavia before its descent into violence.

Transition to a sovereign and fully democratic state never really took place in Bosnia and Herzegovina (as of September 2013). The first multiparty elections (September 14, 1990) brought to power three nationalist parties, representing Muslims, Serbs, and Croats, respectively.[2] The same political parties and/or their factional offsprings continue to rule Bosnia and Herzegovina to this day—despite the war, genocide, and the oversight of the international community. In the words of David Chandler (2000), Bosnia's de facto protectorate status means that everyone in its political life—representatives of the international community and local actors—are simply faking democracy. Mnemonic wars are fierce, but they focus on the events from the last war, such as Srebrenica. Although internationally recognized as the site of the worst genocide in Europe since World War II, Srebrenica remains in the territory of Republika Srpska, and Serb politicians refuse to use the word "genocide" when referring to it. Denials are built upon allegations that the list of victims in the memorial cemetery in Potocari includes people who are still alive and/or complaints that the Serb victims of the war have never been properly acknowledged and recognized. For their part, some Bosnian historians and politicians have been building their capital on victimhood and constant reminders of the war (Nettelfield 2010). Throughout the 2000s, television news in the Muslim-dominated part of Bosnia continued to be dominated by reports from endless deadlocked political meetings among the representatives of ethno-nationalist parties, reports from excavations and/or identification of bodies from mass graves in Srebrenica and elsewhere, and equally contentious and ethnically tinted sports news.[3]

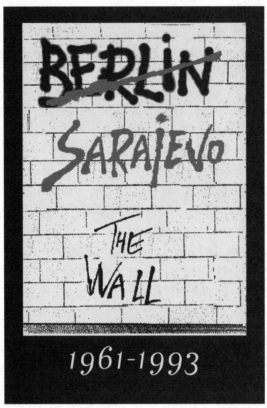

PICTURE 11.1 Sarajevo, Bosnia and Herzegovina, 1993. "It Happened Elsewhere," wartime postcard. *Source:* Design/Trio, Sarajevo.

Twenty years after 1989, the sentiment that the fall of the Berlin Wall was too distant from Bosnian reality to be a part of its internal political discussions had not changed. For Bosnians, political walls—internal and external—continued to be just as real as the graves from the last war. Although governed by an EU-dominated body, the Office of the High Representative, Bosnians were internally divided and tangibly separated from Europe by the Schengen wall ever since the Dayton Peace Agreement. The memory of Europe's indifference to the war and the shameful withdrawal of Dutch troops from Srebrenica made Berlin and united Europe seem distant and irrelevant. The most impressive commemorative event was the visit by Berlin's Schaubühne Theatre—one of the first events in Europe to mark the anniversary of 1989. A world-renowned theater troupe, Schaubühne presented three plays in Sarajevo—Shakespeare's *Hamlet*, Arthur Miller's *Death of a Salesman*, and Falk Richter's *Under Ice*. The performances attracted several thousand people, but some of the local press did not miss the irony that two of the plays dealt with the darkest sides of capitalism (*Nezavisne Novine* 2009a).

The only other commemorative events worth mentioning were conferences and meetings, sponsored by the Heinrich Böll Foundation and the Goethe Institute. One of the conferences, organized by political science faculty in Sarajevo, was appropriately entitled "1989–2009, Years of Upheaval: Beginning of Inclusion or Exclusion?" The other event, cosponsored by the Bosnian P.E.N. Club, had an even more telling title: "What is the Berlin Wall to Us?" (P.E.N. International 2009). In both gatherings, participants brushed upon the ongoing debate about consociationalism as the solution to the Bosnian fractured state but mostly focused on Bosnia's relation to Europe. If the fall of the Berlin Wall brought about the "general 'space of freedom,' " asked organizers of the Heinrich Böll conference (Grünther-Djecevic and Mujagic 2009), then "what kind of freedom did it bring to the EU-supervised Bosnia?" Was it "the freedom to segregate children along ethnic lines, the freedom of ignorance, freedom in conformism, freedom in opportunism?" In other words, was Bosnia, with its internal divisions and ethnically cleansed areas, an anomaly in the new Europe or emblematic of its history? "Would it be possible," asked Bosnian political theorist Asim Mujkic (2009), "no matter how fantastic or utopian it may sound, that those last, 'circumvented' yet-not-European countries find a new strength in their multi-culturalism and offer a plausible model for Europe of tomorrow?" Can Europe, asked several participants, citing French philosopher Etienne Balibar, "recognize in the Balkan situation not a monstrosity grafted to its breast [...] but rather an image of effect of its own history?" Will Europe "undertake to confront it and resolve it" or will it "continue to treat the problem as an exterior obstacle to be overcome through exterior means, including colonization?" (Balibar 2002).

And so, in 2009, just as in 1989, Bosnian intellectual conversations provoked by the fall of the Berlin Wall focused not on regime or regime change but on the fate of little people in Europe's periphery. Meanwhile, ethno-nationalist parties in power paid no attention to events in Europe or to the memory of communism: faking democracy, dividing the spoils of war, and sabotaging Bosnia's entry into the EU consumed all of their political time.

Serbia

As indicated in the introduction to this chapter, 1989 was a significant year in Serbia, but for reasons very different than in other parts of Eastern Europe. Slobodan Milošević solidified his position as Serbia's most important politician by organizing "spontaneous protests" in his support. Serbs celebrated the six hundredth anniversary of the Battle of Kosovo, where they fought against the Ottomans, and Milošević abolished Kosovo's autonomy and instituted the state of emergency in the

Albanian-dominated province. Thus, while other Yugoslav republics made their first baby steps toward democracy by organizing the first free elections, Milošević used the charade of the free elections to establish even firmer control not just over Serbia, but over the political project known as Greater Serbia.

The media in Serbia followed the events in Eastern Europe with great interest, but the events were interpreted with a surprising twist. In his brilliant analysis of the Serb coverage of 1989, anthropologist Ivan Čolović (2009, 2010) demonstrates how the Serb media followed the events in Eastern Europe with great sympathy toward the protestors. By contrast, Ceaușescu's reluctance to inform his people about the events in Berlin was harshly criticized. However, the language used to describe the demands of Eastern German protestors echoed the language used to describe Milošević's "happenings of the people" over the previous year. "It was all presented in such a way," says Čolović, "that one could easily think that people protesting on the streets of East Berlin represented just a German version of the Serb's 'happenings of the people.' Everything we read led to the conclusion that the events in Eastern Europe had actually been initiated by the Serbs" (Čolović 2009).

The subsequent ten years in Serbian politics were marked by similar national-ist fantasies, which perpetually placed the Serbs at the center of the history of the universe and excused them from participation in any crimes. The trend continued even after the October 5 revolution in 2000, which toppled the Milosevic regime. The regime change of 2000 entailed a number of compromises between democratic opposition and Milošević's followers. The assassination of Prime Minister Zoran Djindjić in 2003 cast a long shadow on Serbia's political leaders, including some of Djindjić's former allies. The coalition government formed in 2008 included repre-sentatives of Milošević's party; their leader, Ivan Dačić, became Serbia's Minister of Interior. The so-called Second Serbia—intellectuals, lawyers, civil society leaders who had been the most vocal opponents of Serbia's "official" politics and the war-riors for public acknowledgment of the state's involvement in crimes—were trau-matized by Djindjić's assassination and marginalized by their own friends who were now in power. Their positions in Serbia's mnemonic wars did not go as far as World War II or even the communist period: They were still asking for the accounting of the crimes committed under Milošević's watch and even more so during the reign of his democratic successors responsible for Djindjić's death.

The anniversary of 1989 was, therefore, not the cause for political debates in Serbia. The only official event took place in Belgrade. The Göethe Foundation com-missioned a German artist—Frank Belter—to build a small cardboard replica of the Berlin Wall on Belgrade's main square. It was planned that the wall would be three meters high and forty meters long. Belgrade citizens were supposed to write graffiti on just one side of the wall, the one representing West Germany. They were then expected to participate in the wall's destruction and feel empowered by their actions (Radio-televizija Srbije 2009a). However, as a proof that reality is always more fantastic than art, the wall was blown away by heavy winds before its demolition could even begin. The artist, Frank Belter, said that he had expected that the changing weather conditions could alter his work, symbolizing political changes, but he had not thought that the wall could just fly away. Trying to save the concept, the organizers used pieces of the wall to create an improvised Belgrade Museum of the Wall. The museum was opened by the German ambassador, who recalled The Scorpion's song "Winds of Change," which was written during the band's 1989 visit to Moscow and then served as the unofficial anthem of German reunification. "The winds of change," said the ambassador in his opening remarks, "are blowing very hard through Belgrade these days" (Blic 2009). Contradicting the ambassador, a group of Young Serbian Communists appeared at the end of the event with a large banner saying "The Wall Fell on the Wrong Side" (English Café 2009).

And while political and other winds preoccupied official Serbia, the imagination of ordinary people was captured by another upcoming event—the abolishment of visas for Serbian citizens traveling to EU countries (Pavićević 2009; *Nezavisne Novine* 2009b; E-Novine 2009). After twenty years, on December 19, 2009, the Schengen visa restrictions were removed for Serbs, Montenegrins, and Macedonians. The Serbs could again go shopping in the West. Travel agencies lured customers with advertisements for New Year's Eve celebrations in EU countries, as even respectable newspapers and magazines cherished the opportunity to publish new guides about the best places abroad to buy cheese, salami, and brand-name products!

The lack of public debates about 1989 and its meaning for Serbia should not be particularly surprising. For Serbian elites, both former communists and new democrats alike, there was nothing to be gained by rekindling the images of 1989. Commemorating 1989 could have invoked troubling memories of Milosevic's rise to power and his immense popular support at the time—but also of the subsequent wars, the collapse of Yugoslavia, and the de facto loss of Kosovo. There were also no political benefits to reminiscing about communism. Tanja Petrovic (2012b), a researcher with the Slovene Academy of Arts and Sciences, convincingly argues how "Milosevic made it impossible after 'democratic change' in 2000 for the new political elite to use socialist symbols and keep continuity in the Serbian identity politics." Thus, writes Petrovic, despite the fact that "Serbia is considered (and self-perceived) as a successor of Yugoslavia," remnants of its socialist past have been "almost completely eradicated from public spaces."[4] Instead, Serbian elites have turned to their nineteenth-century legacy of uprising against the Ottomans and the constitutional founding of the modern Serbian state as a way to bridge the potentially conflicting demands of their post-2000 intranational reconciliation and pro-European identity.

Hence, reflecting upon 1989 and its winds of change could be left to German foundations. The Serbian elites preferred to skip the last century and to link the memory of Serbia's nineteenth-century turn to Europe with its twenty-first-century prospects for a future within the EU.

Montenegro

It is not easy to describe—and even less so to assess—democratic transition in Montenegro, the smallest of the ex-Yugoslav republics. The first and the most important reason is that Milo Djukanović, alternately Montenegrin prime minister and president, and a former head of the Communist Party of Montenegro, was the only politician in the post-communist world who had never been out of power between 1989 and 2009. The second reason is that Montenegro did not become independent until 2006, so its politics remained entangled with Serbian politics for most of the post-1989 period.

Djukanović came to prominence as a young communist politician organizing Milošević's "happenings of the people," known in Montenegro as the "anti-bureaucratic revolution." Djukanović's party, which is the successor party to the Montenegrin Communist Party, was renamed as the Democratic Party of Socialists (DPS) in 1991. It splintered into two political parties in 1998; one maintained a pro-Serbian stance, while the other, ruled by Djukanović, became pro-European. Djukanović's wing never lost power, regardless of the momentous changes in Montenegro itself and in its neighborhood, sometimes initiated by the party itself (Bieber 2003).

It is alleged that Djukanović was a close business associate of Milošević's son Marko and that his brother, with Djukanović's knowledge, organized a sophisticated cigarette smuggling business that financed Serbia's wars and, later, Montenegro's bid for independence (Hozić 2004). Indicted in Italy on smuggling charges, Djukanović for years avoided court appearances by hiding behind his diplomatic immunity. He continued to build the Montenegrin economy with wild privatization, an ever expanding illicit and informal economy, and the influx of Russian capital. In a country with 600,000 people, where the strength of Granovetter's (1973) "weak ties" is particularly pronounced, the popularity and longevity of DPS could be best explained by the number of people whose livelihood was dependent on the party's licit or illicit proceeds. Likewise, it is easy to understand why political battles have been focused on the distribution of those profits rather than the ways in which they were accumulated.

There were no public manifestations to mark the anniversary of 1989 and no contestations over its memory. Opposition newspapers rehashed the history of

Djukanovic's rise to power, lamented the power of unnamed Montenegrin tycoons, and pondered the force of political continuity rather than change in their country. Djukanovic's press focused on developments in the European Union, Montenegro's prospects of joining the Union, and rebuttals of Djukanovic's Italian indictment. What exactly 1989 symbolized and why others made such a fuss about it were never addressed publicly on its twentieth anniversary in Montenegro.

Macedonia

Macedonia—the only former Yugoslav republic entirely left out of the wars in its neighboring states during the 1990s—is another republic where it is difficult to speak about regime change. If 1989 was happening elsewhere for the other Yugoslav republics, it might as well have happened on another planet as far as the Macedonians were concerned. Throughout the 1990s, Macedonian politics was the paradigmatic case of continuity with the defunct communist regime. The country's president, Kiro Gligorov, a popular communist politician and diplomat, kept the country out of trouble and stayed in power for eight years—from 1991 to 1998. The country's government was also dominated by the Social Democratic Union of Macedonia, a successor party to the Communist Party. So it was only after Gligorov's voluntary departure in 1998, that the opposition, nationalist Macedonian party—Vnatrešna Makedonska Revolucionerna Organizacija (VMRO)—was able to win both parliamentary and presidential elections, ushering in a period of several years of less stable coalitions and coinciding with the period of violence between ethnic Albanians and Macedonians.

In August 2001, the EU-sponsored Ohrid Framework Agreement ended Albanian armed insurgency and created novel power-sharing political institutions in Macedonia, thus ensuring continuous representation of Albanians in Macedonian government. Despite marked improvements in minority employment and education opportunities, the political and economic situation in the country remained complex and potentially unstable. As is the case in other quasi-consociational arrangements (Lebanon, Bosnia-Herzegovina, Ireland, to name just a few), Macedonian power-sharing institutions diffused some of the tensions while generating new ones. In 2009, eight years after Ohrid, politics in Macedonia was further ethnified and completely dominated by ethno-nationalist parties; most ethnic Albanians were not satisfied with the speed or the depth of the reforms, while many ethnic Macedonians resented the compromises imposed upon them by the Framework Agreement; and finally, the state—as the largest employee in the country—continued to act as the main provider of stability and the key instigator/object of ethno-political contention.

Early parliamentary elections in 2008, supported by the ruling Vnatrešna make-donska revolucionerna organizacija—Demokratska partija za nacionalno edin-stvo (VMRO-DPNE) party, sought to capitalize on the popular resentment caused by NATO's refusal to invite Macedonia into its membership because of the long-standing dispute with Greece over the country's name. In elections marred by violence, the VMRO-DPNE-led coalition won a decisive majority in the parliament. Following the elections, VMRO-DPNE invited the smaller of the two main Albanian parties—Democratic Party of Albanians (DPA)—into the government. The decision to ignore the larger (and politically more salient, as it was formed by the leaders of the 2001 armed insurgence) of the two Albanian parties—Democratic Union for Integration (DUI)—led to protests and renewed threats of violence, especially by the leaders of the more radical wing of DUI (Ragaru 2008).

From 2006 until the time of this writing, the VMRO-DPNE government has been led by former Finance Minister Nikola Gruevski. Many observers of Macedonian politics characterize Gruevski's leadership style as populist. His government engaged in permanent campaigning and dominated the quasi-independent Macedonian media with its massive and perpetual political advertising. As Sasho Ordanoski, a well-known political analyst and editor of privately owned Alsat TV, put it in an IREX (2009, 69) report on Macedonian media: "The public is mesmerized by the government campaigns. This is a populist model of ruling the country. The government's approach to the media is a populist one, and the objective is not to promote the values of liberal democracy but to mobilize the masses on the ground behind the government's policies." Government control of the media through advertising, threats to journalists and limits to their freedom of speech, a declining level of professionalism among journalists, and the concentration of media ownership in few, politically partisan hands have led the IREX team to reduce Macedonian media sustainability ratings in 2009 and to declare that the country had "regressed into an unsustainable, mixed [media] system" (IREX 2009, 67).

As an added flavor to its populism, the ruling party used the dispute with Greece over the country's name for domestic purposes, re-writing the history back into a glorious B.C.E. era, and explicitly or implicitly approving the invention of "Ancient Macedonians" as an ethnic category. In 2006, the government renamed the largest airport in the country Alexander the Great and in 2009 planned to build a six-story statue of Alexander the Great on the main square in the capital city of Skopje. As one of my interviewees in 2009 noted, "the Government has placed ethnic Macedonians into a time-capsule and sent them off to space with little or no regard as to what will happen when they discover that there is no there-there." Needless to say, the invention of "Ancient Macedonians" has created many new loyal followers for the government while generating new identity divisions in Macedonia, not only between minorities and ethnic Macedonians, but among ethnic Macedonians themselves.

Macedonia has been an EU candidate country since 2005, and issues related to EU accession and integration continue to dominate Macedonian politics. The name dispute with Greece remains one of the key obstacles to Macedonia's accession to the EU, a goal shared by the majority of Macedonian citizens but (like NATO membership) particularly coveted by Macedonian Albanians. The latter have little understanding for the name game as currently played by Gruevski's government. Other much discussed issues in Macedonian daily politics include decentralization and local provision of services mandated by the Ohrid Agreement, minority integration and/or segregation in education, and public service reform.

In the country that aspires toward EU membership while fighting mnemonic and cultural wars over ancient history and the identity of Mother Teresa (an ethnic Albanian born in the Macedonian capital, Skopje, albeit during Ottoman times) (Wood 2003), neither 1989 nor its twentieth anniversary could get much traction. On September 24, 2009, the Konrad Adenauer Stiftung (2009) sponsored a forum about the collapse of communism in Skopje, and on November 14, they brought Greek, Macedonian, German, Serb, and Albanian students together to discuss "often very intensely—what is to be learned from the events 20 years ago, when courage and decisiveness brought down the Berlin Wall and ended the communist system." According to the Foundation's website, the students demonstrated that "despite the differences in opinion today about the name issue, Kosovo or any other current challenges, the walls can be torn down, when talking and working together." The Foundation also sponsored a publication of a journal, *Politička Misla* (Political Thought), inspired by the fall of the Berlin Wall—an uneven mix of articles about lustration, transitions, revolutions, Romanian perceptions of détente, and Balkan geopolitics. More important, perhaps, the journal issue was prefaced by Henri Bohnet (2009), chairman of the Konrad Adenauer Stiftung for Serbia and Macedonia, who stressed the need for "these countries" to learn from their past in order not to repeat it but also to be able to meet "Europe's high standards of democracy and the rule of law." The journal ended with a reprint of the European Parliament Resolution 1481 (2006) on the "need for International Condemnation of Crimes of Totalitarian Communist Regimes" (*Politička Misla* 2009).

The only official statement about 1989 was a letter sent by Macedonian president Gjorge Ivanov (a VMRO politician and a political science professor) to his German counterpart, Horst Köhler. In his letter, Ivanov praised the process of European reunification—"Europe without borders, walls or prejudices"—triggered by the fall of the Berlin Wall. But then he also reminded the German president that "the citizens of Macedonia are awaiting their day of major significance—the day when the

Schengen wall will be lifted. A wall that prevented my countrymen to feel the bene-fits of united Europe for too long" (MIA 2009; *Macedonia Daily* 2010). And so, just as for many ordinary citizens of Serbia and Montenegro, 1989 and its anniversary really arrived in Macedonia on December 19, 2009, when the EU finally removed its restrictions on their travel to the Schengen countries.

Politics of Commemoration in the Former Yugoslavia

Confrontations with history burst onto Yugoslav's political scene almost immedi-ately after Tito's death in 1980. In the political vacuum created by Tito's departure and filled by grave economic woes, a range of theatrical works, novels, political memoirs, and new historical accounts began to address both previously glossed-over crimes of Nazi collaborators in World War II (the Croatian Ustashe, Serbian Chetniks, and the Muslim Handžar division) *and* previously unmentioned communist crimes. In the years that followed, further complicated by new wars, new violence, and new state crimes, battles over collective memory included naming and renaming of streets, retouching of photographs and historical records, purges of public libraries and bookstores, rewriting of textbooks, cleansing and reconstruction of museum spaces, destruction and rebuilding of monuments, and massive movements of living and dead bodies. Commenting upon the frenetic confiscation of memory, which, for the most part, meant complete erasure of the common socialist past, Croatian scholar and novelist Dubravka Ugrešić (1996, 33) wrote: "Seen from outside […] the Balkan peoples resemble demented gravediggers. They appear stubbornly to con-firm the dark stereotypes others have of them. […] Through their activity of digging up and ritually mourning human bones and burying fresh ones without funeral rites, the Balkan peoples are spinning in a diabolical circle: it is impossible for them to come to terms with their own past, present and future."

It is, therefore, puzzling—in the context of this volume and in the context of the ex-Yugoslavs' preoccupation with the past—that the anniversary of 1989 did not lead to soul-searching and politically heated discussions about the end of commu-nism, about the role of the Yugoslav Communist Party at home and in the world, or about the enduring and abandoned legacies of Titoism. As a Croatian political com-mentator said on the occasion of one of those discussions about "twenty years after," it was somewhat astonishing that, in such a context, there were no debates about what had been accomplished during those twenty years of Croatian independence, and particularly no assessments as to where Croatia stood vis-a-vis its communist "prehistory" (Čulić 2009). It is almost as if those forty-five years of post–World War II developments under communism had never happened. Therefore, in this last section of the chapter, I would like to offer two possible explanations of the peculiar course that commemorations took in the former Yugoslavia—one that confirms the hypothesis offered by the editors of this volume, and another that somewhat exceeds the bounds of their framework.

First, it is important to note that all of the newly founded Yugoslav states appear to have fractured *mnemonic fields* on most issues, but relatively unified *regimes* when it comes to the memory of 1989. They are unified by their abnegation of this anniversary. The only possible exception is Montenegro, where it is difficult to speak of a mnemonic regime of any kind in respect to 1989. Second, given that contestations in some cases concern simultaneously several layers of history, it is not always easy to identify mnemonic actors: mnemonic warriors on one issue (e.g., Bleiburg in Croatia) may also be abnegators when it comes to crimes committed by Croats in the latest wars. Mnemonic pluralists (e.g., pro-democracy forces in Slovenia, Serbia) may easily overlap with prospectives (e.g., leave the past behind—whether it is Kočevski Rog or Srebrenica—and look forward to the EU).

Kubik and Bernhard's explanations of the varied cultural fields of memory politics in post-communist countries rely for the most part on the ways in which particular countries extricated themselves from the old regime: the type of transition, the role of the former communist parties; the tactical choices made by the successors of the former ruling party after transition; and ideological orientations and relative strengths of political actors at any given time after the transition. In the analysis of the six former Yugoslav states, one of these factors seems to be far more important than the others: *the role of the former communist parties*. Despite variations in the mode of transition or the quality of their newly achieved democracy, the six Yugoslav cases do not exhibit particularly significant differences in their desire to address and directly confront communist legacy. This lack of meaningful commemorations or even discussions about the moment of regime change—either in Eastern Europe or in the former Yugoslavia itself—is most easily explained by the continued political presence of the former communist parties in all six former Yugoslavia republics. From Slovenia to Macedonia, ex-communist parties have occupied important political offices for a good part of the last twenty years. They may have renamed themselves, made different re-branding choices (embracing or rejecting nationalism), maintained power or returned to it as democratic reformers, but they have never been completely defeated, marginalized, or truly forced to account for their past—if there was something to account for.

One ideological well that successors to the Yugoslav Communist Party have continued to draw on is Yugoslav exceptionalism. In Slovenia, Yugoslav difference from other communist countries has been at the front and center of battles between the Center-Right and the Left over communist crimes, lustration, and memories of World War II. Already in the 1990s, President Milan Kučan, a former communist, a political reformer, and a Slovene nationalist, argued that laws about lustration implemented in other communist countries were not applicable in Slovenia since the nature of the regime in Yugoslavia was different (Državni zbor Republike Slovenije, 1997). Needless to say, throughout the years, the Slovene Right has insisted upon the opposite—trying to prove, in every instance, that Yugoslavia was a totalitarian country like all other countries in the Eastern bloc, and that Tito's foreign policy separation from Stalin was never a domestic separation from the Stalinist political methods.

In other ex-Yugoslav republics, debates about Yugoslav exceptionalism are colored with nationalism and mementos of the most recent war. Some flirt with Yugo-nostalgia, either viewed as the equivalent of desire for renewed Serb domination or as a much-needed mnemonic device to counterbalance the virulent nationalism of the new states. Nationalists, for their part, also have difficulties confronting communist legacy: If their nations were as perfect as they assume, how could they have succumbed to forty-five years of voluntary servitude in the former Yugoslavia? Finally, in relation to 1989, arguments about Yugoslav exceptionalism echo the idea held by most Yugoslavs in 1989, that political events in the East had nothing to do with them. As Croat philosopher Žarko Puhovski (2009) eloquently described it, "When the Wall was breached, it was seen here as something happening to the worst examples of Soviet Communism—and had nothing to do with us. 'We' were something else in the eyes of most of the citizens of Yugoslavia. […] We saw them [people in the streets in the East] as trying to establish something we already had." As I have already mentioned, Serbian anthropologist Ivan Čolović (2009, 2010) persuasively argued that Milošević's propaganda machine used the events of 1989 so deftly that it really seemed as if the uprisings in the East had been initiated by the Serbs, as if the Germans were just imitating Milošević's own "happenings of the people." Twenty years later, with nationalism and wars as replacements for transition (Kennedy 2002), the anniversary of the fall of the Berlin Wall was still perceived as a *déjà vu* unrelated to the lived realities of peoples in the former Yugoslavia.

And, to make it worse, it was a bitter *déjà vu*. To the degree that they cared, the anniversary was a reminder that in that year Yugoslavs lost all that had previously made them so different and so exceptional: their unique place in Europe. The loss was not just a very significant change in Yugoslavs' geo-strategic position (a position of considerable—perhaps undeserved—privilege, which allowed Yugoslavia, as I heard an EU official say in 1989, to eat from both sides of the banquet table). It was also the loss of personal freedoms for ordinary Yugoslavs. From 1989 on, Yugoslav citizens gradually lost what they had treasured the most—freedom to travel without visas anywhere in the world. In 1989, West Germany was the first Western European country to introduce visas for Yugoslav citizens. It was quickly followed by France, and then by other Western European countries. By the end of the wars, with the exception of Croats and Slovenians, no citizens of former Yugoslav countries could enter Europe without humiliating waits for Schengen visas (Hozić 2011). The Schengen wall was accompanied by other imperceptible walls, which painted former Yugoslav citizens and polities as culturally different from the rest of Europe: wars, poverty, "ancient ethnic hatreds," Balkanism, Islam, and criminality. The expulsion from Europe, which Yugoslavs once saw as their rightful home, may explain why discussions about regime change were so easily substituted by discussions about Europe. The very ambivalence of the ex-Yugoslav's status within Europe since 1989 questioned the linear narrative of the events about Europe's reunified identity, now upheld by multiple new walls.

The theme of Europe's old and new walls brings me to the second possible explanation of why the commemorations of 1989 in the former Yugoslavia took the course that they did: *the transnationalization of mnemonic politics in Europe.* First, it should be obvious, even from this relatively brief overview of events in the former Yugoslav republics, that there would have been almost no public events marking the end of communism and the fall of the Berlin Wall had it not been for the German foundations and cultural institutions—the Konrad Adenauer Stiftung, an offspring of the Christian Democrats, the Heinrich Böll Stiftung, related to the Green Party, or the Göethe Institute. While the foundations allowed for a multiplicity of perspectives on the wall to be aired, it is difficult not to think that the way in which the anniversary of 1989 was marked in the former Yugoslavia was still just an echo of pre-scripted narratives, closely entwined with Europe's own reinvented common past.

Second, and perhaps ironically given the collective disregard for 1989 as a symbolic marker in the former Yugoslavia, mnemonic politics and practices in this defunct country still broadly conform to the processes of "Europeanization" of memory, currently under way through formal and informal institutions of the European Union. Ever since the hearings on "Crimes Committed by Totalitarian Regimes" initiated by Janez Janša and held during the Slovenian presidency of the EU Council in 2008, a broad coalition of European political parties (EPP—European People's Party, ALDE—Alliance of Liberals and Democrats, EFA—The Greens-Europeans Free Alliance, and UEN—Union for Europe of the Nations), with the notable exception of the Socialists, has been pushing for a common platform on European memory and conscience. On April 2, 2009, the European Parliament passed a resolution in favor of the initiative, recognizing that the "20th anniversary of the collapse of the Communist dictatorships" provided "an opportunity to enhance awareness of the past [...] and strengthen feelings of togetherness and cohesion." The resolution emphasized that "Europe will not be united unless its is able to reach a common view of its history, recognized Communism, Nazism and Fascism as a shared legacy and conduct an honest and thorough debate on all totalitarian crimes of the past century" (European Parliament 2009). After a series of follow-up events and initiatives, the platform was established in 2011 as an educational project of the EU. Under the auspices of the Polish presidency, the platform linked a number research centers throughout Europe, all specializing in the history of totalitarian regimes—such as the research arm of the Hungarian House of Terror, the Polish Institute of National Remembrance, the Romanian Institute for the Investigation of Communist Crimes, the Slovenian Study Center for National Reconciliation, and dozens of other similar institutions throughout the former communist world.

The thread connecting all these commemorative initiatives and research is the equalization of communist and Nazi crimes. As a process of memory creation, it has important—and some would say problematic—implications (Uhl 2009; Radonić 2012; Petrović 2012a, 2012b): By putting a premium on intra-national reconciliation, it promotes national homogenization and, frequently, externalizes responsibility for crimes (to the Germans or the Soviets); by equating Nazi and fascist collaborators and anti-fascists, it erases the memory of resistance (and sometimes criminalizes it); by individualizing victimhood ("from the perspective of the victims, it is immaterial which regime deprived them of their liberty") (European Parliament 2009), it institutionalizes the forgetting of crimes committed against particular groups (e.g., Roma, homosexuals, Slavs, communists), and precludes possible discomforting comparisons with the present treatment of minorities. Mostly, by emphasizing World War II and communist crimes, it deals with the communist past parenthetically, limiting serious and critical inquiry of everyday practices that sustained and undermined communist regimes for over fifty years.

Thus, mnemonic politics and practices in the former Yugoslav states, approached in this chapter through the investigation of public commemorations of 1989—confiscation of memory about communism (Ugresić 1996), obsession with intra-national reconciliation (Jansen 2010), externalization of guilt and responsibility for state crimes (Radonić 2012), placating of contemporary war crimes with narratives of previous wars or ancient glory (Petrović 2012b)—no longer seem particularly unique. For ex-Yugoslavs, 1989 might have happened elsewhere, taking them far away from Europe, where they thought they had rightly belonged—but their nationalist politics of memory, built as much on remembering as on denials, reaffirms that they have a rightful place in Europe, a continent obsessed with the dilemmas of collective memory and amnesia.

NOTES

1. On November 2, 2009, the Pew Global Attitudes Project published results of a survey conducted in nine former "Iron Curtain countries" (East Germany, Russia, Poland, Czech Republic, Slovakia, Hungary, Lithuania, Bulgaria, and Ukraine). The findings suggested that "the initial widespread enthusiasm about these changes [transition to democracy and capitalism] has dimmed in most of the countries surveyed; in some, support for democracy and capitalism has diminished markedly" (Pew, 2009). Approval of changes to democracy and capitalism most markedly declined in Ukraine, Bulgaria, Russia, Lithuania, and Hungary—while Czechs and East Germans still seemed reasonably content with results of their post-1989 political and economic transition. Many East Europeans (and the rate varied from 35 percent in Poland to 72 percent in Hungary) also thought that they were economically worse off in 2009 than in 1989.

2. In the 1990 elections, seven members of the Bosnian Presidency were elected from three political parties—Party of Democratic Actions (SDA, Muslim) won three seats, while Serb Democratic Party (SDS) and Croat Democratic Party (HDZ) won two seats each. The same three parties secured control over the Assembly of Bosnia and Herzegovina—both in the Council of Citizens and in the Chamber of Municipalities. Former Communist Party and Reform Party, led by then Prime Minister Ante Markovic, won very few seats. In the Chamber of Municipalities, Communist Party and Reform Party won only five seats out of 110 (Arnautovic, 2007).

3. In a country governed by ethnic quotas, sports too are dominated by ethno-politics. Due to its immense popularity (and money-making potential), soccer was most obviously affected by ethnic wrangling. Until 2002, there was no national soccer league in Bosnia and Herzegovina (teams from Croat-dominated Herceg-Bosna and Serb-dominated Republika Srpska refused to participate in joint competitions until 1999 and 2002, respectively). Violent incidents in soccer stadiums were frequent. In 2009, a young man—Vedran Puljic—was killed by hooligans at a soccer match in Siroki Brijeg, nominal capital of Herceg Bosna. It took years for the Bosnian national team to be recognized as such by Bosnian Serbs and Croats, and then it was fractured by demands for ethnic parity. In 2011, the Bosnian soccer association was suspended from the two most important international soccer organizations—UEFA (Europe) and FIFA (world)—because it refused to change its statutes according to UEFA/FIFA rules and to replace its three-member presidency with a single president.

4. Available at: http://www.iwm.at/read-listen-watch/transit-online/serbias-quest-for-a-usable-past/. Accessed on February 11, 2014.

4 Conclusions

12 The Politics and Culture of Memory Regimes
A COMPARATIVE ANALYSIS
Michael Bernhard and Jan Kubik

IN THE CONCLUDING chapter, we set out to do four things. First, we discuss the results of the case studies and provide a synthetic overview of them with an eye toward answering the question of why a given country ended up with a fractured, pillarized, or unified memory regime.[1] Second, we analyze whether and how the factors we identified in Chapter 1 have an impact on the memory regime outcomes, using qualitative comparative analysis (QCA). We identify one single-country configuration of conditions (Ukraine) and four distinct patterns,[2] two that produced fractured memory regimes and two that did not. Third, we discuss the relationship between the cultural content (framing) of memory regimes and national cultures, understood as discursively established "points of concern." Finally, we offer brief concluding reflections on the relationship between the type of mnemonic regime and democracy.

Fractured, Unified, and Pillarized Memory Regimes in the Commemoration of the Fall of State Socialism

In this section we analyze our outcome of interest: the political form of the *memory regime pertaining to the fall of state socialism* that emerged in the countries covered in the book (hereafter: memory regime). In each case the reconstruction of this regime is based primarily on the observation of the commemorations of the twentieth anniversary. In the country study summaries that follow, we present observations on the nature of key mnemonic actors (warrior, pluralist, abnegator) and their mixes that generate each memory regime. The presentation is organized according to regime outcomes in order to facilitate the testing of our assumption that the configuration of actors' strategies corresponds to regime outcomes. There are three possible forms that the regime can take: fractured, pillarized, or unified. At the same time, we systematically review the issues on which the mnemonic actors engaged and the conditions under which they waged their political struggles. The goal is to detect patterns of conditions that drive the choice of strategies by actors in the construction of the historical visions that they employed in their struggles for power.

Fractured Memory Regimes

There are a total of nine fractured memory regimes in the seventeen countries we considered. In 2009, Hungary had one of most strongly polarized and fractured memory regimes in the post-communist world. Political struggle pitted the post-communist Hungarian Socialist Party against a powerful Hungarian Right, embodied primarily in the Fidesz-Hungarian Civic Union, a party whose origins stem back to the opposition of the late communist period. The party-political Gyurcsány government, which had been re-elected in 2006, was removed in favor of a more technocratic cabinet, under Gordon Bajnai, that avoided a large public celebration. The Socialists, who presided over the Roundtable that had ended state socialism in Hungary twenty years earlier, were interested in promoting a pluralist interpretation of 1989, one in which political actors of different orientations compromised for the good of the nation to restore democracy and sovereignty. Their credibility had been damaged by revelations concerning former Prime Minister Gyurcsány's lies about the economy during the electoral campaign in 2006 and the ensuing mass protests by Fidesz and a new party of the Far Right, Jobbik.

Fidesz completely blunted this pluralist strategy by taking the position of a memory warrior for whom the pacted transition of 1989 had been a rotten compromise that yielded a political system in which ex-communists retained too much power (both officially and unofficially). They attempted to delegitimate their ex-communist opponents by casting doubt on whether they were "truly" Hungarian. In Fidesz's narrative this was linked rhetorically to the crushing of the Hungarian revolution of 1956 by the Soviet Union, and the reassumption of power by the communists, who presided over a "normalized" country from 1956 to 1989. The transition of 1989 was portrayed as a second betrayal, somehow akin to that of 1956. As a result, the only unproblematic commemorations of 1989 had to do with the opening of the barbed wire fence between Hungary and Austria, and the role that this played in the events that led up to the fall of the Berlin Wall that autumn.

The focal point of contentious commemoration in 2009 was the anniversary of the start of the 1956 revolution on October 23. Its commemoration in 1989, like the Nagy reburial, had been a watershed event in the Hungarian transition. It cemented 1956 as a foundational event in the Hungarian struggle for national sovereignty and democracy. In 2009, the government, Jobbik, and Fidesz held separate commemorations. The governmental ceremony was an austere and lightly attended affair with little public enthusiasm. The separate party political celebrations by Fidesz and Jobbik were fierce and confrontational, linking the communist betrayal of the 1956 revolution to their continued domination of politics, made possible by a transitional pact that perpetuated their privilege and unjust grip on power beyond 1989.

Poland also had a highly fractured memory regime during the commemorations of 1989. The main cleavage here was between two political parties that descended from Solidarity, the centrist Civic Platform (PO) and the rightist Law and Justice (PiS). This partisan divide was reinforced and intensified because the two parties were cohabitating in a semi-presidential regime. The commemoration brought heightened visibility to both President Lech Kaczyński (PiS) and Prime Minister Donald Tusk (PO). As PO by and large descended from the reformist wing of Solidarity that had been central in negotiations with the communists, PiS used the commemorations as an opportunity to attack the Roundtable Agreement of 1989 as a corrupt compromise that left the ex-communists with too much residual power.

Unlike in Hungary, where such attacks were highly successful, Tusk skillfully disarmed the memory warriors of PiS. First, by abnegating on the commemoration of the Roundtable, which was a pact that provided de facto guarantees to the communists, Tusk was able to avoid the controversies inevitably stoked by this commemoration. Second, by leading national and international commemorations of the election of June 1989, which in some sense destroyed those guarantees because of Solidarity's stunning success, he was able to outflank Kaczyński and look like an inclusive leader not tainted by the stigma of rotten compromise.

Romania's mnemonic regime was also fractured. Here, however, the issue was not the assessment of the events of 1989, but a question of who had the right to give voice to its recollection. For the vast majority of Romanians, despite a lack of clarity on what precisely 1989 was (coup, revolution, or something else), there was general agreement that the elimination of Ceauşescu in 1989 was a positive step in the transformation of the country. The configuration of forces did not fall simply along communist/anti-communist or regime/opposition lines. Two major sets of actors, derived from the National Salvation Front (FSN) that had taken power after the removal of Ceauşescu, were major antagonists, and the commemoration became contextually intertwined with the presidential election of 2009.

There were two sets of memory warriors. On one side was the Democratic Party (later the Democratic Liberal Party) led by President Băsescu, who took one wing of the former FSN in a Center Right, nationalist direction. After moving to the Right, Băsescu attempted to use a re-examination of the communist past as a means to discredit his opponents, the Social Democratic Party (PSD), a more leftist successor to the National Salvation Front. Commemoration became intertwined with the second round of presidential elections in December 2009, when the National Liberal Party (PNL), the strongest anti-communist party, agreed to support Mircea Geoană, the candidate of the PSD, in an attempt to prevent Băsescu's re-election. Self-described as the "Partnership for Timişoara," the two parties tried to present their coalition as a second opportunity for Timişoara to overthrow a dictator. The presidential campaign degenerated into a debacle of charges and countercharges, with both sides adopting warrior strategy as they tried to tar the other with charges of association with the Securitate state. The final denouement came when the "Partnership for Timişoara" attempted to hold an anti-Băsescu rally in Timişoara itself, and was harassed by local activists and actual veterans of the 1989 rebellion. According to the latter, the Partnership's attempts to present itself as a legitimate heir to the "Timişoara revolution" was a mockery of what the people of the town had done in 1989 and a debasement of a truly heroic moment for partisan political purposes. This intervention took the wind out of Geoană's sails, undermined his warrior strategy, and helped to carry Băsescu to a second term.

Slovakia featured a fractured memory regime as well. Generally speaking, there was a positive presentation of the twentieth anniversary in the media and a set of upbeat official public commemorations. However, in the face of the upcoming parliamentary elections of 2010, the divide emerged in the sphere of party competition, where the opposition engaged in mnemonic warfare and used the occasion to attack Robert Fico, the prime minister, for his ambiguous stance and behavior during the commemorations and his fitness to lead a national commemoration. In 1989 Fico was a young communist and his party Smer includes many other former communists.

The memory war in Slovakia manifested itself in competing celebrations. Fico was absent from the country during the anniversary, making state visits to both Russia and England, in a very short succession. In England, he spoke on the Gentle Revolution, presented a pluralistic vision of communist Slovakia that contained both positive and negative elements, and thus interpreted the necessity of regime change in 1989 in an ambiguous fashion. In contrast, the Center-Right opposition to Smer organized their own celebration, whose most important theme was

Fico's and Smer's lack of legitimacy to lead a commemoration of 1989. This warrior strategy bore fruit, and Fico's coalition lost support in the parliamentary election of 2010. Three parties that strongly attacked him in 2009, the Slovak Democratic and Christian Union (SDKÚ), Christian-Democratic Movement (KDH), and the Party of the Hungarian Coalition (SMK), joined the coalition government that replaced him under Iveta Radičová of the SDKÚ. In 2011 this government held an even more elaborate commemoration of 1989 on its twenty-second anniversary.

In Latvia and the other Baltic States we observe a different and somewhat more complex pattern of fractured memory, due to the impact of extant ethno-national cleavages. As in Hungary, the way in which most recent events were commemorated was embedded in a memory field in which a momentous, traumatic, and antecedent historical event, in this case the annexation of the three independent Baltic Republics by the Soviet Union in 1940, looms large. The struggle for the restoration of independence and democracy in the Baltic States during the Perestroika period, 1986–1991, was a protracted civil society battle with the Soviet state. The national fronts that waged that struggle encompassed groups that after the recovery of independence and the emergence of competitive politics would find themselves at odds, not unlike Poland.

In the period of run-up to independence from 1989 to 1991, differences between ideologically diverse factions among the Latvians, Lithuanians, and Estonians, as well as differences between them and Russians and other Slavic populations, intensified. Ethno-national differences that had grown systematically during the postwar period remained largely submerged in the conflict with the center. The anniversaries of three watershed events of this period, the Baltic Way human chain in 1989, the Latvian and Lithuanian barricades in January 1991, and independence in the summer of 1991, all became the subject of contested commemorative events twenty years later.

Commemorations in the Baltic States activated two sets of contested cleavages, ethnic and socioeconomic. This combination provoked a trifurcated memory regime, each of its components with a distinct narrative. Eglitis and Ardava (in Chapter 6) call the first of these the "ethnic elite political narrative." The source of this narrative is the titular elite in each republic. The Soviet occupation of 1940 figures here as a national calamity that is overcome by reassertion of independence by the opposition in 1991. The post-1991 period is treated euphorically as an era of "progress" and "freedom."

However, there is also dispute within the Baltic community over the meaning of the post-1991 period. This "political and economic alienation narrative" among the Estonians, Latvians, and Lithuanians also recognizes 1940 as a national catastrophe and positively assesses the 1986–1991 period and the opposition's goals of independence, democracy, and a market economy. Where this story diverged from the ethnic elite narrative is in the assessment of the post-1991 period. It was more critical, due to the uneven performance of the post-communist economy and the distributional consequences of market reforms. Unhappiness in this regard revolved around the emergence of a prosperous elite, while the living standards of the masses did not improve as fast, or, in some cases, at all. This narrative disagreed with the titular elite narrative in seeing the promise of the independence struggle as not fully realized.

Finally, there is the "ethnic alienation narrative." It has the greatest resonance among Russophone populations. They tend not to dwell on the events of 1940 and often will commemorate the victory in the "Great Patriotic War" in 1945, which they see as liberation from Nazi occupation. In contrast, many Balts see 1945 as a moment when one oppressive master was exchanged for another. For Russophone citizens, many of whom are working-class, these differences are exacerbated by their declining position in the "old" economy, which has deteriorated as heavy industry has contracted.

These memory divisions became politicized on specific anniversaries between 2009 and 2011. The "Heartbeats for the Baltics" in 2009, the commemorative run along a part of the 1989 Baltic Way human chain, divided Balts and Russians due to its close coincidence with the seventieth anniversary of 1940. Here, the different interpretations, strongly correlated with ethnicity, were reflected in the discussion of the anniversary of 1940 organized at the "Moscow House." There, differences between Russian and Latvian interpretations of 1940 stood in stark contrast. In the Russian narrative, 1940 was construed as an attempt to avoid the outbreak of war, and the Baltic and Polish elites of the time were held responsible for provoking a defensive Soviet reaction. For many Russians, especially Red Army veterans, the old Soviet narrative of 1940 as a year of necessary defensive action and 1945 as a year of liberation remained central to their vision of the past.

In 2011, Eglitis and Ardava note, the commemorations of barricade battles of January 1991 in Lithuania and Latvia were romantic and emotional celebrations of the recovery of national independence. Those who perished in the name of Baltic independence were celebrated as martyrs. There was strong tension over the fatalities inflicted by the Soviet armed forces in the failed hard-line crackdown on the movements for independence. In particular, calls for punishment of the Soviet-era officials responsible for the deaths of those killed while defending Baltic independence in January 1991 exacerbated the existing ethnic division. Many ethnic Russians saw such calls as punitive retribution.

The commemoration of the de facto achievement of Baltic independence in the late summer of 1991 was less controversial, though the ethnic divide remained not far from the surface. In Latvia, the commemoration was relatively inconspicuous, in contrast to the far less controversial and more lavishly celebrated eight hundred tenth anniversary of the capital city of Riga earlier in August 2011. The public commemoration of independence was smaller, more elite in nature, and clearly not embraced by the Russian minority. While there were no conspicuous conflicts, the Russian language press commented on feelings of exclusion experienced by its readers.

In Estonia celebrations were less controversial. The main commemoration was a songfest conducted in a rather festive mood. This lack of controversy was likely a product of the relatively good state of the economy, which meant that economic divisions among Estonians were less salient, and divisions between Estonians and Russians concerned only identity issues at that juncture. Despite the drop in contentiousness, during the celebration President Ilves talked about those who "remain stuck in the past." This was a strong assertion of the primacy of the Estonian reading of history over that of the Russophone population. It is unclear at this stage if the drop in contentiousness over the anniversaries was the beginning of an evolution of the memory regime away from fractured toward pillarization. It could also represent the ascendance of titular narratives of independence over Russian attempts to preserve elements of the Soviet-era memory field.

Ukraine, too, had a fractured mnemonic regime when it came to the fall of communism. While Shevel (in Chapter 7) does discuss the emergence of a general sense of Ukrainian national identity and an embrace of independent statehood, the country is deeply divided on the issue of the Soviet past and by conflicting evaluations of the performance of an independent Ukraine. The fissures here are geographic and linguistic, pitting the Ukrainian-speaking southwest against the Russophone northeast, while the hybridized center of the country displays some independent features.

In 2011, there were two sets of memory warriors who offered radically different assessments of Ukraine's experience in the former USSR and of the fall of the old system. The first was the unreformed communists of the Communist Party of the Ukraine (KPU), who were nostalgic and unapologetic enthusiasts for the former USSR. They depicted the breakdown of the Soviet Union and rise of independent Ukrainian statehood as a disaster. The second was the national and national-democratic Right, for whom Ukrainian history has been a series of unsuccessful campaigns to secure independence from a series of occupiers (Tatars, Poles, Russians). For this group, organized mostly in the Ukranian Popular Movement (Rukh), the Soviet Union represented the last version of foreign occupation, whose end was finally achieved with the attainment of independence in 1991. In 2011, both of these groups were highly critical of the poor state of Ukraine's post-independence economy. The former saw the economic travail as a result of the end of socialism, whereas the latter defined it as a product of the power that the Soviet-era economic nomenklatura had managed to retain. Former Soviet apparatchiks, the key group within the corrupt economic elite, were seen as subverting national economic interests while reaping enormous material benefits for themselves.

Curiously, neither of these two groups was the dominant political actor in 2011. That position was held by a third group, culturally quite amorphous, that included both a large number of former apparatchiks and many new businessmen. Their political formation, a classical party of power, has dominated power in Ukraine since Kuchma's assumption of the presidency in 1994 and has engaged in mnemonic abnegation.[3] It did not have strong doctrinaire views on the past but occasionally engaged in memory politics when a salient issue could be turned to its political advantage. The party of power was not above either playing the nationalist card or waxing nostalgic about aspects of the Soviet past if that could bring political gain. Since the split in the party of power dating back to the Orange revolution, its elements made alliances with both the Left and Right. The Tymoshenko faction found common cause with Rukh, thus subscribing to the negative view of the Soviet past and positive assessment of the old system's collapse. The ruling group around Yanukovych espoused a less negative interpretation of the Soviet past while often bemoaning the breakup. The alternations in power since the revolution have meant that both memory warriors were strengthened, and that left the memory regime concerning the breakup of the former Soviet Union deeply fractured.

Shevel argues that these political maneuvers, reflected also in zig-zags of sharply divisive mnemonic conflict, left the population at large rather disenchanted. Her examination of public opinion data suggest that Ukrainian society in 2011 was much more plural in its view of the past than its contending representations in the fractured mnemonic regime constructed by the feuding elites. People held different opinions but were more open to the perspectives of others than the politicians. She suggests that this holds out the possibility of the emergence of a pillarized memory regime, if the staging of mnemonic warfare becomes a liability for politicians whose divisive narratives are out of sync with the much more tolerant set of popular beliefs. The existence of such an "open" popular climate, at least among a significant segment of the population, constitutes an opening for a mnemonic entrepreneur to propose a pluralist view of the past and to try to build a pillarized regime in the future.

Finally, in the former Yugoslavia, Slovenia was the one country that had a fractured memory regime on the issue of 1989. And the fracturing was so strong that there was no major public commemoration of the country's first steps toward democracy and eventual independence (the ending of the communist monopoly of political organization and creation of a multiparty system). The ruling Social Democrats (SD), as successors to the Slovenian League of Communists, tended to play up their role as leading reformers and celebrated the peaceful and evolutionary path of Slovenia out of Yugoslavia and its rapid integration into the European Union. In 2009, the SD saw democracy as a national triumph in which they were full partners. The opposition, particularly the former Prime Minister Janša and the Slovenian Democratic Party, construed the Social Democrats as unreconstructed totalitarians and secret police agents unjustly taking credit for the changes since 1989. These sharply divergent interpretations of 1989 were made manifest in the controversy over the Ertl affair and became central in the disputes between the Slovenian Left and Right over killings in the aftermath of World War II and the Yugoslav revolution.

Pillarized Memory Regimes

At the beginning of the second decade of the twenty-first century, pillarized memory regimes were rare in post-communist Europe. This is not surprising given that all the countries in the region experienced major systemic changes just twenty years earlier. Pillarization, a mnemonic regime in which difference becomes accepted and institutionalized, does not seem like the sort of arrangement that comes together in the short term. The one case where it occurred was the Czech Republic.

O'Dwyer shows (in Chapter 8) that in the Czech Republic there was a consensus on how the Velvet Revolution was remembered, though not on how it was supposed to be commemorated. This is an important distinction in the Czech case. With the exception of the communists who accepted the post-1989 democracy while not fully rejecting the pre-1989 system, the events of 1989 were remembered as a highly positive and critical watershed in Czech history. The communists, largely isolated in the post-1989 politics of the country, took a pluralist stance. They accepted the larger consensus, but within the range of acceptable "pasts" they tried to create room for their own, constructed around an assessment of the pre-1989 period that was not entirely negative.

The tensions that emerged during commemorations did not involve political parties and were thus non-partisan, in contrast to the countries with fractured memory regimes. The division manifested itself, however, as a tension between political society (political elites) as a whole and specific groups in civil society. O'Dwyer depicts the official commemorations as lacking in spirit and enthusiasm due to disarray among the political parties over the collapse of the government and a series of political scandals in the run-up to the anniversary. The dominant stance of the parties was abnegation. Neither of the two major parties, the Social Democrats nor the Civic Democratic Party, saw any political advantage in trying to politicize the event.

Instead, student groups played the leading role in a series of anti-political protests that coincided with the official commemoration. They organized their own celebrations of the spirit of 1989, which tried to recapture the idealistic anti-political enthusiasm of the protests that brought an end to communist rule in Czechoslovakia. The highly satirical, ironic, critical, but also irreverently carnivalesque performances put on by two major student groups, staged against the background of the lackluster official commemorations, glamorized 1989 as a moment of idealized "anti-political" revolutionary purity. Whereas the official commemorations treated "normal" democratic politics in the Czech Republic as an edifice built on the foundation of the Velvet Revolution, the students treated the post-revolutionary reality, full of flaws in their view, as a corruption of the ideal. While pointing out the shortcomings of post-revolutionary politics, they were not mnemonic warriors who sought partisan political advantage by trying to impose their vision of the past—as the "truth"—on others. They instead tried to prod the political class into living up to its pedigree stemming from 1989. But the students also kept their political distance from the communists and offered a starkly critical assessment of the period prior to the 1989 revolution.

A gap opened between the visions of the past presented in student performances and the "official" vision of the political establishment, but it was nonetheless built on a unified recollection of the past, in which the Velvet Revolution was seen as a common achievement of the people who rejected the unwanted system. The students were critical, not of the way state socialism was disposed of, but of the realization of the promise embedded in the ideals that made this possible. On the other hand, no major political actors attempted to play the mnemonic card and use the memory of the fall of communism in a way that could enhance its short-term political prospects. The Czech political landscape in 2011 was thus devoid of mnemonic warriors who would seek to turn the differences in assessment of the pre-1989 period and the transition process into a salient political cleavage. Dominated by abnegators and pluralists, the memory regime remained pillarized rather than fractured. Three different visions of the past coexisted peacefully, that of the two major political parties, that of the student protestors, and that of the communists.

Unified Memory Regimes

The book documents seven unified memory regimes build around the twentieth-year anniversary. The first of these is found in Germany. Despite the historic importance of German unification, the events of 1989–1990 did little to disrupt the existing memory politics of the pre-1989 Federal Republic of Germany. The post-unification German memory field remained remarkably similar to the one that had been developed earlier in the Western part of the country. While there was some anxiety across Europe that unification would lead to a more triumphalist German nationalism, such fears seem unfounded in retrospect. Unification did not dislodge West Germany's *culture of contrition* as the dominant narrative of the German quest to come to terms with the Nazi past (*Vergangenheitsbewältigung*). The memory regime constructed to commemorate the fall of the Berlin Wall was absorbed by the existing German mnemonic field permeated by the themes of the culture of contrition.

The new element in the German mnemonic field after the unification was the legacy of the German Democratic Republic (GDR). In the twenty years following the 1989 revolution, it continued to be an unresolved issue. Germans were to some extent divided over whether the GDR should be understood as an illegitimate state (*Unrechtsstaat*) or as a flawed state whose social system had some positive features. While the issue had not yet become salient by the time of the twentieth anniversary celebrations, it still has the potential to become so. There have been a series of low-level debates about certain politicians from the East who worked as informants for the Stasi. There has also been a discussion about whether the Left Party (*die Linke*), a small leftist-socialist party, should be treated as a normal party. The Left Party was formed by disenchanted social democrats from the West, independent leftists, and members of the Party of Democratic Socialism (PDS), the successor to the former East German ruling communist party. By 2009, the issue of how to treat this party would become locally salient only when the Left Party held the key to a ruling coalition at the level of state (*Land*) governments. It has yet to emerge as an issue nationally. However, it has the potential to open a new and divisive dimension in memory politics. It will probably take a big event like the Left Party becoming critical for the formation of a government on the national level. Under such circumstances one could imagine the Christian Democrats using a mnemonic warrior strategy to undermine such efforts. However, this has yet to happen.

In 2009, the year 1989 was celebrated as a watershed political event in Germany. However, as David Art points out (in Chapter 9), given the coincidence with the anniversaries of Kristallnacht and the German Revolution of 1918, November 9 is likely to remain a low-key celebration, at least as long as the culture of contrition sets the tone for the politics of memory in Germany. At least until other events make the extant differences of the recollection of the GDR a salient political issue, it is likely that the anniversary of the breach in the Wall will remain uncontroversial and devoid of deeper partisan political meanings. All political actors chose to abnegate, not to politicize, the anniversary of the events of November 1989. At least for now, the memory regime around 1989 avoided fracturing by those who could potentially use it as part of either a new nationalist gambit to weaken the culture of contrition or a narrative of indignation against the loss of nostalgically recollected aspects of life in the GDR.

Bulgaria, too, had a unified memory regime. On the twentieth anniversary of November 10, 1989, the resignation of communist leader Todor Zhivkov was celebrated in a weak and understated manner. Ganev (in Chapter 10) explains this as a product of a hegemonic discourse in which the communist past is valorized over the present-day reality. The proponents of this discourse are largely former members of the Bulgarian Communist Party or the communist-era secret service who have benefited from the privatization of state assets, especially the media.

While the Bulgarian Right and Center-Right might not have agreed with this nostalgic recollection, it chose not to challenge it. The government that was in place during the celebrations, led by the Center-Right Citizens for the European Development of Bulgaria (GERB), chose a strategy of abnegation. It either decided not to engage on issues of commemoration or equivocated publicly, as seen in the contradictory statements of Prime Minister Boyko Borisov on the anniversary. Seeing no possibility of turning memory politics to their advantage, GERB chose not to engage on this issue. Given the powerful mnemonic hegemony—the valorization of socialist nostalgia, as Ganev calls it—GERB's abnegation was a successful strategy that gave them an electoral success on the basis of a non-ideological program that stressed pragmatism, competence, and the attainment of European norms.

Hozić (in Chapter 11) identifies five unified memory regimes in the former Yugoslavia with regard to 1989. This does not mean, however, that the memory fields of these countries are unified with regard to other events. All of them have hotly contested and divisive mnemonic issues that produce fractured memory regimes. But in 2009, 1989 was simply not one of them. In Croatia there was little more than some notice of 1989 in the newspapers, with essays written by important intellectuals offering different interpretations of its meaning. However, this did not extend into the competitive world of political society, and no party tried to make the anniversary an issue. In this sense, 1989, a potentially divisive memory, was displaced in Croatia by the disputes around ethnic and ideological warfare from the time of World War II and its aftermath. There was a consensus, at least tacit, among major political actors that the interpretation of 1989 was not important enough or useful to fight over. They had other, in their eyes, bigger issues to contest.

In Bosnia-Herzegovina, the anniversary of 1989 hardly had any impact. The ethno-nationalist parties that controlled parts of the still trifurcated political community paid the anniversary little or no attention. The focus of mnemonic politics was on the genocide and violence perpetrated during the Yugoslav Wars of the 1990s, which remained fresh yet unresolved in the frozen political situation in the trifurcated republic. In Serbia, 1989 was an eventful year. As Hozić notes, it included Milosević's inflammatory "Field of Blackbirds" speech, as well as the orchestrated campaign of popular happenings that served to consolidate his power. Twenty years hence, no political actor found it advantageous to commemorate or criticize this past, given the tense state of Serbian politics torn between nationalist and pro-European formations. The pattern of disinterest and abnegation was also discernible in both Montenegro and Macedonia.

In all five cases we see a universal stance of abnegation leading to unified mnemonic regime of forgetting of 1989. One wonders if the anniversary would have been noticed at all if the EU and the German foundations had not sponsored several commemorative events. The general apathy toward these efforts seems to be a product of the larger issues with which the successor states to Yugoslavia have had to contend since the wars of the 1990s.

Patterns and Explanations: Qualitative Comparative Analysis (QCA)

There are two important observations that emerge from a close reading of the seventeen case studies of commemorations of 1989 and 1991 covered in the previous chapters. The first concerns the *political form* of the mnemonic regime. In our theoretical framework, we understand fractured memory regimes as the product of the emergence and activity of a particular kind of political actor, memory warriors. On an observational level, we expect fractured memory regimes to be characterized by sharp internecine battles over the nature of the past and its impact on the present. This often takes the form of culture wars that color the stances of other political actors (whether or not they are warriors) on other important political issues. Had we found polities where celebrations of the twentieth anniversary of the fall of communism took the form of culture wars but without clearly identifiable mnemonic warriors, this would have undermined our definition of memory regimes based on specific combinations of mnemonic actors. That we see a universal concordance between this kind of cultural politics and the presence of a mnemonic warrior in our fractured cases validates our starting assumptions.[4]

The second observation is about the *cultural content* of the mnemonic regime. It is composed of cultural themes and forms that belong to a "national" repertoire shaped by history. We discovered that the set of issues, their salience, and their framing—in short, the content of the mnemonic contest in which actors engage—is highly country-specific, and it is hard to find any generalizable patterns.

We hypothesized at the outset of this project that the political form of the memory regime should be determined by the interaction of factors belonging to three distinct clusters: (1) structural constraints, (2) cultural constraints, and (3) cultural strategies. These factor clusters influence the choice of mnemonic strategy by actors operating within a specific national context and ultimately determine the type of mnemonic regime that emerges.

In order to prepare the coding for QCA, we read the case studies closely to characterize the factors we selected for the final analysis in the theory chapter in the binary fashion required. To reiterate, these factors were: (1) the type of state socialism that existed in a given country prior to 1989/1991, (2) the mode of extrication from state socialism, (3) the nature of the cleavage structure at the time of commemoration (Left-Right; ethnic, religious, linguistic; both, or neither), (4) the nature of the communist successor party, and (5) the existence and intensity of memory layering during commemoration and its nature.[5] We then verified these codings with the authors of the chapters on each country or set of countries. This generated a qualitative assessment of each case, which was then categorized as the presence (1) or absence (0) of the conditions for use in QCA (see Table 12.1).[6]

In our theory, the central defining feature of the political form of memory regimes is the mix of actors engaged in memory politics. We will now engage in a more general analysis across cases to see if the potential causal factors listed in Table 12.1, or combinations of them, generate different actor outcomes. We do this using crisp algorithm QCA.[7] QCA uses Boolean algebra and set theory to examine systematically both simple and complex conjunctural causal patterns, most effectively in small- and medium-n analysis (Ragin 1987, 2000; Rihoux and Ragin 2009; Schneider and Wagemann 2012). We present separate Boolean analyses for fractured and not-fractured (unified and pillarized combined) memory regimes. We decided to combine the analysis of unified and pillarized regimes because in our cases there was only one pillarized outcome, the Czech Republic.[8] We thus focus on the question of whether or not a memory warrior emerged, distinguishing the causal patterns that lead to fractured and non-fractured memory regimes constructed around the commemoration of the twentieth anniversaries of the fall of state socialism.

Having verified that our definition of the political form of memory regimes through actor configuration was congruent with the case findings, we then turned to the analysis of conditions that explain the emergence/non-emergence of a memory warrior in the set of cases analyzed in the book. By logically minimizing truth tables, we identified *five configurations* (four patterns and one singular configuration) of conditions: three that promoted the emergence of mnemonic warriors and thus fractured memory regimes, and two which did not and thus yielded in their absence unified or pillarized regimes. More technically, we produced Boolean truth tables for the emergence/non-emergence of memory warriors and thus fractured or non-fractured outcomes, and then conducted a QCA analysis designed to identify both parsimonious and intermediary configurations of sufficient conditions (Schneider and Wagemann 2012, 60).

Analysis of Fractured Memory Regimes

We began by first seeing if any of the potential causal factors was a necessary condition for warrior emergence. Our initial analysis showed little of interest.[9] Later, when we explored the cases in more detail, we found that all fractured memory

TABLE 12.1

Potential Conditions Leading to the Emergence of Different Memory Regimes

State	State Socialism	Mode of Extrication	Polarizing Cleavage 2009/2011	First Communist Successor Party	Memory Layering	Mnemonic Warrior?	Memory Regime
Estonia	Hard-line	Regime Collapse	Ethnic	Social Democrats	Yes	Present	**Fractured**
Hungary	Reformed	Negotiated	Political	Social Democrats	Yes	Present	
Latvia	Hard-line	Regime Collapse	Ethnic + Political	Social Democrats + Neo-communists	Yes	Present	
Lithuania	Hard-line	Regime Collapse	Ethnic + Political	Social Democrats	Yes	Present	
Poland	Reformed	Negotiated	Political	Social Democrats	No	Present	
Romania	Hard-line	Regime Collapse	Political	Party of Power	No	Present	
Slovakia	Hard-line	Regime Collapse	Political	Social Democrats	Yes	Present	
Slovenia	Reformed	Negotiated	Political	Social Democrats	Yes	Present	
Ukraine	Hard-line	Elite Control	Linguistic + Political	Party of Power + Neo-communists	Yes	Present	
Bosnia	Reformed	Regime Collapse	Ethnic/Religious	Social Democrats	Displacing	Absent	**Unified**
Bulgaria	Hard-line	Elite Control	None	Party of Power	No	Absent	
Croatia	Reformed	Regime Collapse	Ethnic + Political	Social Democrats	Displacing	Absent	
Germany	Hardline	Regime Collapse	None	Social Democrats	Yes	Absent	
Macedonia	Reformed	Elite Control	Ethnic + Political	Party of Power	Displacing	Absent	
Montenegro	Reformed	Elite Control	Ethnic	Party of Power	Displacing	Absent	
Serbia	Reformed	Elite Control	Ethnic + Political	Party of Power	Displacing	Absent	
Czech Rep.	Hardline	Regime Collapse	None	Neo-communists	No	Absent	**Pillarized**

regimes shared an extant polarized cleavage (either Left-Right or ethnic/linguistic/religious). And a subsequent necessary condition analysis confirmed that all fractured memory regimes had one or both of these conditions. The question remained as to whether such cleavages were sufficient as well.[10]

Our reduction of the truth table for warrior emergence, conducted to identify sufficient causes, returned both parsimonious and intermediate solutions.[11] The former are simply minimal configurations of conditions whose presence is sufficient for the emergence of memory warriors. Among them, we found several combinations that included the non-appearance of a displacing memory layer. We did not find these findings particularly enlightening given that the existence of a displacing memory layer in the field of memory would mean that the commemoration of the twentieth anniversary of the extrication from communist regimes was suppressed or overwhelmed by other issues in the memory field.[12] One other pair of conditions that emerged as a parsimonious solution was the combination of the absence of a reform socialist past and the presence of an ethnic cleavage. This pairing is quite important in the Baltic countries and will figure prominently in our following discussion.

When Boolean analysis is used to test existing theory, parsimonious solutions allow one to see if the configurations of sufficient conditions specified in theory are confirmed by the case analyses. However, in studies where there are not strong theoretical priors and the researcher is breaking new theoretical and empirical ground, it is important to compare the parsimonious minimal formulas (prime implicants) generated by the Boolean analysis with three richer models of the analyzed material: (1) descriptive (or primitive) formulas (conjunctions representing a full row in a truth table), (2) intermediate solutions (products of partial logical reduction), and (3) case narratives provided by country experts.[13] This is in line with the methodological guidance provided by the pioneers of qualitative comparative analysis:

> An important part of the research dialogue in Boolean analysis, therefore, concerns the comparability of cases. By specifying the assignment of cases to different causal paths, the Boolean approach establishes the boundaries of comparability. Thus Boolean analyses simultaneously identify key cases and key causal conjunctures, which can then be examined in more detailed case-oriented studies. In general the identification of different causal conjunctures provides a basis for delineating types and subtypes of social phenomena. Specifying types, in turn, establishes the necessary bridge between the diversity that exists in a given category of historical outcomes and social scientists' attempts to produce theoretically relevant generalizations about events and processes around them. (Ragin 1987, 168)[14]

By focusing on the intermediate results, we are able to simultaneously compare systematically the presence and absence of factors in groups of cases *and* anchor our Boolean analysis in the causal narratives produced for specific countries. This allows us to better understand the contextualized causal mechanisms that produce the outcomes. In brief, QCA is designed to elucidate what is essential in the cases analyzed, while providing the researcher with an opportunity to contextualize the findings by returning to the evidence in the case studies.

The intermediate solution for the emergence of a mnemonic warrior and thus a fractured memory regime is presented in Table 12.2. Based on these results and our understanding of the case material, we identify two patterns of conditions and one unique case configuration that led to the emergence of memory warriors and thus fractured memory regimes.

The unique configuration of conditions that led to the emergence of fractured memory regime in Ukraine is presented in the center of the table.[15] The rest of the cases are grouped into two subsets, each with its own distinct causal pattern that resonates with our understanding of post-communist politics and is congruent with at least one of the causal narratives in the case chapters.

Poland, Hungary, and Slovenia constitute the first sub-set (bottom of Table 12.2). This pattern combines four factors—reformed communism, negotiated extrication, a strong ex-communist social democratic party, and a strong existing Left-Right cleavage (refsoc * trann * pcsd * lrclev).[16] In all three cases, the post-communist space on the Left was dominated by an ex-communist social democratic formation, there was a strong existing structure of cleavages, and no displacing layer emerged.

One can see the origins of this pattern in the *negotiated extrication from reformed communism*. All three countries had reform-oriented communist parties that exhibited a relatively high degree of liberalization (Przeworski 1991) prior to the changes of 1989–1991. This higher degree of liberalization meant that all three communist parties were able to negotiate an end to their formal monopoly of political organization with civil society actors that could be seen to represent important parts of already highly independent and contentious societies. In Poland and Hungary these negotiations were actually formalized in Roundtables, whereas in Slovenia they were more informal. Under these conditions, as they exited power, the reform-oriented communists chose to recast and reorganize themselves as social democratic parties that became electorally viable contenders for power (Grzymała-Busse 2002).

Thus, in this group of countries the major contenders for power in the post-communist period have included both the ex-communist successor parties and the parties that emerged from the civil society–based opposition. This pattern helped to produce a strong Left-Right political cleavage (lrclev) in all three societies where more nationalist and conservative political parties were able to gain political traction by attacking not only ex-communist social democrats, but also those parties derived from the communist-era opposition that were created by the negotiating partners of the communists in the extrication pact from communist rule.[17] By painting those pacts as "rotten deals" that resulted in "unfinished," "corrupt," or "stolen" revolutions and/or processes of democratization, more nationalist and conservative parties initiated a mnemonic war and created a highly effective platform to justify their claims for power. These actors—Law and Justice in Poland, Fidesz in Hungary, and the Slovenian Democratic Party—emerged as powerful warriors in all three commemorations in 1989.

The second pattern is presented in the top section of Table 12.2. Here the fractured memory regime resulted from the *ideological or ethnic polarization in the countries that emerged from hard-line state socialism via regime collapse* (~refsoc * tranrc * (lrclev+ethclev)). None of these is a country that had a strong tradition of reform under communist rule (~refsoc), which disposed them toward regime extrication via collapse (tranrc). In Romania and Slovakia this was largely due to the hard-line character of their communist parties, whereas in the three Baltic States this was because of resistance by Soviet hard-liners to increased autonomy or sovereignty of republics. Under such conditions, when at least one strong polarizing cleavage existed, either ideological (Left-Right—lrclev) or sociocultural (ethnic, religious, or linguistic—ethclev), a memory warrior emerged. In the three Baltic countries there was the ethnic cleavage between Balts and Russians, overlaid with post-communist distributional struggles in the wake of free-market reform in Lithuania and Latvia. In these three cases, warriors emerged over the differing ethnic interpretations of the events of 1991.

In Romania and Slovakia the cleavages were purely Left-Right. In the former, the successors to the post-transition party of power, the National Salvation Front, engaged in multiple rounds of internecine political battles, and just prior to the commemoration of 1989 the Democratic Party, led by Trajan Băsescu, moved in a more conservative direction, while the more traditionally socialist Social Democratic Party (PSD) entered into a tactical alliance with the traditionally anti-communist National Liberal Party (PNL). In this unexpected realignment of the Romanian political society, the two sides, while both defending the ambiguous revolution that removed Ceaușescu, attempted to paint the other as an illegitimate heir to the "revolution." In Slovakia, it was a classic Left-Right struggle between liberal forces that had previously unseated Vladimír Mečiar and a new catch-all party of the Left, Smer.

To summarize, we see in this group of cases three different patterns of conflict leading to the emergence of warriors and fractured regimes. In the Baltics this includes titular-national defenders of market liberal reform, titular actors who are disappointed with the economic results despite independence, and Russians (and

TABLE 12.2

Boolean Truth Table for Memory Warrior Emergence

Country Cases	Configurations of Causes										
Estonia, Lithuania	~refsoc	~tranec	~trann	tranrc		ethclev	pcsd	~pcpp	~pcnc	layer	~display
Lithuania, Latvia	~refsoc	~tranec	~trann	tranrc	lrclev	ethclev	pcsd	~pcpp	~pcnc	layer	~display
Romania	~refsoc	~tranec	~trann	tranrc	lrclev	~ethclev	~pcsd	~pcpp	~pcnc	~layer	~display
Slovakia	~refsoc	~tranec	~trann	tranrc	lrclev	~ethclev	pcsd	~pcpp	~pcnc	layer	~display
Ukraine	~refsoc	tranec	~trann	~tranrc	lrclev	ethclev	~pcsd	pcpp	pcnc	layer	~display
Hungary, Poland, Slovenia	refsoc	~tranec	trann	~tranrc	lrclev	~ethclev	pcsd	~pcpp	~pcnc		~display

Note: Each line presents a set of conditions that together (logical AND) produce the outcome.

Abbreviations: ~ = not, refsoc = reformist socialism, tranec = elite controlled transition, trann = negotiated transition, tranrc = transition by regime collapse, lrclev = strong Left-Right cleavage at point of commemoration, ethclev = strong ethnic, religious, or linguistic cleavage at point of commemoration, pcsd = emergence of social-democratic post-communist party soon after transition, pcpp = emergence of party-of-power-type post-communist party soon after transition, pcnc = emergence of neo-communist post-communist party soon after transition, layer = layering of twentieth anniversary commemoration with other important mnemonic events, display = layered mnemonic event displaces anniversary in memory regime.

other minorities) who are disappointed by economic change and uncomfortable with the reassertion of the titular culture. In Slovakia we see a pattern that is close to the post-communist/liberal opposition divide. However, it diverges from the classic version of this divide, because the liberal side of this conflict cut its political teeth resisting the establishment of a dictatorship of the nationalist Mečiar and not the ex-communist Left. Mečiar and his party, the Movement for a Democratic Slovakia (HZDS), as a third force on the political scene, one that valorizes independence over democracy in its approach to commemoration, complicates the picture as well. Romania, with its startling realignments of forces from the old National Salvation Front and its opponents, represents the most idiosyncratic of these actor-issue patterns.

In the cases of Romania and Slovakia, the polarized ideological cleavage seems to have greater independent causal leverage than in the grouping of Poland, Hungary, and Slovenia, where this cleavage is at least partially the product of a negotiated extrication from reform communism. On the other hand, the Baltic States differ from Romania and Slovakia by having a more politically salient ethnic cleavage, whose significance was amplified by aggressive Soviet behavior during the waning years of the empire. Here the Czech case (discussed later in our account of cases where a memory warrior did not emerge) provides a highly useful comparison because it also combines an absence of reform socialism with extrication by regime collapse. It differs from Romania and Slovakia in that strong Left-Right and ethnic cleavages were absent in the run-up to commemoration. The result there was a pillarized regime (see the line for Czech Republic in Table 12.3 for comparison with the five cases that fall into the causal configuration discussed here).[18] This contrast provides evidence that the existence of powerful cleavages (ethnic or religious) is important in the fracturing of the memory regimes around the commemoration of the end of communism.

Analysis of Non-fractured Memory Regimes

There are two types of non-fractured memory regimes (where no memory warrior emerged), unified and pillarized (Table 12.3). The only case of pillarization is the Czech Republic. Here, too, we began with an analysis of necessary conditions. In this case we found none. As with the fractured memory regimes, our truth table reduction yielded both parsimonious and intermediate solutions. And again, we begin by reporting on the parsimonious solution, but find that consideration of the intermediate solution in concert with the knowledge provided by the case analyses allows for a richer, more contextualized comparative discussion of why the commemorations did not produce a fractured memory regime on 1989 twenty years later.

The parsimonious solution yielded, however, several important insights. First, a warrior and thus a fractured memory regime did not emerge if there was a displacing memory layer. This finding helps to specify one of the critical mechanisms for the emergence of a unified memory regime: If other memory regimes in the field are already highly polarizing and politically combustible, and their content is highly salient, there is a strong disincentive for the pursuit of a warrior strategy. It is as if potential warriors were saying: "let's call a truce here." We will develop this argument about the layering of memory regimes and their potential displacing effects in our discussion of the intermediate solution.

Another parsimonious solution is the absence of strong Left-Right and ethnic/religious/linguistic cleavages at the time of the commemoration (~lrclev * ~ethclev). This is strongly congruent with our earlier discussion of their presence as a necessary condition for the emergence of memory warriors. A third parsimonious result is that a warrior does not emerge when a reform socialist tradition is combined with the presence of an ethnic cleavage (refsoc * ethclev). This regularity will be discussed in more detail, as it is central for the understanding of several cases from the former Yugoslavia.

A fourth parsimonious result is the combination of reform socialism and the lack of a negotiated exit from communism (refsoc * ~trann). This is again a strong regularity in all the former Yugoslav cases except Slovenia. The negotiated extrication from communism in Slovenia explains why it is the one former Yugoslav case in which the memory regime that emerged on the twentieth anniversary of the events of 1989 was fractured. The collapse of Yugoslavia in the other five successor states blocked a negotiated exit from communist rule despite the reform socialist tradition. This is because disintegration, ethnic conflict, and looming war neutralized conflicts between the ruling communists and the opposition.

The contrast between the fractured cases of Poland, Hungary, and Slovenia and the unified cases from the former Yugoslavia is highlighted in another parsimonious solution—the combined absence of a social-democratic successor party and a Left-Right cleavage (~pcsd * ~lrclev). The non-emergence of these factors in most post-Yugoslav cases, whose presence was fundamental to the fracturing of the other cases emerging from reform socialism, again demonstrates the powerful effect of the dissolution of Yugoslavia on the memory regime that emerged around 1989 twenty years later.

Another parsimonious solution is that extrication procedures that involve elite continuity are important to the non-emergence of warriors. In no case of elite controlled extrication do we see a fractured memory regime. A slightly more complex solution (tranec * ~pcnc) pinpoints extrication with elite continuity and the lack of a neo-communist successor party.[19] However, we do not find the absence of a neo-communist successor party to be an interesting explanatory factor, because such parties are not particularly consequent actors in almost all of the cases studied in the book (Ukraine being the one exception). This signifies that where a unified ex-communist elite maintains control after transition, a fractured politics of memory is unlikely to emerge. We see this pattern in four cases (Macedonia, Serbia, Montenegro, and Bulgaria), but for different reasons. The three Yugoslav cases show a more general pattern of deliberate abnegation by all memory actors, whereas Bulgaria falls into a pattern of depoliticization. We will further discuss these two general patterns responsible for the emergence of non-fractured memory regime.

The causal impact of all the elements and their configurations are more easily visualized and understood more holistically through a presentation of the intermediate solution. There are two discernible broader configurations leading to the emergence of non-fractured memory regimes. The first is unique to the former Yugoslavia (without Slovenia). It can be characterized as *deliberate abnegation* of the twentieth anniversary celebration. The second pattern can be called *depoliticization*.

In the top section of Table 12.3 we see five countries (Croatia, Bosnia, Serbia, Montenegro, and Macedonia), all of which were parts of Yugoslavia with its specific form of reformed state socialism (refsoc). All of the cases share a history of reformed socialism and a heavily layered memory field with powerful memory regimes built around a series of highly salient ethnic cleavages that displace the commemoration of 1989 (refsoc * ethclev * layer * display). The effects of years of war, genocide, and ethnic strife in the region manifest themselves in persistent, highly polarized ethnic, linguistic, and religious cleavages (ethclev). The strength of these cleavages in 2009 was such that it displaced a serious commemoration or re-examination of the events of 1989 (layer, display). Rather than reconsider the painful and destructive disintegration of Yugoslavia, all political actors of consequence in these five countries were abnegators when it came to the anniversary. The unified memory regime with regard to 1989 in these cases is one of "let's not go there." As a result, the few commemorative events that we saw in these countries were sponsored by outside actors (the EU and German foundations) and were not particularly contentious. They were met, on balance, with apathy, irony, or both, by the elite and the population at large.

In the bottom part of Table 12.3 are three cases in which warriors did not emerge due to the mechanism we call depoliticization. All three had hard-line communist regimes, but most of all, at the time of commemoration all lacked sharply polarizing cleavages founded on either an ideological, ethnic, linguistic, or religious basis (~refsoc * ~lrclev * ~ethclev). Two of them, Bulgaria and Germany, are unified, whereas the Czech Republic is pillarized. None of these cases was reformist in orientation under communism, but that is where any consistent similarity of legacies

TABLE 12.3

Boolean Truth Table for Absence of a Memory Warrior

Country Cases	Configurations of Causes										
Croatia, Bosnia	refsoc	~tranec	~trann	tranrc	ethclev		pcsd	~pcpp	~pcnc	layer	display
Serbia, Montenegro	refsoc	tranec	~trann	~tranrc	ethclev		~pcsd	pcpp	~pcnc	layer	display
Macedonia	refsoc	tranec	~trann	~tranrc	ethclev	lrclev	pcsd	~pcpp	~pcnc	layer	display
Bulgaria	~refsoc	tranec	~trann	~tranrc	~ethclev	~lrclev	~pcsd	pcpp	~pcnc	~layer	~display
Czech Republic, Germany	~refsoc	~tranec	~trann	tranrc	~ethclev	~lrclev	~pcsd	~pcpp	pcnc	layer	~display

Note: Each line presents a set of conditions that together (logical AND) produce the outcome.

Abbreviations: ~ = not, refsoc = reformist socialism, tranec = elite controlled transition, trann = negotiated transition, tranrc = transition by regime collapse, lrclev = strong Left-Right cleavage at point of commemoration, ethclev = strong ethnic, religious, or linguistic cleavage at point of commemoration, pcsd = emergence of social-democratic post-communist party soon after transition, pcpp = emergence of party-of-power-type post-communist party soon after transition, pcnc = emergence of neo-communist post-communist party soon after transition, layer = layering of twentieth anniversary commemoration with other important mnemonic events, display = layered mnemonic event displaces anniversary in memory regime.

from extrication ends. What they all share is a depoliticized field of memory politics at the time of the commemoration. In none of them did we detect strongly polarizing salient cleavages at that time, and in all three this absence promoted a consensus about 1989.[20] This clearly played a role in providing a strong disincentive to political actors to take a warrior stance.

In Bulgaria there was general disappointment with its unfulfilled promise, which Ganev describes (in Chapter 10) as leading to a powerful (and sometimes imaginative) nostalgia about the past. Actors who dissented from this interpretation of the past found no political gain to be had in challenging this status quo. In the Czech Republic, the majority of the population remembered the 1989 "Velvet Revolution" fondly and its effects were positively evaluated. The student organizations that were most visible in organizing innovative protest events around the commemorations shared a positive view of 1989, but used the public gatherings as a means to talk about the shortcomings of the political class in living up to the ideals of the Velvet Revolution. A disconnect between political society and civil society emerged, which the former chose not to address. This uncoupling of the two spheres (political and civil) and the toleration of three differing discourses lead to the characterization of the Czech Republic as pillarized rather than fractured.

Finally, Germany, as Art points out (in Chapter 9), is locked into a culture of contrition that has allowed it both to come to terms with its difficult past and to find its place in a unified Europe. This strong equilibrium, while not fully displacing a celebration of November 1989, meant that its potential for being hijacked by ambitious mnemonic warriors was very small. The politicization of 1989 would have represented a challenge to the culture of contrition, entrenched in the whole memory field, and this would be potentially dangerous for any political actor in Germany. Art does point out how the reconsideration of the GDR's past could re-emerge as an important issue, but shows that in 2009 the culture of contrition remained dominant and that all actors took a stance of abnegation, not challenging that consensus. The existence of memory layering did not result in displacing the commemoration of the events of 1989, but channeled them in a particular manner that contributed to the emergence of a unified memory regime.

The absence of warriors in the memory regimes in the Czech Republic, Bulgaria, and Germany seems contingent on the continued depoliticization. Were it not for the lack of salient cleavages, the configuration in the Czech Republic would resemble the pattern we found in Slovakia, Romania, and the Baltics. Bulgaria would more closely follow the pattern found in Ukraine. Thus the way in which existing cleavage structures interact with other key features of the memory regimes seems an important factor in determining whether those regimes fractured in countries without a reform socialist past.

Mnemonic Regimes and Dominant Cultural Cleavages

From its inception, this project intended to break new conceptual ground and generate systematic, comparative evidence of the kind needed to develop new theoretical insights concerning the politics of memory. The richness and comparability of the empirical evidence that our team collected allowed us both to corroborate some existing generalizations as well as develop several new, more precise formulations. We confirmed, for example, that the polities that emerged from state socialism, when studied up close, look remarkably different from each other. Yet, among the political-institutional factors/conditions hypothesized to be consequential in shaping memory politics, we detected distinct sets of configurations that led to the emergence of meaningful types of political forms of memory regimes.

While we discovered common patterns in our analysis of the *political form* of mnemonic regimes, we did not discern any clear patterns in the formation of *cultural content* of the twentieth anniversary commemorations; in fact, each country celebrated in its own manner, organized around a set of mnemonic markers associated with selected major events in its history. Despite this lack of cross-case commonalities with regard to the cultural content, there is an apparent and unmistakable generalization to be made: The cultural tenor of commemorations was often embedded in the structure of a major cleavage in the country's "national culture." For example, the young Czechs were irreverent against the "serious" establishment, the Poles solemnly heroic in a reenactment of a basic cleavage of their culture, and the Germans solidly organized around the still dominant culture of contrition.

This congruence between the tone of the twentieth anniversary commemorations, taken to be representative of the "1989/1991" memory regime, and the more general tenor of "national culture" is striking. It is notoriously difficult, however, to write about it, as the entities called "national cultures" are almost impossible to characterize without invoking worn-out clichés or misguided stereotypes. Each country's culture can be and is characterized in many different ways and upon closer inspection proves to be composed of many subcultures. And yet many influential authors see patterns in their data that are conspicuous enough to try to formulate some generalizations, despite obvious conceptual dangers.[21]

Being aware of these dangers, we decided nonetheless to propose some conclusions on the link between the commemorations and some prominent features of national cultures, particularly the dominant cleavages that structure them. Importantly, we do not treat national culture as a more or less immutable pattern detected in the attitudes of people from a given country, but as a large field of discourses, "where different views of the nation compete and negotiate with each other. The ultimate outcome of these discursive struggles—which are embedded in social and political structures and backed by institutional power—is the creation of the nation as a compelling symbolic configuration" (Zubrzycki 2009, 519). Competing "national" discourses generated by cultural entrepreneurs—including mnemonic actors—constitute *cultural contexts of action* both for them and other political actors,[22] and are powerful weapons in shaping attitudes of various publics. Our formulation is built around an insight succinctly expressed by Laitin: "Culture instills not values to be upheld but rather points of concern to be debated" (1988, 589). While some, perhaps most, cultural-political entrepreneurs are busy reproducing the existing discourses to reinforce their positions in the debates on "points of concern" and thus achieve hegemony, others try to challenge the existing hegemonies and convince people to accept counter-hegemonic themes and scripts.[23]

Governments, political parties, churches, schools, families, museums, and so on, work hard to reproduce both the *themes* (cultural heroes, myths of origin, narratives of greatness, etc.), that are defined as constitutive units of one or more specific versions of "national heritage," and *scripts* or *scenarios of action* that together amount to what is often defined as (a version of) the "national character." While such themes and scripts (for example, "heroism" in Poland) evolve as they are reproduced, their reproduction tends to be dominated by repetition rather than innovation. That is the source of the path-dependent character of cultural reproduction and the strong impression of immutability and persistence of "national cultures," including the main cleavages detectable in them.

Given all these reservations, we want to offer a few cautious generalizations about the relationship between the cultural tenor of the twentieth anniversary commemorations and the dominant cleavages of national cultures that are strongly suggested by the studies collected in this volume. These statements are best taken as preliminary hypotheses derived from an unsystematic examination of some discourses circulating in the countries and among their observers, both internal and external.

We first began thinking about historically established cultural cleavages and their reflection in the twentieth anniversary commemorations, while comparing the Czech and Polish events. The Czech commemorations, organized by two student groups, were full of irreverent humor, critical and mocking distance to the authorities, and even a carnivalesque status reversal. It is hard not to think about an important strand of the Czech culture, expressed in the self-ironic tenor of Hrabal's novels, early Forman films, or—most important—that quintessential Czech character, Hašek's good soldier Švejk.[24] The main message of this version of Czechness is that mockery, satire, and auto-irony are handy political weapons. It is employed by actors who are comfortable invoking the irreverent pole of the Czech national culture, one of several potentially usable reservoirs of enactable scripts of action (or specific points of concern). In this "Švejkian" vision of national identity "the strength of the nation is not in its moral victories…, but in its ability to survive three hundred years of Habsburg oppression, six years of German occupation, and forty-three years of communism through pretended loyalty and tacit or explicit collaboration" (Holy 1996, 130). In 2009, the students commemorating the twentieth anniversary of the fall of communism did not invoke the "heroic" version of Czech history (see Holy 1996), but its Švejkian rendition, albeit combined with a public stance inspired by the Havelian spirit of "anti-politics."[25]

By contrast, a solemn battle of competing commemorations that we observed in Poland constituted—inadvertently perhaps—yet another round in the contentious process of self-examination of the essence of Polishness that has been going on at least since the early nineteenth century. The tension generated by one of the central cleavages of Polish culture and identity, which can be conceptualized as the grand split between Romanticism and Positivism, flared up again, as Kaczyński and PiS struck the tone of romantic rebellion (suffused with the elements of nationalistically interpreted Catholicism and messianism),[26] while Tusk and PO performed the role of sober, pragmatic positivists cum liberals.[27] Moreover, while both parties hail their roots in Solidarity, Kaczyński and his party often portray their more liberal opponents with Solidarity pedigrees as the "impure" associates of ex-communists. The commemoration of 2009 provided one of the principal stages where this symbolic drama, built around competing version of Polishness, was performed for the broader public.

In Hungary, the commemorations were to a large degree a ritual of re-enactment and reinforcement of the cleavage observed in many other areas of public and political life (Csepeli and Murányi 2013; Palonen 2009). As in other countries, this cleavage can be described in several ways, but it is often presented as a split between populism-nationalism and urbanism-cosmopolitanism. Palonen, for example, writes:

> Often the two sides in Hungary are signified as the urbanist and the national-populist sides (urbánusok and népiek), following a distinction made within the dissident groups in the 1980s, but with roots in the interwar period, particularly Hungarian literary tradition and canons, and even in the Hungarian peasant revolts of the sixteenth century and anti-Habsburg riots of the seventeenth century. (2009, 322)[28]

Csepeli sees an affinity between populism, the "Trianon narrative," and a high level of support for more extreme forms of nationalism, combined with tolerance for authoritarianism. By contrast, the urbanism tends to be combined with the "Holocaust narrative," and the more cosmopolitan, inclusive forms of patriotism.[29]

As Seleny shows (in Chapter 2), the 2009 commemorations of the fall of communism organized by the rising Fidesz and its leader, Victor Orbán, quite clearly championed the first syndrome.

In post-1989 Romania, most if not all discursive positions detectable in political debates and battles evolved toward the decisive rejection of communism (even by ex-communists). And in many instances this rejection was associated with adopting some version of nationalistically defined Romanianness. The idiom of nationalism, Pop-Eleches notes (in Chapter 4), has been used in Romanian political life long before the demise of state socialism, producing "Ceauşescu's national communism." For example, many intellectuals, as Verdery observed in her work on Romanian political discourses in the 1980s, tended to draw "upon personal concerns and traditions of inquiry that made the Nation a continuing and urgent reality for them despite its official interdiction. They were also engaged in conflicts among themselves for which, as before, the Nation provided the basic idiom" (1991, 122). It is thus not surprising that for many mnemonic actors who were framing the symbolic struggles around the twentieth anniversary of the fall of communism, nationalist narratives (in one of its version) provided "points of concern to be debated."[30]

In Bulgaria, in a sharp contrast to its Romanian neighbor and many other countries studied in this volume, nationalism was not a major reference idiom for political debates. It is the only country in which we detected considerable and multilayered nostalgia for state socialism, with powerful consequences for the way the anniversary of the fall of state socialism was celebrated. As Ganev argues (in Chapter 10), it was not only expressed, in various forms, in the discourses spawned by quite a few public officials; it was also shared by a large segment of the Bulgarian population. For example, over 24 percent of the respondents—a plurality—surveyed in 2010 regarded September 9, 1944—the day when the communist party staged a successful coup and won power—as the most important event in modern Bulgarian history. This figure illustrates well the strength of the "socialist nostalgia" in Bulgaria, a sentiment hard to find in any other post-communist country in our sample. Consider, for example, that in a 2008 survey, the plurality of Poles (24 percent) regarded "the abolition of communism, the fall of Polish People's Republic" as the "most important event" in the last 100 years of Polish history.[31] The existence of this nostalgia in Bulgaria helps to explain the rather lethargic tone of the commemoration of the fall of communism and the dominant role of mnemonic abnegators in the "1989" memory politics.

While we discovered rather clear patterns in the *political form* of mnemonic regimes, the *cultural content* of these regimes (reconstructed mostly on the basis of our analyses of the twentieth anniversary commemorations) proved to be highly idiosyncratic. Yet the tensions or outright symbolic conflicts detected in the commemorations were clearly reflective of and contributing to at least one major cleavage identifiable in "national culture," understood as a field of competing discourses about national identity. As we argue in the next section, such debates and symbolic contests are highly relevant for the consolidation and quality of democracy (Tismaneanu 1998).

Are Fractured Memory Regimes a Threat to Democracy?

At the end of our theoretical chapter, we discussed the implications of fractured memory regimes for the quality and prospects for democracy. We argued that fractured memory regimes could have important impacts on both the national discursive field and even on institutional frameworks, especially the party system. And indeed, there was ample evidence of this in the chapters.

When actors choose a warrior strategy, it has a powerful effect on the cleavage structure in a country. The structural basis of underlying social cleavages may not be changed, but their cultural and political articulations are affected. This means that elite choices concerning the manner of engagement in mnemonic politics have an important framing effect on the stakes in the broader political game. Warriors are polarizing political actors, and polarization has been shown to be one of the great destabilizers of democracy (Sartori 1976; Linz 1978). Bermeo (2003), in her account of the collapse of democracy in interwar Europe and Latin America in the 1960s and 1970s, argues that conflicts in democracies under stress do not automatically lead to the defection of the masses from support for democracy. Instead, she recasts crises of polarization as the choices of elites who substitute more extreme views on the nature of conflict within democratic systems for those of the electorates. In doing so, they increase the stakes of such conflicts, and this can have strongly negative effects on democratic performance and stability.

Warriors change the discursive field and thus influence how the electorate judges democracy. It is important to remember that democracy is, first and foremost, a set of procedures and institutions that are designed to guarantee free and fair competition between political rivals for control of government. If it brings substantive benefits to the people it is because its built-in mechanisms provide a degree of responsiveness between voters and their rulers. It is a self-adjusting system in which the failure of elites to provide desirable substantive outcomes subjects them to recall through periodic elections. Memory warriors demonize their political competitors whose substantive failures are framed as consequences of their (specifically interpreted) political genealogies, rather than errors of policy design or implementation. Demonizing discourses are focused on delegitimizing opponents as "unfit" to hold and exercise power. From there it is a short step to prioritizing substantive outcomes to the detriment of the procedural norms of democracy.

Democracy, at minimum, requires opponents to accept and respect the outcomes of elections. Attempts to change those outcomes ex post facto or to bias them ex ante undermine democracy (Przeworski 1991). This does not mean that the political opposition under democracy should not use their positions in the system to block or change policies with which they disagree. Nor does it mean that they should abstain from extra-institutional forms of resistance (e.g., protests, demonstrations, strikes, boycotts, expression of dissenting opinion, and other forms of individual or collective action) available under the rule of law. The danger appears when, by using various cultural (symbolic, discursive) strategies, one actor delegitimizes opponents as somehow "essentially" unfit for being players in the game of democracy. Since mnemonic warriors routinely employ such strategies, memory politics should be included in the study of democratic consolidation and the quality of democracy.

The party system is the first place where mnemonic delegitimation strategies may have a powerful impact. Party systems are intrinsic to the smooth functioning of democracy. They are the central mediating institution for the provision of both responsiveness and accountability, as well as essential to stable governance (Mainwaring and Scully 1995; Sartori 1976; Cox 1997). Post-communist Europe is considered to have weaker, less institutionalized party systems than other regions, even those that have also recently adopted democracy. The party systems of the region are marked by a high rate of volatility (vote switching from one party to another), frequent extermination of parties, and the lowest rate of government incumbency in the world (Bernhard and Karakoc 2011).

Successful democratization entails the institutionalization of a well-functioning party system, and fractured memory regimes complicate the realization of this task. Memory warriors consistently question the legitimacy of their competition. This raises the stakes of electoral competition through rhetoric that often calls on voters literally to drive opponents out of the polity (Wasilewski 2010). It is essential for the institutionalization of a democratic party system that all actors accept not only the outcomes of elections but also the actors against whom they compete as legitimate (Mainwaring and Scully 1995). Elections cannot be seen as a legitimate means to attain and transfer power if the parties do not see their opponents as worthy of holding power if they win the election. The ramifications of a lack of trust between competing parties are apparent in the accounts of fractured memory regimes in this volume. For at least some of the countries discussed here, these problems have been exacerbated in the period since the twenty-year anniversaries.

As this book shows, fractured memory regimes—including those constructed around a single event or process, such as the fall of the old regime—may threaten or even undermine democracy. Hungary, as the sharpest case of a fractured memory regime, provides strong evidence of this. As Seleny documents (in Chapter 2), the flagrantly mendacious behavior of Prime Minister Ferenc Gyurcsány in the electoral campaign of 2006 exposed and intensified a major divide in Hungary between the ruling MSZP and the political right, both Fidesz and the newer, extremist Jobbik. For the right, MSZP represented continuity with the failure of the revolution of 1956 and the entrenchment of those forces associated with the normalization of Communist rule. The removal of Gyurcsány by his own party in a constructive vote of no-confidence and his replacement by a more technocratic MSZP-led cabinet under Gordon Bajnai did little to alleviate this tension. This was made manifest in the separate and highly contentious commemorations of that year, in which the Right presented the events of 1989–1990 as a preservation of the ancient regime rather than its replacement.

The elections of 2010 put a mnemonic warrior in firm control of the government. Fidesz not only formed the next government (in conjunction with its Christian-democratic allies) but also won a landslide victory that gave it a two-thirds supermajority in Parliament and the power to rewrite the constitution. This is precisely what the government of Viktor Orban, Hungary's leading memory warrior, did. The measures it has adopted are designed to deny its competitors the ability to regain power and, in the case that they do, the ability to change the policies that Fidesz has put in place. Orban's government has changed appointment procedures to state institutions so as to embed its supporters in key positions in the state bureaucracy and consequently make power less subject to the electoral results. It has also changed the electoral law to its advantage and has worked to undermine the autonomy of the judiciary, by subjecting it to a considerable level of control by the executive branch. If successful, this would represent a change of political system—from liberal democracy to majoritarian democracy and perhaps even competitive authoritarianism—under the cover of legality (Rupnik 2012; Bánkuti, Halmai and Scheppele 2012; Balogh 2013).

And Hungary is not an isolated case. In Romania, the government of Victor Ponta has also attempted to undermine democracy in yet another case that experienced highly fractured "1989" memory regime in 2009. Pop-Eleches' account of the commemorations of 2009 (in Chapter 4) showed it to be highly politicized due to the upcoming elections that pitted an unlikely alliance of the Social-Democrats (PSD) and the National Liberals (PNL) against the Democratic Party (PD). Both sides challenged the legitimacy of the other to speak in the name of the Revolution of 1989. The struggle was resolved to the advantage of the PSD-PNL when the election of 2012 led to the formation of a government under PSD leader Victor Ponta, which was able to increase its parliamentary advantage by subsequently triggering a round of defections from other parties. The Romanian system is semi-presidential, and

Ponta has chafed at sharing power with the sitting president, Trajan Băsescu of the PD. The political struggle between the two sets of memory warriors has remained quite contentious, and Ponta has pursued several measures to undermine the division of powers within the Romanian system.

As in Hungary, we see a change in the balance of power between the actors who are also committed memory warriors in a highly contentious and polarized polity. They try to pre-ordain political outcomes by legislation that undermines fair competition. The new cabinet put other branches on notice that it was in charge, replacing the speakers of both houses of the bicameral parliament, as well as the government ombudsman, an autonomous office that investigates citizen complaints of government misconduct. They also passed a law barring the high court from considering whether legislation is constitutional and threatened its justices with impeachment. The parliament then passed a law making it easier to remove the president from office, and used it to impeach Băsescu. Though he lost the plebiscite vote on his retention, the president retained his office because turnout did not reach the 50 percent threshold mandated by the constitution. The parliament has also changed the electoral law to enhance the chances of the government for re-election (Scheppele 2012a; Tismaneanu 2013). These moves represent an attempt to entrench the current government in power ex ante, prior to the next election, and to enhance its autonomy from the other powers in the system ex post facto.

Does the fracturing of memory regimes by warriors necessarily lead to problems with effective and stable democratic governance? Just as Capoccia (2007) has shown for the interwar period in Europe, polarized polities, even those under extreme economic stress, can overcome challenges to democratic stability. It is important that elites take effective steps to minimize the destabilizing effects of memory wars. Perhaps the best example of such action is found in Poland. Here the government of Donald Tusk effectively blunted the attempts of the Kaczyński brothers to use the anniversaries of 1989 to recapture power after the PiS-led government fell in 2007. By staying out of the dispute on the Roundtable Agreement but engaging vigorously on the anniversary of the June 1989 elections, Prime Minister Tusk effectively neutralized the attempts of the Kaczyńskis to use a radical reinterpretation of democratization in Poland to delegitimize their competitors. This effective strategy boomeranged on PiS when Bronisław Komorowski was able to defeat Jarosław Kaczyński in the presidential elections of 2010 and when, later that year, PO won its second consecutive election and Tusk became the first incumbent prime minister in post-1989 Poland to be re-elected. And it is important to note that in this period the Polish party system has been remarkably stable, something that had eluded Polish democracy until the last several years. Time will tell if this will remain a stable outcome or if the PiS will be able to capitalize on the slowdown in the Polish economy that came in 2013.

Clearly, fractured memory regimes do not inevitably pose a threat to democracy. However, by exacerbating the polarization of existing political and/or cultural cleavages, they have the potential to do so. As in all cases of polarization, the response of elites to such situations, as is made clear by the recent work of scholars such as Bermeo and Capoccia, is instrumental. Politicians who choose to cast political competition as a zero-sum game and treat the loss of power as a problem that requires ex ante institutional fixes that improve their chances of staying in power are highly likely to be mnemonic warriors as well. That is why the study of memory politics—particularly the conditions under which mnemonic wars are waged and won—is an important component of any study of democratization.

NOTES

1. Due to the constraints of our sample (only one pillarized case), in the Boolean analysis presented later in the chapter we reduce these three categories to two and focus our analysis on the emergence of memory warriors (or not) and the comparison of two causal paths, leading to fractured or non-fractured mnemonic regimes.

2. A configuration is "a combination of conditions relevant for a given outcome." Conditions "are explanatory variables that may affect the outcome" (Rihoux and Ragin 2009, 182). If a configuration occurs in more than one case, we call it a pattern.

3. Some interpretations of the aftermath of the Orange revolution would see the period directly after as a break from this pattern. Others see control by the alliance of Yushchenko and Tymoshenko as a continuation.

4. This was confirmed by a necessary condition analysis using the fs/QCA software package that included warrior as a condition for an independently coded characterization of the regime as the outcome of interest. Similarly, we found the absence of a warrior to be a necessary condition for a unified or a not-fractionalized (unified and pillarized combined) memory regime.

5. This intensity is defined as high and coded as "1" when memory of another event or process "displaces" the commemoration of the twentieth anniversary and the memory regime around the latter event is not formed.

6. Our coding of the data for crisp analysis is reproduced in Appendix A.

7. We also ran multivalue QCA and attempted a fuzzy analysis. We used two different programs—fsQCA for the crisp and fuzzy and Tosmana for both crisp and multivalue. We had initially hoped to run both crisp and fuzzy versions with fsQCA, but were unable to run fuzzy-set QCA because of an absence of a sufficient number of patterns that met standard consistency cut-offs (see Ragin 2008; Rihoux and Ragin 2009). Tosmana also allows one to run multivalue QCA, which uses scaled variables and fuzzy logic algorithms (see Cronqvist 2007).

8. We also performed a separate analysis for the non-emergence of warriors for unified regimes. The inclusion of the Czech Republic in this analysis (e.g., for non-fractured rather than unified regimes) did not yield any substantive changes of note.

9. The absence of a displacing memory (~display) emerged as a necessary condition. We discuss why this is a trivial finding later in the text when we discuss the parsimonious solution to the truth table. The results of the necessary condition analyses are presented in Appendix B.

10. The full power of QCA is demonstrated in the analysis of sufficient conditions, as it allows the researcher to identify multiple causal paths leading to the same outcome (equifinality).

11. The parsimonious solutions are presented in Appendix C, and we use the intermediate solution in tabular form to present our findings in this and the next section.

12. These pairings included the absence of a displacing memory layer with Left-Right cleavage, ethnic cleavage, a social democratic successor party, and the absence of both an elite-controlled transition and a neo-communist successor party.

13. See Ragin (1987, 98 and 112–113); and Rihoux and De Meur (2009, 65–66). We focus our analysis on conjunctions of causes that are relatively complex; we avoid maximal parsimony. Moreover, we do not seek maximal parsimony through the analysis of logical remainders (on this topic see Ragin 1987, 104–123, and Schneider and Wagemann 2012, 151–177). We analyze only "conservative solution terms," in Schneider and Wagemann's sense, as in our analysis we refrain "from making assumptions about any logical remainder" and are "exclusively guided by the empirical information at hand" (2012, 162). The reason for this is that we are not interested in proposing a parsimonious theory of mnemonic politics, but rather in identifying causal patterns in the material derived from our rigorously compared seventeen cases. We also want to avoid excessive simplification of the case material.

14. Wagemann and Schneider elaborate this characterization of the method: *"QCA as a research approach* refers to the iterative process of data collection, model specification, case selection and re-conceptualization of the conditions and the outcome which are of central importance for any QCA-based research design. This aspect of QCA stems from its 'qualitative roots,' since it is a common strategy in traditional qualitative comparative research to exclude and/or add cases from the analysis during an ongoing research process; to re-code values for certain cases; or to re-conceptualize entire variables. In contrast, most of these operations are usually strictly forbidden in quantitative, statistically oriented research" (n.d., 2–3).

15. The country had no reformist socialism before 1991 (~refsoc); its transition was elite controlled (tranec); at the point of commemoration it had two strong cleavages: Left-Right (lrclev) and ethnic (ethclev); a strong social-democratic post-communist party did not emerge after transition (~pcsd); a party power did emerge (pcpp); a neo-communist party also played an important role in politics (pcnc); and the memory of the fall of communism was layered with memories of other important mnemonic events (layer).

16. The absence of the other factors is not germane to the analysis we present. The three extrication variables are mutually exclusive, so we would expect the presence of one with the absence of the other two.

17. We are aware of many criticisms waged against describing this cleavage as Left-Right. However, we believe that this language approximates the reality better than competing methods of labeling.

18. The German case also shares this structure (no reform socialism, extrication by regime collapse, and no powerful cleavages). The isomorphism is hard to sustain because of the presence of a displacing set of layered memory events in Germany, as noted by David Art in Chapter 9 in this volume.

19. The parsimonious solution also returned the term "~trann * ~tranrc * ~pcnc." This expression is identical to "tranec * ~pcnc" because of the mutually exclusive nature of the three extrication patterns.

20. Of course in Bulgaria this depoliticization broke down in a big way during the huge demonstrations in the summer of 2013. Ganev's nostalgic consensus gave way to a highly innovative contentious politics.

21. Inglehart and other authors working within the socio-psychological approach to political culture conceptualize "national cultures" as somewhat coherent syndromes discovered via surveys of attitudes. We do not work with this conceptualization here, though we find some of Inglehart's observations helpful: "I suggest that that cultural component of these cross-national differences reflects the distinctive historical experiences of the respective nationalities. Long periods of disappointed expectations give rise to dissatisfied attitudes. These orientations may be transmitted from generation to generation through preadult socialization. In so far as early learning is relatively persistent, this contributes to the stability of distinctive cultural patterns. [...] They remain distinctive cultural characteristics with important behavioral consequences" (1988, 1207).

22."What we term the cultural context of action, to begin with, encompasses those symbolic configurations or formations that constrain and enable action by structuring actors' normative commitments and their understandings of the world and of their own possibilities within it" (Emirbayer and Goodwin 1996, 365).

23. Laitin defines hegemony as "the political forging—whether through coercion or elite bargaining—and institutionalization of a pattern of group activity in a state and the concurrent idealization of that schema into a dominant symbolic framework that reigns as common sense" (1986, 183).

24. Jedlička, a Czech scholar and essayist, outlines the two options available to Czechs: "It's not our fault if we are really to some extent the nation of Svejks. Moreover, 'Švejkování' (Švejk-like behavior) is not in itself a way of resistance that deserves substantial rejection. But it would be our fault, if we wanted to stay the nation of Svejks. It is after all better to create your own history than to be Svejks in the context of other nations' histories" ("Ono je přece jenom asi lepší vytvářet vlastní dějiny, než se cizími dějinami prošvejkovat") (Jedlička 2009, 53).

25. Without this public protest dimension, "Švejkism" can be seen as a strategy of con artists who think only about their individual survival (Klicperova-Baker 1999, 13).

26. As Zubrzycki observes in her work on Poland: "Although the Church had neither created nor openly endorsed this fusion of Catholic symbols and practices with Romantic messianism, Catholicism became the 'carrier' of what Ewa Morawska (1984) named 'romantic civil religion'" (2011, 28).

27. The origins and content of this particular duality are examined in Porter (2000). In her study of elite political discourses, Kurczewska (2002, 132) traces the echoes of a related debate, initiated by Jerzy Gedroyć, about the most important coffins in Polish history: Dmowski's and Piłsudski's. The former represents the more exclusive, nationalistic (and often xenophobic) trend in Polish self-identification, while the latter stands for a more cosmopolitan, inclusive version of Polishness. There exist other conceptualizations of the basic cleavage in Polish culture. Król, for example, argues that the romantic spirit permeates all aspects of this culture, but it can be "used" in two different ways: either as a tool for providing spiritual foundation for liberal-democratic politics or as a weapon in the politics of division (1998, 175).

28. Palonen rightly warns that this distinction should not be treated as an "essential" feature of the Hungarian culture. Like her, we only observe that some version of this cleavage is repeatedly invoked by various cultural-political entrepreneurs and therefore constitutes a recurring theme in the Hungarian political discourse. In her book on Eastern European dissidents, Falk writes: "The populists saw themselves as the representatives of *volkisch* Hungarian traditions, epitomized by their valorization of rural and village life. The urbanists, on the other hand, positioned their axis

on life in Budapest, were disproportionately Jewish and politically more leftist than nationalist" (2009, 125).

29. Personal communication. Csepeli and Murányi explain: "The 'Trianon narrative' and the 'Holocaust narrative' consequently clashed. The 'Trianon narrative' ignores the responsibility of the Hungarian society for the Holocaust, and cheers the revision of the Trianon treaty while the 'Holocaust narrative' ignores the revisionist claims and blames the Hungarian state and society for sending almost half a million Jews into death camps (2013, 23).

30. Nationalism permeated also the celebrations organized in the Baltic states of Lithuania, Latvia, and Estonia. The celebrations of 1991 were powerfully layered: national independence, Soviet (Russian) occupation vs. liberation.

31. "Spojrzenie na Miniony Wiek w Historii Polski," Komunikat z Badań, CBOS BS/166/2008, 4. In the same survey, 45 percent of the respondents chose the "dependence on the Soviet Union" as the main weakness of Poland in the last 100 years (8).

Appendices

Appendix A

Data

TABLE A.I

Data Matrix for Boolean Analysis

Country	refsoc	tranec	trann	tranrc	lrclev	ethclev	pcsd	pcpp	pcnc	layer	display	warrior	abnegator	pluralist	fractured	unified	pillarized
Estonia	0	0	0	1	0	1	1	0	0	1	0	1	0	0	1	0	0
Hungary	1	0	1	0	1	0	1	0	0	1	0	1	0	1	1	0	0
Latvia	0	0	0	1	1	1	1	0	0	1	0	1	0	0	1	0	0
Lithuania	0	0	0	1	1	1	1	0	0	1	0	1	0	0	1	0	0
Poland	1	0	1	0	1	0	1	0	0	0	0	1	1	1	1	0	0
Romania	0	0	0	1	1	0	0	0	0	0	0	1	0	1	1	0	0
Slovakia	0	0	0	1	1	0	1	0	0	1	0	1	1	1	1	0	0
Slovenia	1	0	1	0	1	0	1	0	0	1	0	1	1	0	1	0	0
Ukraine	0	1	0	0	1	1	0	1	1	1	0	1	1	0	1	0	0
Bosnia	1	0	0	1	0	1	1	0	0	1	1	0	1	0	0	1	0
Bulgaria	0	1	0	0	0	0	0	1	0	0	0	0	1	1	0	1	0
Croatia	1	0	1	1	1	1	1	0	0	1	1	0	0	0	0	1	0
Germany	0	0	0	1	0	0	0	0	1	1	0	0	1	0	0	1	0

(Continued)

Country	refsoc	tranec	trann	tranrc	lrclev	ethclev	pcsd	pcpp	pcnc	layer	display	warrior	abnegator	pluralist	fractured	unified	pillarized
Macedonia	1	1	0	0	1	1	1	1	0	1	1	0	1	1	0	1	0
Montenegro	1	1	0	0	0	1	0	1	1	1	1	0	1	1	0	1	0
Serbia	1	1	0	0	1	1	0	1	0	1	1	0	1	1	0	1	0
Czech	0	0	0	1	0	0	0	0	1	0	0	0	1	1	0	0	1

Abbreviations: refsoc = reformist socialism, tranec = elite controlled transition, trann = negotiated transition, tranrc = transition by regime collapse, lrclev = strong Left-Right cleavage at point of commemoration, ethclev = strong ethnic, religious, or linguistic cleavage at point of commemoration, pcsd = emergence of social-democratic post-communist party soon after transition, pcpp = emergence of party-of-power-type post-communist party soon after transition, pcnc = emergence of neo-communist post-communist party soon after transition, layer = layering of twentieth anniversary commemoration with other important mnemonic events, display = layered mnemonic event displaces anniversary in memory regime, warrior = presence of mnemonic warrior, abnegator = presence of mnemonic abnegator, pluralist = presence of mnemonic pluralist, fractured = fractured memory regime outcome, unified = unified memory regime outcome, pillarized = pillarized memory regime outcome.

Appendix B

Necessary Condition Analyses

TABLE B.1

Outcome Variable: Warrior

Conditions Tested	Consistency	Coverage
refsoc	0.333333	0.375000
~refsoc	0.666667	0.666667
tranec	0.111111	0.200000
~tranec	0.888889	0.666667
trann	0.333333	1.000000
~trann	0.666667	0.428571
tranrc	0.555556	0.555556
~tranrc	0.444444	0.500000
lrclev	0.888889	0.727273
~lrclev	0.111111	0.166667
ethclev	0.444444	0.444444
~ethclev	0.555556	0.625000
pcsd	0.777778	0.700000
~pcsd	0.222222	0.285714
pcpp	0.222222	0.400000

(*Continued*)

Conditions Tested	Consistency	Coverage
~pcpp	0.777778	0.583333
pcnc	0.222222	0.500000
~pcnc	0.777778	0.538462
layer	0.777778	0.538462
~layer	0.222222	0.500000
display	0.000000	0.000000
~display	1.000000	0.750000
ethclev+lrclev	1.000000	0.642857

TABLE B.2

Outcome Variable: ~Warrior

Conditions Tested	Consistency	Coverage
refsoc	0.625000	0.625000
~refsoc	0.375000	0.333333
tranec	0.500000	0.800000
~tranec	0.500000	0.333333
trann	0.000000	0.000000
~trann	1.000000	0.571429
tranrc	0.500000	0.444444
~tranrc	0.500000	0.500000
lrclev	0.375000	0.272727
~lrclev	0.625000	0.833333
ethclev	0.625000	0.555556
~ethclev	0.375000	0.375000
pcsd	0.375000	0.300000
~pcsd	0.625000	0.714286
pcpp	0.375000	0.600000
~pcpp	0.625000	0.416667
pcnc	0.250000	0.500000
~pcnc	0.750000	0.461538
layer	0.750000	0.461538
~layer	0.250000	0.500000
display	0.625000	1.000000
~display	0.375000	0.250000

Appendix C

Parsimonious Solutions (fs/QCA)

TABLE C.I

Parsimonious Solution to the Truth Table for Warrior Emergence

Frequency cutoff: 1.000000

Consistency cutoff: 1.000000

	Raw Coverage	Unique	
		Coverage	Consistency
lrclev *~display	0.888889	0.000000	1.000000
ethclev *~display	0.444444	0.000000	1.000000
~refsoc *ethclev	0.444444	0.000000	1.000000
pcsd *~display	0.777778	0.000000	1.000000
~tranec *~pcnc *~display	0.777778	0.000000	1.000000

Solution coverage: 1.000000

Solution consistency: 1.000000

TABLE C.2

Parsimonious Solution to the Truth Table for Non-Warrior

Frequency cutoff: 1.000000

Consistency cutoff: 1.000000

	Raw Coverage	Unique Coverage	Consistency
display	0.625000	0.000000	1.000000
~lrclev*~pcsd	0.500000	0.000000	1.000000
~lrclev*~ethclev	0.375000	0.000000	1.000000
refsoc*~trann	0.625000	0.000000	1.000000
tranec*~pcnc	0.500000	0.000000	1.000000
refsoc*ethclev	0.625000	0.000000	1.000000
~trann*~tranrc*~pcnc	0.500000	0.000000	1.000000

Solution coverage: 1.000000

Solution consistency: 1.000000

Abbreviations: * = Boolean multiplication (the logical "and"), ~= not, refsoc = reformist socialism, tranec = elite controlled transition, trann = negotiated transition, tranrc = transition by regime collapse, lrclev = strong Left-Right cleavage at point of commemoration, ethclev = strong ethnic, religious, or linguistic cleavage at point of commemoration, pcsd = emergence of social-democratic post-communist party soon after transition, pcnc = emergence of neo-communist post-communist party soon after transition, display = layered mnemonic event displaces anniversary in memory regime.

Bibliography

20. výročie novembra 89 (Košice)—Zostrih, 2009. December 1. Accessed February 19, 2011. http://il.youtube.com/watch?v=oTToLXYNhDY&feature=related.

"21. augustā svinēs Latvijas neatkarības de facto atjaunošanas 20. gadadienu." 2011. *nra.lv*, August 19, 2011. Accessed February 2012. http://zinas.nra.lv/latvija/54013-21-augusta-sv ines-latvijas-neatkaribas-de-facto-atjaunosanas-20-gadadienu.htm.

24 Chasa. 2009. "Litzata na prehoda se razpoznaha v snimki," October 27, 1.

88Studio Radio. 2012. "Berlinski zid i Stari most: Šta se izgradilo a šta srušilo u mom životu?" Accessed March 27. http://www.studio88.ba/bh/50/llfstyl/15800/.

Adamson, Kevin, and Dejan Jovic. 2004. "The Macedonian-Albanian Political Frontier: The Re-Articulation of Post-Yugoslav Political Identities." *Nations and Nationalism* 10 (3): 293–311.

Adevarul. 2009. "Scandal în Parlament între Ion Iliescu şi revoluţionarul Dumitru Dincă." December 17. Accessed February 7, 2013. http://adevarul.ro/news/eveniment/scandal-parlament-ion-iliescu-revolutionarul-dumitru-dinca-1_50ad79187c42d5a66395d27c/index.html.

Aguilar Fernandez, Paloma, and Carsten Humlebaek. 2002. "Collective Memory and National Identity in the Spanish Democracy: The Legacies of Francoism and the Civil War." *History and Memory: Studies in Representation of the Past* 14: 121–164.

aktualne.SK. 2007. "Výročie masakry v Černovej si pripomenuli tisíce ľudí." Accessed October 27. http://aktualne.centrum.sk/domov/politika/clanek.phtml?id=1145054.

Amar, Tarik Youssef Cyril, Ihor Balyns'kyi, and Iaroslav Hrytsak. 2011. *Strasti za Banderoiu.* Kyïv: Hrani-T.

Anderson, Benedict. 1983. *Imagined Communities.* London: Verso.

Anderson, Jeffrey J. 2010. "The Federal Republic at Twenty: Of Blind Spots and Peripheral Vision." *German Politics and Society* 28 (2): 17–33.

Androlova. 2010. "9ti septemvri e No.1? Tova e infektzjia!" *24 Chasa*, January 11, 3.

Antonevičs, Māris. 2011. "Svētku ēnā." *Latvijas Avīze*, August 23.

Appel, Hilary. 2005. "Anti-communist Justice and Founding the Post-communist Order: Lustration and Restitution in Central Europe." *East European Politics and Societies* 19: 379–405.

Ardava, Laura. 2009. "'Mēs'—'Viņi' diskursa konstrukcija 1989. gada 23. augusta akcijai "Baltijas ceļš" veltītajās publikācijās 1989. un 1999. gadā." *Latvijas Arhīvi* 4: 121–145.

Ardava, Laura. 2011. "Etnogrāfu piezīmes: 16. marta un 8./9. maija komemorācijas prakses un rituāli Latvijā (2010–2011)." In *Karojošā piemiņa: 16. marts un 9. maijs*, ed. Nils Muižnieks and Vita Zelče, 349–365. Rīga: Zinātne.

Arel, Dominique. 2006. "La face cachée de la Révolution Orange: l'Ukraine en négation face à son problème régional." *Revue d'études comparatives Est-Ouest* 37 (4): 11–48.

Arendt, Hannah. 1977. *Eichmann in Jerusalem: A Report on the Banality of Evil.* New York: Penguin Books.

Arnautović, Suad. 2007. *Ten Years of Democratic Chaos: Electoral Process in Bosnia and Herzegovina from 1996 to 2006: Essays, Analyses, Comments.* Sarajevo: Promocult.

Aronoff, Myron J., and Jan Kubik. 2013. *Anthropology and Political Science: A Convergent Approach.* New York: Berghahn Books.

Art, David. 2006. *The Politics of the Nazi Past in Germany and Austria.* Cambridge, UK: Cambridge University Press.

Ash, Timothy Garton. 1993. *The Magic Lantern: The Revolution of '89 Witnessed in Warsaw, Budapest, Berlin, and Prague.* New York: Vintage.

Ash, Timothy Garton. 2009. "1989!" *The New York Review of Books* 56, no. 17. Accessed September 14, 2012. http://www.nybooks.com/articles/23232.

Assmann, Jan. 1995. "Collective Memory and Cultural Identity." *New German Critique* 65: 125–133.

Auers, Daunis, and Jānis Ikstens. 2005. "The Democratic Role of Political Parties." In *How Democratic is Latvia: Audit of Democracy*, ed. Juris Rozenvalds, pp. 89–98. Rīga: LU Akadēmiskais apgāds.

Avotiņš, Viktors. "*Baltijas ceļa* čaumala." *Neatkarīgā Rīta Avīze*, August 22, 2009.

B92. 2009. "I u Beogradu simbolično srušen zid." November 9. Accessed March 27, 2012. http://www.b92.net/info/vesti/index.php?yyyy=2009&mm=11&dd=09&nav_category=12&nav_id=391592.

Baeva, Iskra. 2010. "Protest sreshtu nalaganeto na novi istini." *24 Chasa*, January 11, 2.

Baeva, Iskra, and Evgenia Kalinova. 2010. "Bulgarian Transition and the Memory of the Socialist Past." In Maria Todorova, ed., *Remembering Communism: Genres of Representation*, pp. 57–94. New York: Social Science Research Council.

Bailey, F. G. 1981. "Dimensions of Rhetoric in Conditions of Uncertainty." In *Politically Speaking: Cross-Cultural Studies of Rhetoric*, ed. by Robert Paine, pp. 25–38. Philadelphia: Institute for the Study of Human Issues.

Balibar, Etienne. 2002. *At the Borders of Europe.* Lecture delivered on the invitation of the Institut Francais de Thessalonique and the Department of Philosophy of Aristotle University of Thessaloniki. French text first published in Transeuropéennes 17 (1999–2000): 9–17. Translated by Erin M. Williams, originally appeared under the title World Borders, Political Borders, *PMLA* 117: 71–78. Accessed October 6, 2012. http://make-worlds.net/node/80.

Balogh, Eva S. 2009a. "Hungarians and the Extreme Right." *Hungarian Spectrum*, June 4. Accessed October 15, 2011. http://hungarianspectrum.wordpress.com/2009/06/04/hungarians-and-the-extreme-right/ .

Balogh, Eva S. 2009b. "Hungary and the East German 'Tourists.'" *Hungarian Spectrum*, June 28. Accessed October 15, 2011. https://hungarianspectrum.wordpress.com/2009/06/28/hungary-and-the-east-german-tourists/.

Balogh, Eva S. 2009c. "Viktor Orbán's Speech on the Anniversary of the October Revolution." *Hungarian Spectrum*, October 24, 2009. Accessed October 15, 2011. http://hungarianspectrum.wordpress.com/2009/10/24/viktor-orbans-speech-on-the-anniversary-of-the-october-revolution/.

Balogh, Eva S. 2011. "Hungarian Democracy in Tatters." *The Dissident Blog*, December 21, 2011. Accessed October 15, 2012. http://www.dissidentblog.org/en/articles/hungarian-democracy-tatters.

Balogh, Eva S. 2013. "President János Áder's Visit to Berlin and the 'Stormy Meetings' with German Politicians." *Hungarian Spectrum*. Accessed March 14, 2013. http://hungarianspectrum.wordpress.com/2013/03/13/president-janos-aders-visit-to-berlin-and-the-stormy-meetings-with-german-politicians/.

"Baltic Presidents Urge Citizens to Remember 'Baltic Way.'" *Earth Times*, August 17, 2009. Accessed January 2011. http://www.earthtimes.org/articles/news/281690,baltic-presidents-urge-citizens-to-remember-baltic-way.html.

"Baltics Celebrate 20 years of Independence." *The Baltic Times*, August 22, 2011. Accessed February 2012. http://www.baltictimes.com/news/articles/29352/.

"Baltics Run for Unity." *The Baltic Times*, August 18, 2009. Accessed January 2011. http://www.baltictimes.com/news/articles/23359/.

"Baltijas vienotība gadu tūkstošu mijā. Valsts prezidentes Vairas Vīķes–Freibergas un Ministru prezidenta Andra Šķēles runas Latvijas Inteliģences apvienības 29. konferencē 1999. gada 23. augustā." *Lauku Avīze*, August 24, 1999.

Bánkuti, Miklós, Gábor Halmai, and Kim Lane Scheppele. 2012. "Disabling the Constitution." *Journal of Democracy* 23(3): 138–146.

Baudrillard, Jean. 1981. *For a Critique of the Political Economy of the Sign*. St. Louis: Telos Press.

Baudrillard, Jean. 1994. *Simulacra and Simulation*. Ann Arbor: University of Michigan Press.

Baudrillard, Jean. 1998. *Consumer Society: Myths and Structures*. Thousand Oaks, CA: Sage.

BBC. 2010. "Yanukovych u PARE: henotsydu ukraiintsiv ne bulo." April 27. Accessed September 15, 2013. http://www.bbc.co.uk/ukrainian/news/2010/04/100427_yanukovych_pace_bt.shtml.

Békés, Csaba. 2002. "Back to Europe: The International Background of the Political Transition in Hungary, 1988–1990." In *The Roundtable Talks of 1989: The Genesis of Hungarian Democracy: Analysis and Documents,* ed. András Bozóki, pp. 237–272. Budapest: Central European University Press.

Benziger, Karl P., n.d. "Imre Nagy and the Unsettled Past: The Politics of Memory in Contemporary Hungary." Accessed July 7, 2011. http://www.newschool.edu/nssr/historymatters/papers/KarlBenziger.pdf.

Bermeo, Nancy. 2003. *Ordinary People in Extraordinary Times: The Citizenry and the Breakdown of Democracy*. Princeton, NJ: Princeton University Press.

Bernhard, Michael. 2005. *Institutions and the Fate of Democracy: Germany and Poland in the Twentieth Century*. Pittsburgh: University of Pittsburgh Press.

Bernhard, Michael, and Ekrem Karakoc. 2011. "Moving West or Going South? Economic Transformation and Institutionalization in Postcommunist Party Systems." *Comparative Politics* 44: 1–20.

Bērziņš, Indulis. 1999. "Baltijas ceļš nākotnē." In *Baltijas ceļš—pirms desmit gadiem, tagad un nākamajā gadu tūkstotī ieejot*, ed. Aija Kalniņa, 57–60. Rīga: Latvijas Inteliģences apvienība.

Bevc, Vladislav. 2008. *Smiling Slovenia: Political Dissent Papers*. New York: Peter Lang Publishers.

Bieber, Florian. 2003. "Montenegrin Politics since the Disintegration of Yugoslavia." In *Montenegro in Transition: Problems of Identity and Statehood*, ed. Florian Bieber. Baden-Baden: Nomos Verlagsgesellschaft.

Bielasiak, Jack. 2010. "The Paradox of Solidarity's Legacy: Contested Values in Poland's Transitional Politics." *Nationalities Papers* 38: 41–58.

Billig, Michael. 1995. *Banal Nationalism*. London: Sage Publications.

Biondich, Mark. 2004. "'We Were Defending the State': Nationalism, Myth and Memory in Twentieth-Century Croatia." In *Ideologies and National Identities: The Case of Twentieth-Century Southeastern Europe*, ed. John R. Lampe and Mark Mazower, pp. 55–82. Budapest: Central European University Press.

Bjelajac, Mile, and Ozren Žunec. 2009. "The War in Croatia 1991–1995." In *Confronting the Yugoslav Controversies*, ed. Charles Ingrao and Thomas A. Emmert, pp. 231–270. West Lafayette: Purdue University Press.

Bleiere, Daina. 2005. "Latvija PSRS sastāvā (1945–1990)." In *Latvijas vēsture. 20. gadsimts.* 2nd ed., ed. Daina Bleiere, Ilgvars Butulis, Inesis Feldmanis, Aivars Stranga, Antonijs Zunda, pp. 294–408. Rīga: Jumava.

Blic Online. 2009. "Muzej Beogradskog zida." November 9. Accessed March 27, 2012. http://www.blic.rs/Vesti/Beograd/119756/Muzej-Beogradskog-zida.

BNS. "Ar plašu programmu svinēs Latvijas neatkarības de facto atjaunošanas svētkus." *Diena.lv*, August 21, 2011. Accessed February 2012. http://www.diena.lv/latvija/zinas/ar-plasu-progra mmu-svines-latvijas-neatkaribas-de-facto-atjaunosanas-svetkus-13899119.

Boguszewski, Rafał, Ewelina Kuźmicz, and Michał Strzeszewski. 2009. "Ocena Skutków Transformacji." In *Dwadzieścia lat przemian ustrojowych w Polsce. Opinie i Diagnozy Nr 15*. Warsaw, CBOS.

Bohnet, Henri. 2009. "Introduction." *Politička Misla*, Special Issue "20 Years after the Fall of the Berlin Wall" 7: 9–12. Accessed December 26, 2012. http://www.kas.de/wf/doc/kas_17542-1522-2-30.pdf?090918140748.

"Bonfires for Freedom." 2011. *The Baltic Times*, January 19, 2011. Accessed January 2012. http://www.baltictimes.com/news/articles/27769/.

Bos, Stephan. 2011. "Lithuania Commemorates 20th Anniversary of Soviet Crackdown." *VOANews.com*, January 13, 2011. Accessed February 2012. http://www.voanews.com/english/news/europe/Lithuania-Commemorates-20th-Anniversary-Of-Soviet-Crackdown-113505669.html.

Bourdieu, Pierre. 1993. *The Field of Cultural Production*. New York: Columbia University Press.

Bourdieu, Pierre, and Loïc J. D. Wacquant. 1992. *An Invitation to Reflexive Sociology*. Chicago: University of Chicago Press.

Boyce, Laurence. 2011. "'Song of Freedom' Heads to Tallinn." *The Baltic Times*, August 17, 2011. Accessed February 2012. http://www.baltictimes.com/news/articles/29328/.

Bozóki, András ed. 2002. *The Roundtable Talks of 1989: The Genesis of Hungarian Democracy: Analysis and Documents*. New York: Central European University Press.

Bratkowski, Stefan. Interview by Paweł Kowal. April 25, 2000. Warszawa. University of Michigan Center for Russian and East European Studies, Ann Arbor. This interview and several others cited in this chapter were conducted with support from a contract awarded to Michael D. Kennedy, Brian Porter, and Andrzej Paczkowski from the National Council for Eurasian and East European Research (NCEEER), under the authority of a Title VIII grant from the US Department of State, for the project, "Negotiating Revolution in Poland: Conversion and Opportunity in 1989." Neither NCEEER nor the US Government is responsible for the views expressed here.

Brendese, P. J. 2013. *The Power of Memory in Democratic Politics*. Rochester, NY: University of Rochester Press.

Brewer, John D. 2000. *Ethnography*. Buckingham, UK: Open University Press.

Brier, Robert. 2009. "The Roots of the 'Fourth Republic': Solidarity's Cultural Legacy to Polish Politics." *East European Politics and Societies* 23: 63–85.

Brubaker, Rogers, and Margit Feischmidt. 2002. "1848 in 1998: The Politics of Commemoration in Hungary, Romania, and Slovakia." *Comparative Studies in Society and History* 44 (4): 700–744.

Brubaker, Rogers, Margit Feischmidt, Jon Fox, and Liana Grancea. 2006. *Nationalist Politics and Everyday Ethnicity in a Transylvanian Town*. Princeton, NJ: Princeton University Press.

Brudny, Yitzhak and Yevgeny Finkel. 2011. "Why Ukraine is Not Russia. Hegemonic National Identity and Democracy in Russia and Ukraine." *East European Politics and Societies* 25 (4): 813–833.

Brüggemann, Karsten, and Andres Kasekamp. 2008. "The Politics of History and the War of Monuments in Estonia." *Nationalities Papers,* 36: 425–448.

Bruszt, Laszlo. 1992. "The Negotiated Revolution in Hungary." In *Post-Communist Transition: Emerging Pluralism in Hungary,* ed. András Bozóki et al. London: Pinter Publishers.

BTV Novinite. 2009. November 10. Accessed June 10, 2012. http://www.youtube.com/watch?v=K29lMerSMMk&feature=related.

Buchert, Viliam. 2009. "Vyprázdněná politika je příležitost pro 'havlismus', říká Václav Klaus" [The Emptying Out of Politics Is an Opportunity for "Havlismus"]. *Mladá fronta dnes.* November 16.

Bulgarian Parliament, 2008. Parliamentary Proceedings, February 28. Accessed June 10, 2012. http://www.parliament.bg/bg/plenaryst/ID/396.

Burawoy, Michael, and Janos Lukacs. 1992. *The Radiant Past: Ideology and Reality in Hungary's Road to Capitalism*. Chicago: University of Chicago Press.

Burch, Stuart. 2008. "An Unfolding Signifier: London's Baltic Exchange in Tallinn." *Journal of Baltic Studies* 39: 451–473.

Buric, Fedja. 2010. "Dwelling o the Ruins of Socialist Yugoslavia: Being Bosnian by Remembering Tito." In *Post-Communist Nostalgia,* ed. Maria Todorova and Zsuzsa Gille, pp. 227–243. New York: Berghan Books.

Butković, Davor. 2009. "Kako smo osnivali HSLS (i je li umro)?" *Jutarnji List*, February 2. Accessed March 27, 2012. http://www.jutarnji.hr/kako-smo-osnivali-hsls--i-je-li-umro--/287821/.

Bútora Martin, Zora Bútorová, Miroslav Kollár, and Grigorij Mesežnikov, eds. 2010. *Kde sme? Mentálne mapy Slovenska*. Bratislava: Inštitút pre verejné otázky a vydavateľstvo Kalligram.

Bútorová, Zora. 2010. "Verejna mienka: zdroj pohybu, sila zotrvacnosti." In *Kde sme? Mentálne mapy Slovensk*, ed. Martin Butora et al. Bratislava: Inštitút pre verejné otázky a vydavateľstvo Kalligram.

Calinescu, Matei, and Vladimir Tismaneanu. 1991. "Epilogue: The 1989 Revolution and the Collapse of Communism in Romania." In *The Romanians: A History,* Vlad Georgescu. Translated by Alexandra Bley-Vroman, pp. 279–297. Columbus: The Ohio State University Press.

Capoccia, Giovanni. 2007. *Defending Democracy*. Baltimore: The Johns Hopkins University Press.

Capoccia, Giovanni 2010. "Normative Frameworks, Electoral Interests, and the Boundaries of Legitimate Participation in Post-Fascist Democracies" (manuscript).

Carnahan, Robin, and Judith Corley. 1992. "Czechoslovakia, June 8 and 9, 1990," In *The New Democratic Frontier: A Country by Country Report on Elections in Central and Eastern Europe*, pp. 112–134. Washington, DC: National Democratic Institute for International Affairs.

Castle, Marjorie. 2003. *Triggering Communism's Collapse: Perceptions and Power in Poland's Transition*. Lanham, MD: Rowman and Littlefield.

CBOS. 2008. "Spojrzenie na miniony wiek w historii Polski," Warsaw: CBOS.

CBOS. 2009a. "Opinie i diagnozy 15: Dwadzieścia lat przemian ustrojowych w Polsce." Warsaw: CBOS.

CBOS. 2009b. "Preferencje partyjne w czerwcu 2009." Warsaw: CBOS.

CBOS. 2013 Komunikat z Badań BS/73/2013. "Czy warto było zmieniać ustrój? Społeczna ocena przemian po 1989 roku." Warsaw: CBOS.

Cenckiewicz, Sławomir, and Piotr Gontarczyk. 2008. *SB a Lech Wałęsa. Przyczynek do biografii*. Warsaw: Instytut Pamięci Narodowej.

Central Committee of the Communist Party of the Soviet Union. 1989. "PSKP CK paziņojums par stāvokli Baltijas padomju republikās." *Padomju Jaunatne*, August 29, 1989.

Centrum Politycznych Analiz. 2010a. "Home." Accessed December 27. http://cpa.info.pl/index. php?option=com_content&view=category&layout=blog&id=1&Itemid=2.

Centrum Politycznych Analiz. 2010b. "Konferencja z okazji 20-ej rocznicy rozpoczęcia obrad Okrągłego Stołu." Accessed December 27. http://cpa.info.pl/index.php?option=com_conten t&view=article&id=4:wpis-numer-jeden&catid=1:newsy&Itemid=2.

Centrum Politycznych Analiz. 2010c. "Rada Programowa." Accessed December 27. 2010. http:// cpa.info.pl/index.php?option=com_content&view=article&id=2&Itemid=4.

Cera, Evija. 2004. " 'Baltijas ceļam" jākļūst par iedvesmu nākotnei." *Neatkarīgā Rīta Avīze*, August 24, 2004.

Černič, Jernej Letnar. 2009. "Responding to Post-Second World War Totalitarian Crimes in Slovenia." *International Law Observer,* June 22. Accessed March 27, 2102. http:// internationallawobserver.eu/2009/06/22/responding-to-post-second-world-war-totali-tarian-crimes-in-slovenia/.

Chandler, David. 2000. *Bosnia: Faking Democracy after Dayton*. London: Pluto Press.

Cheskin, Ammon. 2010. "The Discursive Construction of 'Russian-speakers': The Russian-language Media and Demarcated Political Identities in Latvia." In *Shrinking Citizenship: Discursive Practices that Limit Democratic Participation in Latvian Politics*, ed. Maria Golubeva and Robert Gould, pp. 133–154. New York: Rodopi.

Chrzanowski, Wiesław. 1999. Interview by Marjorie Castle, April 10, 1999. University of Michigan Center for Russian and East European Studies, Ann Arbor.

Ćirić, Miloš. 2012. "Bombardovanje za početnike." *Peščanik*, March 24. Accessed March 29, 2012. http://pescanik.net/2012/03/bombardovanje-za-pocetnike/.

Cohen, Shari. 1999. *Politics Without a Past: The Absence of History in Postcommunist Nationalism.* Durham, NC: Duke University Press.

Čolović, Ivan. 2002. "The Politics of Time." In *Politics of Identity in Serbia.* New York: New York University Press.

Čolović, Ivan. 2009. "Sve je počelo u Srbiji." In *Zid je mrtav, živeli zidovi!,* ed. Ivan Čolović, pp. 37–57. Beograd: Biblioteka XX vek.

Čolović, Ivan. 2010. "Berlinski zid i Srbija." *Peščanik,* October 26. Accessed March 27, 2012. http://pescanik.net/2010/10/berlinski-zid-i-srbija/.

Comisia Prezidentiala pentru Analiza Dictaturii Comuniste din Romania. 2006. *Raport Final.* Bucharest: Office of the President.

Cox, Gary. 1997. *Making Votes Count: Strategic Coordination in the World's Electoral Systems.* Cambridge, UK: Cambridge University Press.

Cronqvist, Lasse. 2007. *Tosmana: Tool for Small-N Analysis. User Manual (Version 1.3 beta, Release: 5th).* Marburg: Institute for Political Science.

Cruz, Consuelo. 2000. "Identity and Persuasion: How Nations Remember Their Pasts and Make Their Futures." *World Politics* 52 (April): 275–312.

Cruz, Consuelo. 2005. *Political Culture and Institutional Development in Costa Rica and Nicaragua: World-Making in the Tropics.* New York: Cambridge University Press.

Csepeli, György, and István Murányi. 2012. "New Authoritarianism in Hungary at the Beginning of the 21st Century." *Central European Political Review* 13: 65–95.

Čulić, Marinko. 2009. "Berlinski zid nam se srušio na glavu?" *Politika,* November 12. Accessed March 27, 2012. http://www.h-alter.org/vijesti/uvodnik/berlinski-zid-nam-se-srusio-na-glavu.

Czyrek, Józef. Interview by Robert Pytlos. Warszawa, December 20, 1999. University of Michigan Center for Russian and East European Studies, Ann Arbor.

D'Anieri, Paul. 2007. *Understanding Ukrainian Politics: Power, Politics, and Institutional Design.* Armonk, NY: M. E. Sharpe.

Davioliute, Violeta. 2011. "Vienna and Vilnius: The Values Gap." *Transitions Online,* July 29, 2011. Accessed February 29, 2012. http://www.tol.org/client/article/22587-vienna-and-vilnius-the-values-gap.html.

Davis, Eric. 2005. *Memories of State: Politics, History, and Collective Identity in Modern Iraq.* Berkeley: University of California Press.

De Brito, Alexandra Barahona, Carmen Gonzalez Enriquez, and Paloma Aguilar, eds. 2001. *The Politics of Memory: Transitional Justice in Democratizing Societies.* Oxford: Oxford University Press.

De Brito, Alexandra Barahona, and Lawrence Whitehead. 2012. "Transitional Justice: Reframing the Debate." In *After Oppression: Transitional Justice in Latin America and Eastern Europe,* ed. Vesselin Popovski and Monica Serrano, pp. 439–462. Tokyo: United Nations University.

Deegan-Krause, Kevin, and Tim Haughton. 2010. "A Fragile Stability: The Institutional Roots of Low Party System Volatility in the Czech Republic, 1990–2009." *Czech Journal of Political Science* 3: 227–241.

Deep White Public Relations. 2010. "Heartbeats for the Baltics—Best International Communications Campaign for 2009." Accessed January 4, 2012. http://www.deepwhite.lv/en/news/.

Demokratska stranka. 2010. "Srbija na pravom putu: Dvadeset godina Demokratske Stranke." Published as a supplement of magazine Vreme, February 4. Accessed March 27, 2012. http://www.slideshare.net/demokrate/20-godina-demokratske-stranke-srbija-na-pravom-putu.

Didanović, Vera. 2009. "Sada i zauvek: Crna Gora, dve decenije vlasti Demokratske Partije Socijalista (DPS)." Vreme, April 2. Accessed March 27, 2012. http://www.vreme.com/cms/view.php?id=855733.

Die Zeit. 2009a "Triumph der offenen Gesellschaft." November 5. Accessed January 3, 2011. http://www.zeit.de/2009/46/Revolution-1989.

Die Zeit. 2009b. "Ostdeutsche haben positives DDR-Bild." June 26. Accessed January 3, 2011. http://www.zeit.de/online/2009/27/ddr-bild-positiv-2.

Die Zeit. 2010. "20 Dinge, die wir bei der nächsten Wiedervereinigung besser machen." September 23. Accessed January 3, 2011. http://www.zeit.de/2010/39/Einheit-20-Jahre.

Doerschler, Peter, and Lee Ann Banaszak. 2007. "Voter Support for the German PDS over Time: Dissatisfaction, Ideology, Losers and East Identity." Electoral Studies 26: 359–370.

Domański, Henryk. 2004. "Problemy wspólnoty a struktura społeczna." Res Publica Nowa. Accessed June 17, 2005. http://respublica.onet.pl/1838,dzial.html.

Dragović-Soso, Jasna. 2002. 'Saviours of the Nation': Serbia's Intellectual Opposition and the Revival of Nationalism. London, UK: Hurst & Company; Montreal & Kingston, Canada: McGill-Queen's University Press.

Državni zbor Republike Slovenije. 1997. "Pismo Predsednika Republike Milana Kučana o predlogih zakona in resolucije o komunističnem totalitarnem režimu." Ljubljana. Accessed February 12, 2013. http://www2.gov.si/up-rs/2002-2007/bp-mk.nsf/priponke/2582BDF045 9B8687C1256EE400361CF9/$FILE/1997-03-lustracija-pismo.pdf.

Durzhaven vestnik. 2009. No.103, December 29, 16.

Dutceac Segesten, Anamaria. 2011. "Nationalism in Romanian Textbooks." In Cultural Transformations after Communism: Central and Eastern Europe in Focus, ed. Barbara Törnquist-Plewa and Krzysztof Stala, pp. 2–50. Lund: Nordic Academic Press.

Dutsyk, Diana. 2011. "20 rokiv Nezalezhnosti: u poshukah pozytyvu." Ukrains'ka pravda, August 23. Accessed July 15, 2012. http://www.pravda.com.ua/columns/2011/08/23/6522431/.

E-Novine. 2009. "Pad viznog zida." Fotogalerija, December 19. Accessed March 27, 2012. http://www.e-novine.com/fotogalerija/fotogalerija-srbija/33352-Pad-viznog-zida.html.

Egle, Ināra. 2011. "Barikāžu laiks visilgāk paliek cilvēku sajūtās." Diena, January 12, 2011.

Eglitis, Daina S. 2002. Imagining the Nation: History, Modernity, and Revolution in Latvia. University Park: Pennsylvania State University Press.

Eglitis, Daina S. 2011a. "The Baltic States: Changes and Challenges in the New Europe." In Central and East European Politics: From Communism to Democracy, ed. Sharon L. Wolchik and Jane L. Curry, pp. 231–249. New York: Rowman & Littlefield.

Eglitis, Daina S. 2011b "Class, Culture, and Consumption: Representations of Stratification in Post-Communist Latvia." Cultural Sociology 5: 423–446.

Ehala, Martin. 2009. "The Bronze Soldier: Identity Threat and Maintenance in Estonia." Journal of Baltic Studies 40: 139–158.

Eichler, Pavel. 2009. "Extremisté v Praze napadali policisty, téměř 50 jich skončilo v cele" [Extremists Attack Police in Prague; Almost 50 Arrested]. Mladá fronta dnes. November 17.

Ekiert, Grzegorz. 1996. State Against Society. Princeton, NJ: Princeton University Press.

Ekiert, Grzegorz, and Jan Kubik. 1999. *Rebellious Civil Society, Popular Protest and Democratic Consolidation in Poland, 1989–1993*. Ann Arbor: University of Michigan Press.

Elkin, Abik. 1998. "Barrikady proshlogo i nastoyashchego." *SM–Segodnya*, January 20, 1998.

Elkin, Abik, and Vadim Fal'kov. 2004. "Dainis Ivans: 12 let—pod oligarkhami." *Vesti segodnya*, August 26, 2004.

Emirbayer, Mustafa, and Jeff Goodwin. 1996. "Symbols, Positions, Objects: Toward a New Theory of Revolutions and Collective Action." *History and Theory* 35: 358–374.

Encarnación, Omar G. 2014. *Democracy Without Justice in Spain. The Politics of Forgetting.* Philadelphia: University of Pennsylvania Press.

English Café (Blog). 2009. "Twenty Years Since the Fall of the Berlin Wall." November 15. Accessed March 29, 2012. http://www.englishcafe.com/blog/twenty-years-fall-berlin-wall-41264.

European Commission. 2010. "Report from the Commission to the European Parliament and to the Council. The Memory of Crimes Committed by Totalitarian Regimes in Europe." *Brussels*, December 12. Accessed March 27, 2012. http://ec.europa.eu/commission_2010-2014/reding/pdf/com(2010)_873_1_en_act_part1_v61.pdf.

European Parliament. 2009. "Joint Motion for a Resolution. European Parliament Resolution on European Conscience and Totalitarianism." March 30. Accessed March 27, 2012. http://www.europarl.europa.eu/sides/getDoc.do?type=MOTION&reference=P6-RC-2009-0165&language=EN.

Evans, Martin. 2006. "Memories, Monuments, Histories: The Re-thinking of the Second World War since 1989." *National Identities* 8: 317–348.

Eyal, Gil. 2004. "Identity and Trauma: Two Forms of the Will to Memory." *History & Memory* 16: 5–36.

Falk, Barbara. 2009. *The Dilemmas of Dissidence in East-Central Europe: Citizen Intellectuals and Philosopher King.* Budapest: Central European University Press.

Fedosseev, Leonid. 1999. "Na seredine Puti." *Chas*, August 23.

Fesenko, Volodymyr. 2011. "Suspil'stvo i nezalezhnist'." *Ukrains'ka pravda*, September 7. Accessed March 23, 2012. http://www.pravda.com.ua/articles/2011/09/7/6566102/.

Fink-Hafner, Danica. 2006. "Struktura i karakteristike razvoja politickog pluralizma u Sloveniji 1989–2004." In *Razvoj Politickog Pluralizma u Sloveniji i Bosni i Hercegovini,* ed. Danica Fink-Hafner and Mirko Pjeanovc, pp. 17–37. Sarajevo: Promocult.

Fink-Hafner, Danica. 2010. "Slovenia since 1989." In *Central and Southeast European Politics since 1989,* ed. Sabrina Ramet. Cambridge, UK: Cambridge University Press.

Fish, M. Steven. 2005. *Democracy Derailed in Russia: The Failure of Open Politics.* Cambridge, UK: Cambridge University Press.

Frankfurter Allgemeine Zeitung. 2009. "Im Herzen Europas." November 10. Accessed on February 9, 2013. http://www.faz.net/themenarchiv/2.1278/20-jahre-mauerfall-im-herzen-europas-1879978.html.

Fulbrook, Mary. 2005. *The People's State: East German Society from Hitler to Honecker.* New Haven, CT: Yale University Press.

Gabanyi, Anneli Ute. 1990. *Die Unvollendete Revolution.* Munchen: Serie Piper.

Gadamer, Hans-Georg. 1989. *Truth and Method.* New York: Crossroad.

Gallagher, Tom. 1995. *Romania after Ceauşescu.* Edinburgh, Scotland: Edinburgh University Press.

Ganev, Venelin. 2007. *Preying on the State: The Transformation of Postcommunist Bulgaria.* Ithaca, NY: Cornell University Press.

Ganev, Venelin I. 2012. "The Valorization of Nostalgia," paper presented at the annual conference of the Council for European Studies, Boston, March 23.

Gawin, Dariusz. 2010. "Legitimizacja i pamięć." In *Legitimizacja w Polsce. Nieustający kryzys w zmieniających się warunkach?* ed. Andrzej Rychard and Henryk Domański, pp. 7–29. Warsaw: iFiS PAN.

Gazeta Wyborcza. 2009a. "Dyskusja o Okrągłym Stole: Potrzebny nam dziś taki dialog." February 5. Accessed February 9, 2009. http://wiadomosci.gazeta.pl/Wiadomosci/2029020,80269,6240567. html.

Gazeta Wyborcza. 2009b. "'Efekt domina'—upadły reżimy komunistyczne Europy." June 5. Accessed November 21, 2010. http://wiadomosci.gazeta.pl/Wiadomosci/1,80708,6689791,_ Efekt_domina____upadly_rezimy_komunistyczne_Europy.html.

Gazeta Wyborcza. 2009c. "Jan Hałas nie przyjął medalu od prezydenta." June 4. Accessed November 21, 2010. http://wiadomosci.gazeta.pl/Wiadomosci/1,80708,6686615,Jan_Halas_ nie_przyjal_medalu_od_prezydenta.html.

Gazeta Wyborcza. 2009d. "Jaruzelski: Okrągły Stół to jedno z największych wydarzeń w historii Polski." February 3. Accessed February 9, 2009. http://wiadomosci.gazeta.pl/ Wiadomosci/2029020,81048,6233381.html.

Gazeta Wyborcza. 2009e. "Kilka tysięcy związkowców na ulicach Katowic." June 4. Accessed November 21, 2010. http://wiadomosci.gazeta.pl/Wiadomosci/1,80708,6687899,Kilka_ tysiecy_zwiazkowcow_na_ulicach_Katowic.html.

Gazeta Wyborcza. 2009f. "Kwaśniewski: Okrągły Stół to było spotkanie patriotów." February 6. Accessed February 9, 2009. http://wiadomosci.gazeta.pl/ Wiadomosci/2029020.90269,6243189.html

Gazeta Wyborcza. 2009g. "Kwaśniewski: Okrągły Stół pierwszym udanym bezkrwawym powstaniem." February 5. Accessed February 9, 2009. http://wiadomosci.gazeta.pl/ Wiadomosci/2029020,81048,6240490.html.

Gazeta Wyborcza. 2009h. "Premier: do końca zabiegałem, aby każdy zaproszony znalazł się na Wawelu." June 4. Accessed November 21, 2010. http://wiadomosci.gazeta.pl/Wiadomosci/1,8 0708,6685553,Premier__do_konca_zabiegalem__aby_kazdy_zaproszony.html.

Gazeta Wyborcza. 2009i. "Prezydent: Magdalenka nie była zdradą." February 5. Accessed February 9, 2009. http://wiadomosci.gazeta.pl/2029020,80269,6242714.html.

Gazeta Wyborcza. 2009j. "Prezydent: obchody były niedobre, bo nie w Stoczni." June 5. Accessed November 21, 2010. http://wiadomosci.gazeta.pl/Wiadomosci/1,80708,6690096,Prezyd ent__obchody_byly_niedobre__bo_nie_w_Stoczni.html.

Gazeta Wyborcza. 2009k. "Prezydent ma swoją konferencję o Okrągłym Stole." February 6. Accessed February 9, 2009. http://wiadomisci.gazeta.pl/Wiadomosci/2029020.80708,6244364.html.

Gazeta Wyborcza. 2009l. "Roszkowski: Okrągły Stół to porozumienie elit, 4 czerwca przemówił lud." February 6. Accessed February 9, 2009. http://wiadomosci.gazeta.pl/ Wiadomosci/2029020,81048,6244806.html

Gazeta Wyborcza. 2009m. "Sejm: rozpoczęła się konferencja z okazji 20-lecia Okrągłego Stolu." February 2. Accessed February 9, 2009. http://wyborcza.pl/2029020,91446,6238749.html

Gazeta Wyborcza. 2009n. "Uroczystości rocznicy 4 czerwca w Sejmie—prezydent i premier wyszli." June 3. Accessed January 15, 2011 http://wyborcza.pl/1,76842,6681931,Uroczystosci_ rocznicy_4_czerwca_w_Sejmie____prezydent.html

Gazeta Wyborcza. 2009o. "Wałęsa: Nie warto sądzić generałów, bo jeszcze dopłacać trzeba." February 6. Accessed February 9, 2009. http://wiadomosci.gazeta.pl/ Wiadomosci/2029020,80708,6243907.html

Gazeta Wyborcza. 2009p. "Wałęsa o rocznicy Okrągłego Stołu: Mając kaca moralnego...." February 5. Accessed February 9, 2009. http://wiadomosci.gazeta.pl/Wiadomosci/2029020,80269,6240920.html

Gazeta Wyborcza. 2009q. "W Sejmie rocznicowe obchody, bez prezydenta i premiera." June 3. Accessed November 21, 2010. http://wiadomosci.gazeta.pl/Wiadomosci/1,80708,6680912,W_Sejmie_rocznicowe_obchody__bez_prezydenta_i_premiera_.html.

Gdula, Andrzej. Interview by Michael Kennedy. Warsaw, Poland, October 8, 1998. University of Michigan Center for Russian and East European Studies, Ann Arbor.

Geida, Aija. 2009. "Guva prieku un spēku." *Latvijas Avīze*, August 26.

Gellner, Ernest. 1983. *Nations and Nationalism*. London: Basil Blackwell.

George, Alexander, and Andrew Bennett. 2005. *Case Studies and Theory Development in the Social Sciences*. Cambridge, MA: MIT Press.

Gerring, John. 2004. "What Is a Case Study and What is it Good for?" *American Political Science Review* 98: 341–354.

Gillis, John, R. 1994. "Memory and Identity: A History of a Relationship." In *Commemorations. The Politics of National Identity*, ed. John R. Gillis, pp. 3–24. Princeton: Princeton University Press.

Głębocki, Henryk. 2008. "O 'politykę kontraktu społecznego...' Memoriał Bronisława Geremka z maja 1988 r." *Biuletyn Instytutu Pamięci Narodowej* 88–89: 183–200.

Gomon, Dmitrii. 2010. "Nastoiashchii dom Simonenko—s mramornymi perilami i bez bashen na kryshe." *Segodnia*, December 2. Accessed July 21, 2012. http://www.segodnya.ua/news/14200858.html.

Gordy, Eric. 1999. *The Culture of Power in Serbia: Nationalism and Destruction of Alternatives*. College Park: Pennsylvania State University Press.

Gospodinov, Georgi. 2009. "1989—drugite dati," *Dnevnik*, November 11, 6.

Graan, Andrew. 2010. "On the Politics of 'Imidž': European Integration and the Trials of Recognition in Postconflict Macedonia." *Slavic Review* 69 (4): 835–858.

Granovetter, Mark. 1973. "The Strength of Weak Ties." *American Journal of Sociology* 78: 1360–1380.

Grass, Günter. 2002. *Crabwalk*. New York: Harcourt.

Gross, Jan Tomasz. 2001. *Neighbors: The Destruction of the Jewish Community in Jedwabne, Poland*. Princeton, NJ: University Press.

Gross, Mirjana. 2007. "Europa izgrađena na namjernoj amneziji." *Jutarnji List*, March 23. Accessed March 27, 2012. http://www.jutarnji.hr/template/article/article-print.jsp?id=218787.

Gross, Toomas. 2002. "Anthropology of Collective Memory: Estonian National Awakening Revisited." *Trames* 6: 342–354.

Grünther-Dječević, Mirela, and Nermina Mujagić. 2009. "Preface." In *1989–2009 Years of Upheaval: Beginning of Inclusion or Exclusion*. Proceedings from a conference. Foundation Heinrich Böll. Sarajevo. Accessed March 27, 2012. http://www.boell.de/publications/publications-7802.html.

Grzymala-Busse, Anna. 2002. *Redeeming the Communist Past*. Cambridge, UK: Cambridge University Press.

Halbwachs, Maurice. 1950. *La mémoire collective*. Paris: Presses Universitaires de France [*The Collective Memory*. 1980. New York: Harper & Row Colophon Books].

Halbwachs, Maurice. 1952. *Les cadres sociaux de la mémoire*. Paris: Presses Universitaires de France [originally published in *Les Travaux de L'Année Sociologique*, Paris, F. Alcan, 1925, and translated as *On Collective Memory*. 1992. Chicago: The University of Chicago Press].

Halbwachs, Maurice. 1992. *On Collective Memory*, trans. Lewis A. Coser. Chicago: University of Chicago Press.

Haran', Oleksii, and Oleksandr Maiboroda, eds. 2000. *Ukrains'ki livi: mizh leninizmom i sotsial-demokratieiu*. Kyiv: KM Academiia.

Haraszti, Miklós. 2011. "Is Europe's Democratic Revolution Over?" *Transitions Online*, May 9, 2011, panel 1, transcript p. 7. http://www.tol.org/client/article/22386-is-europes -democratic-revolution-over.html.

Haughton, Tim, Tereza Novotná, and Kevin Deegan-Krause. 2011. "The 2010 Czech and Slovak Parliamentary Elections: Red Cards to the 'Winners.'" *West European Politics* 34(2): 394–402.

Havel, Václav. 1990. "The Power of the Powerless." In *Without Force or Lies: Voices from the Revolution of Central Europe in 1989–90*, ed. William Brinton and Alan Rinzler, pp. 43–127. San Francisco: Mercury House.

Herf, Jeffrey. 1997. *Divided Memory: The Nazi Past in the Two Germanies*. Cambridge, MA: Harvard University Press.

Hobsbawm, Eric, and Terence Ranger, eds. 1983. *The Invention of Tradition*. Cambridge, UK: Cambridge University Press.

Hockenos, Paul. 2003. *Homeland Calling: Exile Patriotism and the Balkan Wars*. Ithaca, NY: Cornell University Press.

Holy, Ladislav. 1996. *The Little Czech and the Great Czech Nation: National Identity and the Post-communist Transformation of Society*. Cambridge, UK: Cambridge University Press.

Honcharuk, Hryhorii, and Olena Shanovs'ka. 2004. *Natsional'na ideia i Narodnyi Rukh Ukrainy*. Odesa: Astroprynt.

Horáková, Pavla. 2009. "Student Activists Unveil "Present" Received for Velvet Revolution Anniversary." *Czech Radio 7, Radio Prague*. http://www.radio.cz/en/article/122062.

Horn, Miriam. 1990. "Campaign Carnival: A Velvet Election." *The New Republic* 203, no. 6: 11–13.

Hotnews.ro. 2009. Ion Iliescu pentru presa rusa: "Nu stim cine a tras la Revolutie, este o enigma. Probabil au fost oameni extrem de devotati lui Ceausescu." December 22. Accessed February 7, 2013. http://www.hotnews.ro/stiri-esential-6753081-ion-iliescu-pentru-presa-rusa-nu-stim-cine-tras-revolutie-este-enigma-probabil-fost-oameni-extrem-devotati-lui-ceausescu. htm.

Hough, Dan, and Michael Koss. 2009. "Populism Personified or Reinvigorated Reformers? The German Left Party in 2009 and Beyond." *German Politics and Society* 27 (2): 76–91.

Hozić, Aida A. 2004. "Between the Cracks: Balkan Cigarette Smuggling." *Problems of Post-communism* 51 (3): 35–44.

Hozić, Aida A. 2011. "Travel for Ordinary Comforts." *Cambridge Review of International Affairs* 24 (4): 613–628.

Hrib, Štefan. 2000. "Som pripravený byť predsedom vlády rozhovor Roberta Fica so Štefanom Hríbom." *Domino Fórum* 9 (50): 4–5.

Hrytsak, Yaroslav. 2004. "Dvadtsiat' dvi Ukrainy." In *Strasti za natsionalizmom*. ed. Yaroslav Hrytsak, pp. 216-228. Kyiv: Krytyka.

Hudyma, Dmytro. 2010. "'Syndrom Bandery': Nepolitychni koreni vidomoi problemy," *Ukrains'ka pravda*, April 25. Accessed December 3, 2010. http://www.pravda.com.ua/columns/2010/04/25/4961778/.

Huntington, Samuel P. 1991. *The Third Wave: Democratization in the Late Twentieth Century.* Norman: University of Oklahoma Press.

Huyssen, Andreas. 2000. "Present Pasts: Media, Politics, Amnesia." *Public Culture* 12(1): 21–38.

Ijabs, Ivars, and Juris Rozenvalds, eds. 2009. *Latvia Human Development Report 2008/2009: Accountability and Responsibility.* Riga: University of Latvia, Advanced Social and Political Research Institute.

Iliescu, Ion. 1995. *Momente de istorie.* Bucuresti: Editura Enciclopedica.

Inglehart, Ronald. 1988. "The Renaissance of Political Culture." *American Political Science Review* 82, 4 (December): 1204–1230.

Inventura demokracie. 2009a. "What Is Democracy Czech-Up?" Accessed February 1, 2013. http://en.inventurademokracie.cz/.

Inventura demokracie. 2009b. "Student Declaration on the 20th Anniversary of the Velvet Revolution." Accessed February 1, 2013. http://en.inventurademokracie.cz/.

IREX. 2009. "Media Sustainability Index (MSI)—Europe and Eurasia 2009—Macedonia." Accessed December 26, 2012. http://www.irex.org/system/files/EE_MSI_09_se_Macedonia. pdf.

Ivanova, Ilze. 2004. ' "Baltijas ceļš" vienoja nākotnei." *Latvijas Avīze*, August 24.

Jambrek, Peter, ed. 2008. "Crimes Committed by Totalitarian Regimes: Reports and Proceedings of the 8 April Public Hearing European Public Hearing." *Ljubljana, Slovenian Presidency of the Council of the European Union.* Accessed March 27, 2012. http://www.mp.gov.si/fileadmin/ mp.gov.si/pageuploads/2005/PDF/publikacije/2008_11_14_publika.tot.rezimi.pdf.

Janša, Janez. 2009. "Did the Berlin Wall Really Come Down on Both Sides?" *European View* 8: 203–210. Accessed March 27, 2012. http://www.culturaldiplomacy.org/academy/content/articles/speakers/detailed/janez-jansa/publications/janez-jansa-20091105-Did-the-Berlin-Wall-really-come-down.pdf.

Janša, Janez, Ivan Borštner, and David Tasić. 1995. *7 let pozneje.* Ljubljana: Založba Karantanija.

Jansen, Stefan. 2010. "Of Wolves and Men: Postwar Reconciliation and the Gender of Inter-National Encounters." *Focaal: Journal of Global and Historical Anthropology* 57: 33–49.

Jedlička, Josef. 2009. *České typy a jiné eseje.* Prague: Nakladatelství Plus.

Jutarnji List. 2009a. "20 godina od pada Berlinskog zida." Accessed March 27, 2012. http://apps. jutarnji.hr/berlinski_zid/index.php.

Jutarnji List. 2009b. "Čak 49% Istočnih Nijemaca misli da im je bilo bolje u komunizmu." November 6. Accessed March 27, 2012. http://www.jutarnji.hr/dvadeset-godina-nakon-z ida/337013/.

Jutarnji List. 2009c. "Slavenka Drakulić: Zapadni Nijemci I danas istočnu braću smatraju gradjanima drugog reda." November 6. Accessed March 27, 2012. http://www.jutarnji. hr/slavenka-drakulic--zapadni-nijemci-i-danas-istocnu-bracu-smatraju-gradanima-drugog-reda/336980/.

Jutarnji List. 2009d. "Žive dulje pet godina i opet nezadovoljni." October 11. Accessed March 27, 2012. http://www.jutarnji.hr/zive-dulje-5-godina-i-opet-nezadovoljni/344020/.

Jutarnji List. 2009e. "Žižek: Crveni su i dalje na vlasti, prerušeni u menadžere." November 6. Accessed March 27, 2012. http://www.jutarnji.hr/slavoj-zizek---crveni-su-i-dalje-na-vlasti--preruseni-u-vlasnike-i-menadzere/337073/.

Kabuce, Liene. "Vienotības ceļš." *Latvijas Avīze*, August 24, 2004.

Kaczynski, Lech. 2009. "Polski rok 1989." *Rzeczpospolita.* June 5. http://www.rp.pl/ artykul/259388.html?print=tak.

Kansteiner, Wolf. 2002. "Finding Meaning in Memory: A Methodological Critique of Collective Memory Studies." *History and Theory* 41 (2): 179–197.

Kapliuk, Kateryna. 2010. "Perepysana istoriia Ukraiiny. Versiia epokhy Dmytra Tabachnyka." *Ukrains'ka pravda*, August 28. Accessed July 15, 2012. http://www.pravda.com.ua/articles/2010/08/26/5332444/.

Karabeg, Omer. 2011. "Jugonostalgija i strah od Jugoslavije. Radio Slobodna Evropa." October 9. Accessed October 6, 2012. http://www.slobodnaevropa.org/content/most_rse_jugonostalgija_i_strah_od_jugoslavije/24353669.html.

Kasianov, Heorhii. 1995. *Nezhodni: ukrains'ka intelihentsiia v rusi oporu 1960–1980kh rokiv*. Kyiv: Lybid'.

Katchanovski, Ivan. 2006. "Regional Political Divisions in Ukraine in 1991–2006." *Nationalities Papers* 34 (5): 507–532.

Katka, Krzysztof, Magdalena Kursa, and Maciej Sandecki. 2009. "Rząd świętuje, 'S' gwiżdże—podsumowanie obchodów 4 czerwca." *Gazeta Wyborcza*, June 5. Accessed November 21, 2010. http://wyborcza.pl/1,76842,6689263,Rzad_swietuje___S__gwizdze___podsumowanie_obchodow.html.

Kattago, Siobhan. 2008 "Commemorating Liberation and Occupation: War Memorials along the Road to Narva." *Journal of Baltic Studies* 39: 431–449.

Kennedy, Michael D. 2002. *Cultural Formations of Postcommunism: Emancipation, Transition, Nation, and War*. Minneapolis: University of Minnesota Press.

Kennedy, Michael, and Brian Porter, eds. 2000. *Negotiating Radical Change: Understanding and Extending the Lessons of the Polish Round Table Talks*. Ann Arbor: Regents of the University of Michigan. http://webapps.lsa.umich.edu/ii/PolishRoundTable/pdf/negotiatingradical-change.pdf.

Khan, Paul W. 2011. *Political Theology: Four New Chapters on the Concept of Sovereignty*. New York: Columbia University Press.

King, Charles. 2007. "Remembering Romanian Communism." *Slavic Review* 66 (4): 718–723.

Kiscsatári, Marianna. 2009. "Annus Mirabilis: The Year 1989 in Photos, Part 3, The Opening of the Border." *Hungarian Quarterly Volume* L (Autumn 195).

"Klaus varoval před zhoubnými ideologiemi, Havel připomněl mrtvé" [Klaus Warned Against Destructive Ideologies, Havel Remembered the Dead]. 2009. *Mladá fronta dnes*. November 17.

Klicperova-Baker, Martina. 1999. "Post-Communist Syndrome." Paper. Research Support Scheme. Open Society Institute.

Klumbyte, Neringa. 2010. "Memory, Identity, and Citizenship in Lithuania." *Journal of Baltic Studies* 41: 295–313.

Kmu.gov.ua. 2005. "Uriadova komisia skhvalyla fakhovyi vysnovok robochoi hrupy istorykiv z vyvchennia dial_nosti OUN i UPA." October 14. Accessed December 3, 2010. http://www.kmu.gov.ua/control/uk/publish/news_article?art_id=22511532&cat_id=35883.

Kohl, Helmut. 1990. "Television Address on the Eve of the Day of Unity." In *German Unification and Its Discontents: Documents from the Peaceful Revolution*, (1996), ed. Richard Gray and Sabine Wilke, pp. 263–265. Seattle: University of Washington Press.

Kołakowski, Leszek. 2008, "Kołakowski: Pamięć kształtuje narody" [Memory Shapes Nations]. *Gazeta Wyborcza*. April 25. Accessed October 29. http://wyborcza.pl/1,100556,5155479.html?as=1&startsz=x.

Komárek, Martin. 2009. "Proč nechceme vidět, že to bylo skvělé" [Why Don't We Want to See That It Was Great?]. *Mladá fronta dnes*. November 19.

Komunist. 2011. "Petro Symonenko: Richnytsia nezalezhnosti—tse sviato dlia oligarkhiv ta iikhnikh poplichnykiv." September 4. Accessed July 15, 2012. http://www.komunist.com.ua/article/15/42/9855_u.htm.

Kondrāts, Ģirts. " 'Cerību ceļš.' " *Cīņa*, August 25, 1989.

Konrad Adenauer Stiftung Macedonia Office. 2009. "20 Years after the Fall of the Berlin Wall: Lessons for the Balkans." Macedonian-Greek Conference (event announcement). Accessed December 26, 2012. http://www.kas.de/mazedonien/en/publications/18121/.

Kopecký, Josef. 2009. "Topolánek: Žijeme v nejlepší době, jen ovce to vidí jinak" [Topolánek: We Live in the Best Era; Only Sheep See it Otherwise]. *Mladá fronta dnes*. November 17.

Kopstein, Jeffrey, and Daniel Ziblatt. 2006. "Honecker's Revenge: The Enduring Legacy of German Unification in the 2005 Election." *German Politics and Society* 24 (1): 134–147.

Kornai, János. 2010. "Szamvetes" [Taking Stock]. *Nepszabadsag*, January 6, 2010. Accessed January 11, 2010. http://www.nol.hu/index.html.

Kosmeanu, Marijus. 2009. "Preimenovanje ulica na Balkanu." *E-Novine,* November 27. Accessed March 27, 2012. http://www.e-novine.com/drustvo/32637-Preimenovanje-ulica-Balkanu.html.

Kostelanský, Ľuboš. 2008. "Na oslavách v Mikuláši viali vlajky Smeru a SNS." *spravy/pravda. sk,* May 13. Accessed February 19, 2011. http://spravy.pravda.sk/na-oslavach-v-mikulasi-vi ali-vlajky-smeru-a-sns-flo-/sk_regiony.asp?c=A080513_192852_sk_regiony_P04.

Kotliar, Alla. 2011a. "Dialektyka nezalezhnosti." *Dzerkalo Tyzhnia*, August 19. Accessed March 23, 2012. http://gazeta.dt.ua/SOCIETY/dialektika_nezalezhnosti.html.

Kotliar, Alla. 2011b. "Ukraina posidaie mistse." *Dzerkalo Tyzhnia*, August 19. Accessed March 23, 2012. http://gazeta.dt.ua/SOCIETY/ukrayina_posidae_mistse.html.

Krapfl, James. 2009. "Civic Forum, Public Against Violence and the Struggle for Slovakia." BPS Working Paper Series, Institute of Slavic East European and Eurasian Studies, Berkeley. Accessed January 29, 2011. http://iseees.berkeley.edu/sites/default/files/u4/bps_/publications_/2009-08-Krapfl.pdf.

Krapfl, James. 2010. "Commemorating the Great November Velvet Revolution." Paper presented at the annual conference of the Association for Slavic, East European, and Eurasian Studies, Los Angeles, California, November 18–21.

Kratochvíl, Luboš. 2009. "Nedělej ostudu! a Ať žije Klaus! křičeli na prezidenta na Národní" ['Don't Embarrass Us!' and 'Long Live Klaus!' They Cried to the President on *Národní Třída*]. *Mladá fronta dnes*. November 17.

Kratochvíl, Luboš and Ondřej Bezr. 2009. "Trasu Albertov—Národní prošly po 20 letech tisíce lidí, většinou nepamětníků" [Over 20,000 People March from Albertov to Národní]. *Mladá fronta dnes*. November 11.

Kraus, Michael. 1995. "Settling Accounts: Postcommunist Czechoslovakia." In *Transitional Justice: How Emerging Democracies Recon with Former Regimes. Volume II: Country Studies,* ed. Neil J. Krtitz, pp. 542–544. Washington, DC: United States Institute of Peace.

Krawchenko, Bohdan and Jim A. Carter. 1983. "Dissidents in Ukraine before 1972: A Summary Statistical Profile." *Journal of Ukrainian Studies* 8 (2): 85–88.

Kreituse, Ilga. 2009. *Pagājušo gadu Latvija 1945–1990: kā dzīvojām, no kā iztikām, ko apsmējām, par ko priecājāmies*. Rīga: Zvaigne ABC.

Krivokapić, Boro. 1986. *Dahauški Process*. Beograd: Prosveta.

Król, Marcin. 1998. *Romantyzm: Piekło i niebo Polaków. Polskie obrachunki na koniec millenium.* Warsaw: Res Publica.

Krsnik, Vjekoslav. 2009. "Berlinski zid u Hrvata još nije srušen." *Politika*, November 9. Accessed March 27, 2012. http://pollitika.com/berlinski-zid-u-hrvatskoj-jos-nije-srusen.

Kubik, Jan. 1994. *The Power of Symbols Against the Symbols of Power: The Rise of Solidarity and the Fall of State Socialism in Poland.* University Park: The Penn State University Press.

Kubik. Jan 2003. "Cultural Legacies of State Socialism: History-making and Cultural-political Entrepreneurship in Postcommunist Poland and Russia." In *Capitalism and Democracy in Central and Eastern Europe: Assessing the Legacy of Communist Rule*, Grzegorz Ekiert and Stephen E. Hanson, eds., pp. 317–351. Cambridge, UK: Cambridge University Press.

Kubik, Jan, and Amy Linch. 2006. "The Original Sin of Poland's Third Republic: Discounting "Solidarity" and its Consequences for Political Reconciliation." *Polish Sociological Review* 1 (153): 9–38.

Kuchins, Andrew. 2005. "Europe's Last Geopolitician." Accessed January 5, 2013. http://www.carnegieendowment.org/2005/05/09/europe-s-last-geopolitician/5ub.

Kultura. 2011. "Kalina Androlova: Banichari v mediinija biznes," February 2, 3.

Kulturny živo.t. 1992. "Fedor Gál: Mojou vlast'ou je Česko-slovensko." September 10.

Kulyk, Volodymyr. 1999. *Ukrains'kyi natsionalizm u nezalezhnii Ukraini.* Kyiv: Tsentr doslidzhen' natsional'noi bezpeky pry Natsional'nomu universyteti "Kyievo-Mohylians'ka akademiia."

Kundera, Milan. 1985. *The Book of Laughter and Forgetting.* Translated by Michael Heim. New York: Penguin.

Kunze, Thomas. 2010. "Democracy Full Steam Ahead: When the Iron Curtain Fell in Europe." In *Perspectives 1009*, Konrad Adenauer Stiftung. Accessed October 6, 2012. http://www.kas.de/upload/dokumente/jahresbericht2009/englisch/perspectives.pdf.

Kurczewska, Joanna. 2002. *Patriotyzm(y) Polskich Polityków.* Warsaw: IFiS PAN.

Kuzio, Taras and Andrew Wilson. 1994. *Ukraine: Perestroika to Independence.* Toronto: Canadian Institute of Ukrainian Studies Press.

Lācis, Boļeslavs. "To nedrīkst aizmirst." *Liesma*, August 20, 1999.

Laitin, David. 1986. *Hegemony and Culture: Politics and Religious Change among the Yoruba.* Chicago: The University of Chicago Press.

Laitin, David. 1988a. "Political Culture and Political Preferences." *American Political Science Review* 82 (2): 589–597.

Laitin, David. 1998b. *Identity in Formation: The Russian-Speaking Populations in the Near Abroad.* Ithaca, NY: Cornell University Press.

Landsbergis, Vytautas. "The Roaring Year." *Mercator net*, October 16, 2009. Accessed February 2011. http://www.mercatornet.com/articles/view/the_roaring_year/.

Langenbacher, Eric. 2008 "Twenty-first Century Memory Regimes in Germany and Poland." *German Politics and Society* 26: 50–81.

Langenbacher, Eric. 2010. "The Mastered Past? Collective Memory Trends in Germany since Unification." *German Politics and Society* 28 (1): 42–68.

Larson, Jonathan. 2010. "Debating a Debate That Is No Debate? Censure, Publication and the Contexts of a Moral Order in Slovakia's Velvet Revolution." *Journal of Linguistic Anthropology* 20: 134–148.

Lasansky, D. Medina. 2004. *The Renaissance Perfected: Architecture, Spectacle, and Tourism in Fascist Italy.* University Park: Penn State University Press.

Latvian People's Front. 1989. '"Baltijas ceļš" par brīvību un neatkarību." *Literatūra un Māksla*, August 19.

Latvian Television (LTV). 2003. Television discussion *"Baltijas ceļš šodien,"* dedicated to the 15th anniversary of the Latvian People's Front, *Latvian Television*, August 23.

Laudin, Radek. 2009. "Komunista vyrobil k 17. listopadu pamětní medaile, nahází je do Vltavy" [Communist Creates Memorial Medal for November 17th Anniversary, Throws It into the Vltava]. *Mladá fronta dnes*, November 11.

Lebow, Richard N. 2006. "The Memory of Politics in Postwar Europe." In *The Politics of Memory in Postwar Europe*, ed. Richard N. Lebow, Wulf Kansteiner, and Claudio Fogu, pp. 1–39. Durham, NC: Duke University Press.

Lebow, Richard N., Wulf Kansteiner, and Claudio Fogu, eds. 2006. *The Politics of Memory in Postwar Europe*. Durham, NC: Duke University Press.

Lehti, Marco, Matti Jutila, and Markku Jokisipila. 2008. "Never-Ending Second World War: Public Performances of National Dignity and the Drama of the Bronze Soldier." *Journal of Baltic Studies* 39: 393–418.

Lengyel, László. 2009. "A Third Nationalist Wave?" *HVG,* January 8, 2009, Accessed March 14, 2012. http://hvg.hu/english/20090108_László_lengyel_nationalist_wave.

Levi, Pavle. 2007. *Disintegration in Frames: Aesthetics and Ideology in the Yugoslav and Post-Yugoslav Cinema*. Palo Alto, CA: Stanford University Press.

Levitsky, Steven, and Lucan Way. 2010. *Competitive Authoritarianism: Hybrid Regimes after the Cold War*. Cambridge, UK: Cambridge University Press.

Levy-Strauss, Claude. 1966. *The Savage Mind*. Chicago: The University of Chicago Press.

Lijphart, Arendt. 1971. "Comparative Politics and the Comparative Method." *American Political Science Review* 65: 682–695.

Lindstrom, Nicole. 2003. "Between Europe and the Balkans: Mapping Slovenia and Croatia's 'Return to Europe' in the 1990s." *Dialectical Anthropology* 27 (3–4): 313–329.

Lindstrom, Nicole. 2006. "Yugonostalgia: Restorative and Reflective Nostalgia in Former Yugoslavia." *East Central Europe* 32 (1–2): 231–242.

Linz, Juan. 1978. "Crisis, Breakdown, and Reequalibration." In *The Breakdown of Democratic Regimes*, ed. Juan Linz and Alfred Stepan, pp. 1–97. Baltimore, MD: The Johns Hopkins University Press.

Linz, Juan, and Alfred Stepan. 1996. *Problems of Democratic Transition and Consolidation: Southern Europe, South America, and Post-Communist Europe*. Baltimore, MD: Johns Hopkins University Press.

Livitz, Inna. 2006–2007. "Monumental Politics: the Symbolic Political Discourse in Postcommunist Hungary." Accessed February 2, 2011. http://www.fulbright.hu/book4/innal-ivitz.pdf.

Logger, Sam. "Riga's Celebrations Get Under Way." *Baltic Times*, August 10, 2011. Accessed February 17, 2011. http://www.baltictimes.com/news/articles/29268/.

Lowenthal, David. 1986. *The Past Is a Foreign Country*. Cambridge, UK: Cambridge University Press.

Lyotard, Jean F. 1979. *The Postmodern Condition: A Report on Knowledge*. Minneapolis: Minnesota University Press.

Macedonia Daily. 2010. "Ivanov: EU Without Macedonia: Unfinished Story." June 12. Accessed March 27, 2012. http://macedoniadaily.blogspot.com/2010/06/ivanov-eu-without-macedonia-unfinished.html.

Macedonian Information Agency (MIA). 2009. "President Ivanov Congratulates Berlin Wall Anniversary to German Counterpart." November 9. Accessed March 27, 2012. http://www.mia.com.mk/default.aspx?mId=30&vId=68957119&lId=2&title=MACEDONIA+-+FOREIGN+AFFAIRS+.

Maier, Charles. 1988. *The Unmasterable Past: History, Holocaust and German National Identity.* Cambridge, MA: Harvard University Press.

Mainwaring, Scott, and Timothy Scully. 1995. "Introduction: Party Systems in Latin America." In *Building Democratic Institutions: Party Systems in Latin America*, ed. Scott Mainwaring and Timothy Scully, pp. 1–36. Stanford, CA: Stanford University Press.

Mareček, Lubomír. 2009. "V Brně to vřelo Havlovými postřehy i velkým koncertem." *Mladá fronta dnes.* November 19.

Mark, James. *The Unfinished Revolution: Making Sense of the Past in Central-Eastern Europe.* New Haven, CT: Yale University Press, 2010.

Marsovszky, Magdalena. 2011. "Hungary: Where Is the Enemy?" Accessed September 27, 2012. http://www.hagalil.com/archiv/2011/02/24/hungary-7/.

Matsuda, Matt K. 1996. *The Memory of the Modern.* Oxford: Oxford University Press.

McAdams, A. James. 2010. "The Last East German and the Memory of the German Democratic Republic." *German Politics and Society* 28 (1): 30–41.

Media Centar Sarajevo. 2009. "Pad berlinskog zida u štampi SFRJ." November 16. Accessed March 27, 2012. http://www.media.ba/mcsonline/bs/tekst/pad-berlinskog-zida-u-medijima-ex-yu.

Mediafax.ro. 2009. "FOCUS: Incidente la marşul de comemorare a eroilor din Decembrie 1989." December 21. Accessed February 7, 2013. http://www.mediafax.ro/main-story/focus-incidente-la-marsul-de-comemorare-a-eroilor-din-decembrie-1989-5196030.

Mediapool, 2008. "Dneshnite bulgarski komunisti: s pravo izbivahme na 9ti, 10ti i 11ti septemvri." February 22. Accessed June 10, 2012. http://www.mediapool.bg/show/?storyid=136518&srcpos=2&p=27.

Mediapool, 2010. "Edna stotna ot napravenoto ot Zhivkov da storim, shte e goljam uspeh." November 7. Accessed January 28, 2013. http://www.mediapool.bg/show/?storyid=172219&srcpos=5.

Mediņa, Iveta. "Ilūzijas zaudētas, ideāli snauž." *Neatkarīgā Rīta Avīze*, January 20, 2011.

Meier, Victor. 1999. *Yugoslavia: A History of its Demise.* Translated by Sabrina Ramet. London: Routledge.

Merkel, Jacek. Interview by Robert Pytlos, May 24, 2000. Warszawa. University of Michigan Center for Russian and East European Studies, Ann Arbor.

Merkl, Christian, and Dennis Snower. 2008. "Escaping the Unemployment Trap: The Case of East Germany." *Journal of Comparative Economics* 36: 542–556.

Mesík, Juraj. *The Election Is Over: What Is Ahead for Slovakia?* Prague: Heinrich Boll Stiftung, 2010. Accessed February 19, 2011. http://www.boell.cz/web/52-902.html.

Michnik, Adam. 1985. "A Letter to General Kiszczak, 1983." *Letters from Prison and Other Essays*, trans. Maya Latynski, pp. 64–70. Berkeley: University of California Press.

Ministerstvo vnitra *České republiky.* 2009. "Senát—konference a výstava Cesta z okovů" [Senate Conference 'The Path from Shackles']. Accessed February 1, 2013. http://www.mvcr.cz/clanek/senat-konference-a-vystava-cesta-z-okovu.aspx.

Mink, Georges, and Laura Neumayer. 2013. *History, Memory and Politics in Central and Eastern Europe.* London: Palgrave Macmillan.

Močs, Dzintars. "Baltijas ceļš: no sirds uz sirdi, no paaudzes uz paaudzi." *Liesma,* August 22, 2009.

Monitorul de Cluj. 2009. "Geoana, huiduit la Timisoara." December 2. Accessed February 7, 2013. http://www.monitorulcj.ro/cms/site/m_cj/news/geoana_huiduit_la_timisoara_77608.html.

Monroe, Alexei. 2005. *Interrogation Machine: Laibach and NSK.* Cambridge, MA: MIT Press.

Moran, John P. 1994. "The Communist Tortures of Eastern Europe: Prosecute and Punish or Forgive and Forget?" *Communist and Post-Communist Studies* 27: 95–109.

Morvai, Krisztina. 2009. "Morvai 2 Krisztina 2009 október 23 Kossuth tér 18630p NJA." October 23. Kossuth Square 6:30 PM NJA. Accessed June 12, 2012. http://www.youtube.com/watch?v=1vsAPX27y5g.

Mosse, George L. 1975. *The Nationalization of the Masses: Political Symbolism and Mass Movements in Germany, from the Napoleonic Wars Through the Third Reich.* New York: Howard Fertig.

Mujkic, Asim. 2009. "Der Untergang: 1989–2009–20 Years of Liberalisation or Canibalisation?" In *1989–2009 Years of Upheaval: Beginning of Inclusion or Exclusion.* Proceedings from a conference, Foundation Heinrich Böll, Sarajevo. Accessed March 27, 2012. http://www.boell.de/publications/publications-7802.html.

Müller, Jan-Werner. 2002. "Introduction: The Powers of Memory, The Memory of Power and the Power over Memory." In *Memory and Power in Post-War Europe: Studies in the Presence of the Past,* ed. Jan-Werner Müller, pp. 1–35. Cambridge, UK: Cambridge University Press.

Musil, Michal, and Vocelka, Tomáš. 2009. "Jakeš: Kdyby zůstal socialismus, všechno by bylo" [Jakeš: If Socialism had Endured, Everything Would Be...]. *Mladá fronta dnes.* November 16.

Nalepa, Monika. 2010. *Skeletons in the Closet: Transitional Justice in Post-communist Europe.* Cambridge, UK: Cambridge University Press.

Navratits, Tibór. 2011. Presentation to Members of the Global Master of Arts Program (GMAP) of the Fletcher School of Law and Diplomacy, Tufts University. September 2, 2011. Budapest: Hotel Meridien.

Nedelsky, Nadya. 2004. "Divergent Responses to a Common Past: Transitional Justice in the Czech Republic and Slovakia." *Theory and Society* 33 (1): 65–115.

Němcová, Barbora. 2009a. "STEM: Na demokracii nejvíc lidí oceňuje nové možnosti" [According to STEM, People Most Value Democracy for New Possibilities]. *Mladá fronta dnes.* November 17.

Němcová, Barbora. 2009b. "Politici vzpomínají na Listopad 89. Svoboda poslouchal Kryla, Paroubek pracoval." *Mladá fronta dnes,* November 17.

Nets-Zehngut, Rafi. 2011. "Origins of the Palestinian Refugee Problem: Changes in the Historical Memory of Israelis/Jews 1949–2004." *Journal of Peace Research* 48 (2): 235–248.

Nets-Zehngut, Rafi. 2012. "The Passing of Time and the Collective Memory of Conflicts: The Case of Israel and the 1948 Palestinian Exodus." *Peace and Change* 37 (2): 253–85.

Nettelfield, Lara J. 2010. "Research and Repercussions of Death Tolls: the Case of the Bosnian Book of the Dead." In *Sex, Drugs and Body Counts: The Politics of Numbers in Global Crime and Conflict,* ed. Peter Andreas and Kelly M. Greenhill, pp. 159–187. Ithaca, NY: Cornell University Press.

New York Times. 2009. "With Wall Just a Memory, German Divisions Fade." November 8. Accessed December 5, 2010. http://www.nytimes.com/2009/11/08/world/europe/08germany.html?pagewanted=all&_r=0.

Nezavisne Novine. 2009a. "Refleksija kapitalizma na zivot." February 14. Accessed April 1, 2012. http://www.idoconline.info/digitalarchive/public/index.cfm?fuseaction=serve&ElementId=540490.

Nezavisne Novine. 2009b. "Put bez viza postao stvarnost." December 20. Accessed March 27, 2012. http://www.scribd.com/doc/24546515/Nezavisne091220.

Nežmah, Bernard. 2009a. "Amnezije preteklosti i sedanjosti." *Mladina* 48, December 3. Accessed March 27, 2012. http://www.mladina.si/49052/amnezije_preteklosti_in_sedanjosti/?utm_source=tednik%2F200948%2Famnezije%5Fpreteklosti%5Fin%5Fsedanjosti&utm_medium=web&utm_campaign=oldLink.

Nežmah, Bernard. 2009b. "Opozicija kot destabilizator države?" *Mladina* 50, December 17. Accessed March 27, 2011. http://www.mladina.si/49174/opozicija_kot_destabilizator_drzave_/?utm_source=tednik%2F200950%2Fopozicija%5Fkot%5Fdestabilizator%5Fdrzave%5F&utm_medium=web&utm_campaign=oldLink.

Nochnykh, Viktor. "Otkuda byli golosa?" *Vesti segodnya*, August 25, 1999.

Nolte, Ernst. 1985. "Between Myth and Revisionism? The Third Reich in the Perspective of the 1980s." In *Aspects of the Third Reich*, ed. H. W. Koch, pp. 36–37. London: Macmillan.

Nora, Pierre. 1989. "Between Memory and History: Les Lieux de Mémoire." *Representations* 26: 7–25.

Nora, Pierre. 2001. "General Introduction." In *Rethinking France: Les Lieux de Mémoire. Volume 1: the State*, ed. Pierre Nora, vii–xxiii. Chicago: The University of Chicago Press.

Norval, Aletta. 1999. "Truth and Reconciliation: The Birth of the Present and the Reworking of History." *Journal of Southern African Studies* 25: 499–519.

Novinar, 2009. "Glasuvame za stroitelen obekt na veka," January 3, 3.

Novy Čas. 2009. "Dzurinda na oslaváchrevolúcie: Fico odvádza pozornosť!" November 18. Accessed January 26, 2011. http://www.cas.sk/clanok/139208/video-dzurinda-na-oslavach-revolucie-fico-odvadza-pozornost.html.

Novy Čas. 2009b. "Politici vzpomínají na Listopad 89. Svoboda poslouchal Kryla, Paroubek pracoval." *Mladá fronta dnes*, November 17.

Novynar.com.ua. 2010. "Symonenko porivniav Den zhovtnevoii revoliutsii z Dnem nezhalezhnosti." October 27. Accessed July 15, 2012. http://novynar.com.ua/politics/139102.

O'Donnell, Guillermo, and Philippe C. Schmitter. 1986. "Tentative Conclusions about Uncertain Democracies." In *Transitions from Authoritarian Rule*, ed. Guillermo O'Donnell, Philippe C. Schmitter, and Laurence Whitehead. Baltimore, MD: The Johns Hopkins University Press. Part IV.

Office of the President of the Polish Republic. 2009. "Rok 1989—narodziny wolności," Debata historyków z okazji 20 rocznicy rozpoczęcia obrad Okrągłego Stołu, Pałac Prezydencki, February 6, 2009. Transcript.

Olczyk, Eliza, and Jerzy Wiatr. 2009. "Staliśmy się elitą III RP, bo nam się to nalezało." *Rzeczpospolita*, June 2. http://www.rp.pl/artykul/259498.html?print=tak.

Olick, Jeffrey K. 1999. "Collective Memory: The Two Cultures." *Sociological Theory* 17 (3, November): 333–348.

Olick, Jeffrey K. 2003. "Introduction." In *States of Memory: Continuities, Conflicts, and Transformations in National Retrospection*, ed. Jeffrey K. Olick, pp. 1–16. Durham, NC: Duke University Press.

Olick, Jeffrey K., and Joyce Robbins. 1998. "Social Memory Studies: From 'Collective Memory' to the Historical Sociology of Mnemonic Practices." *Annual Review of Sociology* 24:105–140.

Olick, Jeffrey K., Vered Vinitzky-Seroussi, and Daniel Levy, eds. 2011. *The Collective Memory Reader.* Oxford: Oxford University Press.

Onken, Eva. 2010. "Memory and Democratic Pluralism in the Baltic States—Rethinking the Relationship." *Journal of Baltic Studies* 41: 277–294.

Opona: A Public Benefit Corporation. 2009. *Annual Report 2009.* January 21, 2011, http://www.oponaops.eu/assets/files/Opona/vyrocni-zprava-2009-en-mensi.pdf.

Orbán, Viktor. 2005. "érzem a puskapor szagát" [I can already smell the gunpowder]. *ma-online*, December 3. Accessed September 22, 2012. http://belfold.ma.hu/tart/prcikk/a/0/135664/1.

Orzechowski, Marian. Interview by Paweł Kowal, Warszawa, February 18, 2000. University of Michigan Center for Russian and East European Studies, Ann Arbor.

Osipian, Ararat, and Alexandr Osipian. 2012. "Regional Diversity and Divided Memory in Ukraine: Contested Past as Electoral Resource, 2004–2010." *East European Politics and Societies* 26 (3): 616–642.

Ost, David. 2005. *The Defeat of Solidarity: Anger and Politics in Postcommunist Europe.* Ithaca, NY: Cornell University Press.

P.E.N. International. 2009. "Šta je nama Berlinski zid?" November 2. Accessed March 27, 2012. http://www.boell.ba/web/index-294.html.

Pakier, Małgorzata, and Bo Strath. 2010. *A European Memory?: Contested Histories and Politics of Remembrance.* New York: Berghahn Books

Palonen, Emilia. 2009. "Political Polarisation in Contemporary Hungary." *Parliamentary Affairs* 62 (2): 318–334.

Pavićević, Borka. 2009. "Dogodilo se na današnji dan." *Peščanik*, December 12. Accessed March 27, 2012. http://pescanik.info/content/view/4111/96/.

Pearce, Susan C. 2010. "Commemorating Revolution and Absence of Revolution: Poland, Germany, Hungary, the Czech & Slovak Republics, Bulgaria, Serbia, and Romania in 2009." Paper presented at the annual conference of the Association for Slavic, East European, and Eurasian Studies, Los Angeles, California, November 18–21.

Peskin, Victor, and Mieczyslav P. Boduszyński. 2003. "International Justice and Domestic Politics: Post-Tudjman Croatia and the International Criminal Tribunal for the Former Yugoslavia." *Europe-Asia Studies* 55 (7): 1117–1142.

Petro, Nicolai N. 2001. "Creating Social Capital in Russia: The Novgorod Model." *World Development* 29 (2): 229–244.

Petro, Nicolai N. 2004. *Crafting Democracy: How Novgorod Has Coped with Rapid Social Change.* Ithaca, NY: Cornell University Press.

Petrović, Tanja. 2012a. *Yuropa: Jugoslovensko nasledje i politike budućnosti u postjugoslovenskim društvima.* Beograd: Edicija Reč.

Petrović, Tanja. 2012b. "Serbia's Quest for the Usable Past: The Legacy of the 19th Century in the Context of the EU Accession." In *Changing Identities in South Eastern Europe*, ed. Hanna Scheck, pp. 92–105. Ljubljana: Austrian Science and Research Liaison Office.

Pew Research Center Publications. 2009. "End of Communism Cheered but Now with More Reservations." November 2. Accessed March 27, 2012. http://pewresearch.org/pubs/1396/european-opinion-two-decades-after-berlin-wall-fall-communism.

PEW Global Attitudes Project. 2009. *Two Decades after the Wall's Fall: End of Communism Cheered but Now with More Reservations.* November 2. Accessed January 26, 2011. http://pewglobal.org/files/pdf/267.pdf.

Plakans, Andrejs. 1998. "Ievads." In *Atmiņa un vēsture: no antropoloģijas lidz psiholoģijai,* ed. Roberts Ķilis, pp. 9–15. Rīga: N.I.M.S.

Planet Siol.net. 2009. "Mednarodna konferenca o odboju po padcu Berlinskega zida." November 26, Accessed March 27, 2012. http://www.siol.net/novice/slovenija/2009/11/v_ljubljani_mednarodna_konferenca_o_obdobju_po_padcu_berlinskega_zidu.aspx.

Plumb, J. H. 2004. *The Death of the Past.* New York: Palgrave.

Polit.ru. 2010. "Kontseptsia novogo uchebnika ukrainskoi istorii. Lektsia Natalii Yakovenko." March 18. Accessed October 10, 2011. http://www.polit.ru/article/2010/03/18/uchebniki/

Politička Misla. 2009. Special Issue "20 Years after the Fall of the Berlin Wall," 7. Accessed December 26, 2012. http://www.kas.de/wf/doc/kas_17542-1522-2-30.pdf?090918140748.

Politika. 2009. "Tadić: Evropa ujedinjena tek sa zemljama zapadnog Balkana." November 8. Accessed March 27, 2012. http://www.politika.rs/rubrike/Politika/Tadic-Evropa-ujedinjena-tek-sa-zemljama-zapadnog-Balkana.lt.html.

Polonski, Antony, and Joanna Michlic. 2004. "Introduction." In *The Neighbors Respond: The Controversy over the Jedwabne Massacre in Poland,* ed. Antony Polonsky and Joanna Michlic, pp. 1–43. Princeton, NJ: Princeton University Press.

Polska Agencja Prasowa. 2009. "Wałęsa jednak przyjechał na konferencję," March 31. Accessed December 24, 2009. http://fakty.interia.pl/raport/20-lat-okraglego-stolu/aktualnosci/news/walesa-jednak-przyjechal-na-konferencje,1283400,5823.

Pop-Eleches, Grigore. 1999. "Separated at Birth or Separated by Birth? The Communist Successor Parties in Romania and Hungary." *East European Politics and Societies* 13 (1): 117–147.

Pop-Eleches, Grigore. 2008. "A Party for All Seasons: Electoral Adaptation of Romanian Communist Successor Parties." *Communist and Post-Communist Studies* 41 (4): 465–479.

Popovski, Vesselin, and Monica Serrano, eds. 2012. *After Oppression: Transitional Justice in Latin America and Eastern Europe.* Tokyo: United Nations University Press.

Porter, Brian. 2000. *When Nationalism Began to Hate: Imagining Modern Politics in Nineteenth-Century Poland.* New York: Oxford University Press.

Portnov, Andrij. 2010. *Uprazhneniia s istoriei po-ukrainski.* Moscow: Memorial.

Potič, Zoran. 2009. "Duh totalitarizma je v Evropi ostal le še v Ljubljani i Moskvi." *Delo,* November 21. Accessed March 27, 2012. http://www.delo.si/clanek/93630.

Pravda. 2007. "KSS: Nežná revolúcia bol podvod na občanoch." 2007. Accessed January 26, 2011. http://spravy.pravda.sk/kss-nezna-revolucia-bol-podvod-na-obcanoch-fi7-/sk_domace.asp?c=A071117_124854_sk_domace_p23.

Pravda. 2009a. "Mečiar: Nemohol som sa vyjadriť k novembru 89, Markíza ma 'zostrihala." November 20. Accessed January 26, 2011. http://spravy.pravda.sk/meciar-nemohol-som-sa-vyjadrit-k-novembru-89-markiza-ma-zostrihala-pyy-/sk_domace.asp?c=A091120_122649_sk_domace_p12.

Pravda. 2009b. "Mečiar pred dvadsiatimi rokmi netušil, kam to dotiahne." November 17. Accessed January 26, 2011. http://spravy.pravda.sk/meciar-pred-dvadsiatimi-rokmi-netusil-kam-to-dotiahne-pd6/sk_domace.asp?c=A091117_121955_sk_domace_p29.

Pravda. 2009c. "Napätie počas osláv pokračuje, KDH odišlo po príchode Schustera a Čiča." November 18. Accessed January 26, 2011. http://spravy.pravda.sk/napatie-p

ocas-oslav-pokracuje-kdh-odislo-po-prichode-schustera-a-cica-1j0-/sk_domace. asp?c=A091118_124028_sk_domace_p23.

Pravda. 2009d. "Treba chrániť ciele novembra, upozorňuje opozícia." November 16. Accessed January 26, 2011. http://spravy.pravda.sk/treba-chranit-ciele-novembra-upozornuje-opozicia-fvc-/sk_domace.asp?c=A091116_163309_sk_domace_p12.

Pravda. 2010a. "Fico: Vládni predstavitelia majú laxný prístup k sviatkom." September 1. Accessed January 26, 2011. http://spravy.pravda.sk/fico-vladni-predstavitelia-maju-la xny-pristup-k-sviatkom-pms-/sk_domace.asp?c=A100901_125706_sk_domace_p58.

Pravda. 2010b. "Slota: Mali by sme oslavovať výročie černovskej tragédie, nie vznik ČSR." October 29. Accessed January 26, 2011. http://spravy.pravda.sk/slota-mali-by-sme-oslavovat-vyrocie -cernovskej-tragedie-nie-vznik-csr-1e3-/sk_domace.asp?c=A101029_113122_sk_domace_p12.

Predsednik Republike Slovenije. 2009a. "Predsednik na slovesnosti ob 20. obletnici padca železne zavese." June 26. Accessed March 27, 2012. http://www.up-rs.si/up-rs/uprs.nsf/dokumentiweb /8AFB7DE8E3DE44D1C12575E4002D291F?OpenDocument.

Predsednik Republike Slovenije. 2009b. "V Ljubljani bi lahko imeli Trg Demosa." December 24. Accessed March 27, 2012. http://www.up-rs.si/up-rs/uprs.nsf/dokumentiweb/0ACFAEFF52 EFC9B7C125769600559624?OpenDocument.

"PŘEHLEDNĚ: Připomeňte si oslavy 20 let od Listopadu na iDNES.cz" [Overview: Commemorate the 20-year Celebration of November in *Mladá Fronta Dnes* online]. 2009. *Mladá fronta dnes*. November 18.

President.gov.ua. 2008. Transcript of the May 8, 2008, television program, "Second World War: Lessons for Ukraine." Accessed April 5, 2009. www.president.gov.ua/news/?cat=28.

Pridham, Geoffrey. "Post-Soviet Latvia—A Consolidated or Defective Democracy? The Interaction Between Domestic and European Trajectories." *Journal of Baltic Studies* 40 (2009): 465–494.

Procházková, Bára. 2009. "Tohle mě nikdo nenaučil" [This No One Ever Taught Me]. *Respekt*. November 22.

Przeworski, Adam. 1991. *Democracy and the Market*. Cambridge, UK: Cambridge University Press. "Pučs beidzies." *Diena*, August 22, 2011.

Puhovski, Žarko. 2009. "In Yugoslavia, Everything Was Viewed Through the Prism of Nationalism." *IP Journal Global Edition*. Accessed March 27, 2012. https://ip-journal.dgap. org/en/article/"-yugoslavia-everything-was-viewed-through-prism-nationalism"-0.

Puisāne, Guna. "Vairot garīgu brīvību." *Neatkarīgā Rīta Avīze,* January 12, 2011.

Radio Svoboda. 2011. "Sutychky pid muzhyku. Chym uviide v istoriiu vidznachennia 20-richchia nezalezhnosti?" August 25. July 15, 2012. http://www.radiosvoboda.org/content/article/24308024.html.

Radio-televizija Srbije. 2009a. "Muzej Beogradskog Zida na Trgu Republike." November 10. Accessed March 27, 2012. http://www.rts.rs/page/stories/sr/story/16/Kultura/286191/%22M uzej+beogradskog+zida%22+na+Trgu+Republike.html.

Radio-televizija Srbije. 2009b. "Dve decenije od proslave na Gazimestanu." June 28. Accessed March 27, 2012. http://www.rts.rs/page/stories/sr/story/9/Srbija/70533/Dve+decenije+od+ +proslave+na+Gazimestanu.html.

Radonić, Ljiljana. 2012. "Standards of Evasion: Croatia and the Europeanization of Memory." *Eurozine*, April 6. Accessed October 15, 2012. http://www.eurozine.com/ articles/2012-04-06-radonic-en.html.

Radstone, Susan, and Katherine Hodgkin. 2003. "Regimes of Memory: An Introduction." In *Regimes of Memory*, ed. Radstone and Hodgkin, pp. 1–22. London: Routledge.

Ragaru, Nadere. 2008. "The Former Yugoslav Republic of Macedonia: Between Ohrid and Brussels." In *Is There an Albanian Question?* ed. Judy Batt, Chaillot Paper 107. Paris: Institute for Security Studies.

Ragin, Charles. 1987. *The Comparative Method: Moving Beyond Qualitative and Quantitative Strategies*. Berkeley: University of California Press.

Ragin, Charles. 2000. *Fuzzy Set Social Science*. Chicago: University of Chicago.

Ragin, Charles. 2008. "User's Guide to Fuzzy-Set/Qualitative Comparative Analysis." Tuscon: Department of Sociology, University of Arizona.

Rainer, János M. 2009. "Was There a 1989?" *Open Society News*, "Eastern Europe: Where Do Open Societies Stand 20 Years Later?" New York: Soros Foundation Network News, Fall.

Ramet, Sabrina P. 1992. *Nationalism and Federalism in Yugoslavia, 1962–91*. 2nd ed. Bloomington: Indiana University Press.

Ramet, Sabrina. 2008. *Serbia, Croatia and Slovenia at Peace and at War: Selected Writings 1983–2007*. Zürich, Berlin: LIT Verlag Münster.

Raudseps, Pauls. 2009. "Baltijas maratons." *Diena*, August 25.

Razumkov Center. 2011. "Suspil'na pidtrymka Nezalezhnosi vysoka, iak nikoly." August 22. Accessed March 18, 2012. http://www.uceps.org/ukr/print.php?lng=UKR&&news_id=375&&address=news.

Reconciliation of European Histories: For a Better Understanding of Shared Histories. Memorandum of an informal group of members of the European Parliament. Accessed March 27, 2012. http://eureconciliation.wordpress.com/about/.

Reuters. 2009. May 22.

Rév, István. 1995. "Parallel Autopsies." *Representations* 49 (Winter): 15–40.

Revista 22. 2009. "Caramitru si Herlea au demisionat din conducerea PNTCD in semn de protest fata de sustinerea lui Geoana." December 3. Accessed February 7, 2013. http://www.revista22.ro/caramitru-si-herlea-au-demisionat-din-conducerea-pntcd-in-semn-de-prot-7196.html.

Riabchuk, Mykola. 2011. "Pro 'nashi' i 'jikhni' zvytiahy." *Zahid.net*, August 25. Accessed March 15, 2012. http://zaxid.net/home/showSingleNews.do?pro_nashi_i_yihni_zvityagi&objectId=1234526.

Riabchuk, Mykola. 2012. "Ukraine's 'Muddling Through': National Identity and Postcommunist Transition." *Communist and Post-Communist Studies* 45: 439–446.

Richardson, Tanya. 2004. "Disciplining the Past in Post-Soviet Ukraine: Memory and History in Schools and Families." In *Memory, Politics, and Religion: The Past Meets the Present in Europe*, ed. Frances Pine, Deema Kaneff and Haldis Haukanes, pp. 109–135. Lit: Munster.

Rihoux, Benoît, and Charles C. Ragin, eds. 2009. *Configurational Comparative Methods: Qualitative Comparative Analysis (QCA) and Related Techniques*. Los Angeles: SAGE.

Rihoux, Benoît, and Gisèle De Meur. 2009. "Crisp-Set Qualitative Comparative Analysis (csQCA)." In *Configurational Comparative Methods. Qualitative Comparative Analysis (QCA) and Related Techniques*, ed. Rihoux and Charles C. Ragin, 33-68. Los Angeles: SAGE.

Rizman, Rudi. 2006. *Uncertain Path: Democratic Transition and Consolidation in Slovenia*. College Station: Texas A & M University Press.

Robertson, Graeme. B. 2011. *The Politics of Protest in Hybrid Regimes*. Cambridge, UK: Cambridge University Press.

Romania Libera. 2009. "Iliescu: Daca as fi inchis pentru Revolutie, ar protesta toata tara." December 18. Accessed February 7, 2013. http://www.romanialibera.ro/opinii/interviuri/iliescu-daca-as-fi-inchis-pentru-revolutie-ar-protesta-toata-tara-172884.html.

Romania Libera. 2010. "Sorin Ovidiu Vîntu, informator al Securității cu numele de cod 'Nuş'" July 12. Accessed February 7, 2013. http://www.romanialibera.ro/actualitate/eveniment/sorin-ovidiu-vintu-informator-al-securitatii-cu-numele-de-cod-nus-193372.html.

Romanian Presidential Election Study. 2009. Three waves panel survey. Financed by Soros Foundation Romania and Romanian National Council for Scientific Research in Higher Education (CNCSIS Research Grant no. 2174/2008, PN II IDEI Program, Director Mircea I. Comsa). Electronic Dataset made available to the author.

Rone, Māra. "Uz Eiropas sliekšņa." *Liesma*, August 26, 1989.

Rossi, Michael. 2009. "Resurrecting the Past: Democracy, National Identity and Historical Memory in Modern Serbia." PhD dissertation, Rutgers University.

Rothstein, Bo. 2000. "Trust, Social Dilemmas and Collective Memory." *Journal of Theoretical Politics* 12 (4): 477–501.

Rozenvalds, Juris. "Par inteliģenci un tās lomu Latvijas politiskajos procesos 1987–2000. gadā." *Latvijas Zinātņu akadēmijas vēstis* 54 (2000): 130–141.

Rožukalne, Anda. 2010. "The Construction of Ethnic Political Identity and the Mechanisms of Exclusion in the Latvian-Language Media." In *Shrinking Citizenship: Discursive Practices That Limit Democratic Participation in Latvian Politics*, ed. Maria Golubeva and Robert Gould, pp. 111–131. New York: Rodopi.

Rupnik, Jacques. 2012. "How Things Went Wrong." *Journal of Democracy* 23 (3): 132–137.

Rusu, Mihai-Stelian. 2011. "The Colonization of the Past and the Construction of Mnemonic Order." *Studia Universitatis Babes-Bolyai. Sociologia* 56 (2): 39–57.

Rzeczpospolita. 2009a. "Debata o Okrągłym Stole w Pałacu Prezydenckim." Accessed June 2, 2009. http://www.rp.pl/artykul/259710.html?print=tak.

Rzeczpospolita. 2009b. "Wałęsa w Koninie o Okrągłym Stole." February 6. Accessed February 9, 2009. http://www.rp.pl/artykul/259749.html?print=tak.

"Sametová revoluce byla zlomová, myslí si dvě třetiny Čechů." [The Velvet Revolution Was a Breakthrough Say Two-Thirds of Czechs]. 2009. *Televiza Nova.* November 12. Accessed January 20, 2011. http://tn.nova.cz/zpravy/domaci/sametova-revoluce-byla-zlomova-mysli-si-dve-tretiny-cechu.html#.

Sandecki, Maciej, and Krzysztof Katka. 2009. "Działo się w Gdańsku." *Gazeta Wyborcza* June 4. Accessed November 21, 2010. http://cjg.gazeta.pl/CJG_Trojmiasto/1,94649,6689315,Dzialo_sie_w_Gdansku.html.

'Sandis,' August 23, 2009, on the *Diena* news portal, available at: www.diena.lv, accessed January 14, 2011. This comment is taken from the commentary page associated with the following article: "Sākas barikāžu divdesmitgades piemiņas pasākumi." *Diena.lv,* January 13, 2011. Accessed February 2012. http://www.diena.lv/izklaide/sakas-barikazu-divdesmitgades-pieminas-pasakumi-763293.

Sartori, Giovanni. 1976. *Parties and Party Systems.* Cambridge, UK: Cambridge University Press.

Scheppele, Kim Lane. 2012a. "Guest Post: Romania Unravels the Rule of Law." Accessed July 6, 2012. http://krugman.blogs.nytimes.com/2012/07/05/guest-post-romania-unravels-the-rule-of-law/.

Scheppele, Kim Lane. 2012b. "Hungary's Constitutional Revolution." February 14. Accessed July 6, 2012. http://lapa.princeton.edu/eventdetail.php?ID=519.

Schneider, Carsten Q., and Claudius Wagemann. 2012. *Set Theoretic Methods for the Social Sciences: A Guide to Qualitative Comparative Analysis*. Cambridge, UK: Cambridge University Press.

Schniererová, Diana, and Lukáš Milan. 2009. "Povstanie si sprivatizoval Smer." August 31. Accessed January 26, 2011. http://spravy.pravda.sk/povstanie-si-sprivatizoval-smer-d45-/sk_ domace.asp?c=A090831_073802_sk_domace_p12.

Schudson, Michael. 1992. *Watergate in American Memory: How We Remember, Forget and Reconstruct the Past*. New York: Basic Books.

Schumpeter, Joseph A. 1991. "Comments on a Plan for the Study of Entrepreneurship." In *The Economics and Sociology of Capitalism*, ed. Richard Swedberg, pp. 406–428. Princeton, NJ: Princeton University Press.

Scott, Paul. 2011. "Lithuania's Winter War, January 13, 1991." *The Lithuania Tribune*, January 10. Accessed January 2012. http://www.lithuaniatribune.com/2011/01/10/lithuania%e2%80% 99s-winter-war-13-january-1991-by-paul-scott/.

SEEcult. 2009. "20 godina bez Berlinskog zida." September 11. Accessed March 27, 2012. http:// www.seecult.org/vest/20-godina-bez-berlinskog-zida.

Sen, Amartya. 2004. "How Does Culture Matter?" In *Culture and Public Action*, ed. V. Rao and M. Walton, pp. 37–58. Stanford, CA: Stanford University Press.

Shevel, Oxana. 2011. "The Politics of Memory in a Divided Society: A Comparison of Post-Franco Spain and Post-Soviet Ukraine." *Slavic Review* 70 (1): 137–164.

Shevel, Oxana. 2011a. *Migration, Refugee Policy, and State Building in Postcommunist Europe*. New York: Cambridge University Press.

Simeonov, Petko. 2010. "Iskahme ot ribi da stanem luvove. Ne mozhe." *Trud*, November 6, 2–3.

"Sirdspuksti savienojas Rīgā," *Diena, August 24,* 2009.

"Skolotajs," August 3, 2009, on *Diena* news portal, available at: www.diena.lv, accessed January 14, 2011. The comment was taken from the commentary page associated with the following article: "Zatlers veic skrējiena pēdējo posmu, piedalījušies 50 000," *Diena*, August 23, 2009; the comment is, however, no longer accessible.

Slapšak, Svetlana. 2009. "Posleratni rat polova: Mizoginija, feministička getoizacija I diskurs odgovornosti u post-jugoslovenskim društvima." In *Zid je mrtav, živeli zidovi!* ed. Ivan Čolović, pp. 281–302. Beograd: Biblioteka XX vek.

Slovak National Party (SNS). 2007. "Home Page." Accessed January 26, 2011. http://www. sns.sk/ *Noviny.sk*. "Slovenský parlament chce uzákoniť Hlinkove zásluhy o SR." September 18, 2007. http://udalosti.noviny.sk/z-domova/18-09-2007/slovensky-parlament-c hce-uzakonit-hlinkove-zasluhy-o-sr.html.

Slovak National Party (SNS). 2009. "SNS si pripomenula udalosti v Černovej." October 28. http://www.mladezsns.sk/uncategorized/sns-si-pripomenula- udalosti-v-cernovej/.

Slovenia Times. 2011. "Philosopher Confronts His Politician Friend." July 15. Accessed April 1, 2012. http://www.sloveniatimes.com/philosopher-zizek-confronts-his-politician -friend-gregor-golobic.

Slyusareva, Elena. 2009. "Istorya rozhdaetsya v sporakh." *Vesti segodnya*, August 22.

Sme.sk. 2009d. *"Nevenujte pozornosť Ficovým rečiam, vyzval Dzurinda."* November 11. Accessed January 26, 2011. http://www.sme.sk/c/5114612/nevenujte-pozornost-ficovym-reciam-vy zva-dzurinda.html.

Smith, David J. 2008. "Woe from Stones: Commemoration, Identity Politics and Estonia's 'War of Monuments." *Journal of Baltic Studies* 39: 419–430.

Snyder, Timothy. 2010. "A Fascist Hero in Democratic Kiev." *New York Review of Books*. February 24. Accessed March 18, 2011. http://www.nybooks.com/blogs/nyrblog/2010/feb/2 4/a-fascist-hero-in-democratic-kiev/.

Sólyom, László. 2009. Speech at the Unveiling of the "Memorial to the Breakthrough to Liberation" on the 20th Anniversary of the Pan-European Picnic at Sopronpuszta, August 19. Accessed June 17, 2011. www.paneuropaipiknki.hu.

Spiegel Online. 2010a. "Ostdeutsche fremdeln mit der Bundesrepublik." August 31. Accessed December 5, 2010. http://www.spiegel.de/politik/deutschland/ sozialreport-ostdeutsche-fremdeln-mit-der-bundesrepublik-a-714860.html.

Spiegel Online. 2010b. "Linken Abgeordnete Preist Stasi-Agenten." May 19. Accessed February 13, 2013. http://www.spiegel.de/politik/deutschland/grusswort-an-ex-auslandsspitzel-linke n-abgeordnete-preist-stasi-agenten-a-695759.html.

Der Spiegel. 2009. "Versöhnung Ernst Nehmen." November 2. Accessed December 18, 2010. http://www.spiegel.de/spiegel/print/d-67596369.html.

Stan, Lavinia. 2002. "Moral Cleansing Romanian Style." *Problems of Post-Communism* 49 (4): 52–62.

Stan, Lavinia. 2013. *Transitional Justice in Post-Communist Romania: The Politics of Memory.* Cambridge, UK: Cambridge University Press.

Stan, Lavinia, and Nadya Nedelsky, eds. 2012. *Encyclopedia of Transitional Justice.* 3 vols. Cambridge, UK: Cambridge University Press.

Stankēviča, Zane. "Ušakovs kļuvis par pozitīvāk vērtēto Rīgas mēru." *LETA*, April 18, 2009. Accessed January 2012. http://www.leta.lv/lat/arhivsn/.

"Staroměstské náměstí ovládla socialistická hesla a veksláci" [Socialist Slogans and Money Changers Overrun Old Town Square]. 1993. *Mladá fronta dnes.* November 17, 2009.

Starr, Frederick. 1991. "A Usable Past." The Soviet System in Crisis: a Reader of Western and Soviet Views, ed. Alexander Dallin and Gail W. Lapidus, pp. 11–15. Boulder, CO: Westview Press.

Štavljanin, Dragan. 2009. "Dvadeset godina od pada bastiona prema Zapadu." *Radio Slobodna Evropa,* November 1. Accessed March 27, 2012. http://www.danas.org/content/berlinski_ zid/1866092.html.

Stokes, Gale. 1993. *The Walls Came Tumbling Down: The Collapse of Communism in Eastern Europe.* New York: Oxford University Press.

Štor, Barbara. 2009. "Enter the Bloody History." *Slovenia Times*, April 3. Acessed April 1, 2012. http://www.sloveniatimes.com/enter-the-bloody-history.

Stoyanov, Petar. 2010. "Izostaviha "Manifesta" za da zapazjat "Kapitala." *24 chasa*, November 4, 1.

Stróżyk, Jarosław. 2009a. "Biała i czarna legenda obrad." *Rzeczpospolita.* February 7. Accessed February 9, 2009. http://www.rp.pl/artykul/259496.html?print=tak.

Stróżyk, Jarosław. 2009b. "Prezydent: to było konieczne." *Rzeczpospolita*, February 7. Accessed February 9, 2009. www.rp.pl/artykul/259963.html?print=tak.

Stróżyk, Jarosław, and Antoni Mężydło. 2009. "Trzeba było dokonać ostrzejszych zmian." *Rzeczpospolita*, February 6. Accessed February 9, 2009. http://www.rp.pl/artykul/259497. html?print=tak.

Swidler, Ann. 1986. "Culture in Action: Symbols and Strategies." *American Sociological Review* 51 (2): 273–826.

Symonenko, Petro. 1996. "Natsional'na idea: mify i real'nist." *Holos Ukrainy*, March 21.

Szacka, Barbara. 2006. *Czas przeszły. Pamięć. Mit.* Warsaw: Wydawnictwo Naukowe Scholar.

Szacki, Wojciech. 2009. "Ten wspaniały przełom 1989 r." *Gazeta Wyborcza*, February 20. Accessed November 21, 2010. http://wyborcza.pl/1,97274,6298318,Ten_wspanialy_przelom_1989_r_.html.

Szájer, József. 2009. Address by József Szájer, Member of the European Parliament, August 19. The Europa Concert at the Cave Theatre in Fertőrákos. Accessed January 24, 2013. http://www.paneuropaipiknik.hu/index.php?site=40.

TA3, 2009. October 26. Accessed January 26, 2011. http://www.ta3.com/sk/diskusie/806_mal-by-r-fico-oslavovat-sviatok-17-novembra-na-slovensku?.s.

Tageszeitung. 2009. "Alles so schön bunt hier." November 11. Accessed February 8, 2013. http://www.taz.de/!43680/.

Tamm, Marek. 2008. "History as Cultural Memory: Mnemohistory and the Construction of the Estonian Nation." *Journal of Baltic Studies* 39: 499–516.

Tănăsoiu, Cosmina. 2007. "The Tismaneanu Report: Romania Revisits Its Past." *Problems of Post-Communism* 54 (4): 60–69.

Tasi, Katalin. 2009a. "Húsz éve nyugszanak arccal az ég felé." *168 Ora*, 2009. június 16. Accessed June 18, 2011. http://www.168ora.hu/cimke/?tagname=forradalom ["For twenty years they have rested with facing the sky," *168 Hours*, June 16, 2009].

Tasi, Katalin. 2009b. "Interjú Nagy Imre unokájával: 'Két kis gyerek vadidegen titkosszolgák-kal'" *168 Ora*, 2009 június 20 ["Interview with Imre Nagy's grand-daughter: 'Two little children with strangers from the secret police,'" *168 Hours*, June 20, 2009]. Accessed June 18, 2011. http://www.168ora.hu/itthon/ket-kis-gyerek-vadidegen-titkosszolgakkal-interju-nagy-imre-unokajaval-38478.html

Terenzani-Stanková, Michaela. 2010. "November '89 remembered." *Slovak Spectator,* November 22. Accessed January 26, 2011. http://spectator.sme.sk/articles/view/40839/2/november_89_remembered.html.

Terzens, Arnis. 2007. *Latvijas Kapitalistiskā republika.* Rīga: Apgāds ARTE.

Times of Israel. 2012. "Why Joachim Gauck Is Wrong for Germany." March 22. Accessed May 24, 2012. http://www.timesofisrael.com/why-joachim-gauck-is-wrong-for-germany/.

Tismaneanu, Vldimir. 1998. *Fantasies of Salvation: Democracy, Nationalism and Myth in Post-Communist Europe.* Princeton, NJ: Princeton University Press.

Tismaneanu, Vladimir. 2008. "Democracy and Memory: Romania Confronts Its Communist Past." *The Annals of the American Academy of Political and Social Science* 617 (1): 166–180.

Tismaneanu, Vladimir. 2013. "Democracy on the Brink: A Coup Attempt Fails in Romania." *World Affairs* (January/February). Accessed March 15, 2013. http://www.worldaffairsjournal.org/article/democracy-brink-coup-attempt-fails-romania.

"The Song of Freedom" website. Accessed February 2012. www.20.ee.

Thompson, John B. 1995. *The Media and Modernity: A Social Theory of the Media.* Stanford, CA: Stanford University Press.

Točs, Sandris. 2011. "Mums aiz muguras." *Diena*, August 23.

Todorova, Maria. 1997. *Imagining the Balkans.* Oxford and New York: Oxford University Press.

Tomić, Ante. 2009. "Zar se Jan Palach spalio zbog McDonald-sa?" *Jutarnji List,* November 14. Accessed March 27, 2012. http://www.jutarnji.hr/zar-se-jan-palach-spalio-zbog-mcd onald-sa/349756/.

Törnquist-Plewa, Barbara, and Krzysztof Stala, eds. 2011. *Cultural Transformations after Communism: Central and Eastern Europe in Focus.* Lund: Nordic Academic Press.

Transitions Online. 2009. "CEE, Slovakia, Where Are They Now? Fedor Gal." November 25. Accessed January 26, 2011. http://20years.tol.org/2009/11/25/fedor-gal/.

Trehub, Olena. 2011. "Natalia Yakovenko: 'V Ukraini diala ne "sovetskaia vlast," a "radians'ka vlada." *Ukrains'ka pravda*, December 6. Accessed December 10, 2011. http://www.istpravda. com.ua/articles/2011/12/6/64212/.

Trifonova, Galya. 2009. "Prehodut svurshi: Interview with Zhelyu Zhelev," *Sega, November 11*, 5.

Troanski, Hristo. 2004. *Ubiistveno cherveno.* Sofia: Izdatelsko atelie Ab.

Trouillot, Michel-Rolph. 1997. *Silencing the Past: Power and the Production of History.* Boston: Beacon Press.

Trud. 2009a. "Polititzi ot vsichki boi pochetoha 10ti noemvri," October 27, 1.

Trud. 2009b. "Vuzmuten sum ot pravitelstvata na prehoda: Interviju s Georgi Atanasov, chast I," November 9, 3–4.

Trud. 2009c. "Zhivkov polozhi usilija da otlozhi otstavkata si: Interviju s Georgi Atanasov, chast II," November 11, 3–4.

Trud. 2009d. "Imalo e kufarcheta, pulni s pari: Interviju s Iordan Iotov, November 26, 2.

Tumarkin, Nina. 1994. *The Living and the Dead: The Rise and Fall of the Cult of World War II in Russia.* New York: Basic Books.

Tusk, Donald. 2009. "Przemówienie premiera Donalda Tuska z okazji 20. Rocznicy wyborów 4 czerwca 1989," Kancelarnia Przes Rady Ministrów. Accessed November 23, 2010. http://www. premier.gov.pl/premier/przemowenia/id:2892.

Ugrešić, Dubravka. 1996. "The Confiscation of Memory." Translated by Celia Hawkesworth. *New Left Review* I/218: 26–39.

Uhl, Heidemarie. 2009. "Conflicting Cultures of Memory in Europe: New Borders Between East and West." *Israel Journal of Foreign Affairs* 3 (3): 59–72. Accessed March 27, 2012. http://israel-cfr.com/documents/issue9-Uhl.pdf.

Ukrains'ka pravda. 2008. "Use men'she ukraintsiv opyraiut'sia statusu voiakam OUN-UPA." January 17. Accessed September 3, 2009. http://www.pravda.com.ua/articles/2008 /01/17/3351003/.

Ukrains'ka pravda. 2010. "Donets'kyi sud vidibrav u Bandery zvannia heroia." April 2. Accessed December 3, 2010. http://www.pravda.com.ua/news/2010/04/2/4906504/

Ukrains'ka pravda. 2011. "28 ukraiins'kykh istorykiv zaiavliaiut', shcho "ne viddadut'" mynule i maibutnie Ukrainy v ruky politykiv." January 24. Accessed September 20, 2013. http://www. istpravda.com.ua/short/2011/01/24/17727/

Ukrains'ka pravda. 2013. "Referendum za nezalezhnist' 1-ho hrudnia 1991. Ahitatsiia i biu-leteni." September 28. Accessed December 10, 2012. http://www.istpravda.com.ua/ artefacts/2012/12/1/102150/#2

Ukrains'kyi instytut natsional'noi pamiati. 2009. *Kontseptsiia ta prohramy vykladannia istorii Ukrainy v shkoli (proekt).* Kyiv: Stylos. Accessed December 10, 2011. http://www.memory.gov. ua/ua/announce/detail/91.htm.

UN High Commissioner for Refugees (UNHCR). 2012. "Hungary as a Country of Asylum" Observations on the Situation of Asylum-Seekers and Refugees in Hungary." Accessed November 11, 2010. http://www.unhcr.se/SE/Protect_refugees/pdf.

Upleja, Sanita. 1999. "Baltijas ceļš: kad apritējuši desmit gadi." *Diena,* August 23.

Ured Predsjednika Republike Hrvatske. 2009. Predsjednik Mesić na Svečanosti obilježavanja 20. obljetnice pada Berlinskog zida (HINA), November 9. Accessed January 22, 2010. http://www.predsjednik.hr/Default.aspx?art=16707&sec=767.

Vatolin, Igor. 2011. "Putchisty i natsionalisty. Chto obshchego?" *Chas,* August 19.

Vaughn, Stephen. 1985. "History: Is It Relevant?" In *The Vital Past: Writings on the Uses of History,* ed. Stephen Vaughn, pp. 1–11. Athens: The University of Georgia Press.

Večernji List. 2009. "Mesić: Pad Berlinskog zida bio je kraj i početak." November 9. Accessed March 27, 2012. http://www.vecernji.hr/vijesti/mesic-pad-berlinskog-zida-bio-je-kraj-pocetak-clanak-47873.

Veidemane, Elita. 1989. "Akcija 'Baltijas ceļš.'" *Atmoda,* August 28.

Verba, Sidney. 1965. "Germany: The Remaking of a Political Culture." In *Political Culture and Political Development,* ed. L. Verba and S. Verba. Princeton, NJ: Princeton University Press.

Verdery, Katherine. 1991. *National Ideology under Socialism: Identity and Cultural Politics in Ceausescu's Romania.* Berkeley: University of California Press.

Vesti.rs. 2009. "Obeležavanje rušenja Berlinskog zida u Beogradu." November 6. Accessed March 27, 2012. http://www.vesti.rs/Kultura/Obelezavanje-jubileja-rusenja-Berlinskog-zida-u-Beogradu.html.

Videkanic, Bojana. 2010. "First and Last Emperor: Representations of the President, Bodies of the Youth." In *Remembering Utopia: The Culture of Everyday Life in Socialist Yugoslavia,* ed. Breda Luthar and Maruša Pušnik, pp. 37–63. Washington, DC: New Academia Publishing.

Vidyakin, Aleksandr. 2009. "Ne pora li postavit' mnogotochie." *Telegraf,* August 24.

Vilikovská, Zuzana. 2009. "Slovak Celebrations of the Velvet Revolution Anniversary Continue." *Slovak Spectator,* November 18. Accessed January 26, 2011. http://spectator.sme.sk/articles/view/37156/10/slovak_celebrations_of_the_velvet_revolution_anniversary_continue.html.

Vogt, Henri. 2005. *Between Utopia and Disillusionment: A Narrative of the Political Transformation in Eastern Europe.* New York: Berghan Books.

Volkov, Denis. 2012. "The Protesters and The Public." *Journal of Democracy* 23: 55–62.

Volkovs, Vladislavs. 1996. *Krievi Latvijā.* Riga: Latvian Academy of Sciences, Institute of Philosophy and Sociology, Ethnic Studies Center.

Volyn'. 2011. "Zvernenniia do hromadian Rivenshchyny z nahody vidznachennia 20 richnytsi nezalezhnosti Ukrainy." August 12. Accessed July 15, 2011. http://volyn.rivne.com/ua/1482.

Vona, Gábor. 2009. "Vona, Gábor 2009 október 23. 1.rész" (Gábor Vona, October 23, 2009, Part 1). Accessed June 12, 2012. https://www.youtube.com/watch?v=1KD8_jNkqeI.

Vorobyeva, Lyudmila M. 2009–2010. *Istorya Latvii ot Rossiiskoi imperii k SSSR.* Moscow: Instoricheskaya pamyat' and Rossiiskii institut strategicheskih issledovanii.

Vujačić, Veljko. 2004. "Reexamining the 'Serbian Exceptionalism' Thesis." Berkeley Program in Soviet and Post-Soviet Studies Working Paper Series. Accessed September 30, 2013. http://iseees.berkeley.edu/bps/publications/2004_03-vuja.pdf.

Vujačić, Veljko. 2006. "Slobodan Milošević: Charismatic Leader or Plebiscitarian Demagogue?" In *World Order After Leninism,* ed. Vladimir Tismaneanu, Marc Morjé Howard and Rudra

Sil. Seattle: Herbert J. Ellison Center for Russian, East European, and Central Asian Studies, University of Washington: In association with University of Washington Press.

Wagemann, Claudius, and Carsten Q. Schneider. n.d. "Standards of Good Practice in Qualitative Comparative Analysis (QCA) and Fuzzy-Sets." Accessed June 14, 2013. http://www.compasss. org/wpseries/WagemannSchneider2007.pdf.

Wanner, Catherine. 1998. *Burden—of Dreams: History and Identity in Post-Soviet Ukraine.* University Park: Penn State University Press.

Wasilewski, Jacek. 2010. "Trudny test demokratycznego elityzmu." In *Legitimizacja w Polsce: Nieustający kryzys w zmieniających się warunkach?* ed. Andrzej Rychard and Henryk Domański, pp. 31–59. Warsaw: iFiS PAN.

Way, Lucan. 2005. "Authoritarian State Building and the Sources of Regime Competitiveness in the Fourth Wave: The Cases of Belarus, Moldova, Russia, and Ukraine." *World Politics* 57 (2): 231–261.

Web Café. 2010. "9ti septemvri e politicheskoto subitie na Bulgaria za 20ti vek," August 1. Accessed January 28, 2013. www.webcafe.bg/id_1827207474.

Wedeen, Lisa. 2002. "Conceptualizing Culture: Possibilities for Political Science." *American Political Science Review* 96 (4): 713–728.

White, Hayden. 1978. *Tropics of Discourse: Essays in Cultural Criticism.* Baltimore, MD: The Johns Hopkins University Press.

Wilde, Alexander. 1999. "Irruptions of Memory: Expressive Politics in Chile's Transition to Democracy." *Journal of Latin American Studies* 31: 473–500.

Wilds, Karl. 2000. "Identity Creation and the Culture of Contrition: Recasting "Normality" in the Berlin Republic." *German Politics* 9 (1): 83–102.

Wiesław Władyka, 2009. "Spojrzenie na Okrągły Stół z perspektywy 2009 roku." *Polityka*. Accessed February 9, 2009. http://www.polityka.pl/polityka/print2.jsp?place=texto3&news_cat_.

Wikipedia. 2012. "Institutul Revoluției Române din Decembrie 1989." Accessed July 23, 2012. http://ro.wikipedia.org/wiki/Institutul_Revolu%C8%9Biei_Rom%C3%A2ne_din_ Decembrie_1989.

Wikiquotes. 2009. "Govor Borisa Tadića na proslavi dvadesetogodišnjice pada Berlinskog zida." November 7. Accessed March 27, 2012. http://sr.wikiquote.org/sr-el/ Говор_Бориса_Тадића_на_прослави_двадесетогодишњице_пада_Берлинског_зида.

Wilson, Andrew. 2000. *The Ukrainians: Unexpected Nation.* New Haven, CT: Yale University Press.

Wilson, Andrew. 2002. "Reinventing the Ukrainian Left: Assessing Adaptability and Change, 1991–2000." *Slavonic and East European Review* 80 (1): 21–59.

Wirnitzer, Jan. 2009. "Oslavy dvaceti let "sametu" nechal stát na lidech" [The State Leaves Celebration of the "Velvet Revolution" to the People]. *Mladá fronta dnes*, November 12.

Wittlinger, Ruth. 2008. "The Merkel Government's Politics of the Past." *German Politics and Society* 26 (4): 9–27.

Wolin, Sheldon S. 1989. *The Presence of the Past: Essay on the State and the Constitution.* Baltimore, MD: The Johns Hopkins University Press.

Wood, Nancy. 1999. *Vectors of Memory: Legacies of Trauma in Postwar Europe.* Oxford: Berg.

Wood, Nicholas. 2003. "Nations Row over Mother Teresa." *BBC News Macedonia*, August 10. Accessed March 27, 2012. http://news.bbc.co.uk/2/hi/europe/3139003.stm.

Woolcock, Michael. 1998. "Social Capital and Economic Development: Toward a Theoretical Synthesis and Policy Framework." *Theory and Society* 27 (2): 151–208.

Woolcock, Michael, and Deepa Narayan. 2000. "Social Capital: Implications for Development Theory, Research, and Policy." *The World Bank Research Observer* 15 (2): 225–249.

Wóycicki, Kazimierz. 2009. "Zagadnienia historiografii pamięci." *Orbis Linguarum* 4: 1–30.

Wprost. 2009a. "20 rocznica wyborów 4 czerwca w Krakowie i Gdańsku," June 4. Accessed November 12, 2010. http://www.wprost.pl/ar/163164/20-rocnicz-wyborow-4-czerwca-w-krakowie-i-gdansku.

Wprost. 2009b. "Konferencja: Okrągły Stoł to fenomen w skali światowej," February 5. Accessed September 2, 2009. http://www.wprost.pl/ar/152567/Konferencja-Okragly-Stol-to-fenomen-w-skali-swiatowej/?O=152567&K=1&KI=91922.

Wujec, Henryk. Interview by Maria Krisan, February 18, 2000. Warszawa. University of Michigan Center for Russian and East European Studies, Ann Arbor.

Wüstenberg, Jenny, and David Art. 2008. "Using the Past in the Nazi Successor States from 1945 to the Present." *The Annals of the American Academy of Political and Social Sciences* 617: 72–87.

Yanukovych, Viktor. 2011. "Dvadtsiat' rokiv Ukrainy: Nash shliakh lyshe pochynaiet'sia." *Dzerkalo Tyzhnia*, August 19. http://gazeta.dt.ua/POLITICS/dvadtsyat_rokiv_ukrayini__nash_shlyah_lishe_pochinaetsya.html.

Yerushalmi, Yosef Hayim. 1982. *Jewish History and Jewish Memory*. Seattle: University of Washington Press.

Zahid.net. 2011. "Derzhavna nezalezhnist' Ukrainy—vybir mizh borot'boiu ta evoliustiieiu." August 31. Accessed March 22, 2012. http://zaxid.net/home/showSingleNews.do?derzhavna_nezalezhnist_ukrayini__vibir_mizh_borotboyu_ta_evolyutsiyeyu&objectId=1234962.

Zakharchenko, Tanya. 2013. "Polyphonic Dichotomies: Memory and Identity in Today's Ukraine." *Demokratizatsiya* 21 (2): 241–269.

Żakowski, Jacek. 2002. *Rewanż pamięci*. Warsaw: Sic.

Žatkuliak, Jozef. 2009. *November '89 : medzník vo vývoji slovenskej spoločnosti a jeho medzinárodný context*. Bratislava: Historický Ústav SAV vo Vydavateľstve Prodama.

Závodná, Michaela. 2009. "Studenti v Brně připomněli výročí revoluce lampionovým průvodem" [Students in Brno Commemorate the Anniversary of the Revolution with Parade of Lanterns]. *Mladá fronta dnes*. November 17.

Zeit Online. 2009. "Der Erinnerungstisch ist reich gedeckt." March 26. Accessed January 3, 2011. http://www.zeit.de/2009/14/DDR-Geschichte.

Zelče, Vita. 2007. "Vēsture un vēsture, un 9. Saeimas vēlēšanas." In *Latvijas Republikas 9. Saeimas vēlēšanu kampaņa: priekšvēlēšanu publiskā telpa*, ed. Inta Brikše and Vita Zelče, pp. 193–216. Rīga: Zinātne.

Zelče, Vita. 2009. "Vēsture—atbildība—atmiņa: Latvijas pieredze." In *Latvija. Pārskats par tautas attīstību, 2008/2009: Atbildīgums*, ed. Ivars Ijabs and Juris Rozenvalds, pp. 42–54. Riga: University of Latvia, Advanced Social and Political Research Institute.

Zepa, Brigita, Evija Kļave, Oksana Žabko, Līga Krastiņa, Iveta Bebriša, Zane Jansone, Lelde Vaivode, and Liene Beriņa. 2008. *Mēs. Svētki. Valsts: Valsts svētku svinēšanas socioloģiska izpēte*. Riga: Baltic Institute of Social Sciences.

Zerubavel, Eviatar. 1996. "Social Memories: Steps to a Sociology of the Past." *Qualitative Sociology* 19: 283–300.

Zerubavel, Eviatar. 2003a. *Time Maps: Collective Memory and the Social Shape of the Past.* Chicago: The University of Chicago Press.

Zerubavel, Eviatar. 2003b. "Calendars and History: A Comparative Study of the Social Organization of National Memory." In *States of Memory: Continuities, Conflicts, and Transformations in National Retrospection*, ed. Jeffery K. Olick, pp. 315–338. Durham: Duke University Press.

Zerubavel, Yael. 1995. *Recovered Roots: Collective Memory and the Making of Israeli National Tradition.* Chicago: University of Chicago Press.

Zhurzhenko, Tatiana. 2002. "The Myth of Two Ukraines." *Eurozine.* Accessed September 20, 2013. http://www.eurozine.com/articles/2002-09-17-zhurzhenko-en.html

Ziare.com. 2009a. "S-a semnat 'Parteneriatul pentru Timisoara:' Geoana, sustinut si de PNTCD." December 1. Accessed July 23, 2012. http://www.ziare.com/pntcd/crin-antonescu/s-a-semnat-parteneriatul-pentru-timisoara-geoana-sustinut-si-de-pntcd-963849.

Ziare.com. 2009b. "Ciuhandu: Cine voteaza cu Basescu voteaza cu comunistii." December 1. Accessed February 7, 2013. http://www.ziare.com/basescu/stiri-traian-basescu/ciuhandu-c ine-voteaza-cu-basescu-voteaza-cu-comunistii-963847.

Zlámalová, Lenka. 2009. "Pokuta pro Topolánkovy ovce." *Lidové noviny.* November 18.

Zubrzycki, Geneviève. 2009. "National Culture, National Identity, and the Culture(s) of the Nation." In *Sociology of Culture: A Handbook*, ed. Laura Grindstaff, John R. Hall, and Ming-cheng Lo, pp. 514–525. New York: Routledge.

Zubrzycki, Geneviève. 2011. "History and the National Sensorium: Making Sense of Polish Mythology." *Qualitative Sociology* 34: 21–57.

"Zuze," August 23, 2009, on the *Delfi* news portal, available at: www.delfi.lv, accessed January 14, 2011. This comment comes from a section linked to the following article: "Skrējienā "Sirdpuksti Baltijai" kopumā piedalijušies vairāk kā 60 000," *Delfi*, August 23, 2009; the comment is, however, no longer accessible.

Zyzak, Paweł. 2009. *Lech Wałęsa—idea i historia. Biografia polityczna legendarnego przywódcy "Solidarności" do 1988 roku.* Kraków: Wydawnictwo Arcana.

Author Index

Page numbers followed by *f, t* or n indicate figures, tables, or notes, respectively. Page numbers in *italics* indicate pictures.

Subject Index

Page numbers followed by *f, t* or n indicate figures, tables, or notes, respectively. Page numbers in *italics* indicate pictures.